Managing the Fiscal Metropolis

Selected Titles in the American Governance and Public Policy Series

Series Editors: Gerard W. Boychuk, Karen Mossberger, and Mark C. Rom

Managing the Fiscal Metropolis

The Financial Policies, Practices, and Health of Suburban Municipalities

Rebecca M. Hendrick

Georgetown University Press/Washington, DC

Georgetown University Press, Washington, D.C. www.press.georgetown.edu

Library of Congress Cataloging-in-Publication Data

Hendrick, Rebecca Martin.
    Managing the fiscal metropolis : the financial policies, practices, and health of suburban municipalities / Rebecca M. Hendrick.
        p. cm.—(American governance and public policy series)
    Includes bibliographical references and index.
    ISBN 978-1-58901-776-4 (pbk. : alk. paper)
1. Local finance—Illinois—Chicago Metropolitan Area—Case studies.   2. Local government—Economic aspects.   3. County services—Economic aspects.
4. Municipal services—Economic aspects.   I. Title.
    HJ9227.H46 2011
    352.4′2169097731—dc22   2011006194

♾ This book is printed on acid-free paper meeting the requirements of the American National Standard for Permanence in Paper for Printed Library Materials.

15 14 13 12 11   9 8 7 6 5 4 3 2
First printing

Printed in the United States of America

To Martin and local government officials everywhere

Contents

Illustrations

Figures

Preface

For many people in the United States, local government affects their lives more directly than other levels of government. Although many of us receive large transfer payments from the state or federal governments for medical services or social security, for instance, the goods and services delivered by all local governments in urban areas affect residents daily and often in very significant ways. Without local government, many of us would have no clean water, garbage pickup, or roads. We depend on local government to protect us and save us from dangers that threaten our health and safety, and we rely on local government to educate our children. These are not trivial services, but their successful provision and production is often taken for granted by citizens and elected officials. We expect our water to be clean, police to respond promptly, and our properties to be protected from fire and other hazards, yet we give little thought to whether the responsible local government has the complete authority or capacity to follow through according to our expectations.

Using suburban municipalities in the Chicago metropolitan area as a laboratory, this book identifies factors that affect the authority, capacity, and even motivation of local government to deliver goods and services from a financial perspective, and the book examines how these factors impact its financial policies and practices. This book also examines how the role and incentives of different government officials and their approaches to governance affect the financial policies and practices of local government that ultimately affect its financial condition. The book's primary purpose is to present a more comprehensive picture of the causes and impacts of financial decisions and financial management practices in local government than has been presented in the past in order to inform the theory and practice of financial management and governance at the local level. The book also identifies state policies and metropolitan features that affect the financial governance, management, and condition of the municipalities in this study.

To accomplish these objectives, I examine the concept of local government financial condition in detail to clarify what is measured, and I develop a framework for understanding events associated with financial decision making that combines several theoretical approaches. This framework draws heavily from accepted ideas about strategic problem solving, strategic management, and local governing institutions to guide what is observed and how observations are interpreted. The book uses many sources of data, both quantitative and qualitative, and inductive and deductive methods to determine what the data reveal about financial condition in suburban municipalities and their financial policies and practices.

Fiscal policy in suburban governments generally and municipalities in particular have been studied before, but prior research has targeted particular fiscal policies, such as property tax levels, or types of services and events at a macro level. It does not often look within the black box to determine how financial decisions are interrelated. For instance, chapter 7 of the book examines the relationship between capital spending and capital financing, and the fiscal and governing factors that drive these decisions. It finds that some of these factors, such as overall fiscal capacity and home rule status, are directly related to spending and capital financing, but others are related indirectly. In this case, home rule status also affects the impact of fiscal capacity on capital spending and financing. The methodology used here allows for a more thorough analysis of such events and better observation of their complex nature, but it also limits the sample of local governments that can be studied within the region.

I have been studying local government in the Chicago metropolitan region since I arrived at the University of Illinois at Chicago (UIC) in January 1998. My research has focused on local governments in the region, and municipalities in particular, and has examined the effects of financial structure, competition, and governing structure on financial policies in the areas of spending, debt, and revenue generation using quantitative data and methods. This book incorporates my prior research and expands on it by observing more areas of policy and practice and using qualitative data sources.

Using one's immediate environment as a laboratory for research is often a good strategy, and the Chicago region offers plenty of opportunity to do this. Living and working in the region allowed me to conduct in-depth interviews of local governments over an extended period of time and gave me a working knowledge of local government and finances in the region and state that was very useful in designing the analyses and interpreting findings. The region also offers opportunities for many of my students to do projects on local government in budgeting and capstone courses. These projects have provided much useful information about local governments in the region that were not interviewed. It should be noted that the approval of interviews in 2003 and 2009 by the Institutional Review Board at the UIC prevents me from identifying interviewees with particular comments. Because interviewees must remain anonymous, there are no citations of quotations from interviewees in the book. I have also kept the confidentiality of governments that were involved in student projects.

Although this book should be of greatest interest to scholars and practitioners in the Chicago area and the state of Illinois, its findings have much relevance for local governments in other metropolitan regions and states. Irrespective of their location in the United States, local governments in metropolitan regions share many features that are not shared by local governments in rural areas. For instance, metropolitan governments are more diverse than rural governments within a defined geographical area, and metropolitan governments have more neighbors and are therefore likely to have more competitive pressure than rural governments. These factors and their effects on financial policies and practices are explored in some detail here. The book also documents how local government is likely to be very different in Illinois, and the Chicago region in particular, to allow readers to judge how the relationships identified here and the book's overall findings may be different in other states and regions.

This book was greatly facilitated by my one year's appointment as a faculty scholar at the Great Cities Institute at UIC during the 2002–3 academic year. This award gave me the time to plan the book and do the interviews. I want to thank my graduate assistant Garrison Marr for his valuable assistance in collecting news reports, and graduate students in my master's and PhD classes for reading and commenting on earlier versions of chapters. I especially want to thank the PhD students in my spring 2006 Advanced Seminar in Financial Management for helping me develop the model of financial condition used here. I also want to thank the external reviewers and series editors who read and commented on the entire manuscript, and the conference discussants who reviewed earlier versions of several chapters. Finally, I want to thank my friends and family for their encouragement and listening, and Vince for his inspiration.

Acronyms

ACIR	Advisory Commission on Intergovernmental Relations
CAFR	Comprehensive Annual Financial Report
CAO	chief administrative officer
CEO	chief executive officer
CFO	chief financial officer
COG	council of government
CPI	Consumers Price Index
EAV	equalized assessed value
EPA	Environmental Protection Agency
FAUI	Fiscal Austerity and Urban Innovation
FDS	financial decision structure
GAAP	generally accepted accounting procedures
GFOA	Government Finance Officers Association
GO	general obligation
ISBE	Illinois State Board of Education
ICMA	International City/County Management Association
IDOR	Illinois Department of Revenue
ILCS	*Illinois Compiled Statutes*
IOC	Illinois Office of the Comptroller
MMC	Metropolitan Mayors Caucus
OLS	ordinary least squares
PCS	permanent community sample
PTAB	property tax appeals board
PTELL	Property Tax Extension Limitation Law
TIF	tax incremental finance district
2SLS	two-stage least squares

Chapter 1

Introduction

This book is about how municipal officials in the suburbs of a large metropolitan region improve, maintain, or fail to maintain the financial health of their governments. Elected and appointed officials at the local level pursue many objectives in their respective roles, but ultimately their governments need to maintain a reasonable level of financial health to achieve many of their goals. Some officials are even elected on platforms to improve government financial health to make the government more sustainable financially. Many more are elected to reduce or limit spending and taxes. Others see political advantages in expanding government's scope and resources, and a small number will even try to divert public funds for personal gain. Whatever their political or professional objectives, however, no government official has a desire to see their government bankrupt, and most will strive to maintain or improve its financial health. But, we know from example that many government officials make decisions that severely undermine the financial condition of their government to the point that their government becomes insolvent or defaults on its debt.

Severe financial crises have been documented in numerous major cities and counties, especially those that have come close to financial collapse.[1] Many people are familiar with New York City's near default on its debt in 1975 from in-depth analyses of the event (Tabb 1982; Brecher and Horton 1985; Shefter 1992). Other visible but less well-documented cases of fiscal crises are Cleveland, Ohio (1978); Philadelphia, Pennsylvania (1991); Orange County, California (1994); Miami, Florida (1996); Buffalo, New York (2003); Pittsburgh, Pennsylvania (2003); San Diego, California (2004); Vallejo, California (2008); and Jefferson County, Alabama (2008). Severe and continuous financial crises have been noted in many smaller, chronically distressed cities such as Flint, Michigan; Hamtramck, Michigan; East St. Louis, Illinois; Bridgeport, Connecticut; West Haven, Connecticut; Camden, New Jersey; and East Cleveland, Ohio. Undoubtedly, there have been many more municipalities and other local governments facing similar circumstances since 1975 that have gone relatively unnoticed by the press and the academy, and the Great Recession of 2007–9 is still producing widespread financial crises at the state and local levels of government at the time of this writing.[2]

The specific reasons for past crises vary tremendously, but there is one obvious similarity. Large cities such as Cleveland, Philadelphia, Buffalo, Pittsburgh, and Detroit and the smaller cities mentioned above (some of which are suburbs) all have entrenched economic deficits that make it very difficult for them to collect enough revenue to cover spending demands irrespective of what is happening with the national economy. Their local economies simply do not provide sufficient wealth for them to draw enough revenues to provide good quality or even adequate services to citizens and property owners. Their situation becomes progressively worse from the continuous exit of wealthier taxpayers, and the remaining taxpayers have greater service needs. These governments must continually raise the tax burden on remaining taxpayers to provide basic and necessary services. These governments may be well-run politically and administratively, but their financial condition severely compromises their ability to provide quality services in a consistent manner. In effect, these governments are not fiscally sustainable in the long run. They also are likely to have significant challenges in managing their financial affairs in the short run, such as cash shortages, that are less likely to be publicized but are an important part of their financial picture and descent into financial crisis.

By comparison, the financial crises in San Diego, Orange County, Miami, and Jefferson County are not rooted in economic deficits and, given each city's relative revenue wealth, seem out of place and very unlikely. The income levels of residents in San Diego and Orange County are some of the highest in the nation, and their revenue resources are more than adequate to meet basic spending needs and citizen demands. Although less wealthy and needier, Miami and Jefferson County also do not have the economic deficits apparent in the northern central cities mentioned previously. So what caused the financial crises in these four cases?

In all instances, the crises were produced by some combination of political fragmentation, lack of fiscal discipline and controls, incompetence, illegal activities, and bad financial decisions. The proximate causes of the crises in San Diego and Orange County were risky investments and in Jefferson County risky borrowing, but the opportunities and incentives to engage in these practices were created by these cities' governing institutions. Similarly, Miami's financial crisis was facilitated by governing institutions that did not promote good financial management practices and sound financial decisions (Dluhy and Frank 2002; Baldassare 1998; Alabama Policy Institute 2008; Hirth 1996; Fields 1996; Whitmire and Walsh 2008; Dewan 2009; *San Diego Union-Tribune* 2006; Perry 2006).

It is also not uncommon for governments with entrenched fiscal deficits to exacerbate their problems with budgeting and financial practices that ignore the economic deficits. Buffalo relied too strongly on state aid and grants to fund critical services, which disappeared when the state of New York had to redistribute resources to New York City to recover from the terrorist attack of 9/11 (Braun 2003; Robinson 2003; *Buffalo News* 2001). Although Philadelphia's divisive politics and strong unions prevented it from making the tough spending and revenue decisions necessary to adapt to a declining revenue base, its financial management system also did not promote decisions or practices necessary to improve efficiency or provide appropriate checks and balances to increase accountability. There were few controls on overtime; little vigilance in collecting many fees and some revenues; and inadequate monitoring of grants, contracts, and cash flow (Inman 1995; Meyers 1990; Williams 1991). Similarly, Pittsburgh avoided operating deficits for a short period of time by using one-shot fixes, such as selling assets and refinancing debt, but eventually recovered by adopting dramatic spending cuts and fundamental changes to its tax structure (Conte 2001; *Pittsburgh Post-Gazette* 2002).

We know from San Diego, Orange County, Miami, and Jefferson County that good external fiscal capacity (defined generally as high revenue wealth and low spending needs) does not always protect local governments from fiscal crisis and poor financial condition.[3] Does it also follow that some governments with poor fiscal capacity or entrenched economic deficits are not destined to experience financial crises? What are the independent effects of politics and administration on financial decisions and financial condition? Besides recessions, what other challenges do local governments face in managing and maintaining financial condition? How do they respond to different financial threats, including recessions, and opportunities? Given the same circumstances, do some responses lead to better financial health and produce governments that are more financially sustainable than others?

Our knowledge of the answers to these important questions with respect to local government, especially suburbs, is somewhat narrow. A lot of research has been conducted on at least part of several questions: What are sources of fiscal stress, and how do governments respond to it? But there has been no investigation of fiscal opportunities or munificence (the opposite of fiscal stress). There is also a large body of research on the effects of governing and administration on financial decisions, but little is known about how these factors affect financial condition. As noted previously, case studies (and news reports) document the financial experiences of large governments during periods of extreme fiscal stress and the negative impacts of decisions on financial condition. But we know little about governments that have successfully negotiated severe fiscal threats to maintain good financial condition, as the failures are much more interesting and thus garner the most attention. Other in-depth research on financial policymaking has produced a broad understanding of how financial context, internal politics and administration, and financial policies in local governments are linked, but the linkage to financial condition is missing, and findings are limited to specific governments (Fuchs 1992; Dluhy and Frank 2002; Levine, Rubin, and Wolohojian 1981; Sharp and Elkins 1987; Chapman 1999; Badu and Li 1994).

This book strives to fill some of the gaps in our understanding of this subject matter through comprehensive investigation of 264 Chicago suburban municipalities from the late 1990s to the end of the first decade of the 2000s.[4] More generally, this book focuses its investigation on four broad areas of financial concern about these governments. First, it identifies and describes the primary contextual factors and events that are likely to affect their financial decisions and financial condition. Some of these factors have been noted or alluded to previously. They include fiscal capacity (internal and external), governing institutions, and administrative approaches, especially with regard to fiscal policy and financial management practices. Fiscal threats, including recessions, and fiscal opportunities, such as grants and population growth that constrain or expand government choices, also are identified and discussed in detail. Current financial condition is another important contextual factor in future financial condition as it establishes the boundaries on officials' financial choices for handling fiscal threats and taking advantage of fiscal opportunities.

Second, this book identifies the financial strategies these governments use to manage financial condition and solve financial problems and the decisions they make in response to fiscal threats and opportunities. Financial decisions (and strategies) examined here focus on fiscal policies about tax rates or debt levels, for instance, changes to fiscal policies (e.g., the decision to raise taxes), and financial management practices such as approaches to budgeting or cash management. Third, this book examines the impact of contextual factors and events on government financial decisions. Finally, it examines the impact of contextual factors, events, and decisions on financial condition overall.

While the main purpose of this book is to improve understanding of the finance and financial management of local governments in general and those in metropolitan settings in particular, the book also has practical and pedagogical value. Understanding the financial decisions these governments make and linking them to context, events, and financial condition provides a sound basis for making recommendations about how suburban local governments should be managing and governing their fiscal affairs. This investigation also yields clues about the minimum capacity requirements for maintaining a reasonable level of financial condition and financial sustainability and what types of governing and administrative arrangements are likely to promote more sound financial decisions at the local level.

This book uses numerous concepts from public finance and financial management to describe the phenomena observed here and to assist with the investigation. By its very nature, this subject matter is laden with concepts and terminology that are explained and applied throughout the book (see glossary). Some of the terms will be known to financial managers. Other terms that are not known will be useful in helping them to think about and understand conditions and events they are likely to encounter.

Other terms such as *financial condition* and *fiscal stress* are used imprecisely throughout the literature and have numerous meanings. These are given precise definitions in the next chapter. For now it is enough to recognize that the concept of financial condition is complex and generally refers to a government's ability to meet current and future obligations. Complete measurement of the concept must take account of different features of government fiscal capacity and fiscal structure, such as debt levels and reliance on different revenues. Investigation of financial condition, especially as a result of financial choices, is complicated further by the fact that many of its aspects are a direct function of government fiscal policies and decisions over time. Thus, investigation of the impact of financial choices on financial condition is limited by the relatively short time period examined here, although the book's findings will help direct future research in this area.

In addition, this research offers some important lessons about financial problems and solutions that may be especially relevant to local governments dealing with the Great Recession that began in late 2007. However, this book is not just about fiscal stress, the causes of financial crises, or municipal governments' responses to negative financial pressures. These situations offer a worthwhile opportunity to observe financial choices in response to fiscal threats in general and the impacts of capacity, politics, governing structure, and administrative conditions on choices and financial condition, but they are not the only circumstances local governments face in managing their finances and maintaining financial health. Indeed, municipalities in the Chicago region experienced a wide range of threats and opportunities during the time period examined, even during the 2001 recession. Although the Great Recession promises to produce more severe financial crises in greater numbers of local governments than observed in previous recessions, local government experiences with this recession and its impacts also are likely to vary greatly. The moral of the story in this case is that it is important to document a wide range of conditions and events to fully understand how and whether municipalities improve, maintain, or fail to maintain financial health.

The Study of Financial Condition and Decisions in Metropolitan Governments

Although the majority of people in the United States live in suburbs, we know little about how suburban governments manage and govern their fiscal affairs, and why some fail and others succeed under different and similar conditions.[5] Much more research in this area has been conducted on central cities and large municipalities (Clark and Ferguson 1983; Barrett and Greene 2000; Burchell et al. 1981; Ladd and Yinger 1989), leaving a gap in our understanding of such events for the type of local governments experienced by most of the US population. Recent trends toward suburbanization have given rise to numerous books and a large volume of published research on suburbs and metropolitan regions in the fields of urban studies, economics, and political science (Orfield 2002; Gainsborough 2001; Oliver 2001; Lewis 1996; Schneider 1989; Weiher 1991; Rusk 1995; Oakerson 1999; Altshuler et al. 1999; Foster, 1997). But knowledge gained from these sources is limited primarily to questions about the gross impacts of fiscal or institutional environments on aggregate behavior (e.g., how do economic and demographic characteristics of suburbs affect expenditures or voting patterns) and how these patterns have changed over time (e.g., inner ring versus outer ring).

Why is it so important to distinguish between large municipalities, especially central cities, and smaller, suburban municipalities in the study of financial condition? First, many contextual factors that are likely to affect financial decisions and conditions are significantly different for central cities than suburban governments. This point is demonstrated by the story of East St. Louis, Illinois, a suburb of St. Louis, Missouri (see Reardon 1997 and www.uic.edu/cuppa/pa/faculty/vitae_pdf/The_Story_of_E_St_Louis.pdf for a detailed description of problems and events in East St. Louis).

From 1980 to 1990, the City of East St. Louis struggled greatly with trying to deliver basic services to citizens and meet payroll. But it was not until 1990 at the urging of its neighbors, including the City of St. Louis, who were tired of dealing with the spillover of problems from the municipality, that the State of Illinois established a means of assisting the seemingly insolvent government. In addition to debt guarantees and loans, part of this assistance included granting a highly coveted riverboat gambling license to the city. However, by late 2005 the city appeared to be heading toward the same level of insolvency it faced in the early 1990s and their financial condition and practices do not seem to have improved substantially in the late 2000s.

Cities and counties that are at the center of a metropolis usually have enough assets, in one form or another, to attract significant investments and financial opportunities from a large set of public and private entities to help solve their financial problems as compared with small suburban governments. To date there is no documentation of a central or major city government having continuous fiscal distress over as long a period of time or at the same level of fiscal insolvency as East St. Louis. Many more parties are likely to have a stake in the financial success of central and major cities compared to small suburban governments, especially ones with as many fiscal problems and as few amenities as East St. Louis.

Although the City of East St. Louis has a council-manager form of government according to statute, its history of machine-style politics based on an aldermanic structure with separate wards promotes a very political approach to policymaking that is most often associated with older and larger central cities such as Chicago and New York (Theising 2003). Such cities tend to be more partisan and patronage based, and also conflict laden. Representation of political interests in policymaking is not inherently bad. Indeed, it is an important tenet of democracy. But the incentives in local governments with strong political systems are structured for political gain, and the importance of financial condition can be overlooked in policy and personnel decisions.

Central and major cities have an advantage in this respect because their large size ensures that professionals with expertise and technical knowledge are represented at high levels of executive and financial decision making (Svara 1999). Such professionals are likely to be better informed than elected officials about what types of fiscal policies and practices are going to help a government maintain or improve financial condition and adapt to changing fiscal environments. Their position also will provide a voice for these options in the political debate. East St. Louis has the disadvantage of being both highly political and nonprofessional administratively. In other words, it has little administrative and technical capacity in areas that would help it maintain or improve financial health.

Central and larger cities with populations greater than seventy-five thousand are also different from smaller, suburban municipalities in that the latter tend to be much more homogenous demographically and economically (Weiher 1991; Lowery 2000). This makes the environment within which most suburbs operate and their options for solving financial problems very different from the governments that have been studied in the past. Compared to each other, however, suburban municipalities within the same metropolitan region are likely to be very fiscally diverse and highly segregated on many dimensions, making it impossible to find the "typical" suburb in any one region (Orfield 2002).

For instance, some suburbs may be predominately commercial or industrial and serve as job or commerce centers for the entire region and beyond. Suburbs within the same region can be rich or poor, rapidly growing or stagnant, old or new, white collar or blue collar, and their residents can have unique tastes and lifestyles that place particular service pressures on the government. Not surprisingly, the governing systems adopted by suburbs can vary as greatly as their socioeconomic and demographic features and reflect a mixture of political (e.g., fiscally conservative or service driven) and administrative approaches (e.g., politically or professionally managed). Such varied conditions make it very difficult to neatly summarize the contextual factors, events, financial decisions, and financial health of all municipalities in one metropolitan region. However, it offers an excellent opportunity to observe a broad range of phenomena and their effects.

There is great disparity of contextual factors that are important to this investigation among suburban municipalities within the Chicago metropolitan area. Table 1.1 shows this disparity for some of these features. It presents the lowest, highest, and median values for six key attributes of the jurisdiction or government in 2000.

In this case, the percent of labor force with managerial and professional occupations reflects whether the jurisdictions are predominately white collar or blue collar.

TABLE 1.1 Lowest, Median, and Highest Values of Key Contextual Factors for 264 Suburban Municipalities in the Chicago Metropolitan Region

	Lowest	Median	Highest
Population	100	10,600	143,000
Total spending	$20,000	$6.9 million	$107 million
Median household income	$17,500	$60,000	$200,000
White population (%)	2	90	99
Labor force with managerial or professional occupation (%)	3	18	39
Equalized assessed value that is residential	3.5	73.5	100

The percent of the *equalized assessed property value* (EAV) that is residential is a measure of the extent to which the jurisdiction is a bedroom community (residential) or industrial and commercial. These features and others that are relevant to financial condition are examined more closely in chapters 2 and 3 and reveal tremendous variation and distinction of characteristics. Some suburbs are exclusive, hyperwealthy enclaves that cater to a population with particular tastes and values (e.g., equestrian activities, boating, or natural settings). Others might be described as, in effect, financially insolvent with very similar experiences and problems to East St. Louis, and others do not exist for their citizens but to serve the larger metropolitan region (commercial, industrial, and entertainment centers).

Focusing the investigation on municipal governments in one metropolitan region allows one to observe the independent effects of contexts and events that are unique to each government more easily because all are subject to the same macrolevel context and events. For instance, state statutory constraints and policies toward municipalities are one of the most important contextual factors affecting many of their financial decisions. State law determines what kinds of taxes and revenues municipal governments may collect, what levels of taxes and revenues they can levy and charge, and how much debt they can issue. Many states also dictate some financial management practices in local government, and states have varying levels of custodial oversight of local financial decisions and fiscal affairs. The vast majority of the population and land area of the Chicago metropolitan region is within Illinois, and examining only municipalities within this state removes the effects of these macrolevel conditions from the investigation.

Local governments in the same metropolitan region also face similar economic pressures and physical conditions that impact revenues and spending. For instance, municipalities in the Chicago region pay similar costs for labor and transportation, and their sources of revenue, such as property values or sales receipts, are likely to be affected similarly by changes in the national economy. The Chicago region also has a particular geography that affects water provision, wastewater and storm-water management, and flooding across municipalities in similar ways. Municipalities in the region experience similar weather and have proximity to Lake Michigan.

Another macrolevel contextual factor to consider here is that municipalities in the Chicago region are part of the same jurisdictional structure that includes the City of Chicago; many overlapping, single-purpose governments (school and special districts);

and a large number of municipalities. A metropolitan region such as this one with a large number of jurisdictions exemplifies a quasi-market for public goods to a greater degree than jurisdictions in rural or small metropolitan regions. This structure increases the likelihood of competition in areas of taxation and economic development (Ostrom 1990; Oakerson 1999), and it provides many opportunities for local governments to develop collaborative networks or other methods of coordinating service provision and fiscal activities with neighboring jurisdictions (Agranoff and McGuire 2003).

Identifying and separating out the effects of state, regional, and local contexts and events is necessary to thoroughly understand why local governments make particular financial decisions that improve, maintain, or fail to maintain their financial health. However, this study investigates only local contexts and events by focusing on one metropolitan region. Incorporating state and regional effects into this study would require examining municipalities in multiple metropolitan regions. Such a comprehensive study would be difficult as it would require many cases and phenomenal amounts of detailed observations. At the same time, circumstances and events that make Illinois and the Chicago metropolitan region unique from other regions and are likely to affect the financial decisions and condition of its municipalities must be acknowledged as part of the larger context.

Explaining Financial Condition and Decisions

Based on the discussion thus far, I can identify four broad and interrelated factors and events that are likely to explain municipal *financial decisions* (financial management practices and fiscal policies) and *financial condition.* These factors are local government *fiscal capacity, administrative capacity, governance* (political and organizational structure and institutions), and *fiscal threats* and *fiscal opportunities.*

To better understand the effects of capacity, governance, and other microlevel factors on municipal financial decisions, this book focuses on how governments with different features respond to threats and opportunities, especially ones with a financial impact. The time period over which the Chicago municipalities are examined includes a recession and a period of financial munificence when the state of Illinois was distributing high levels of grants and *shared revenue* to these governments and local sales receipts were generating relatively high sales taxes. As revealed here, however, these governments face other financial threats and opportunities that can have significant effects on their financial condition, such as population growth and the closing of a major revenue generator.

This book also employs the metaphor of a *fiscal toolbox* to describe the options available to governments to respond to fiscal threats and opportunities. As noted previously, decisions can be fiscal policies, such as tax rates and changes to tax rates, or more mundane financial practices, such as the decision to self-insure or purchase insurance commercially. The fiscal toolbox then contains the set of all financial policies and practices governments could adopt at a point in time. Which policies and practices they pursue are a function of the size and content of the toolbox and the choices they make from among available tools.

As shown by the investigation conducted here, external fiscal capacity is one of the most important factors affecting the size of the fiscal toolbox. It is a function of *revenue wealth* (the level of revenues that the government can generate), *spending needs* or obligations, state-level institutional rules that limit or enhance access to different revenue sources (e.g., home rule), and the level of financial aid received from state government. However, the content of the toolbox also depends on internal fiscal capacity, which is a function of fiscal structure and prior policy decisions. For instance, whether a government can use its *fund balance* to solve the financial problems created by a recession depends upon how much money is in the fund balance, which is directly affected by prior decisions to lower or raise residual dollars to that account. In addition, decisions that affect the fund balance in the near term may reflect broader government policies regarding the appropriate level and use of the fund balance.

The contents of the fiscal toolbox are also affected by fiscal threats and opportunities. Threats such as recessions eliminate revenue options for resolving financial problems, which increases fiscal stress. Opportunities such as population growth expand revenue options and create a more munificent environment. Both threats and opportunities require the government to take action to maintain or improve financial condition. As shown here, governments that are experiencing high population growth and economic development face a unique and powerful set of threats and opportunities compared to others in the region. Governments must successfully adapt to these events if they are to maintain or improve financial condition and be financially sustainable. Also the relationship between government fiscal structure, threats, and opportunities is sometimes not direct. Fiscal structure can make threats more risky and give government greater access to opportunities. For instance, governments that rely heavily on sales taxes will be more exposed to fiscal stress during a recession than those that rely heavily on property taxes.

Administratively, the concept of capacity can be defined in terms of officials' ability to identify opportunities and threats and successfully implement strategies to manage fiscal stress and improve or maintain financial condition. In this case, capacity is a function of financial knowledge and experience or even political inclination. For instance, one might expect professional finance directors to assess tools for solving financial problems differently than mayors. Although many would disagree as to whose approach is likely to be more successful, the views of professional finance directors are likely to be more in line with professional standards. Similarly, an electorate that is more tolerant of tax increases and creative forms of financial management will alter government officials' views of what tools are available for solving financial problems.

In many suburban governments, the level of professionalization of executive and financial decisions is likely to be greater in those with a council-manager form and a finance director than those with a council-mayor form and with no finance director. Therefore, form of government is useful in predicting and explaining governments' choice of tools from the fiscal toolbox. But local governance is much broader than the role of the mayor and other officials in determining financial and other policy choices of government. It encompasses how key personnel in financial decision making are appointed and the government's culture toward accountability and fiscal responsibility. In the model of financial problem solving presented in chapter 4, administrative capacity and governance have more to do with how a government is likely to assess the tools in the fiscal toolbox and the choices it makes than the contents or size of the toolbox. Although governance has different dimensions and is measured in several ways here, its components are treated as a single construct in most cases because of the difficulty of disentangling them in small governments.

One complicating factor in determining the effects of fiscal capacity on financial condition, as demonstrated by this discussion, is that the two concepts are not mutually exclusive. Financial condition can be defined generally as the relative level of assets to liabilities in a government. Governments with better financial condition have more assets than liabilities and therefore greater capacity to leverage opportunities to increase assets and reduce liabilities and also greater capacity to minimize threats that might reduce assets or increase liabilities. In other words, governments with better financial condition have greater capacity to maintain and improve their financial condition.

Looking at the effects of fiscal capacity on financial condition is redundant according to the last statement, but the concept of financial condition is more complicated than this brief discussion suggests. It has multiple features, dimensions, and time frames. The analysis and use of these concepts in this book is based on a model of local government financial condition that recognizes these dimensions and time frames and provides a basis for identifying different sets of factors that are important to the financial condition of municipalities in general and in the Chicago region more specifically. For instance, chapter 6 examines whether governments with revenue diversification are better able to maintain budgetary solvency, which measures near-term financial condition, over a time period that includes the recession in 2001. Other analyses examine whether governments with economic deficits (poor revenue wealth and high spending needs) or low capacity in other areas (e.g., non–home rule and very small) have difficulty maintaining different aspects or time frames of financial condition.

Fiscal stress is another concept that overlaps with financial condition in the literature. As the term is generally applied, governments with severe economic deficits and low fiscal capacity are described as experiencing high fiscal stress. Similarly, a government that is experiencing cash shortages is also under fiscal stress compared to one with a fund balance that contains a year's worth of operating expenditures. However, this book defines fiscal stress specifically as a negative change in fiscal capacity or financial condition more broadly. Fiscal stress is dynamic and does not refer to a steady state in any particular time period. Governments experience fiscal stress when an economic recession reduces their *budgetary solvency* (revenues relative to spending) and the size of their fiscal toolbox. Similarly, governments experience fiscal stress when they are subject to expensive lawsuits and other events that have the potential to change their financial condition.

The Investigation

This book examines how municipal governments in the Chicago metropolitan area have managed and governed their fiscal affairs during the 2000s, focusing on the constraints established or opportunities presented by their fiscal and institutional environments. It addresses the impact of different conditions, events, and choices on policies, practices, and financial condition. It identifies the major financial problems experienced by these governments, the solutions they pursue, and the fiscal outcomes that result from the interplay of decisions and environment.

The primary research questions investigated here are the following: (1) What are the sources of fiscal threats and opportunities in these governments? (2) What tools (policies and practices) do they use to manage fiscal threats and opportunities and maintain financial condition? (3) What effect do contextual factors such as fiscal capacity and governance have on the tools available to them and the tools they use to manage fiscal threats and opportunities and maintain financial condition? (4) What effect do particular tools have on their ability to manage fiscal threats and opportunities and maintain financial condition?

The chapters that follow answer these questions with in-depth analyses using extensive quantitative and qualitative data on the fiscal and governing characteristics and decisions of these governments. The quantitative data are primarily fiscal and span the financial good times of the late 1990s through the middle of the first decade of the 2000s, which includes the 2001 recession. The qualitative data come primarily from extensive interviews of municipal officials and news reporting in the region. Most of this data is from 2000 through the middle of the first decade of the 2000s, but some interviews were conducted and news reports collected in 2009 and 2010 that focus on the Great Recession. However, the continuing and lagged effect of this later recession on municipal governments precludes being able to thoroughly investigate these questions with respect to this major fiscal threat.

The specific research questions I ask in each primary area, the expected answers, and how I define concepts used throughout the book are derived, to a great degree, from empirical research and strong theoretical traditions in economics, political science, and public administration. One body of research I rely on is composed of the many studies on local government fiscal stress and financial condition conducted in the late 1970s and early 1980s. At the time, many believed central cities were dead and revenue from the federal to local governments had declined significantly. This period spawned numerous efforts to develop indicators of fiscal stress and financial condition from different sectors (Burchell et al. 1981; Bahl 1984; Aronson 1984; ACIR 1971, 1979; Groves, Godsey, and Shulman 1981) and led to additional work in the fields of economics and public administration in later years (Groves and Valente 2003; Ladd and Yinger 1989; Brown 1993). A related and important area of research for this book comes from the Fiscal Austerity and Urban Innovation project (FAUI) that supported many studies of fiscal stress and financial strategies in numerous governments in the United States and elsewhere using similar surveys (Clark and Ferguson 1983; Pammer 1990; Hawkins 1989).

The second body of research that informs my research questions and analyses is from the field of strategic management, which views financial decision making as problem solving (Mintzberg 1979; Mintzberg, Raisinghani, and Theroet 1976; Simon and Associates 1986). According to this perspective, financial policies that are adopted and practices that are implemented are in response to financial problems. The problems can be fiscal threats, such as a recession, or fiscal opportunities in the form of large state and federal grant programs.[6] More commonly, the financial problem may involve, for instance, funding needed capital improvements or controlling the financial decisions of others in the government concerning how such funds are managed. The important point here is that the financial decisions government makes are in large part an attempt to adapt to its fiscal environment. Governments in good financial condition will have adapted successfully while those in poor financial condition will not have adapted successfully. Which decisions government makes is a function of the financial tools available to it and its approach to solving financial problems. The latter varies depending upon the heuristics employed by government officials, which is affected by the government's institutions of governance.

A third body of research that informs my research is represented by two streams of studies that both focus on internal governing institutions. One stream is represented by Laurence Lynn and his colleagues, who utilize a particular theoretical approach and framework to derive specific research questions that link management and politics in the study of government and identify important events and factors in the governing process (Lynn, Heinrich, and Hill 2001; Ingraham and Lynn 2004; Lynn and Ingraham 2004; Hill and Lynn 2004; Heinrich and Lynn 2000). This framework "is based on the premise that any particular governing arrangement—within a policy domain, with respect to a type of government activity, within a particular jurisdiction, or within a particular organizational field—is embedded in a wider social, fiscal, and political context" (Lynn, Heinrich, and Hill 2001, 12).

The second stream of research is more specifically focused on management and politics in smaller, local governments (Frederickson, Johnson, and Wood 2004; Folz and French 2005; Frederickson and Nalbandian 2002). As described here, local governments can be arrayed on a continuum of political versus corporate governance that affects how financial problems are solved and, ultimately, which tools officials choose to solve these problems and adapt to their environment. But the Lynn framework does not immediately fit with this continuum and so must be adapted. In this case, smaller, local governments have fewer governance levels and less distinct legislative and executive arenas than what is envisioned by the Lynn framework, which makes the continuum more important in these settings than in larger governments.

Another area of literature that is incorporated into the analyses conducted here would not be described as research by most scholars. Rather this literature represents written standards and opinions about the practice of financial management that are available from organizations such as Government Finance Officers Association (www.gfoa.org), Standard & Poor's (2002), and Moody's Investor Services (2000). Consistent with their mission, these organizations identify critical areas of financial management practices and establish standards for such practices based on many years of expert opinion. I use these standards and opinions, available online or in printed form, to help organize the qualitative data and identify key practices and financial decisions.

The last important body of research for my investigation focuses on understanding local governments, especially those in metropolitan regions, as a part of a larger system of governance. Although this larger system is part of the macrolevel environment that varies by state or region, so its effects cannot be determined in a single-region study, it is critical to assess how this system is likely to be different in Chicago compared to other metropolitan regions. One perspective from this body of research that is useful here views local governments as embedded within a system of nested institutions that includes state or regional governments (McCabe and Feiock 2005). Another perspective views local governments as embedded more specifically within a metropolitan region that contains many local governments that interact with one another on a variety of matters, but especially those with fiscal implications (Oakerson 1999; Ostrom 1990; Boyne 1996). These interactions or relationships can take many forms that exemplify greater or lesser degrees of voluntary collective action, contracting, conflict, and competition that may be driven by the fiscal capacity and governance features of individual governments (including nested features).

This book's empirical observations from which it derives its claims and inferences about the effects of capacity, governance, and other factors on financial decisions and condition come from five primary sources of data: (1) extensive quantitative data from 1997 to 2006 from the state of Illinois that report details of municipal government financial condition, fiscal capacity, and some types of financial decisions that is supplemented with data from the US Census; (2) news reports on the governance, financial decisions (policies and practices), and financial condition of municipalities in the Chicago metropolitan region from more than seventy regional newspapers spanning 2001 (or earlier in many cases) to 2006; (3) semistructured interviews with the chief financial officers in sixty-two specifically selected municipal governments in spring 2003; (4) interviews with executive directors of most of the councils of government in the region in December 2009; and (5) news reports about selected governments from 2009 and 2010.[7] In the 2003 interviews, municipal officials were asked how their governments were handling the 2001 recession and other financial problems, and they were also questioned about the fiscal practices and policies of their governments more generally. In the interviews with the executive directors, they were asked about the level of fiscal stress their member municipalities were experiencing due to the Great Recession and how they were handling it. The executive directors were also asked about collaboration, interlocal agreements, and other forms of collective action that their member governments were engaged in with other local governments.

The quantitative data are used to measure municipal government financial condition, fiscal capacity, fiscal structure, some types of fiscal threats and opportunities, and some aspects of fiscal governance. Analyses with these data help link fiscal capacity, fiscal structure, and governance to government financial condition and some types of financial decisions (e.g., spending and revenue levels, dependence on sales taxes, and fund balance levels) particularly in response to fiscal stress. The qualitative data (news reports and interviews) are used to document other aspects of governance in the municipalities, the fiscal problems they face, and nuanced details about their fiscal practices and policies that cannot be observed from the quantitative data. Analyses with the qualitative data help link capacity and governance more broadly to financial decisions (fiscal policies and practices), strategies for dealing with financial problems, and fiscal outcomes.

The research design for the quantitative analyses is well known to researchers that employ statistical analyses on cross-sectional and time series data. Here I use graphs of aggregate financial features and changes in features over time, and regression analysis of pooled data to observe the independent effects of potential causes of fiscal stress, financial decisions, and financial condition. Being able to observe multiple years of data, even in a narrow time frame, across many municipalities allows me to separate the effects of events in these two dimensions (time and cross-sectional). The 2001 recession, and the Great Recession to a lesser degree, present a form of experimental research design that allows me to observe the effects of these fiscal threats that were common to all governments in the region and periods of financial munificence in the late 1990s and between the two recessions.

Documentation of governance, jurisdictional interactions, fiscal problems, and financial decisions (primarily fiscal practices) is established by coding and summarizing the 2003 interview data and news reports from that period according to definitions and categories of these events that are grounded in both theory and practice. When combined with the quantitative data on capacity and financial condition, the qualitative analysis allows me to describe variation and clustering among municipalities with respect to what one would expect based on theory and practice. For instance, I have observed that many governments compare themselves to other governments on a wide range of financial policies (e.g., tax rates, charges, salaries) and practices (e.g., internal controls), especially when making changes to them, which is a form of competitive interaction between them. I have also observed that lawsuits are a financial drain on many governments and that stable governance may have an effect on financial condition independent of type of governance. Not surprisingly, large governments with high fiscal capacity are more likely to govern in particular ways than small governments and those with low capacity, but irrespective of size, governments with high fiscal capacity experience less fiscal stress than governments with low capacity.

More specifically, I link the qualitative data on governance and capacity to financial decisions—that are often made in response to financial problems—and I link financial decisions to outcomes using two strategies. First, commonalities in practices, policies, and financial condition among governments with similar governance and capacity features are identified and reported. Second, financial decisions and fiscal outcomes (primarily financial condition) are contrasted and compared among municipalities that are grouped according to key governance and capacity features. For example, one strategy I use is to look for similarities in financial decisions and governance features of municipalities that have high capacity but are less fiscally healthy or that experience high levels of fiscal stress. Another strategy I use is to look for similarities in financial decisions and governance features of municipalities that have low capacity but are fiscally healthy even during a recession (Bollen, Entwisle, and Alderson 1993; Miles and Huberman 1994).

There are two primary limitations of my research design and methodology. First, the qualitative data do not represent in-depth case reporting. I am not observing the progression of events in one case over an extended period of time. Case reporting helps to establish the time ordering of events and the mechanisms that lead from one event to another, which can provide a very comprehensive picture of cause and effect. Case reporting would have been very useful to better understand the chain of events in high-growth municipalities or those undergoing significant change in governance or capacity, but the extensive news reports over time for many municipalities helps in this regard. Second, with the exception of the sixty-two municipalities in which interviews were conducted, my sample of information about the other municipalities may not be representative of the true conditions, practices, and policies in these governments. News reports do not constitute a random sample of events but only those that get reported, and the quality or thoroughness of reporting on municipalities certainly varies across the region. Although the high number of cases in this analysis helps to overcome some of these limitations, I must acknowledge that the absence of some events and qualitative features in a municipality as documented by the news reports does not necessarily mean that the event did not happen or the feature does not exist for that government. It may simply be that the event or feature was not reported, and my findings need to be interpreted with this in mind.

The primary reason for using a comparative approach with many cases rather than in-depth analyses of fewer cases is the tremendous variation in capacity, governance features, and fiscal problems of the municipalities in the Chicago metropolitan region. As noted previously, there is no typical suburb or even a limited amount of typical groups of suburbs upon which to base a restricted amount of in-depth case studies. Thus any in-depth comparative case study, even those with more than a few cases, will apply only to a portion of suburban municipal governments in the region. The wide variation of suburban municipalities also means that many capacity and governance features and/or dimensions must be taken into account to explain how they affect municipal financial decisions and financial condition.

Plan of the Book

Chapter 2 presents a framework for conceptualizing local government financial condition and the fiscal toolbox that is used to derive many measures used in this book. This framework is based on a systems approach that provides a means of organizing the phenomenon's complexity and recognizes multidimensional features in varying time frames. The model is used to classify the many measures of financial condition that exist in the literature and to develop measures that are appropriate in different time frames and to municipalities in this region. This chapter also describes and operationalizes all the other indices and variables used in the analyses in this book and maps important features to demonstrate how municipal governments in the region are widely distributed on critical variables.

Chapter 3 presents the first theoretical framework that explains how and why governments choose different tools from the toolbox. It conceptualizes financial decision making as problem solving in the context of strategic management (strategic problem solving). Discussions in this chapter focus on professionalization as a primary factor affecting how officials solve financial problems and other features such as entrepreneurialism and approaches to risk. The research uses professional standards and prior research on managing fiscal stress as a basis for categorizing and analyzing the fiscal policies and practices of Chicago municipalities. The chapter also describes the qualitative data and analysis in more detail.

Chapter 4 presents two other theoretical frameworks that focus on municipal governing structure and institutions as complementary factors in explaining how and why government chooses certain tools and also explains the contents of the fiscal toolbox. One framework specifies a way of conceptualizing the different governing structures and institutions within municipal governments in Illinois. The second framework recognizes the effects of governing structures and institutions on the fiscal toolbox and choice of tools at a more macro level. At a micro level, governing structures and institutions are unique to each municipal government in the study. At a macro level, governments' solutions to financial problems are defined and influenced by other local governments in the metropolitan region and state rules. In this case, the fragmentation of the Chicago region and the decentralization of state-local relations in Illinois must be recognized as key factors in fiscal problem solving by these governments. The chapter also presents a model of financial problem solving that is used to direct the investigation and interpret findings.

Chapter 5 documents the financial threats and opportunities that Chicago municipal governments faced in the late 1990s up to the middle of the first decade of the 2000s, and more recently in 2009 and 2010, using both qualitative and quantitative evidence. It examines financial trends in these governments and assesses the level of fiscal stress these governments experienced during this time period and how they reacted. The qualitative evidence is examined for revenues and spending separately, with particular attention given to home rule and reliance on sales taxes on the revenue side, and lawsuits and political conflict on the spending side. In addition, population growth and development is documented and evaluated in some detail as the threats and opportunities high-growth and developing governments face are so different from other governments, as are the types of decisions that will help them adapt fiscally to growth and development. Finally, the chapter presents a set of regression analyses that examines how factors in the financial decision model affect fiscal stress, measured as changes in budgetary solvency, in Chicago municipal governments from 1999 to 2005.

Chapter 6 documents the policy and practice tools Chicago municipal governments use to manage fiscal stress according to the primary fiscal equation using qualitative evidence and trend analysis. This chapter then presents a set of regression analyses that examines their responses to fiscal stress and munificence with respect to changes in own-source revenue, capital spending, and operational spending.

Chapter 7 documents the policy and practice tools Chicago municipal governments use to manage fiscal stress using qualitative evidence. It also presents a set of regression analyses that examine these governments' fiscal policies regarding own-source revenue, operational spending, capital spending, dedicated capital revenue, total debt, budgetary solvency, and dependence on sales taxes. The chapter documents the practice tools that these governments use to maintain or improve financial condition and focuses on budgeting and planning, financial management practices, and their collaborative/competitive behaviors. Finally, chapter 7 uses two analytical methods to examine multiple indicators of financial condition for different groups of municipal governments and derive conclusions about the effects of fiscal capacity, governance, and other events on the financial health of these governments.

In conjunction, these analyses confirm many things we already know, or think we know, about the impact of such contextual factors on local fiscal policies and practices. That is often the role of scientific investigation. For instance, when faced with fiscal threats, Chicago suburban governments pursue a hierarchy of responses that was identified many years ago (Levine, Rubin, and Wolohojian 1981). But the analyses also reveal some new information about these phenomena, such as the prevalence of competition and the importance of different contextual phases of growth and development. The findings elaborate on existing knowledge by showing the extent to which these impacts are conditional or modified by other factors and the lack of stability in many key factors. Although this makes it difficult to isolate and observe the effects of particular factors on policies and practices, it establishes important qualifications for future research and practice. More generally, the book demonstrates the extent to which the particular frameworks presented here are useful for understanding local government financial condition and how local governments in a metropolitan region solve financial problems. These frameworks help define concepts; identify important factors in the processes examined, or at least show where to find these factors; and provide powerful metaphors for describing events.

Notes

1. Governments cannot really go bankrupt in the same way that a private corporation can and suddenly stop providing services to citizens. The services provided by local governments are guaranteed at some level by state government, which has certain obligations to provide for the health and safety of its citizens, but local governments can declare bankruptcy under Chapter 9 of the bankruptcy code that limits its obligations to repay debt and creditors (Dubrow 2009).
2. The Great Recession officially ended in June 2009 according to the National Bureau of Economic Research.
3. Good internal fiscal capacity refers to surplus internal resources such as the fund balance, excess employees, and flexibility in spending for objects and services.
4. According to the 2007 US Census of Governments, the six-county Chicago metropolitan region had 271 total suburban municipalities.
5. Over 50 percent of the US population lived in suburban areas of metropolitan regions as of 2000, and only 20 percent lived in nonmetropolitan areas. Trends suggest that the percentage of people living in suburban areas is likely to be higher in 2010 (Hobbs and Stoops 2002).
6. "Illinois First" that was implemented in 1999 by Governor George Ryan and the federal American Recovery and Reinvestment Act that was implemented in 2009 distributed a lot of funds to local governments for capital expenditures.
7. It is important to note that the full effects of recessions on municipalities often lag up to two years or more after the recession ends.

Chapter 2
Local Government Financial Condition and Fiscal Stress

To understand how municipal officials in large metropolitan regions improve, maintain, or fail to maintain the financial health of their governments, one must first understand what it means for a municipal government to be financially healthy. Generally speaking, a financially healthy government is one that can meet its financial and service obligations. This description is not very satisfying, however, as it leaves many unanswered questions. What constitutes an obligation? Some obligations are formalized or explicit such as those established by contract, agreement, or statute; others are implied and therefore ambiguous. Do governments have greater obligations to residents than nonresidents? What about obligations to future generations? Are some types of obligations, such as public safety and education, more important than others, such as health and recreation? Is a government in better financial health if it can finance and meet its obligations at a higher level, or are there thresholds at which financial health is considered to be established?

Incorporating answers to all these questions into a definition of financial health and method of measurement is not easy, and may not even be necessary, but deciding what to include and exclude requires informed judgment and logical reasoning. The concept is very complex, and it has many interpretations depending upon one's perspective or assumptions. For instance, state governments are likely to focus on the economic characteristics of local jurisdictions, such as personal income or property values, to evaluate the financial condition of local governments for purposes of distributing grants and aid. They are less likely to monitor local government financial features such as revenues collected, spending, and debt and incorporate these factors into state policies that affect local government. By comparison, local governments monitor their own financial performance much more closely, especially regarding taxes, which are of much interest to voters. Local governments also focus on other areas of financial performance related to fund balances and cash flow, which is of little interest to voters or higher levels of government. Investors who want to purchase municipal bonds will examine a wide range of indicators to assess local government financial health, even examining fiscal attributes of the surrounding region to predict its ability to repay debt.

Rather than present one correct definition of local government financial health, this chapter presents a model of financial condition that identifies its different dimensions or components and organizes them into a comprehensive framework to show the linkages and conditional relationships among its parts. This approach allows for a more comprehensive picture of the concept than is usually found in research on local government finance and financial management. More important, this model also provides a framework for defining and organizing the various measures of financial condition that are specified in different fields, including economics, public administration, and governmental accounting. Some of these measures will be used in the analyses presented in later chapters that link capacity, governance, and other factors to municipal financial decisions and financial condition.

The lesson that can be derived from this chapter is that there is no one best way to define and measure local government financial health. Financial condition, its measurement, and its interpretation may vary depending upon the context, application, and other factors. I also use this model to distinguish financial condition from related concepts such as fiscal capacity and fiscal stress that are applied liberally and often interchangeably in the literature. However, before this framework is presented, it is useful to review definitions and measurement of local government financial health or financial condition from prior research.

Local Government Financial Health in Prior Research

The fiscal pressures faced by central cities in the late 1970s and early 1980s engendered numerous efforts across disciplines and by different government and nonprofit agencies to assess local government financial health and, in some cases, develop sophisticated indices to measure it. Since then, research on the financial condition of local government has been more sporadic but not infrequent. A review of this extensive literature yields three observations. First, many definitions of financial condition and statements about what constitutes good financial health conceptualize the phenomenon as an equilibrium or balance between different financial features of the government and its fiscal environment. Second, assessment and measurement of financial health is often done with respect to a benchmark, which represents a group norm (e.g., average or median), although it can be an agreed upon standard or condition. Third, it is impossible to construct a valid, comprehensive measure of financial condition that takes into account all dimensions and uses of the concept.

One comprehensive and well-recognized work on local government financial condition is Clark and Ferguson (1983) who conceptualize the term very broadly as a balance or equilibrium between local government policies and the private sector environment (44). They develop numerous indicators of fiscal balance using ratios of financial features such as expenditures relative to city wealth or median family income, and expenditures relative to spending needs (functional performance). They also use several ratios of government financial performance and long-term obligations as indicators of financial management problems. They classify the financial health of a sample of sixty-two urban municipalities in the United States with populations greater than fifty thousand residents between 1960 and 1977 using their indicators and investigate the relationships between fiscal stress, financial preferences, political culture, and leadership in these cities.

It is important to note that Clark and Ferguson's approach emphasizes that financial condition is not specifically about the absolute level of resources available to government, their spending needs, or expenditures. Rather, it depends upon whether one set of financial features is appropriate to another. In other words, it depends upon context. In this case, financial condition can refer to whether there are enough resources to meet spending needs, whether revenues collected burden existing resources too much, and whether expenditures are appropriate to spending needs. Financial condition can also be a function of whether liabilities are balanced with assets, whether there is adequate protection against risks, or whether revenues are balanced with spending.

Ladd and Yinger (1989) is another often-cited comprehensive work that measures local government financial condition. They present a method of assessing city financial condition that is also based on the idea of balance, but their focus is on the balance between government policies and exogenous conditions within the jurisdiction. This work is highly sophisticated mathematically and emphasizes precision in measuring the exogenous aspects of financial condition. They distinguish between standardized and actual fiscal health. The calculation of standardized fiscal health is based on the assumption that all cities have access to the same level and types of revenues and have the same set of service responsibilities (103–5). The concept is defined as the difference between standardized revenue-raising capacity and standardized spending need.[1] In contrast, actual fiscal health is the balance between restricted revenue-raising capacity and actual spending need (190–93).

For both standardized and actual fiscal health, spending need is the amount a government must spend to provide a standard level of public services at a standard level of quality, and revenue-raising capacity is defined as the amount of revenue a government can raise with a standard tax burden (Ladd and Yinger 1989, 46). However, restricted revenue-raising capacity takes into account government access to resources as determined by fiscal institutions, and actual spending need takes into account only those services for which government is responsible.

Ladd and Yinger's work represented, in many respects, the dénouement of a large body of research conducted by scholars associated with the US Advisory Commission on Intergovernmental Relations (ACIR 1962, 1971, 1979, 1988; Bahl 1984; Tannenwald and Cowan 1997). The ACIR was established in 1959 by an act of Congress as a permanent, independent, bipartisan, intergovernmental agency to investigate how different levels of government relate to and interact with one another. Terminated in 1996, its broader mission was to encourage a dialogue about how governments at different levels should or could interact with one another in the context of the US federalist system to promote valued and common objectives. Much of this research identified emerging intergovernmental issues and trends that concerned governing institutions and finances and investigated the impacts of such events across levels of government. A significant amount of ACIR research also focused on developing methods of measuring state and local government financial condition that laid the groundwork for much subsequent research on this subject.[2] This work shared a focus with other research on external resources and spending pressures as the primary determinants of government financial condition, although much of it incorporated actual revenues and spending (policy choices) in relation to these exogenous factors to assess financial health.

Figure 2.1 presents the primary causes or components of financial condition and their relationship to each other and the broader concept of financial health as con-

FIGURE 2.1 Primary Attributes of Financial Condition

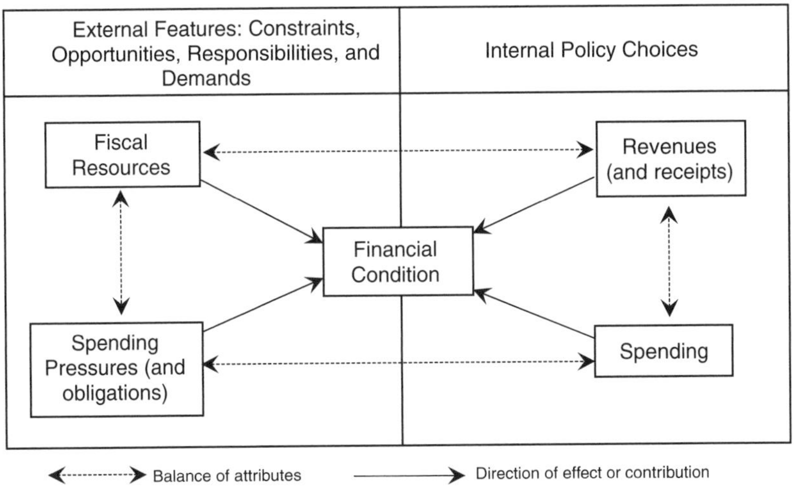

ceptualized by research in this book. The most important external factors in the diagram (exogenous to policy choices) are available fiscal resources and spending pressures, which represent the boundaries of government financial condition. But there is more to financial condition than external factors, and focusing only on the relationship between resources and spending needs overlooks the role of government action in meeting these needs in a way that does not deplete fiscal resources. Financial condition also depends on whether revenues collected are balanced with available fiscal resources and whether spending is balanced with spending needs.[3] In this case, high spending pressures and low fiscal resources do not guarantee poor financial health if the government does not overburden resources and is able to adequately meet service responsibilities.

Berne and Schramm (1986) present another useful framework for assessing government financial health that reviews different ways of thinking about and measuring the concept. They define financial condition as the probability that a government will meet its financial obligations to creditors, consumers, employees, taxpayers, suppliers, and others as these obligations come due (68). Using the balance metaphor, they state that this probability depends on the likelihood that resources and spending needs can be brought into equilibrium. Although Ladd and Yinger recognize some aspects of the policy dimension of financial condition with their measure of revenue effort (revenue collected divided by revenue capacity), Berne and Schramm incorporate the internal side of government financial performance more directly into the discussion and analysis of local government financial condition.

It is the case that local governments rely almost completely on external resources to fund services, but they often have significant internal resources that can supplement revenues when needed. Most governments accumulate surplus funds in their fund balances, which serve primarily to meet short-term obligations, such as accounts payable. But at higher levels these funds can be used to meet broader spending obligations in the near term when fiscal resources decline, such as during recessions. Looking at figure 2.1, the balance between revenues and spending will determine whether government has surpluses or deficits during the fiscal year that increase or decrease the fund balance. A government that does not maintain a structural balance between revenues and spending is not really in good financial condition, even if it has sufficient external resources to meet all spending needs and generate surplus funds. Berne and Schramm also investigate the role of past spending commitments, such as debt and long-term contracts, in local government financial condition. These policy choices can contribute significantly to current spending obligations, although they are not always recognized in assessments of financial condition. In this case, spending obligations in figure 2.1 include past decisions that incur current and future obligations.

More broadly, Berne and Schramm's important contribution to understanding government financial condition is their argument that financial health can exist in different time frames. Assessing government financial position during the fiscal year, for instance, is not going to tell you whether it has the capacity to fund necessary services now and in the future, but acknowledging both factors gives a more complete picture of financial health. Groves and Valente (2003) formalize this perspective of financial condition in different time frames with four concepts of fiscal solvency.[4] *Long-run solvency* refers to the long-term balance between government revenues and spending and emphasizes the ability of government to meet future obligations and handle unknown fiscal challenges for an extended period. *Service-level solvency* refers to the government's ability to provide adequate services to meet the health, safety, and welfare needs of its citizens given its revenue resources. *Budgetary solvency* is defined as the ability to balance the budget or generate enough resources to cover expenditures in the current fiscal year. *Cash solvency* reflects the ability to generate enough cash over thirty or sixty days to pay bills during that time period.

The concepts of fiscal stress and financial condition should be distinguished at this point in the discussion, as the two are often used interchangeably. As conceptualized here, *fiscal stress* is a dynamic event that occurs when governments experience decreasing revenues or increasing spending pressures that move it off-balance or out of fiscal equilibrium in any area of solvency. For instance, if state government slows its payment of shared revenues to local governments, then the latter will have reduced cash solvency, which creates fiscal stress. A recession or the closing of a major taxpaying enterprise within a jurisdiction can temporarily slow or permanently reduce the revenue stream of governments, which reduces long-run solvency and increases fiscal stress. Thus fiscal stress can be defined as a worsening of financial condition, or even the threat of a worsening of financial condition. For instance, some have measured fiscal stress as discretionary tax increases and expenditure reductions, which reflect change in two areas of financial condition (Holcombe and Sobel 1997, 166). On the other side of the spectrum, *fiscal munificence* is the improvement of financial condition or the existence of opportunities to improve financial condition.

Financial condition, then, is the state of equilibrium or balance that exists between different dimensions or components of government's financial sphere of spending pressures and obligations, external fiscal resources, revenues and internal resources, and actual spending. The definition is very broad and vague precisely because it can only be defined specifically for particular types of solvency or particular contexts. The important point is that good financial condition implies balance, and measuring balance is best accomplished using ratios of components, not absolute values (Hildreth 1997).

In conjunction with each other, the concepts of financial condition and fiscal stress or munificence present a view of local government financial health that is more dynamic than prior research. One exception is Clark and Ferguson (1983), who argue that balancing all the components in figure 2.1 is a dynamic process in which government officials make policy decisions that affect current and future spending and revenue that can promote or hinder adaptation to the economic and service environment. Environments change to create fiscal stress and munificence, and cities that cannot adapt or do not adapt rapidly enough will have poorer financial condition than governments that do adapt. Thus *financial health* (financial condition and fiscal stress) is both a state of being and an ongoing process that reflects the extent to which a government fiscal structure is adapted to the environment and whether government maintains or improves this balance in the future. In this case, a government that is experiencing greater fiscal stress will be worse off than one that is experiencing little change in financial condition, and a government whose financial condition is improving might be considered better off than one with stable financial condition. Taking account of changing fiscal states and current financial condition to assess the overall financial health of government is not common and complicates its assessment greatly.

It is also common for financial condition to be measured and defined relative to conditions in a set of governments or an agreed-upon standard. Clark and Ferguson (1983), Ladd and Yinger (1989), and the ACIR (1962, 1971, 1988) measure different aspects of financial condition in each government using the average of those features for a group of governments. For instance, the functional performance index devised by Clark and Ferguson measures spending need in a government as the difference between its actual spending and the average spending of a reference group. The reference group may be all governments in a state or region or even cohorts with similar features. In this case, the average reflects what is normal or typical for that group. Similarly, the ACIR used average tax rates in its representative tax system to measure available fiscal resources. Average tax rates for each type of tax are multiplied by the value of the government's tax base to determine the amount of revenues a government could obtain from each source if it taxed at normal baseline rates. The revenues are then summed across types of taxes to create a composite measure of overall tax capacity.

The discussion thus far demonstrates that financial condition and financial health are complex and multidimensional with varying time frames. Many concepts also are relative rather than absolute because they are meaningful only in comparison to other concepts, and there are multiple reference points for comparison (e.g., group median or past conditions). Conceptualizing these phenomena in a comprehensive manner in order to identify causes and important events will require recognizing different time frames (past, current, future, short-term, and long-term), time lines (static and dynamic), and dimensions. Figure 2.1 is focused primarily on budgetary solvency and long-run financial condition under the assumption that external resources and spending pressures are not likely to change in the short run. But long-run solvency encompasses future states that cannot be known and adds uncertainty or risk to the analysis of financial condition. Specifying the relative impacts of dimensions, time frames, and time lines also is problematic because they often are related in indirect or nonlinear ways. These considerations indicate how difficult it is to fit all these elements together to yield a valid assessment of overall financial health in a government.[5]

For instance, consider the difficulty of comparing the financial health of a government that is in very good financial condition yet experiencing high levels of fiscal stress with one that is in poor but stable financial condition. Which government is in worse shape? Similarly, it is not clear how one would compare the financial condition of a government with poor, long-run solvency but reasonably good cash and budgetary solvency to one with good, long-run solvency but poor cash and budgetary solvency. Governments with poor, long-run solvency due to high spending needs and low levels of available resources are more likely to have low spending effort, high revenue burden, and poor budgetary and cash solvency, but this is not guaranteed. Factors that affect financial condition in different time frames or with respect to different levels of solvency can function somewhat independently, especially in the short run. All of this suggests that it may be impossible to develop a single, meaningful, and valid measure of financial condition or financial health that captures all time frames, time lines, and dimensions of the phenomena.

Brown (1993) and Kloha, Weissert, and Kleine (2005) are examples of comprehensive indicators of financial condition that combine components from different time frames and levels of solvency.[6] The Brown index merges ten different ratios that represent different time frames and endogenous and exogenous causes of financial condition. He assesses each measure by comparing it to others obtained from similar-sized governments (the reference group) and assigns governments a score for each measure based on their location within each distribution. The scores are equally weighted and then summed in a linear fashion for each government. The Kloha, Weissert, and Kleine index is very similar to the Brown index with somewhat different component measures and standards for assigning scores to governments.

Examining the Brown index for 261 municipalities in the Chicago metropolitan region in 2003 reveals some of the problems with this method of assessing financial condition (Hendrick et al. 2006). First, very little variation is observed in the financial condition of these governments. Also many governments in the region that are generally known by financial experts in the region to be in poor financial condition have similar values on the index as those generally known to be in good financial condition. One reason for these problems is that the measure combines so many different dimensions in such an arbitrary way, which makes it unable to distinguish between good and bad financial condition at a comprehensive level. In the parlance of measurement, such measures have poor face validity and are not sensitive enough to factors that produce different levels of financial condition, although these measures can be useful in the hands of knowledgeable users who understand their limitations and are relatively easy to construct.

A Framework for Conceptualizing Financial Condition

Figure 2.2 presents a model of financial condition process that is employed here to better understand its different time frames, dimensions, and their relationship. The model shows that financial condition is shaped by two primary components—the fiscal environment and the policy choices officials make in response to the opportuni-

FIGURE 2.2 The Financial Condition Process

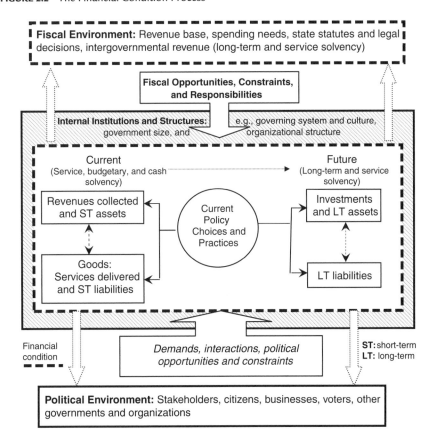

ties, demands, constraints, and responsibilities generated by the fiscal and political environments and prior policy choices.

Current financial policies (and financial management practices) impact the revenue-assets and spending-liabilities dimensions of financial condition in both the current time period and the future. With respect to revenue and assets, government officials determine the level of revenues to be collected and short-term assets to maintain, such as cash on hand, which are direct factors in short-term financial condition or solvency. Officials also determine which investments to undertake, which affects future revenue streams, and make other decisions that affect the future value of long-term assets. Long-term assets include capital infrastructure, pension investments, major equipment, or other resources the government owns that have value over time. Their future value is defined by their future market worth or the increases in revenues that result from these investments minus depreciation and other costs. With respect to spending and liabilities, officials' current decisions regarding debt, pensions, and deferred capital purchase or maintenance can increase or decrease future obligations. Current policies also determine the level of services and goods delivered during the fiscal year and whether to fulfill immediate obligations, such as payment to vendors.

More broadly, government financial policies are choices officials make about government fiscal structure (e.g., decisions about revenues, spending, assets, and liabilities) within the *fiscal policy space*. For instance, governments decide how much tax to collect, how much to depend on particular revenue sources, how much to spend, and how much revenue to reserve. They also decide how much to invest in capital infrastructure and whether to push current obligations to the future. Government *fiscal structure* is the combined outcome of these choices, which has many characteristics that are usually represented in relative terms, such as fund balance relative to total spending and property tax as a percentage of total revenue.

The fiscal environment includes all revenue bases of government, such as property values from which they draw property taxes, sales receipts (sales taxes), and resident income or payroll (income or payroll tax). The fiscal environment also includes spending needs and responsibilities, which are affected by events such as crime level, miles of roads, or age of infrastructure, and it can include imposed legal decisions that create fiscal responsibilities, such as from lawsuits. State statutes that directly constrain or expand revenue capacity, such as property tax limitations and home rule, and establish spending mandates are another feature of the fiscal environment. Intergovernmental revenues, such as grants and shared revenue from other governments, are another important feature of the local fiscal environment.

The political environment also greatly affects policy choices, but it is not a component or dimension of government financial condition in the same manner as the fiscal environment. The political environment consists of external stakeholders, such as residents and businesses within government boundaries, who place fiscal demands and political restrictions on the government through voting or other mechanisms. The political environment also consists of neighboring and overlapping governments and other organizations with which the government interacts and that can affect its financial choices directly or indirectly. For instance, governments in large metropolitan regions may face lots of competition from other governments to attract businesses and, as a result, are under great pressure to offer businesses incentives such as tax reductions to relocate into the jurisdiction. Other interactions can be contractual or collaborative to provide services, or they can be noncooperative such as the threat of a lawsuit.

Officials' policy choices also are constrained and directed by internal institutions and other features that are specific to their organization and government (the endogenous environment of the fiscal policy space). Like the political environment, these features are not part of a dimension of financial condition. Rather, they represent a set of boundaries, rules, and expectations within which financial decisions are made. These institutions and structures include the type of government (e.g., strong or weak mayor) and governing culture and values (e.g., professionally or politically motivated), both of which constrain and define policy options, determine who participates in financial decision making, and establish the rules of choice. For instance, governments that value professionalization or have qualified professionals significantly involved in policy decisions are likely to gravitate toward a different set of policy choices from one that is governed by political values and appointees. Similarly, municipal managers of governments with a council-manager form are going to have more authority over financial policies and the range of policy options considered than governments with a mayor-council form.

Organizationally, the size of the government is another important nonfiscal factor and feature of the government that affects the range of financial options available to officials. Large and complex organizations have more horizontal and vertical linkages than small ones, which increases options and opportunities when making choices (Thompson 1967). Similarly, large governments have a greater volume of activity that increases their capacity to share or trade off among activities and gives them more flexibility than small governments (Mattson 1994; MacManus and Pammer 1990). For instance, small governments are less likely to have surplus personnel who can be dedicated to projects as needed, and they are not likely to be involved in a wide range of fiscal activities (e.g., having multiple forms of debt) compared to large governments.

The dotted arrows between current revenues and spending and future assets and liabilities in the fiscal policy space signify that the two components of each pair are interdependent. Technically state and local governments cannot spend more than they collect in revenues, although certain features of their fiscal structure, as discussed later, provide some short-term flexibility in this matter. Similarly, short-term assets that are necessary to fund government during the fiscal year must be matched with near-term liabilities. Thus choices about current revenues and spending are often made in conjunction, and their outcomes tend to be highly correlated. Choices regarding future assets and liabilities are also interdependent, albeit less so than current revenues and liabilities. Government choices about future liabilities, such as the decision to incur more debt currently, often take the value of long-term assets into account, but sometimes they do not consider these factors thoroughly in making such decisions. In addition, the unpredictability of future states means that officials' decisions about long-term investment and liabilities will always be based on imperfect information, and these events are less likely to be correlated.

Dynamically, good financial health exists when officials' policy choices continuously produce a fiscal structure that is balanced with, adapted to, and even improved by changes in the fiscal environment (fiscal stress or munificence). On a static level, good financial condition reflects the extent to which a government has adapted its current fiscal structure to the demands, pressures, opportunities, constraints, and likely future changes in the environment (Clark and Ferguson 1983). Although environmental changes are not specifically represented in figure 2.2, the solid and thick arrows from the environment to the fiscal policy space demonstrate the direct effects of the former on the latter. In this case, changes in the environment, both positive and negative, establish the need for and induce policy choices that establish fiscal structure.

The nonsolid and smaller arrows from the fiscal policy space back to the fiscal environment indicate that current financial policies and practices have an indirect or less immediate effect on the fiscal environment than on components of the fiscal policy space. In effect, government officials have more control over items in the fiscal policy space and their fiscal structure than features of the fiscal environment. Likewise, officials have less control over the political environment than their own financial policies and fiscal structure. The dotted arrow from current to future fiscal structure shows that, to a great degree, future fiscal structure is a function of current fiscal structure precisely because the options available to government are defined by its current fiscal structure and environment. In other words, the fiscal future will look a lot like the fiscal past. Governments that rely predominately on property tax are not likely to rely predominately on sales taxes next year or even ten years later. Although some aspects of government fiscal structure may change rapidly, such as cash balances, many do not.

Risk and slack are two features of government fiscal structure and environment that are not represented specifically in the diagram but are very important to adaptability. They also represent different sides of the same coin in terms of their opposing effects on government adaptability. More specifically, higher levels of risk reduce adaptability or increase the potential effects of environmental changes on fiscal structure (via policy choices), and higher levels of slack increase adaptability or reduce the potential effects of environmental changes on fiscal structure. Theoretically, slack resources and other sources of fiscal flexibility allow the organization to better absorb positive and negative events by reducing the need for core structural changes (Tsetsekos 1995). Administratively slack provides managers a tool for limiting the disruption of service delivery or production processes that is often caused by environmental and internal changes. Risk and slack are closely related in that higher levels of risk can be balanced with higher levels of slack to improve adaptability, and lower levels of risk require less slack to maintain financial condition.

Theories of organizational behavior often define *slack* as the pool of resources in excess of the minimum necessary to produce a given level of output (Moe 1997; Niskanen 1975). Fiscal slack can be surplus, short-term resources such as the fund balance or rainy day fund or nonmonetary resources such as excess employees. Fiscal slack can also be uncollected revenue from that portion of the revenue base that is available to the government through higher taxation (*revenue reserves;* Berne and Schramm 1986). On the expenditure side, fiscal slack can be discretionary spending such as capital maintenance and travel that can be easily reduced during difficult financial periods (Hendrick 2004). Organizational theory also distinguishes between discretionary slack (e.g., cash, excess capital, personnel, spending, and credit) that is more liquid and fungible and nondiscretionary slack that is more difficult to convert to service production (e.g., specialized employees or restricted investments such as pensions; Sharfman et al. 1988).

Decision theory and public choice define *risk* as uncertainty about the occurrence of events but having knowledge of their probabilities (Luce and Raiffa 1957). In this case, risk is a property of the decision maker. More commonly risk is viewed as a property of the environment, or rather the likelihood of environmental change. In terms of the adaptation metaphor, it is also a function of the organization's exposure or vulnerability to detrimental fiscal shocks and changes in the environment. All other things being equal, a government with a more volatile environment that is also more exposed to its effects will be less able to adapt to negative changes than one that is less exposed. Thus, the government that is more exposed is in worse financial condition than a government with less risk or less exposure. For example, a government that relies heavily on sales taxes that are highly elastic is more vulnerable to declines in the economy than one that relies heavily on property taxes that are more stable and less affected by the economy. Small organizations also face greater risk because of their limited flexibility in compensating for or adapting to shocks and changes. For instance, large governments are more likely to have unfilled positions that can remain unfilled during periods of fiscal decline compared to small governments in which the duties of individual employees will be critical to a broader range of governmental functions.

According to the framework proposed here, governments with more slack are less exposed to risks because it provides them greater flexibility for managing detrimental and volatile environmental changes, at least in the short run. Governments with slack also have greater capacity to take advantage of opportunities and investments that could improve financial condition in the future, such as grants or economic development proposals. Thus slack and risk are important features of several dimensions of financial condition and demonstrate the principal of balance. Financial condition is a function of whether revenues collected are balanced with or appropriate to the revenue base, whether revenues are balanced with spending, and also whether government slack accounts for the risks it faces.

The fiscal structure of government that relies heavily on property taxes but has significant retail sales and the opportunity to levy a sales tax is not balanced with its revenue environment, especially if voters are highly opposed to raising property taxes. Although the government may perceive that it has lower financial risk because property taxes are more stable than sales taxes, it may be unable to raise enough property taxes to cover current or future spending needs. In this case, spending is not balanced with obligations, and the government should consider collecting more sales taxes to generate additional revenue. The government also should increase its surplus funds to mitigate the increased financial risk associated with being more dependent on sales taxes, which then brings its slack into balance with its risk.

Linking Time Frames of Financial Condition and Process

As defined previously, long-run solvency refers to the balance between the collective revenue bases and spending needs of government in the long run and its ability to satisfy future liabilities. Because most factors that generate spending needs and determine the value or size of the revenue bases are fairly stable over time, a government with balanced revenue bases and spending needs will have more long-run solvency than one with higher spending needs than the revenue bases can support. In addition, if a government has maximized the amount of revenue it draws from the revenue bases, then it has no revenue reserves or slack to accommodate increases in spending needs or opportunities (e.g., matching grants) that require additional funds. In this case, the government's long-run solvency is lower because its risk from negative changes in the fiscal environment is higher, and its investment potential is lower.

Long-run solvency also encompasses future assets, liabilities, and events—all of which are unknown. These uncertainties make it hard to assess long-run solvency or financial condition, but if a government has had low resources historically due to poor revenue bases and high spending needs, chances are its future environment will be similar. Unless there is evidence of positive future changes, such as an influx of development that raises property values, this government should limit future liabilities to better ensure a good financial condition down the road and improve long-run solvency.

Service-level solvency, by comparison, focuses on the extent to which governments are balancing near-term spending obligations, actual spending, available revenues, and revenues collected. Although a government with poor, long-run solvency is less likely to provide adequate services and therefore more likely to have poor, service-level solvency (and vice versa), the two events are distinct. For instance, a government with poor or constrained revenue bases can improve its service-level solvency by spending only what it needs to deliver services, reducing liabilities, and increasing surplus internal resources to handle emergencies. One could describe this government as having adapted its fiscal structure to the fiscal environment as evidenced by the balance between revenues collected and revenue bases, expenditures and spending needs, and structural features such as surplus resources. Alternatively, a government with good, long-run solvency may not tax or spend enough due to political constraints to adequately meet the health and safety needs of its citizens.

A wealthy government's fiscal structure may be poorly adapted to the fiscal environment in other ways that demonstrate low, service-level solvency. Due to political pressure, it may spend too much given its needs, not collect enough revenue to cover spending, and try to make up the shortfall with risky, high-paying investments and increases in liabilities (e.g., reduced pension funding). Although this government's revenue bases and spending needs indicate good, long-run solvency, its service-level imbalances due to policy choices have made it quite vulnerable to fiscal stress in the near term. One significant fiscal shock, such as a deep recession or a large number of retirements and lawsuits, could dramatically reduce funding for basic services and reduce the level and quality of services it provides for an extended period of time.

Strictly speaking, budgetary solvency is the level of balance between revenues, expenditures, and surpluses at the end or the beginning of the fiscal year. More generally, it is the "ability to generate enough revenue over normal budgetary periods to meet expenditures and not incur deficits" (Groves and Valente 2003, 1). Normally governments project at the beginning of the fiscal year that revenues will equal expenditures at the end of the fiscal year. But if economic (or political) conditions worsen unexpectedly, or if officials' estimates of revenues and expenditures are simply inaccurate, then the budget will not be balanced at the end of the fiscal year unless other conditions exist. These other conditions include having enough slack in the fiscal structure to lower spending and/or cover the deficit with surplus funds or having enough revenue reserves in the fiscal environment to increase revenues collected (revenue burden). In most cases, raising tax rates during the fiscal year (if state statutes allow for this) will not generate enough revenues to solve midyear fiscal problems due to the cycles of collection. Thus governments often rely on slack in their fiscal structure, such as the fund balance or deferred capital spending, to reduce risk and achieve budgetary solvency. In addition, governments with more stable revenues and better service-level solvency have less risk or exposure and therefore need less slack to be solvent and balanced at this level.

At the most immediate level of financial condition, problems with cash solvency and cash flow emanate from two sources: (1) fiscal shocks that unexpectedly speed up or add payments or slow down and delete revenues, and (2) not functioning with enough slack to cover expected timing differences between revenues coming in and payments going out. Generally, governments with poor service-level and budgetary solvency tend to have poor cash solvency because they tend to operate with less slack and a narrower margin of error, but wealthy governments and those with good budgetary solvency can also have cash flow problems if risks and cash trends are not recognized and planned for. As with the other solvency areas, good cash solvency means having an appropriate fiscal structure and maintaining a balance between short-term assets and near-term liabilities.

It is clear from this discussion that financial condition in the four time frames tends to be positively related. Governments with a poor, long-run solvency will have more difficulty maintaining good financial condition in the near term due to external and uncontrollable characteristics that determine fiscal structure over time. Thus a government with poor long-run and service-level solvency is more likely to have poor budgetary and cash solvency. It is also more likely to have higher future liabilities, greater risk, less slack, and a fiscal structure that is more unbalanced and inappropriate for its environment. Similarly, a government with good long-run and service-level solvency is more likely to have good budgetary and cash solvency and so on. However, examples have shown that these relationships are not absolute.

A government with poor revenue bases and sound financial decisions may find it difficult but not impossible to maintain budgetary and cash solvency. Alternatively, a government with strong revenue bases may have poor, short-term solvency. Over time, sound fiscal practices and policy choices could improve the poor government's service-level solvency, and unsound fiscal practices can threaten wealthy governments' short-term solvency. But long-term financial conditions may also make it impossible for some poor governments to achieve service-level solvency. On the other end of the continuum, it may take more severe, negative environmental changes to weaken the service-level and short-term solvency in wealthier governments, and they may be able to recover balance more quickly than poorer ones.

Measuring Financial Condition

Table 2.1 presents a range of component measures of financial condition that divides the measures along two dimensions. Moving from top to bottom, these measures are organized according to whether they represent resources or assets and expenditures or liabilities. The net financial condition measures link components in the two dimensions to reflect different areas of balance. Moving from right to left in table 2.1, the measures are classified according to time frames or levels of solvency with the attributes or properties of these levels indicated at the bottom of the table. Although the component measures are presented in three groups, their attributes are better represented as continuums rather than discrete groups. Measures on the left-hand side of the table represent aspects of financial condition that are less controllable by government officials, more stable or entrenched, focused on long-term or future events, part of the government's environment, and exogenous. Measures on the right-hand side of the table represent aspects that are more controllable, volatile, focused on short-term or current events, a feature of the government's fiscal structure, and endogenous. It must also be noted that the measures listed in each cell of the table are not exhaustive and represent, in most cases, general types of indicators or areas of measurement rather than specific measures.

TABLE 2.1 Classification and Types of Financial Condition Measures

Long-Term Solvency	Service-Level Solvency	Cash and Budget Solvency
Revenues, assets, and other resources		
Economic and revenue base (and elasticity)	Dependence on inter-governmental revenues	Revenues collected and outstanding
State economy	Tax rates, fees, and charges	Accounts receivable
Revenue capacity	Budgeted revenues	Fund balance and surplus resources
Residents and businesses (growth)	Revenue diversification and fungibility	Cash and ST investments
Physical assets and LT investments	Revenue reserves	
Recurring intergovernmental revenues		
Expenditures and liabilities		
Spending needs and demands, costs	Budgeted expenditures (and fixity)	Accounts payable (terms, fixity)
Residents and businesses (growth)	Spending priorities	ST debt
State and federal mandates		ST liabilities
LT debt (past decisions)		
Unfunded pension liabilities (past decisions)		
Deferred maintenance (past decisions)		
Net financial condition: Balance		
Spending needs relative to revenue wealth	Revenue burden	Liquidity
	Slack relative to risk	Expenditures relative to revenues
	Assets relative to liabilities	ST slack relative to ST risk
Attributes		
Over time/Future	←——————→	Current
Less Controllable	←——————→	More Controllable
External/Environment	←——————→	Internal/Fiscal Structure
Stable	←——————→	Volatile
Exogenous	←——————→	Endogenous

LT: long-term

ST: short-term

Revenues, Assets, and Resources

From an accounting perspective, an *asset* is anything that is owned by the government that can produce an economic benefit. More generally, an asset is any form of wealth and includes external resources that the government has access to or that give it the capacity to meet obligations and improve financial condition. Assets also include short-term investments and cash balances that are used to manage cash flow during the fiscal year, slack resources that help manage budgetary risk, long-term physical assets such as buildings, and revenue reserves. However, revenues are a government's most important asset with respect to financial condition.

Local governments have two basic types of revenue: intergovernmental and own-source. *Intergovernmental revenues* are funds received from the state or federal governments for specific functions (grants) and for general financial assistance (aid). *Own-source revenues* are generated from resources within the local government's jurisdiction, although they can be collected by other governments and distributed to the owner government at regular intervals. Local own-source revenues include property taxes, user fees, and other charges and in some states may include sales and income taxes. Local governments meet most of their service and financial obligations with own-source revenue, but much of their revenue can be intergovernmental in the form of general assistance from state government based on a formula or a share of state taxes and grants from state and federal government.

A local government's *economic base* represents the set of economic resources from which it draws own-source revenue. Its *revenue base* is that portion of the economic base it has access to through specific revenue-raising mechanisms as established by state statute and other legal and institutional constraints. Most local governments have access to property values (property tax), and some have access to sales receipts (sales taxes), resident and nonresident income (payroll tax), and other sectors of the economy (e.g., utility usage and development). Income per capita is also considered to be a good measure of total revenue base wealth in governments with few revenues generated from businesses or nonresidents (Berne and Schramm 1986). The value of many specific revenue bases also are greatly affected by population growth and economic development, which, over time, may increase property values and the revenue generated from fees (e.g., building permits).

Own-source *revenue capacity* reflects that portion of the revenue base the government can collect, which also is established in most cases by state statute. For instance, state governments often limit the maximum property tax rates local governments can levy. Thus a local government's revenue-raising capacity for a particular type of revenue is the maximum level of revenue it could raise from that source. *Actual revenues* are the amount of revenues it actually collects and *revenue reserves* are excess or slack revenue capacity that the government has access to but has not used (reserves = capacity − actual). If a locality tapped its revenue bases to their full potential, actual revenues would equal revenue capacity, and revenue reserves would equal zero. Neither actual revenues nor revenue reserves are really exogenous because elected officials control them through decisions about tax rates, charges, fees, and so on.

Because a significant portion of most local governments' total revenue is from state government, it is an important factor in their financial condition.[7] Grants are one form of state intergovernmental revenue and tend to be one-time or nonrecurring revenues that have specific obligations attached to them. Recurring state aid is another form of state intergovernmental revenue. It has few obligations and is often distributed by population or need. Thus the state economy, which determines the pool of state revenue available to distribute to local government, is another important factor in local financial condition. The other problem with intergovernmental revenue is that local governments do not control how much state revenue is distributed them. History tells us that intergovernmental state and federal funds are not guaranteed and can be withdrawn almost at will. However, to a great extent, local governments do control the degree to which they rely on intergovernmental revenue to meet service and financial obligations. Local governments that rely more on revenue from other governments have a more uncertain and precarious future and therefore face more risk than those that rely less on these revenues.[8]

Governments also rely to a greater or lesser extent on different sources of own-source revenue. Governments that rely equally on many revenue sources have a diversified revenue structure. Whether having a diversified revenue structure is better than relying on one revenue source depends on the elasticity or sensitivity of that revenue source. The concept of *revenue elasticity* indicates the responsiveness of a particular revenue base or revenue source to changes in the national economy, personal income, tax rates, or other economic quantity. The more elastic a revenue source is, the more variability there is in its base and therefore the more variability there is in revenues collected given changes to the economy. In most cases, income taxes have the highest elasticity and property taxes have the lowest elasticity to economic changes. The elasticity of sales taxes also is relatively high, and other taxes and revenues are in the middle.

Revenue fungibility refers to the extent to which revenues from one source can be substituted for revenues from another source. In this case, governments with large enterprises or high levels of earmarked revenues in fund accounts dedicated to particular services have more opportunity to offload expenditures to revenues generated in these accounts. For instance, governments with many funds or accounts can charge varying amounts of salaries, equipment, and supplies to different accounts if personnel perform duties that are funded by more than one account or if equipment and supplies are shared by accounts. The finance director and municipal manager oversee and perform duties in administering the enterprise and roads funds in addition to the general fund. If either or both specialized funds have significant levels of revenues or surplus resources, then greater or lesser portions of the salaries of these individuals can be charged to these funds. Thus revenue fungibility represents a form of slack.

On the right-hand side of table 2.1, assets consist primarily of cash, short-term investments, and surplus resources (fund balances). These assets are exclusively endogenous and represent features of the government's fiscal structure. The value of these assets may change often during the fiscal year. On the balance sheet, fund balances (and retained earnings) are the residual equity or net assets in each account. More generally, residual equity is the difference between all assets and liabilities. Fund balances also represent the accumulation of monetary surpluses (revenues minus expenditures) over time and are easily accessible to meet obligations within accounts during the fiscal year. The fact that most governments have more than one fund balance provides opportunities to borrow across accounts (called interfund transfers) or even sweep some surpluses into other accounts. Other types of assets or conditions that can affect cash and budgetary solvency are the ability to speed up revenue collections (e.g., accounts receivable), short-term investments, and saleable physical assets.

Another consideration in assessing financial condition on the current end of the continuum is the extent to which revenues and fund balances within different accounts are reserved for specific purposes according to state or local statute. For instance, state governments may require that the gasoline taxes they share with local governments be reserved for road maintenance and construction, or local governments themselves may earmark particular revenues for specific purposes. It is especially common for governments to manage the risk of elastic revenues by earmarking these revenues for nonrecurring expenditures (e.g., capital spending). Another useful measure of short-term solvency in the asset category is the ratio of restricted operating revenues to total operating revenues, which indicates government flexibility in meeting short-term liabilities.

Spending and Liabilities

As reflected by the second section in table 2.1, a *liability* is anything that is owed by the government to another party. More specifically, a liability is the sacrifice of current or future economic benefits to satisfy current and past obligations. Liabilities on the left-hand side of the table represent fiscal obligations covering an extended period of time, such as the obligation to deliver services in the long run and meet future obligations including pensions, repayment of debt, and capital replacement. Liabilities on the right-hand side of the table represent obligations that must be met within a time frame that is shorter than the fiscal year, such as accounts payable or short-term debt.

Similar to the left-hand side of the assets category, most of the liabilities on the left-hand side represent environmental conditions over which government has less control and which tend to be stable over time. Spending needs are exogenous and determined by environmental conditions that dictate the level of expenditures required by local government to adequately provide for the health, safety, and welfare of its residents and visitors. For instance, spending needs for police services are affected by crime levels. Spending for fire services, public works, building inspection, and capital spending are affected by the age of the infrastructure. Population growth and economic development also greatly increase government spending needs, especially for the construction of infrastructure.

The costs of personnel, materials, supplies, equipment, and other items used in service delivery are another source of government spending needs. Costs also are a significant factor in capital outlays for construction and land acquisition. Other spending needs may be dictated by federal or state mandates that specify the types or levels of services local governments must provide. Spending mandates imposed on local government exist in a variety of areas but are especially prevalent for pensions, health care, and water and sewerage services. Which services local governments provide in a state depends on state statute, how their roles have evolved over time, and the existence of overlapping local governments—counties, townships, municipalities, and special districts. *Spending demands,* in contrast, reflect the spending priorities of its residents, clients, and other stakeholders who influence government expenditures through the political process.

Past decisions to issue debt, underfund pension obligations, and defer infrastructure maintenance and replacement are other obligations that are not controllable by government officials in the current time period. Although current decisions to create these obligations for the future are controllable, governments faced with obligations to repay past debt or make up for past underfunding of pensions and infrastructure repair have limited control over the pressure this places on current spending. In contrast, the level of spending governments undertake to meet current service obligations is more controllable.

Not all cities facing similar spending needs are going to fund current service obligations at the same level due to variations in spending demands, which are filtered through the political process and transformed into expenditure priorities.[9] To some extent, spending priorities can be observed by the percentage of total spending budgeted for different services, programs, or areas of spending, once a government's service needs and other fixed liabilities are taken into account. Spending for services is also affected by how fixed current spending obligations are relative to each other (called short-term *spending fixity*). Personnel expenditures and repayment of debt, for instance, are relatively fixed in comparison to maintenance and equipment expenditures that can be deferred more readily. The level of fixed liabilities relative to other liabilities represents the ease with current spending in different areas or for different objects that can be altered in the near term to react to fiscal shocks and take advantage of fiscal opportunities. Thus, low spending fixity is a form of slack. Similarly, different types of accounts payable also have different levels of fixity. For instance, some bills or amounts owed during the fiscal year must be paid immediately or regularly (e.g., wages), and other payments can be delayed to improve cash flow in the short run.

Net Financial Condition

The last section in table 2.1 represents measures that can be used to reflect whether a government's fiscal structure is balanced with its environment or other conditions relevant to the different types of solvency. On the left-hand side of the table, long-run solvency could be assessed by measures that examine aggregate spending needs relative to total revenue wealth. For instance, measures such as the age of infrastructure and crime per capita could be used as indicators of overall spending needs. These measures then could be compared to total assessed value or income in a municipality to determine a government's long-run solvency. Looking at future obligations, one can compare long-term liabilities (e.g., debt) to long-term relevant assets (e.g., value of infrastructure minus depreciation) to determine the long-run solvency of physical assets. More generally, one might even attempt to forecast future service needs and revenue wealth based upon demographic trends.

With respect to service-level solvency, *revenue burden*—the ratio of actual revenues to revenue base or revenue capacity—is one of the most important measures of financial condition in the literature. Tax or revenue burden for individual revenue bases is the same thing as the tax or charge rate. Total revenue burden, which was one of the composite indicators of financial condition developed by Ladd and Yinger, is the sum of all tax rates or the sum of all revenues relative to the sum of all revenue capacities. This measure is presented in the center of this category because its numerator (actual revenues) is relatively controllable and endogenous, but its denominator (revenue bases) is exogenous. On the spending side, comparing actual spending to spending needs would indicate government *spending effort,* or the extent to which its service obligations are being met.

Measures of slack relative to risk are also important for assessing service-level solvency. For instance, surplus funds, such as rainy day funds and fund balances, could be compared to dependence on elastic or uncertain revenue sources (e.g., percent of total revenue that is intergovernmental) to determine if governments have enough slack to maintain adequate service levels during economic recessions. Theoretically, slack could be measured with a composite indicator that incorporates different types of slack including the fund balance, capital spending, and discretionary spending (Hendrick 2006). A similar composite indicator could be constructed for risk, but it would have to recognize uncertainty about future events.

Cash and budgetary solvency are assessed primarily by examining features of government fiscal structure that affect its ability to balance its budget and pay its bills during the fiscal year. Measures of short-term solvency, also called its operating position, include liquidity, fund balances, operating deficits or surpluses, short-term borrowing, fixity of accounts payable, and dependability of accounts receivable. Liquidity is the ratio or balance of cash and current assets to current liabilities. Operating deficits and surpluses measure whether revenues are balanced with expenditures; however, they are more meaningful if they are considered in conjunction with the fund balance. As emphasized previously, fund balances must be compared to other features of the government's fiscal structure and environment to assess short-term and even midterm financial condition. Similarly, high levels of liquidity may not be necessary in governments with stable revenue streams and spending.

One final consideration in assessing financial condition is that all the measures represented in table 2.1 can be examined over time to determine rates of change and, to some extent, be used to predict future fiscal states. However, as discussed previously, incorporating dynamic states into an assessment of current financial condition or overall financial health is not straightforward. Are current fiscal states more relevant to financial condition than the degree of change in past fiscal states? Similarly, how important is long-run solvency relative to budgetary and cash solvency? Are local governments with long-run solvency likely to remain that way regardless of fiscal shocks and poor cash or budgetary solvency? To what extent does poor cash or budgetary solvency threaten a government's service-level solvency? How should we integrate the time dimension (past, current, and future) and different types of solvency into our assessment of overall financial condition? Unfortunately, the profession does not have clear answers to these questions, which suggests that measures of current conditions and changes from past conditions should be examined separately. Similarly, the distinct nature and potential effects of different features in different time frames on overall financial condition and their nonlinear (contingent) relationships make a case for assessing financial condition within each area of solvency separately rather than trying to combine measures across time frames into a single composite measure.

Municipal Financial Condition in the Chicago Region

This section of the book defines and operationalizes the different measures of financial condition used in the analyses and explains how these measures are affected by the municipal governments' being in the state of Illinois and a large metropolitan region.

Unique Features of Illinois and the Chicago Region

Before presenting the measures of financial condition used in the analyses here, it will be useful to review state statutes and revenue-sharing conditions that directly affect local government finances in the state of Illinois. These features change the fiscal environment in significant ways for municipalities in Illinois as compared to other states. Thus they are important to consider when assessing long-run and service-level solvency of municipalities in the Chicago region. As is so often noted, local governments are creatures of the state, which means that states control many aspects of local financial condition. State statutes that dictate the types and levels of revenues local governments can collect are most important to local financial condition. Another factor to consider in measuring financial condition of municipalities in the Chicago region is that they are suburbs. Suburban municipalities are more diverse comparatively, and some have very unique roles within the regional economy, which can distort financial condition measures when applied to these governments.

Illinois is somewhat unique compared to other states in that its municipalities may levy many types of taxes, and they are relatively free to establish charges and fees for many services (Wandling 2001). In addition to the property tax, Illinois municipalities may levy taxes on cigarettes, photo finishing, motel occupancy, automobile rental, and utilities (telephone, natural gas, and electricity). But home rule municipalities can levy even more taxes, including sales and real estate transfer taxes.[10] They also have additional powers regarding contracts, regulation, and economic development that may affect financial condition indirectly through impacts on financial management practices and other fiscal policies. Most important, home rule municipalities in Illinois are not subject to property tax limitations that restrict local governments from increasing property taxes by more than 5 percent or the rate of inflation, whichever is less.[11] Because home rule privileges greatly alter the number and diversity of municipal revenue bases and capacity in Illinois, it is very important to consider this factor in assessing levels of solvency and financial condition of Chicago governments.

Home rule status is automatically granted to municipalities with populations greater than 25,000, but smaller municipalities can obtain home rule status via referendum, and larger governments can repeal home rule through referendum (Keane and Koch 1990). As of 2003, 39 percent of the 264 municipal governments in the Chicago metropolitan region were home rule, and 30 percent had a population greater than 25,000.

Another factor to consider is that all Illinois municipalities receive state-levied sales taxes in proportion to the amount of sales transactions that occur within their boundaries, although only home rule governments may increase sales tax rates on retail sales within their boundaries independent of referenda.[12] Municipal governments receive 1 percent of the sales receipts generated within the jurisdiction from the state sales tax. Although non–home rule municipal governments do not control sales taxes rates, except through referenda, these taxes are considered to be own-source for all municipal governments in the sense that the amounts they collect depend on the resources within their jurisdiction. Similarly, municipal governments are considered to own replacement taxes even though the rates applied are determined by state law.[13]

Compared to property and sales taxes that are owned (or semiowned) by municipalities in Illinois, they do not own income or motor fuel taxes distributed by state government. The latter taxes are distributed according to municipal population as a proportion of the total state population and therefore are not generated by financial resources owned by the government. However, population changes within the jurisdiction will directly affect the level of state revenue they receive from these sources.[14]

Responsibility for water and sewer services is another important feature that affects the fiscal structure and financial condition of Chicago municipal governments. This matter is discussed in more detail in chapter 5, but it is important to note now that these services are fairly decentralized in the Chicago region compared to many other regions in the United States where such services are delivered and coordinated by regional authorities, districts, or even counties. Although water and sewer services are a fundamental responsibility for most municipal governments in the United States, about 90 percent of Chicago municipal governments spend for water or sewer services according to the 2007 US Census of Governments.[15] Also, high-population densities throughout the region do not allow many municipal governments to push such responsibilities onto the homeowner (private well and septic), which greatly increases the level of services many of them must provide. As in many other metropolitan regions in the United States, water and sewer are costly services, but Chicago municipal governments spend a lot by comparison.[16] As a result, the enterprises that municipal governments in the region administer to deliver water and sewer often represent a significant portion of their total revenues (plus receipts) and expenditures (plus expenses), and these systems are often responsible for the majority of municipal government debt.

The fact that the municipalities studied in this book are suburbs within the same region also must be recognized in assessing their financial condition. Economic theory and current research demonstrate that local jurisdictions in large metropolitan areas are likely to fragment and segregate such that the demographic and socioeconomic features of their populations become more homogenous when examined internally but more differentiated when compared to each other (Tiebout 1956; Rusk 1995; Orfield 2002). Suburban municipalities also may become unique in other ways, such as land use, as the region grows economically and in overall population. For instance, business employment and payroll levels that are used to assess the financial health of central cities may not be relevant to suburbs, especially if the suburbs are primarily residential. Similarly, per capita measures may distort conditions in suburban municipalities that are primarily industrial, commercial, or provide services for the larger region.

A good example of a very specialized municipality in the Chicago metropolitan region is the Village of Rosemont, which had an estimated population of about 4,200 but had a budget of $96 million for enterprise and governmental operations in 2005. This makes total spending per person in Rosemont equal to almost $23,000 in that year! Since its incorporation in 1956, Rosemont has developed into a convention and tourism center for the region due to its proximity to the main airport. In fact, the government's home page is merely a link to the home page of the Rosemont Convention and Tourism Bureau. It boasts that "with a population of 4,000, the village's leadership has created a top meeting/convention/tradeshow and entertainment center, hosting an average 50,000 visitors a day." Bedford Park is another municipality that serves the region more than its residents. Its population was only 550 in 2005, but its total spending was $46 million, or $83,600 per person. Its crime rate per 1,000 people was about 900 in the same year, which is meaningless in this case. Unlike Rosemont, Bedford Park has a very large industrial sector that provides jobs to people throughout the region. Only 5 percent of its equalized assessed value is residential, and 85 percent is industrial.

Although both municipalities are very unique, they underscore the problem of constructing valid measures of financial condition of suburban governments and the difficulty of comparing measures across all jurisdictions. This is particularly an issue for per capita measures that are often used as components of more comprehensive indicators of long-run and service-level solvency. Bedford Park's expenditures per person of $83,600 does not really mean that the village spends that much on services for its residents, nor do 90 percent of residents experience a violent crime. Rather, the government spends a lot on providing services to nonresidents who visit the jurisdiction and businesses within its borders.

Assessments of financial condition of municipalities in this region must also recognize the uniqueness of Cook County. As shown in figure 2.3, there are six counties in the metropolitan area, but Cook County is the largest according to population (66% of regional) and land area (25% of regional). It also contains 45 percent of the region's municipalities and is dominated by the City of Chicago politically and economically. More important to the finances of municipal governments within its boundaries, Cook County is responsible for property assessments (townships everywhere else in the state), and its property classification system and assessment ratios for each class are very different from those of other counties in the state.

Cook County had twelve different classifications of property as of 2010, compared to six classes in other counties. Its assessment ratio (as a percentage of market value) also varies by class in a manner that is contrary to state law. By statute, the assessment ratio of all nonfarm property in Illinois should be 33.3 percent. But the assessment

FIGURE 2.3 Chicago Metropolitan Region Municipalities and Counties

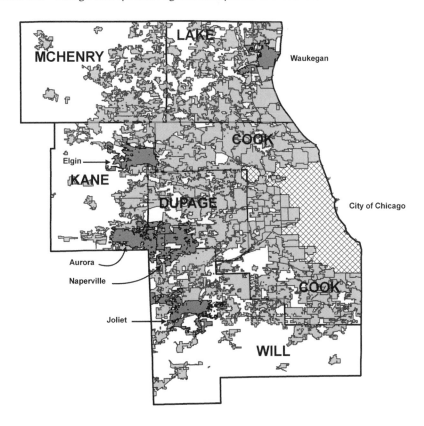

ratios for the different classes of property in Cook County range from 10 percent to 36 percent. The state's equalization factor for the county, which is used to bring the average level of property assessments to 33.3 percent for purposes of equalizing of tax rates and distributing of grants and aid, was 2.97 in 2008 and 2.18 in 2000. By comparison, the equalization factors for all Illinois counties in 2000, which was the last time the state published these figures, ranged from .93 to 1.17, with the majority of factors equaling 1.0.[17]

Measures of Municipal Financial Condition

Appendix 1 presents the calculation rules and information about the data used to construct the financial condition indicators of Chicago municipal governments. It also explains other important variables used in the analyses in the book and identifies variables that might be used to represent a concept but were not employed here (identified by bullet points). Readers are referred to the appendix for details on how all indicators were constructed, but it is important to explain some methods more thoroughly.

First, most per capita measures were multiplied by percent residential equalized assessed value (EAV) to correct for the distortions in per capita measures described previously. When multiplied by percent residential EAV, which is used to measure the "residentialness" of a jurisdiction, the per capita measures for municipalities that are highly residential will be inflated, and the per capita measures for nonresidential (industrial or commercial) jurisdictions will be deflated. These corrected per capita measures are, in effect, weighted by the level of residentialness in the jurisdiction.

The appendix shows that there are four primary indicators of long-run solvency. The two most important primary indicators are revenue wealth and spending needs. Both of these indices are complex in that they are constructed by aggregating component measures into a single value for each government. However, the component measures for each index also are used separately in some cases. Other indicators of long-run solvency used here are debt per capita (total, total bonds, and GO) and the balance of revenue wealth and spending needs. Because general obligation (GO) debt is guaranteed by property taxes in Illinois, total bonds include GO debt, revenue debt (guaranteed by enterprise charges), and alternate revenue debt (guaranteed by other local taxes). The balance indicator of long-run solvency is the ratio of the revenue wealth index to the spending needs index and shows the extent to which a government's revenue wealth can cover or meet its spending needs.

Revenue wealth measures government capacity to generate own-source revenues from different revenue bases in 2000. The four sources of own-source revenue for municipalities in this state are property tax, sales tax, nontax revenue (e.g., fines, licenses, and charges), and other tax sources (e.g., utility and real-estate transfer taxes). Property tax capacity is measured as EAV per square mile and weighted sales receipts per capita measures the wealth of the sales tax revenue base.[18] The appropriate base for nontax revenue and other taxes is not clear given that much of it may be exported to nonresidents and persons doing business within the community. In this case, income per capita may be the best measure of revenue capacity for revenue other than property or sales taxes (Berne and Schramm 1986; Rafuse and Marks 1991). This measure of revenue wealth must also take into account that home rule governments in Illinois have much greater access to these revenue bases than non–home rule governments.

The wealth index was created by converting the three component measures into Z values (and percent of the median) to standardize their distributions. The Z values for each component are then weighted by a standardized regression coefficient and summed. The regression coefficients were obtained from a regression analysis with corrected own-source revenues per capita as the dependent variable, the three component indicators as independent variables, and run separately for home rule and non–home rule governments (see appendix 1 for more details about how this index is constructed).

Spending needs is constructed from the following seven variables: median age of housing, weighted crime rate per capita, population density (population/square miles), miles of roads per square mile, and whether a municipality is in a fire, library, or parks district.[19] Measures of spending needs developed in prior research for larger municipalities and central cities target many more factors such as age of the population, poverty, and employment that may not be relevant to suburban governments that do not provide extensive social or health services (Ladd and Yinger 1989; Rafuse and Marks 1991). In this case, prior analyses of spending in the Chicago suburbs indicate that age of housing and crime rate have a significant effect on expenditures, whereas other variables such as age of the population and poverty have no effect. Past studies have shown crime rate to be a good general indicator of public safety expenditures (e.g., police, fire, and inspection) and age of housing is often used to measure infrastructure and public works maintenance needs (Clark and Ferguson 1983).[20] Miles of roads is included as another measure of public works needs. Population density measures the economies of scale for service delivery—the more people per square mile, the less costly it is to deliver services (Berne and Schramm 1986). Finally, municipalities that are in special districts that provide municipal services, especially fire services, will have substantially reduced spending needs for salaries, equipment, and pension obligations. Similar to the wealth index, the spending need index for 2000 is created by converting the seven component indicators into Z values, weighting them with standardized regression slopes (corrected expenditures per capita as the dependent variable), and then summing the weighted values.

Fiscal stress with respect to long-term solvency is measured as change in revenue sources and population. The variable *change in revenue sources* is measured as an index of the combined ratio change in the three main revenue sources, which are sales receipts, EAV, and intergovernmental revenue. Also each ratio is multiplied by the proportion that the revenue source is of total revenues before constructing the index.[21] Similar to the indices for revenue wealth and spending needs, this index was constructed by weighting the change in revenue bases (multiplied by proportion of total revenue) by the standardized regression slopes calculated from regression analyses, using ratio change in total revenue as the dependent variable, and run separately for home rule and non–home rule governments. These new weighted values, recalculated as Z scores or percent medians, are then summed to create the index. More generally, change in revenue wealth is measured as a function of change in each revenue base, weighted by the contribution of each revenue source to total revenue regressed against change in total revenue. Percent change in population is used separately to measure changes in spending needs and growth and development more generally. However, as examined in chapter 5, it is correlated with changes in different revenues collected by the municipal governments.

Service-level solvency is measured with sixteen different indicators, three of which are composites. Some indicators measure overall service-level solvency, and others measure specific components of this solvency that are tied to particular revenue sources, capital investments, slack, or risk. Revenue burden measures the level of revenues collected relative to the wealth of the revenue base and is calculated as the ratio of total own-source revenues per capita (corrected for nonresidential distortion) to revenue wealth. Both the numerator and denominator are calculated as a percent of the median of the distribution because of the problem of using negative Z values in ratios. Spending effort measures the degree to which spending needs are met and is calculated as the ratio of operational spending per capita (weighted) and spending effort (numerator and denominator as percent medians).

None of the measures associated with revenue or spending slack (fungibility or fixity) are used here because they were not found to be important to this dimension of financial condition, but different measures of revenue risk are used in the analyses. *Revenue diversification* is a composite measure of the diversity of government revenue structure based on the Hirschman-Herfindahl Index that is widely used in the finance sector to measure market share of firms in an industry (Suyderhoud 1994). Here it is used to measure share of total revenue for the four different revenue sources owned by the government—property tax, sales tax, other taxes, and nontax revenue. Fiscal stress with respect to service-level solvency is also measured by examining ratio changes in different types of revenue, but no index is created to produce a composite measure of this concept.

Short-term solvency (budgetary) is measured with three different indicators. Overall budgetary solvency is defined as the ability to cover current spending with current resources, and it is measured as fund balance plus revenue divided by spending. Fiscal stress with respect to budgetary solvency is the change ratio of the budgetary solvency measure. Fund balance and deficit or surplus (revenue − spending) are also used separately in the analyses. Finally, because cash solvency has more to do with financial condition during the fiscal year, which can vary greatly throughout the fiscal year, no measures of cash solvency are used here.

To some degree, all of the indicators of service-level solvency and the long-run solvency measures of debt reflect policy choices made by government over several years. For instance, revenue burden is determined in part by the level of revenue wealth (denominator) that is available to the government. But government officials decide each year how much revenue to collect to fund operations and capital spending. Similarly, government officials decide each year how much debt to issue, how much they should rely on sales taxes, and how much they should spend on capital purposes. Some of these indicators may not vary greatly over several years, especially operational spending and revenues, as they reflect policy choices government officials make over many years.

Financial Features of Municipalities in the Chicago Region

In addition to the counties, figure 2.3 shows all 270 suburban municipalities in the Chicago metropolitan region as of 2005, with important municipalities indentified in dark gray. The City of Chicago, which is excluded from most analyses in this book, is the area represented by the crosshatched area. The *satellite cities* of Waukegan, Elgin, Aurora, and Joliet are shown in gray, as is Naperville, which is the second-largest suburb of the region. Aurora is the largest suburb in the region with a population of about 192,000 in 2010. The satellite cities existed before growth emanating from the City of Chicago reached out to these areas, and their economic bases were somewhat independent from the City of Chicago until they were absorbed into the larger metropolitan region. The satellite cities also have their own suburbs.

Figure 2.4 shows how the municipalities are distributed according to quintiles of per capita income in 1999. Residents in the suburbs on the north shore of Lake

FIGURE 2.4 Income per Capita, 1999

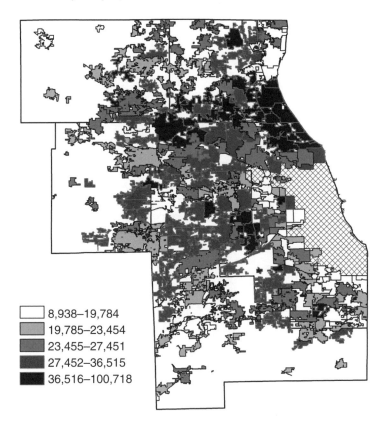

	8,938–19,784
	19,785–23,454
	23,455–27,451
	27,452–36,515
	36,516–100,718

Michigan are some of the wealthiest in the region, with continuing pockets of personal wealth in south Lake County and northwest Cook County. The lowest levels of personal income exist in south Cook County, just west of the City of Chicago, and near Lake Michigan by the Wisconsin border. Areas furthest away from the City of Chicago have less wealth but are not the poorest. However, high residential wealth does not translate directly into high government revenue wealth or a low revenue burden.

Figure 2.5 shows the distribution of the revenue burden measure (no. 7 in appendix 1) in quintiles. Revenue burden is the ratio of own-source revenues divided by the revenue wealth index (no. 1 in appendix 1). This measure reflects revenue capacity the government is using up, or how much of a burden it is placing on the revenue base. The figure shows that revenue burden is high among the governments in south Cook County and municipalities elsewhere with high poverty levels. It also shows that many governments with wealthy residents have low revenue burden, but many have high revenue burden. The satellite cities also have relatively high revenue burden. The governments with the lowest revenue burden tend to have high levels of commercial activity that allow them to export some burden to nonresidents.

FIGURE 2.5 Own-Source Revenue Burden, 2000

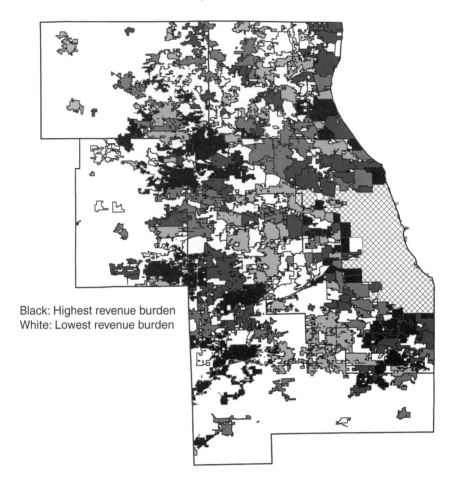

Black: Highest revenue burden
White: Lowest revenue burden

Figure 2.6 shows how land use is distributed in the region according to whether the jurisdictions are predominately residential, industrial, commercial, or a mixture of one or more uses based on percentages of EAV. The majority of the suburbs are mixed use, but there are several industrial suburbs just west of the City of Chicago. Highly commercial jurisdictions are scattered throughout the middle ring of suburbs that encircle the city, and suburbs that are predominately residential exist throughout the region but are concentrated somewhat in the northwest.

Finally, figure 2.7 shows a map of the percent change in population of jurisdictions in the region between 2000 and 2005. The pattern shown here is similar to the pattern that has existed for many years in which residents migrate further away from the city of Chicago and nearby suburbs. Also one can discern three rings of development according to the map. Suburbs near the central city with population decline or little growth constitute the first ring and the first wave of development

FIGURE 2.6 Land Use, 2004

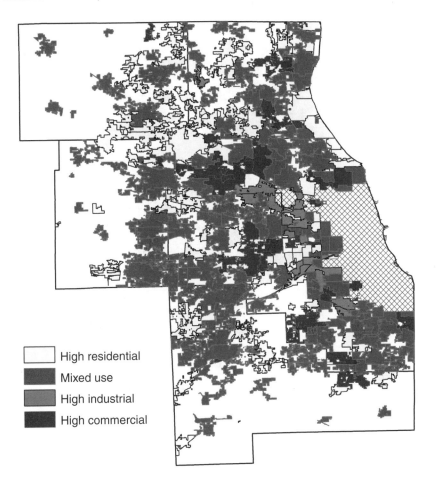

- High residential
- Mixed use
- High industrial
- High commercial

in this pattern. The second ring of suburbs, which is more neutral grey, represents the second ring and wave of development. The third ring is furthest from Chicago and represents areas where development and population growth are greatest. It is also apparent from the map that the greatest population growth has been in the southwest part of the region.

Conclusion

This chapter lays the groundwork for how to think about and measure financial condition and fiscal stress in local governments with particular focus on municipal suburban governments in the Chicago metropolitan region. Application of this framework to other local governments, and especially local governments in other states, is not

FIGURE 2.7 Percent Change in Population, 2000–5

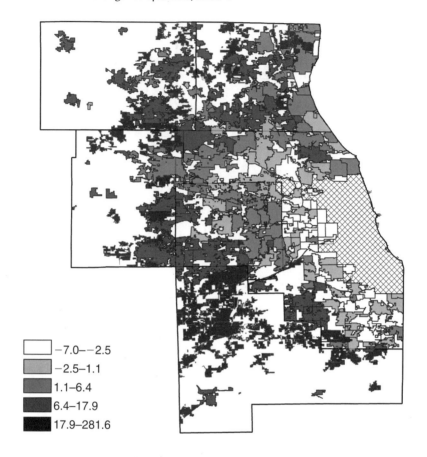

Legend:
- −7.0−−2.5
- −2.5−1.1
- 1.1−6.4
- 6.4−17.9
- 17.9−281.6

automatic. Rather it must be done logically, drawing from the theories and concepts proposed here to accommodate circumstances in other metropolitan regions and states. This may not be satisfying, as there is often a need to assess and compare the financial condition of local governments in different states. However, the discussion of financial condition and fiscal stress presented here suggests that this endeavor may be constrained by the inability to easily measure multiple dimensions of these concepts in a manner that is comparable across fundamentally different contexts.

The system of measurement proposed by Ladd and Yinger (1989) provides a mechanism to account for different local tax privileges—the fact that, for instance, municipalities in Wisconsin can levy only a property tax, but those in Missouri can levy taxes on property, general sales, and income. However, their system misses important financial factors, such as variation in home rule privileges or differences in tax and expenditure limitations that can impact the financial condition of local governments in ways that are not linear or straightforward.

With respect to the financial condition and fiscal stress of municipal governments in the Chicago metropolitan region, the important conclusion here is the tremendous variation that exists among them for many of the ratios and indices in appendix 1. The maps do not make this as apparent as a close examination of the measures themselves. This variation facilitates many analyses in this book, especially those using quantitative data and answering questions for which this data are appropriate. The next chapter lays out the theoretical framework used to think about and understand financial decision making and management in suburban, municipal governments.

Notes

1. Standardized refers to a group norm or benchmark in this case.
2. See Burchell et al. 1981; Aronson 1984; and Ross and Greenfield 1980 for comprehensive summaries and critiques of the many composite measures developed during this period. Composite measures include the urban hardship and economic index (the Brookings Institute), the fiscal need index (Congressional Budget Office), the fiscal strain index (US Department of Treasury), and a financial condition classification system (Touche Ross–First National Bank).
3. The term *revenue* as used here includes receipts from enterprises and charges. Spending includes expenditures and enterprise expenses.
4. This framework is based on one developed by the Municipal Finance Officers Association in conjunction with Peat, Marwick, Mitchell & Co. in 1978.
5. Technically speaking, financial condition is not a latent variable because it does not underlie the observable variables that comprise the composite measure of financial condition. Rather, the causal flow runs from observable variables to financial condition as indicated in figure 2.1.
6. The Civic Federation in Chicago also examines many measures of different dimensions of local government financial health, similar to those of Brown and Kloha, Weissert, and Kleine, but they do not combine measures across dimensions to form a single index (Bowman, Calia, and Metzgar 1999).
7. An analysis of US Census of Governments data for 2007 shows that, at the median, 32 percent of revenue for all local governments comes from state government. About 19 percent of municipal revenue comes from state government, and about 31 percent of county revenue comes from state government.
8. Chapman (1999) refers to this type of risk as *local fiscal immunity autonomy.*
9. A well-articulated example of this is developed in Stonecash and McAfee (1981).
10. Non–home rule municipalities may levy a sales tax, but it requires voter approval and cannot exceed 1 percent.
11. Non–home rule governments in Illinois are subject to the Property Tax Extension Limitation Law (PTELL). Increases in taxes that result from new growth in the municipality versus inflation or appreciation in assessed value are not subjected to PTELL. One side effect of PTELL is that it limits general obligation debt for non–home rule governments, which is guaranteed by property taxes. As a result, Illinois designates *alternate revenue debt* as being guaranteed by other own-source revenues and not charges for enterprise services. Total property tax rates in non–home rule governments are also constrained by maximum designated rates for particular services.
12. In Illinois, sales taxes are a combination of occupation taxes that are imposed on sellers' receipts and use taxes that are imposed on purchasers.
13. Replacement taxes are revenues collected by the state and paid to local governments to replace money that was lost by local governments when their powers to impose personal

property taxes on businesses were taken away in 1976. Portions are distributed based on the share of personal property tax collections at that time, but the actual levels depend on the amount of personal property owned by businesses within municipal boundaries. Gaming taxes are another example of state taxes that are distributed based upon the size of the municipal base.

14. Expenditures of motor fuel taxes must be earmarked for transportation services and roads.

15. Examining the 125 largest metropolitan regions in the United States based on population levels in 2006, about 90 percent of the municipalities in half of these regions provide some level of water and sewer services. The average per capita spending for both services combined in the Chicago region is about $350, which is the twentieth from the highest spending per capita in all regions (although the median spending per capita at $168 is relatively low). Calculations based on downloadable data released from US Census Bureau to the author via e-mail on March 9, 2010. Source of finance data for individual governments is 2007 Census of Governments. The website where data are located is password protected: http://harvester.census.gov/filedownload/2007cog_finance_individual_units.zip.

16. Many areas of the region also have water table limitations, radon and other contaminants, and state and federal environmental protection mandates, all of which add significant costs to water production and sewer and wastewater management.

17. Generally speaking, an equalization factor of 1.0 means that properties within a county are assessed at 33.3 percent. An equalization factor of 2.0 means that the assessed values of properties must be doubled to equal 33.3 percent of market value. *Equalized assessed value* (EAV) of a property is then the assessed value of a property after the equalization factor has been applied.

18. EAV per square mile is used because multiplying EAV per capita by percent residential EAV to correct for the distortion of per capita measures yields residential EAV per capita, which is not appropriate here.

19. Median age of housing and population density is reversed to make their effects consistent with other component measures.

20. About twenty-five municipalities contract with the county to provide police services, so separate crime statistics are not reported for them. Most of these municipalities have populations less than one thousand and are in Lake County. To avoid eliminating these governments from the analyses, their crime rates are estimated using regression analysis, and these estimates are then used in the regression analyses to construct the spending needs indicators.

21. Ratio changes are used rather than percent change because these variables are logged in many cases to compensate for the high level of skewness in these distributions. Negative values that result from percent change calculations cannot be logged.

Chapter 3

Financial Decision Making in Municipal Government

The previous chapter talked about what it means for local governments to be financially healthy and identified environmental and structural features that establish the boundaries of fiscal capacity and spending obligations (current and future). The key attributes of financial condition according to chapter 2 are revenue wealth, or the capacity of the environment to generate revenues; the level of spending needs within the jurisdiction; state-imposed rules that limit access to revenues and establish local spending responsibilities; and the government's fiscal structure. This chapter presents a framework for describing and explaining financial decisions about policies and practices that affect financial condition. This framework is based on the concepts of strategic management and problem solving and focuses on qualities of the decision process and framing rather than qualities of the environment within which decisions occur.

Financial decision making is conceptualized here as strategic problem solving in which government officials have a toolbox of options they can use to solve financial problems and achieve financial goals. The toolbox consists of different fiscal policies and practices for solving financial problems, which are determined by government's financial attributes, in part, and by their institutional and governing environments. Officials' choices among these options depend to a great degree on their approach to financial problem solving and their preferences for particular solutions. The latter is shaped by their institutional and governing environments, which is examined in more detail in chapter 4.

The metaphors of problem solving and strategic management are based on large bodies of empirical research with well-developed theoretical foundations and provide a rich framework for explaining and interpreting local government financial decisions (Jones 2001). Strategic management is oftentimes viewed as a prescriptive approach to managerial decision making because it advocates designing decisions to strategically position the organization to leverage strengths, overcome weaknesses, take advantage of opportunities, and minimize threats. However, this approach also is used to describe and explain managerial decisions in terms of the adaptation of an organization's internal features (e.g., fiscal structure) to external conditions (Mintzberg 1990). With respect to financial problems and goals of municipal government, the strategic problem to be solved is to adapt government fiscal structure to the fiscal and political environments (see figure 2.2). What is considered a preferred solution in this regard depends on decision makers' assessments of risks and knowledge of how or whether options from the fiscal toolbox will solve financial problems and achieve their goals.

The problem-solving metaphor, by comparison, views decisions as a series of iterative subchoices of establishing goals, finding or designing courses of action, and evaluating and choosing among alternative options (Mintzberg, Raisinghani, and Theroet 1976; Simon and Associates 1986; Smith 1988). This approach is often used to describe and understand decisions or decision processes that are complex, novel, and unstructured rather than routine, simple, and structured. This approach also emphasizes the role of heuristics that, like threats and opportunities, directs consideration of financial options as solutions to financial problems. As recognized by cognitive psychology, heuristics are guides, and professionalism and professional training are important sources of heuristics for strategic solutions to government financial problems.

More generally, strategic management is concerned with the content and outcomes of decisions more than decision process, whereas problem solving focuses more on process than content and outcomes. These two metaphors are discussed first, and the qualitative data and methodology used to document and explain financial choices within the governing and fiscal environments are discussed at the end of this chapter.

Strategic Management and Risk

Many local practitioners will be familiar with the concept of strategic management from the practice of strategic planning, which is a formalized method of developing policies and other broad strategies at the top levels of government and organizations. The intellectual roots of strategic management go back to Frederick Taylor and the concept of scientific management (1911), but the elaboration and study of strategy making by managers and policymakers continue at a high level today. In fact, one of the field's most prolific contributors has noted ten distinct schools of strategy formulation. Most of these schools share several common perspectives on how to describe decision making in organizations or what to prescribe about how decisions should be made (Mintzberg and Lampel 1999).

One shared view is that the development of business strategies and their implementation are the mechanisms by which organizations adapt to their competitive environments. Another view is that successful business strategies will bring organizational processes and structure in line with the environment. This is not to say that only one set of strategies will be appropriate, or that only certain processes and structures will work in particular environments, but the end result for whatever strategy is implemented should be an overall fit or match between the organization's internal environment (structure and process) and external environment.

For instance, some research has shown that decentralized organizations perform better than centralized organizations in turbulent environments because the former has greater flexibility and can respond faster to changing circumstances. Research also suggests that decentralization is more effective when organizations are large, employees are professional, and the work is service rather than manufacturing (Huber, Miller, and Glick 1990). Departmentalization and specialization of tasks, interdependence among units, and slack resources are other internal features studied in this context (Scott 1998).

From a prescriptive perspective, the premise underlying the field of strategic management is that business strategies should align the organization's internal competencies (strengths and weaknesses) to environmental *threats* and *opportunities* (Mintzberg 1990). Descriptively, the field examines strategies, strategic choice process, and structural/procedural adaptation (success) to determine their features and relationships in different settings. Research in this area is vast, especially with respect to firms and the business sector in general, but there are a significant number of studies of strategic management of public organizations and governments (Nutt and Backoff 1987, 1992; Meier et al. 2007; Andrews et al. 2009). Based on the seminal works of Mintzberg (1979) and Miles and Snow (1978), research on both sectors views strategic choice about internal structure, processes, and tasks as being constrained by both the external and internal environments.

Dimensions of the external environment that are particularly important to this perspective are munificence scarcity, stability variability, and threat security (Pfeffer and Salancik 1978; Lawrence and Lorsch 1967; Thompson 1967). Borrowing from this approach, fiscal stress is defined here as the worsening of financial condition brought about by negative changes in the fiscal environment and related threats. Fiscal munificence is the opposite—an improvement in financial condition brought about by positive changes in the fiscal environment and related opportunities. External threats and opportunities also trigger strategic decisions (Chattopadhyay, Glick, and Huber 2001).

Important dimensions of the internal environment include some of the structural and procedural conditions mentioned previously—centralization-decentralization, professionalization of employees, and interdependence of units (loose versus tight coupling). The internal environment also encompasses how employees, tasks, and processes are organized, the processes and rules used to coordinate and control events, and specific characteristics about internal elements, such as the capacity of employees or the tasks they engage in. More generally, the internal environment consists of strengths and weaknesses that the organization brings to the table in dealing with threats and opportunities.

As described here, strategic decisions are better thought of as a stream of major and minor decisions made by managers and policymakers rather than a formal activity such as strategic planning, although strategic planning is an internal process that can elicit major decisions by an organization. Strategic decisions attempt to position the organization to be successful in (adapt to) the competitive environment or, in the case of public organizations, to be successful in (adapt to) the public domain of constituencies (including voters), other governments, service responsibilities, and revenue capacity. Strategic decisions focus on changing organizational structures, processes, and tasks to accommodate the competitive environment or public domain, although they can target changes to the external environment more directly. Most important, strategic decisions take place within boundaries and stimuli determined by environmental constraints, opportunities, and threats (Child 1972, 1997; Bluedorn et al. 1994).

An important elaboration of the basic framework of strategic management is made by Miles and Snow (1978), who identify the basic strategies of defender, prospector, analyzer, and reactor from observed patterns of decision making in business organizations. Defender strategies focus on improving the efficiency of existing operations and defending product domain rather than searching for opportunities or new solutions. Prospector strategies emphasize innovation and product-market development and are somewhat opposite of defender strategies. Reactor strategies are in contrast to proactive strategies that involve some level of planning or anticipation, and analyzer strategies share traits with defenders in stable situations and prospectors in more volatile circumstances. This typology has been extensively applied in research on strategic decision making and has generally been supported (DeSarbo et al. 2005; Boyne and Walker 2004). As will be discussed in chapter 6, both the defender and prospector strategies have been observed in the municipalities in the Chicago metropolitan region.

These four strategies have been associated more recently with different managerial perspectives on risk and risk taking. In classical decision and game theory, risk is conceptualized narrowly as decision makers not knowing outcomes of choices with certainty, but knowing the probabilities of possible outcomes. The expected value of a choice for a decision maker is the payoff that will occur as a result of the decision, multiplied by the probability of that outcome. In this case, the desirability of a strategy is a function of both the likelihood of an outcome and the payoff to the decision maker. This view of decision making under risky conditions depicts the process as being very rational, which may be the way decisions should be made, but it is not how decisions are actually made in most cases.

Studies of decision making in the field of cognitive psychology and strategic decision making recognize that perceptions of risks and propensity for risk can vary across individuals and context. Both depend on individual personality, the way in which problems are framed, the value of expected gains or losses, and other conditions. For instance, individuals tend to ignore events that are very unlikely or remote, evaluate more certain outcomes as more likely to occur than is the case, and associate risk with the magnitude of negative outcomes or losses rather than probabilities of events (Tversky and Kahneman 1981; March and Shapira 1987; Chattopadhyay, Glick, and Huber 2001). Similar to problem solving, individuals apply heuristics to simplify their thinking about risks, which creates biases and inaccuracies in assessing them.

Perceptions of risk have also been linked to threats and opportunities. Kahneman and Tversky (1979) first proposed that individuals assign value to gains or losses rather than outcomes and that they will be more risk accepting when facing losses and threats but more risk averse when facing favorable conditions and opportunities. In the first case, when individuals perceive they have little to lose from negative outcomes due to threats, they will take more risks. In the second case, they perceive greater losses from negative outcomes when pursuing opportunities, so they take fewer risks. In effect, rather than having propensity for more or less risk, individuals are biased against losses and lack regret over missed gains (Tversky and Kahneman 1991).

These biases have been observed in many organizational settings and have been linked to prospector and defender management strategies in several ways (March and Shapira 1987). First, organizations and individuals that are prospectors are more risk accepting, whereas defenders are more risk averse. Second, prospector strategies are more likely to be externally directed and progressive in response to threats and possible losses, whereas defender strategies are directed internally and conservative in response to taking advantage of opportunities and favorable external conditions (Krause 2003; Wiseman and Gomez-Mejia 1998). Others have found that organizational slack (as defined in chapter 2) lessens the perceived dangers of risk by making losses seem less painful or negative. Thus defender strategies may become more prospective regarding opportunities if organizations have discretionary or nondiscretionary slack (Chatto-padhyay, Glick, and Huber 2001; Singh 1986; March and Shapira 1987).

Problem Solving

The study of decision making as problem solving is most closely associated with the field of cognitive psychology and relies heavily on experimental designs to observe how individuals make decisions under different constructed circumstances. Herbert Simon, who is one of the most celebrated and seminal scholars of public administration, was an early pioneer in the field of cognitive psychology and human problem solving (Newell and Simon 1972).[1]

Building on the work of Simon and others, Mintzberg, Raisinghani, and Theroet (1976) observed three primary phases and several subphases of problem solving in twenty-five different organizational decisions that laid the foundation for much future research and thinking about strategic decision making in the management field (Rajagopalan, Rasheed, and Datta 1993). These decisions included building a new airport runway, developing an urban renewal program, purchasing new equipment for a hospital, firing a radio announcer, developing a new product, and acquiring a firm. These phases are similar to descriptive models of decision making developed by others in the field (Schwenk 1984) and are outlined below:

1. Problem identification
   - ▼ Decision recognition: Opportunities, problems, threats, and crises are recognized, which evokes decision and mobilizes resources
   - ▼ Diagnosis: Comprehension of problem and determining cause-and-effect relationships, clarifying and defining the problem by tapping existing information and opening channels to create new information, e.g., creating task force
2. Development: Heart of decision making that leads to development of one or more solutions to the problem or elaboration of an opportunity that includes two somewhat mutually exclusive processes
   - ▼ Search: Finding ready-made solutions to a problem
   - ▼ Design: Develop custom-made solutions or modify ready-made ones
3. Selection: May be bound up with the development phase if the latter involves factoring decisions into subdecisions, with each requiring selection
   - ▼ Screen: Reduce number of potential solutions to a few feasible ones through elimination
   - ▼ Evaluation-choice: Investigate the feasible alternatives and select course of action using judgment, bargaining, and analysis
   - ▼ Authorization: Ratify the chosen course of action at a higher level

Four points must be emphasized about this process. First, decision making and analysis often proceed across and within phases in an iterative, nonlinear manner. However, the process is basically sequential rather than anarchic (Pinfield 1986). Second, not all decisions follow this path. Mintzberg and colleagues distinguish between opportunity decisions that are purely voluntary and crisis decisions that are made under extreme pressure. The selection phase for opportunity decisions may be somewhat predetermined, requiring little problem identification, development, screening, or evaluation. Decisions during crises may not have the time or resources to engage in all phases, and the overall process may be truncated. Third, the development phase consumed the greatest amount of decision making resources and so is discussed in more detail subsequently. Finally, strategic decisions are important, nonroutine, complex, ill-structured, precedent setting, and commit substantial resources from the organization (Schwenk 1988; Hickson et al. 1986).

Dividing decision problems into separate phases is one method of managing the complexity of the problem and decision making and represents how "people cut problems down to size" (Simon and Associates 1986). Another method is heuristic search, which is an important component of the development phase. With respect to problem solving, a *heuristic* is "any principle or device that contributes to the reduction in the average search for solutions" (Simon, Newell, and Shaw 1982, 152). More generally, heuristics are techniques and cognitive shortcuts used to simplify problem solving. Heuristics direct problem-solving activities and the judgment of decision makers, such as with search, but also in other areas including screening, diagnosis, and evaluation. Heuristics suggest which paths of analysis should be tried first, which leads are promising, which solutions are likely to be successful, and how to structure a problem to resolve it more easily. Heuristics are controllers that guide or establish problem-solving procedures and thus systematically influence and bias decisions in particular ways.

The following are examples of heuristics that have been studied empirically in numerous settings and mathematically (Simon 1962; Kahneman, Slovic, and Tversky 1982; Gigerenzer 2004):

▼ Search for solutions locally or focus on solutions that are easiest to implement.
▼ Perform trial and error to find solutions over time using feedback from successive choices.
▼ Apply brainstorming as a method of designing a solution.
▼ Use scenarios and other mental models to judge outcomes of choices and events.
▼ Apply simple analogies to diagnose problems and design solutions.
▼ Screen or search based on categorizations of solution features.
▼ Consult colleagues, friends, or reference manual.

Another example is the *availability* heuristic in which people view events that are more common in their experience as more likely. This approach to problem solving is apparent in the aphorism "If the only tool you have is a hammer, then every problem looks like a nail." People apply the *representativeness* heuristic when they view new events as related because their experience or training places the event in the same class as other events. Police use of profiling when stopping motorists is a good example of the representativeness heuristic. *Anchoring and adjustment* occurs when individuals anchor search and design for solutions to initial suggestions or current conditions (Tversky and Kahneman 1974).

The heuristic process and decision makers' choice of heuristics are shaped by the task, decision setting, cognitive structure (e.g., beliefs, causal maps, frame of reference) and personality traits of the decision maker, and less cognitive sources of knowledge such as intuition and common sense (Walsh 1995). This knowledge is influenced greatly by experience and training, although current research sometimes distinguishes between heuristic judgments that are automatic and innate rather than problem-solving heuristics that are cognitive and deliberate (Keren and Teigen 2004).

Some heuristics are more powerful than others. For instance, the heuristics used by experts are more efficient and effective than the heuristics used by novices. The newer or more unfamiliar the problem, the more likely individuals are to use time-consuming heuristics such as trial and error or crude mental models to solve problems. Heuristics become more selective and systematic as the novice gains experience. Consider the heuristics used by a grand master chess player versus someone who has played chess only a few times. The grand master is able to comprehend and interpret the entire board, eliminate undesirable moves, and focus attention on particular sets of moves very quickly. By comparison, the novice is more likely to assess all moves individually and sequentially (Simon 1962; Day and Lord 1992).

Heuristic judgment and problem solving by experts is not always better, however. It can produce its own biases with detrimental consequences. Although experts' assessments are often more accurate than laypersons', experts tend to be overconfident in their estimates of events. Expertise also can create myopia that focuses attention on certain diagnoses and areas of search or design at the expense of others. For instance, doctors often do not consider the cost of medical tests or the impact of false positives, and regulatory agencies may not see targeted events in a broader context (Rachlinski 2004.)

Financial Decisions and Strategic Problem Solving

How do these theoretical perspectives apply to fiscal policy and practices in suburban local governments? First, one has to be comfortable with the notion that financial decisions can be conceptualized as risky (probabilistic outcomes) solutions to fiscal problems affecting the strategic position of government within the financial and governing environments. Additionally, financial decisions or strategies may be conceptualized as choosing one or more tools from the fiscal toolbox as part of a broader strategy or solution to maintain or improve financial condition. Although many financial decisions are routine, simple, and nonstrategic, many others are nonstandard and strategic decisions about broad-based or important events that can affect one or more levels of financial solvency and other strategic concerns of a financial nature.

For instance, on the one hand, checking an encumbrance with equity in the equipment fund to determine if there is enough money to enter into an obligation to buy a copier is a routine financial decision. On the other hand, instituting a policy that encumbrances will always be checked with fund equity for every transaction more than $10,000 is not routine. Similarly, calculating quarterly pension payments to employee trust funds is simple, but deciding how to invest these funds or whether and at what level to consciously underfund future obligations is not standard. Both decisions in the first set help maintain short-term solvency by reducing the likelihood of overspending, and both decisions in the second set affect long-term solvency, but only the second decision in each set constitutes financial problem solving that is strategic.

Many financial decisions, especially policy-level choices about revenues, debt, service levels, infrastructure, and financial performance goals, can be conceptualized as strategic solutions to financial problems with probabilistic outcomes. Similarly, decisions about internal controls, how to develop a budget or financial plan, and other financial management practices are risky solutions to problems with strategic implications.

Professionalization and Heuristics

This chapter also has noted the importance of heuristics to financial problem solving, including the assessment of risks and the choice of fiscal tools and strategies. What qualities about suburban government officials are likely to affect the heuristics they use to make financial decisions? One of the most important features is officials' knowledge of local public finance and standards of financial management practice, which is influenced greatly by their professional training and experience. According to Hansell (2002), a professional is someone who has four characteristics: (1) mastery of a body of knowledge appropriate to their job, (2) formal admission to the profession via certification of competence (strong form) or membership in a professional group (weak), (3) acceptance of a code of ethics and standards of practice promoted by the profession, and (4) maintenance of skills and knowledge through continuing professional development. These characteristics are developed or obtained through extensive formal training, experience in the field, and interaction with colleagues in the profession.

More important to strategic fiscal problem solving and consistent with the characteristics described by Hansell, professionalization is likely to cultivate a very different set of heuristics compared to those used by nonprofessionals resulting in systematic differences in preferred solutions to the same financial problems. For instance, professional finance directors may assess the risks of debt financing of capital infrastructure very differently from mayors with little knowledge of and experience with how debt financing works or the options associated with this solution to the problem of capital financing. Professional finance directors with degrees in accounting and experience with implementing financial management practices in government also may be more sensitive to the need for internal controls and how best to structure them than village managers with degrees and experience in public administration.

Although the manager in a council-manager form of municipal government may not be a professional as defined previously, it is more likely especially as the municipality becomes wealthier and larger. Similarly, a mayor-council government is more likely to have a professional chief administrator as the municipality becomes larger because the financial problems are more complicated and larger governments face special administrative challenges (Svara 1999).

An individual with the title of village/city manager or administrator is the chief administrative officer (CAO). Assuming the CAO is a professional, one would expect that professional heuristics are more likely to be employed when solving administrative and financial problems in municipalities in governments with a CAO. Alternatively, professional heuristics are less likely to be employed in governments without a CAO. Compared to professional CAOs, however, professional finance officers are likely to have a set of heuristics even more honed toward solving financial problems. There is no evidence to support this claim on a broad scale, but the qualitative evidence gathered for this book (as described in the section on qualitative methodology) suggests the patterns of professionalization described here. This evidence led to the development of a key measure to capture systematic differences in financial heuristics in these governments.

Preparations for choosing governments to interview in late 2002 revealed that certain structural features seemed to impact the kinds of financial decisions being made in governments of different size and composition. The variable *financial decision structure* (FDS) was created with five different categories to reflect these features, and all municipalities in the region were classified based on whether they had the following: (1) a municipal manager and finance director, (2) a municipal administrator and finance director, (3) a municipal manager or administrator but no finance director, (4) a finance director but no municipal manager or administrator, and (5) no municipal administrator, manager, or finance director (mayor only). Municipalities were assigned a category based on examining websites, news reports, and making phone calls if necessary.

Although having a designated finance director, administrator, or manager does not guarantee that the official will be a professional, it does indicate that the government considers these positions to require more responsibility and administrative expertise than a financial coordinator, bookkeeper, or office manager. This is especially true for the positions of village or city manager and administrator that are commonly recognized terms applied by elected and appointed government officials to designate an appointed person with significant responsibility for government operations. The distinction between an administrator and manager is less clear but is also important as it designates different levels of administrative and policymaking authority (Ammons 2008).

In the ideal type council-manager form of government, a city manager or village manager is the chief administrative officer and assumes some of the mayor's executive authority. Municipal governments in Illinois that operate under the managerial form of government, as recognized by Illinois state statutes (65 ILCS 5/, Illinois Municipal Code), must appoint a manager with the authority to hire and remove all departmental heads. The municipal manager also owns the executive budget, which is the cornerstone of fiscal policy and other critical financial decisions, and participates in policymaking at all board meetings.

Municipal governments in Illinois that do not adopt the council-manager form by statute may still appoint a city or village manager with most of these powers and are included in the category of governments with a manager form.[2] DeSantis and Renner (2002) consider these governments to have a council-manager form with an empowered mayor. By comparison, municipal administrators have no executive authority. Mayors in these governments have full control over the budget and appointment of departmental heads, and they may share administrative duties with the administrator, especially in economic development.

The position of an appointed finance director is not as well recognized as the positions of municipal manager or administrator, but the pattern of finance directors having formal training, experience, and a level of professionalization that is greater than other financial positions is borne out by the qualitative evidence and years of student budgeting projects on local governments in the region. In addition, unlike the position of manager or administrator, that of finance director is associated with very specific tangible skills and technical knowledge that require a relatively high level of training and experience. For instance, it is not unusual for municipal administrators and managers in the Chicago region to have been mayors previously, or even to be the current mayor of another municipality. However, a government is much less likely to appoint someone as a finance director who has not studied formally or obtained years of experience in accounting and other areas of financial management. Alternatively, some municipalities may have an elected treasurer that is a financial professional and so have no need to appoint a finance director.

The issue of elected treasurers being professionals and managers or administrators being nonprofessional, political appointees means that professionalization will not correlate exactly to the FDS categories, but it is a good approximation. Furthermore, professional treasurers can lose elections, and politically appointed managers and administrators can disappear with the election of a new mayor or council. It is also not unusual for elected officials in smaller, wealthier suburbs who are financial professionals to take a more active role in the financial management of their government, which reduces the need to hire a financial professional. Another common practice is for municipalities with an administrator or manager (usually the former) to hire an assistant executive administrator with financial skills and knowledge and forgo the finance director or to forgo the finance director if the executive administrator has a strong financial background. Thus one would have to survey elected officials and the chief executive and financial administrators in all municipalities to obtain a better measure of the level of financial professionalization and experience in these governments.

Table 3.1 shows how municipal governments are distributed across the five categories of FDS in 2003 according to the population of the jurisdiction and government spending in 2000. Overall, 78 percent of the 264 municipalities in this study have populations less than 25,000 and 72 percent have budgets less than $15 million. The table shows that the highest portion of municipalities in the region have both a finance director and manager or a mayor only, followed by no finance director with a manager or administrator. Very few of the municipalities have a finance director only. With respect to population, municipalities with a manager and finance director are the largest, followed by those with a finance director only and those with both an administrator and finance director. By comparison, municipalities without a finance director are much smaller, with mayor-only governments being the smallest according to median population and spending values. However, looking at the minimum and maximum population and spending values in the table shows how much variation there is in municipal size within each category.

Professional Financial Heuristics

How does professionalization alter the choices government officials make about fiscal policy and practice? In other words, how does formal training and/or years of experience, interaction with other professionals, and other characteristics of professionalization alter financial problem solving? How does professionalization alter decision

TABLE 3.1 Municipal Population and Government Spending for Categories of Financial Decision Structure: 264 Municipal Governments in the Chicago Metropolitan Area

Number and percent of governments in 2003	Manager and Finance Director 75, 28%		Administrator and Finance Director 40, 15%		Administrator or Manager, No Finance Director 56, 21%		Finance Director, No Manager or Administrator 18, 7%		No Finance Director, Manager, or Administrator 75, 28%	
2000	Pop.	Spending	Pop.	Spending	Pop.	Spending	Pop.	Spending	Pop.	Spending
Mean	31,844	$24,958,047	17,795	$11,922,850	7,565	$4,645,566	37,248	$31,230,488	6,328	$4,113,857
Median	24,554	$17,014,637	15,609	$10,703,435	5,449	$3,467,019	23,171	$18,682,343	3,553	$1,884,564
Minimum	2,494	$2,898,187	1,429	$2,588,115	574	$830,976	2,134	$2,630,513	106	$20,449
Maximum	128,358	$95,209,436	56,321	$42,309,007	26,999	$17,326,794	142,990	$107,277,520	32,776	$28,297,264

ANOVA

Population, F = 30.8, p = .000

Spending, F = 32.6, p = .000

recognition (what is a fiscal threat or opportunity), search for a solution, screening (what is an acceptable financial solution), and final selection to produce choices that are different from governments without professionals? The profession of governmental financial management has several groups that codify recommended financial practices and policies for state and local levels of government based on general agreement from their membership and bodies of highly qualified members. In effect, these recommended practices and policies represent idealized solutions to financial problems that may not be appropriate for all contexts, but they do provide anchors to guide development or search for solutions to financial problems in all local settings.

Government Finance Officers Association (GFOA; 2001) is the broadest group in terms of the financial professionals it represents and its financial foci.[3] As of the end of 2009, GFOA had almost 150 recommended fiscal practices and policies across the following categories: (1) accounting, auditing, and financial reporting; (2) budgeting and fiscal policy; (3) cash management; (4) debt management; (5) economic development and capital planning; and (6) retirement and benefits administration. Development of these recommendations, which are very detailed, was initiated by the National Advisory Council on State and Local Budgeting under the leadership of GFOA (Esser 1997).[4]

Although the recommendations do not advocate specific taxing or spending policies, as political preferences matter greatly in these decisions, the recommendations do state that governments should adopt revenue, spending, and debt policies that promote sustainability (environmental and fiscal) over time and for future generations. As discussed in the recommendations, sustainability is about maintaining balance between the economy, the environment, the community, and the government's financial structure. The recommendations also suggest that financial professionals have a public duty to express their opinions about decisions they believe would threaten sustainability. Certainly, the financial profession would disapprove of raising debt levels beyond what is likely to be repaid in the future, or spending levels beyond what revenues can support. Other recommendations, such as basing financial decisions on long-term financial planning and allocating sufficient funds to capital maintenance and replacement, also are very general, although they can be politically charged, as elected officials may not want to commit to particular solutions or ways of solving financial problems. However, the majority of recommendations covers relatively nonpolitical, financial management practices such as using managed competition and shared service delivery, maintaining appropriate fund balance levels, and using appropriate methods of applying and analyzing financial data.

Bond rating agencies such as Standard & Poor's and Moody's are another important source of heuristics for financial and administrative professionals in local government. Governments that undergo bond ratings, even periodically, become educated about particular solutions to financial problems, especially regarding financial threats and acceptable opportunities. For instance, Moody's lists potential signs of distress that would lead the agency to downgrade a government's credit rating, such as being self-insured with no corresponding reserves, having significant pending litigation and settlements, being at or close to tax ceilings (no revenue reserves), and having high reliance on operating transfers from other funds (Moody's Investor Services 2000; Standard & Poor's 2002).

Compared to the GFOA sanctioned practices, which are closer to the definition of heuristics as decision-making rules, the bond rating criteria target policy outcomes that affect the financial condition of government. To some extent, the bond rating agencies care less about the process of financial decision making than the outcomes, but emphasizing particular outcomes can have a large effect on the search phase of government fiscal policymaking. For example, one decision rule used by government officials to guide financial policies or practices might be "Consider financial actions that would downgrade bond rating only as a last resort." Also the qualitative evidence presented here shows that maintaining bond rating is very important to both elected and appointed governments officials, which then become important anchors for officials' search, screening, and selection of financial options.

Table 3.2 presents four broad areas of financial decision making as derived from the bond rating criteria and GFOA's recommended budgeting practices. It is assumed that these areas represent fundamentally different types of financial problems and solutions (policies and practices).[5] Financial problems and solutions in category A focus on budgeting and planning. For instance, how the government projects revenues and spending for upcoming budgets would be included here. Other problems and solutions in category A would concern whether the government has a capital program, states fiscal policies, engages in formal planning exercises, and uses the appropriation ordinance as the budget.[6] Category B focuses on problems and solutions associated with financial and managerial control of operations and transactions such as internal controls and accounting methods. Category C focuses on how and whether governments monitor and assess financial, operational, and programmatic performance and use this information in problem solving. Category D represents government policies and practices that more directly affect the financial stability and condition of local government in the long run and the short run. Government policies and practices in this area are further subdivided into the four problem spheres shown for this category in the table.

Entrepreneurialism and Risk

Consistent with Miles and Snow's observations about types of business strategies and their relationship to risk preferences or propensities toward risk, special attention is given to risk in the analysis of financial problem solving in Chicago governments. Also risk taking is a fundamental component of many financial management and fiscal policy choices. Decisions about how to structure debt, investments in cash and long-term assets, and how much insurance to buy incorporate risk directly and involve assessing risk. However, the decision to underfund pension liabilities also is a risk these liabilities can be paid in the future, and the decision to postpone capital maintenance risks higher increases in expenditures down the road or even user safety. Similarly, the decision to raise taxes is risking that it will produce enough revenues in the long run and not be detrimental at election time. Thus whether the chief financial officer and other government officials are defenders (risk averse) or prospectors (risk seeking) will be relevant to understanding fiscal practices and policies in local government.

The concept of entrepreneur is very similar to the prospector defined by Miles and Snow (1978), but with greater emphasis on innovation. An entrepreneur is very alert to opportunities for change and willing to take risks in pursuit of opportunities

TABLE 3.2 Categories of Financial Practices and Policies

(A) Planning and Budgeting: Practices and Process

A multiyear perspective on budgeting and other areas of financial management, meaningful and comprehensive assessment of future revenues and expenditures, recognize future impact of current decisions
- Projection of revenues and spending
- Budget versus appropriations ordinance, comprehensive budget document
- Capital budget or program
- Strategic planning or planning exercises
- Long-range financial planning
- Formal statements of goals and objectives (programmatic and fiscal)
- GFOA budget and CAFR award

(B) Fiscal Accountability and Control

Methods of financial and managerial control of operations and transactions (accounting) including reporting, auditing, and transparency
- Accounting for purchasing and contracts
- Internal auditing procedures
- Monitoring of overtime and hours worked
- GAAP and basis of accounting
- Auditor's role in reporting and fiscal operations (independent?)
- Website information on budget or CAFR and other fiscal info to public
- Illegal activities
- Presence of financial information systems
- Existence of checks and balances
- Formal policies regarding accountability and control
- Recording of transactions and midyear reporting

(C) Assessing Financial and Programmatic Performance

Systematic monitoring and assessing, obtaining and using information to guide operational and financial decisions, types of information gathered and how it is used
- Performance, outcomes, productivity (programmatic, operational, and financial)
- Costs and benefits of fiscal operations and policies
- Rate studies, cost accounting
- Assess financial status—sources of problems and financial resources, long-term trends
- Assess future capital needs, pension obligations, debt burden
- Assess and monitor risk, transaction costs, cash flow

(D) Financial Stability and Health

Practices and policies that affect current and future long-term and short-term solvency in areas of cash management, risk management, debt, capital investment and maintenance, pensions, revenues, and spending
- Capital equipment and infrastructure and debt: Maintenance, condition (liability), funding mechanisms (e.g., grants, earmarking, pay as you go)
- Fund balance and reserves: Function—cash management, rainy day, capital savings; how manage cash flow—tax anticipation notes, line of credit, reserves
- Fiscal policies and priorities on spending and revenues: Tax and spend priorities, use of grants, how utilize revenue increases from late 1990s
- Risk perception and reduction: Reliance on sales taxes, revenue diversification, risk reduction programs (e.g., working safety), funding of liability and health insurance (e.g., self-insured)

(Schneider, Teske, and Mintrom 1995, 8). Entrepreneurs have the ability to frame issues and problems in ways that emphasize change from the status quo. One might say that their heuristics are more sensitive to opportunities and the possibilities that ensue from pursuing them than the average individual. Strategically, their orientation should be more toward the external environment (Bruton and Hildreth 1993).

There is also a range of entrepreneurialism that involves different levels of risk. On the risky side are highly innovative entrepreneurs that create totally new solutions and institutional forms to resolve problems and pursue their vision. On the less risky side are entrepreneurs that borrow solutions from others and adapt them to their own circumstances rather than create something new. In this case, the less risky entrepreneur shares characteristics with the analyzer, which describes "managers who watch competitors closely for new ideas, then rapidly adopt those that appear to be the most promising" (Miles and Snow 1978, 29). Leadership ability is another important feature noted about entrepreneurs because they are able to coordinate the actions of other people to implement solutions.

The study of entrepreneurial behavior by Schneider, Teske, and Mintrom (1995) is particularly relevant to the study of Chicago suburbs because their unit of analysis is suburban governments in the one hundred largest metropolitan regions in 1970. They conducted a survey of municipal clerks in 1991 asking them about entrepreneurs in their government and their opinions about its governing and political characteristics. Their findings distinguished between political and managerial entrepreneurs, and between progrowth and antigrowth entrepreneurs. Although both appointed and elected officials can be progrowth or antigrowth entrepreneurs, it is usually elected officials that handle growth in an entrepreneurial manner because it offers so many opportunities from which they can benefit. Growth and economic development can create jobs, stabilize or reduce taxes, improve the business climate, and provide different forms of payoffs to supporters, all of which become leverage and resources at election time.

However, there also are significant political and financial risks in growth and development. Residential and commercial development alters a jurisdiction's physical environment and constituencies, which can change the quality of life for existing residents dramatically and add new residents who place very different demands on the government. This often produces significant political conflict that transforms governing institutions, especially in small, less-developed jurisdictions that are in the path of the regional growth machine (MacManus 2004). High population growth and commercial development create a political minefield for municipal officials and have profound effects on the government's fiscal environment. Such changes will alter its fiscal structure, creating another minefield for officials to negotiate—that of maintaining the government's financial condition during the growth period and after the growth has slowed. For instance, growing municipal governments in the Chicago region that do not balance commercial with residential development run the risk of having few commercial services for residents in the future and being unable to change their dependency on property taxes once they are fully developed.

For many governments, therefore, growth and development present as many political and financial threats as opportunities. Negotiating the growth and development minefields can be a significant challenge even for experienced and knowledgeable government officials. For this reason, it is important to examine financial policies, practices, and conditions in governments that are undergoing high growth and development separately from governments with little or no growth. Indeed, the qualitative data show the nature and extent of fundamental differences between Chicago governments in different stages of maturity. In effect, each stage presents a different set of fiscal problems to be solved. Using the balance metaphor, growth and development requires governments to adapt institutionally and financially to maintain long-term solvency. One key question here is whether government adaptation to growth and development is better achieved with different types of financial decision structures, fiscal strategies, or sets of practices than others.

Low-growth governments that are in poor financial condition and have changed their FDS are another place to observe entrepreneurialism and its effects on financial policies and practices. The qualitative evidence on Chicago municipal governments shows numerous instances of governments hiring professional financial and administrative officials specifically to help them improve financial decisions and condition. It is interesting that the individuals who were hired in these cases often exhibited entrepreneurial characteristics, although the willingness to work for communities with very poor financial condition, and often high levels of political conflict, does not seem like an entrepreneurial choice according to the picture of the entrepreneur provided by Schneider and his colleagues. That picture stresses leadership and, consistent with the Miles and Snow concept of prospector, an external focus.

Alternatively, the entrepreneurial managers observed in low-growth and poor governments seem closer to the picture of entrepreneurs provided by Levin and Sanger (1994). They observed entrepreneurs who create mission, are biased toward action, are opportunistic, take risks, and underestimate obstacles. Although research from the business sector finds little psychological difference between entrepreneurs and managers, entrepreneurs in fiscally stressed governments seem to embrace challenges more than other officials who were interviewed in Chicago (Busenitz and Barney 1997). However, McCue (2000) finds that, irrespective of their personal disposition toward risk and entrepreneurial qualities, local government financial officers defer to the public interest when making investment decisions.

Prior research on strategic decision making shows that entrepreneurs do not have greater propensity toward risk taking. Rather, they tend to view situations more favorably and perceive risks as lower, which accounts for their overconfidence. Entrepreneurs are likely to see greater strengths than weaknesses, more opportunities than threats, and greater likelihood of future improvement than decline. From a problem-solving perspective, current theory and empirical findings suggest that entrepreneurs employ more biases and heuristics in decision making, especially regarding their greater tendency to generalize from limited experience and information (the representative heuristic) (Busenitz 1999).

Level of Fiscal Stress and Responses

Although the claim that fiscal stress (change in financial condition) will affect the fiscal policies and practices of government seems self-evident, there has been very little research since the late 1980s into how different levels of fiscal threat systematically impact financial choices. That condition may change as practitioners and scholars work to better understand how state and local governments handle the Great Recession. Thus it is useful to revisit what we know about how governments adapted to an earlier period of economic decline.

In his seminal article "Organizational Decline and Cutback Management" and subsequent works, Charles Levine claimed that governments respond to fiscal stress in a hierarchical and sequential pattern that depends on the degree and persistence of resource decline (Levine 1978, 1980; Levine, Rubin, and Wolohojian 1981). In the first stage governments employ *delaying* tactics hoping the problems will be temporary and denying the seriousness of fiscal problems. In the second phase governments employ *stretching and resisting* tactics to do more with the same amount of resources and avoid deep cuts and visible tax increases. The last phase targets *cutting and smoothing* tactics to constrain and directly counter the effects of severe fiscal stress. Essentially governments begin coping with changes in financial condition by pursuing options that are the easiest to implement, least intrusive to operations and financing, and least visible to the public. Assuming fiscal stress continues or worsens by the time they reach the last phase, governments have used up options that do not involve painful cuts in services, increases in taxes, and changes to internal process and structure. Alternatively, governments may pursue tactics in stage three more quickly to the extent that they recognize that fiscal problems are too severe to be alleviated with less profound and more desirable options. Table 3.3 summarizes Levine's inventory of specific tactics or options in each phase and adds a fourth category or phase of financial tactics (Levine 1978; Levine, Rubin, and Wolohojian 1981).

The last category, *escapist and survival mode,* contains tactics that are more likely to be seen in governments that are in a constant state of fiscal crisis and close to insolvency, such as exists in some municipalities in the Chicago metropolitan region. The condition that Schick (1980) described as *total scarcity,* which occurs when resources are not adequate to fund services at a minimum level, may apply in these cases. Such governments cannot deliver a level or quality of services necessary to meet baseline needs with all the resources at their disposal because they are too poor, their spending needs are too high, and they have no remaining slack. Because the problem is more severe than filling a budget gap, it is futile for governments in this situation to try to balance their budget, so they will paper it over with choices based on unrealistic and inaccurate assessments that are often dishonest and corrupt. At this level, budgeting and financial management is more escapist, and financial decisions focus on cash flow and simply having enough cash to pay the bills.[7]

Schick (1980) also documents other levels of scarcity that elicit different ways of solving financial problems and correspond to some extent to the phases in table 3.3. *Chronic scarcity* occurs when funds are sufficient to continue services at existing levels but insufficient to cover program expansion, growth in demand and needs, or costly new initiatives. Enough slack exists in the budget to avoid reducing service levels or quality to cover modest spending increases over time or greater spending increases for a short time. Under these conditions the budgetary focus is on controlling spending and funding modest expansion, but planning, analysis, and evaluation are not used to make decisions. *Acute scarcity* exists when governments do not have sufficient resources to absorb incremental increases in service delivery costs and therefore find it difficult to maintain

TABLE 3.3 Options for Handling Fiscal Stress

Delaying Near-term strategies for least-severe fiscal stress or to buy time to consider more strategic or dramatic cuts in the future	Artful budget manipulation, creative financial management, one-time solutions ▼ Short-term notes and fund transfers ▼ Delay capital spending ▼ Draw down fund balance ▼ Charge outlays to next fiscal year ▼ Optimistic revenue and spending forecasts ▼ Charging more internal services to fiscally healthy funds ▼ Limit discretionary spending, e.g., travel ▼ Pursue more grants
Stretching and resisting Midterm strategies for continuing financial decline and more severe fiscal stress	Strategic, innovative, and selective revenue and spending changes ▼ Long-term debt for operating expenditures ▼ Salary and hiring freezes ▼ Reduce employees through attrition ▼ Reduce administrative staff ▼ Increase benefit and retirement contributions from employees ▼ Rationing services, e.g., limiting hours or availability of service ▼ Increasing fees, fines, and other less visible revenues ▼ Efficiency reforms—changes in process and service delivery, e.g., contracting, collaborating, greater use of technology ▼ Across-the-board or selected cuts ▼ Reduce overtime ▼ Decreasing pension contributions
Cutting and smoothing Remote strategies for long-term fiscal stress and most severe financial decline	Visible and/or dramatic cuts in services and revenue increases ▼ Sell assets ▼ Layoffs ▼ Close facilities ▼ Terminate programs ▼ Transfer services to other units of government or other sectors ▼ Increasing most visible revenues, e.g., income and property taxes ▼ Decreasing visible and important services, e.g., police, snowplow ▼ Institute furlough days and reduce compensation
Extreme survival Total scarcity and constant fiscal crisis	Unrealistic, escapist, and radical measures to function at minimum level ▼ Illegal, prohibited, or dishonest actions, e.g., destroying or losing financial records, falsifying financial information ▼ Fake budgets: Budgets based on unrealistic projects and financial assumptions ▼ Nonbudgets: Not operating on a budget or having no intention of sticking to the budget as passed ▼ Focus on cash, e.g., not paying bills or relying on transfers of funds from all sources

current service levels or quality. Fiscal conservatism increases in governments that are experiencing acute scarcity, and the main focus of budgetary problem solving is to align funding with spending through nonpermanent reductions on the spending side. *Relaxed scarcity,* which cannot be described as fiscal stress, exists when governments have sufficient resources to continue services at current or higher levels, absorb normal cost increases due to growth or inflation, and undertake new commitments. Schick claims that under these circumstances, budgetary decisions will be based more on planning and oriented toward multiple years, but there will be little review or evaluation of existing programs or incentive to economize and alter existing fiscal practices.

As presented here, these phases of strategies for dealing with fiscal stress are consistent with the problem-solving perspective and suggest that local governments' fiscal toolboxes are hierarchical. Cyert and March (1963) and March and Simon (1958) argue that the search for solutions to organizational decline tends to be hierarchical, focusing first on options that are more familiar and immediately accessible than those that vary significantly from the status quo, are more risky, or require greater effort to fulfill. The prevalence of this broad-based heuristic was documented by much subsequent research on business behavior that links decline in organizational performance with different levels of response, risk taking, innovation, and slack (Whetten 1987; Weitzel and Jonsson 1989; Wiseman and Bromily 1996; Deephouse and Wiseman 2000). Overall, this literature argues that organizational decline and hostile (versus munificent) environments reduce risk taking and innovation, but the relationship is often curvilinear with less risk taking and innovation occurring in both more hostile and munificent environments (Kreiser, Marino, and Weaver 2002).

As described in chapter 2, higher levels of slack can provide organizations more time and flexibility to adapt to hostile environments (a form of organizational learning), but here too there is an inverse U-shaped relationship—too much and too little slack will reduce performance and innovation (Nohria and Gulati 1996; Tan and Peng 2003). With respect to the phases of fiscal strategies in table 3.3, governments are more likely to innovate in response to fiscal threats during the stretching and resisting phase. In this case, higher levels of slack resources, both discretionary and nondiscretionary, allow governments to postpone their search for more drastic and less innovative cutting and smoothing strategies in order to maintain financial condition.

Although business and government organizations share many characteristics, recommendations for improving the performance of organizations during times of fiscal stress or other hostile situations that are derived from research on businesses will not always apply to governments. Governments simply do not have the same level of discretion over their actions and domains as do organizations in the private and nonprofit sectors. The logical question here is what do we know about the strategies and success of government in dealing with fiscal stress generally and periods of retrenchment more specifically? Surprisingly, the picture is not very complete beyond what Levine and Schick outlined many years ago.

Numerous studies on the causes and impacts of fiscal stress on local government financial strategies were conducted in the late 1980s in conjunction with the seminal work of Clark and Ferguson (1983). Clark and colleagues initiated a broad-based collaborative effort among scholars in the United States and internationally to examine and report on these events in municipalities and US states.[8] Although this research yielded important insights into why governments pursue some strategies over others, as explained below, the results were mixed and often weak. In addition, we know lots of details about the causes of and solutions to fiscal stress from other research, but our knowledge applies only to a few larger municipal governments that have experienced severe retrenchment during the last thirty years of the twentieth century, especially New York City (Gramlich 1976; Levine, Rubin, and Wolohojian 1982; Tabb 1982; Shefter 1992).

Using a variety of methodologies, much of the collaborative research on fiscal stress sought to explain different categories of more than thirty fiscal strategies with socioeconomic, demographic, political, intergovernmental, and institutional variables (Clark and Walter 1991; Downing 1991; Pammer 1990; Hawkins 1989; Morgan and Pammer 1988; Appleton and Williams 1986). The categories of strategies were constructed using statistical methods that determine how strategies are observed to group together across surveyed governments that evaluate the importance of each strategy to their operations. In support of Levine's phases of responses to fiscal stress, many of these studies found that the strategies fit a hierarchical pattern of least extreme to most extreme and with revenue strategies sometimes grouped separately from expenditure strategies.

Such a survey was sent to all municipalities in the Chicago metropolitan region in late 1993 through 1994 and yielded a response rate of 58 percent (153 of 257 municipalities).[9] A factor analysis was conducted on the responses to the strategy questions that produced the five different groups enumerated below. The median response rate on the level of importance of all strategies in that group is shown in parentheses (on a scale of 1 to 4).[10]

▼ Least extreme revenue and expenditure strategies: seek new revenue; increase charges and fees; reduce expenditures for supplies, equipment, and travel; increase productivity; improve management; reduce expenditure increases (2.8)
▼ Targeted expenditure strategies: selected cuts, shift spending to other organizations, contract out, reduce administration (2.0)
▼ Moderately extreme expenditure strategies: across-the-board cuts, layoffs, freeze wages and hires, attrition, reduce capital expenditures, reduce overtime, control construction (1.9)
▼ Most extreme revenue strategies: increase taxes, draw down surpluses, sell assets, defer payments, short-term and long-term borrowing (1.8)
▼ Most extreme expenditure strategies: reduce compensation, reduce services, eliminate programs, early retirement, deferred maintenance of capital (1.5)

The strategies collected into these categories do not exactly match the level of severity of strategies listed in the categories in table 3.3. For instance, deferred capital maintenance is in the most extreme spending category observed in the Chicago region but is listed in the delaying category in table 3.3. Also increasing productivity and improving management are in the least extreme category here but are in the moderately extreme strategy in the table. However, such surveys are particularly vulnerable to reporting bias. Most government officials who make financial decisions know that deferring capital maintenance is bad and increasing productivity and improving management is good, so they report the former as less important and the latter as more important than it really is.

Another weakness with this survey and others that were part of the FAUI effort is that the questions about strategies, especially revenue strategies, were not customized to state statutory privileges. For instance, the questions for the Chicago area survey do not distinguish between raising property taxes versus sales or utility taxes. Doing so would have allowed a sharper distinction among types of tax increases, which is particularly important for municipalities in Illinois who view increases in sales taxes as less extreme than increases in property taxes.

More generally, the research that was based on these surveys did not produce convincing or consistent evidence for explanations of the importance of different categories of strategies. One study, for instance, concluded from its findings that the processes that determine financial strategies are unstructured, confused, and support a "garbage can" explanation (Morgan and Pammer 1988). Other studies conclude that the financial strategies governments pursue seem to depend upon circumstances relevant only to those strategies or particular time periods (Hawkins 1989; Clark and Walter 1991).

There are, however, two fairly consistent sets of findings in this research that suggest more predictable patterns of strategic behavior. One is the significance of level of fiscal stress, defined objectively or measured by the perceptions of survey respondents, to the importance of different categories of strategies (Morgan and Pammer 1988; Clark and Walter 1991; Hawkins 1989). This finding was supported by later research on the conditions under which officials implement different types of strategies to deal with fiscal stress (Forrester and Spindler 1990; Cooper 1996; Maher and Deller 2007). The second set of notable findings concerns the causal order of the various explanatory factors being tested. Studies that examine causal order find that local, internal, or controllable factors are more directly related to the types of financial strategies pursued than broad-based, external, and uncontrollable factors (Clark and Ferguson 1983; Clark and Walter 1991; Hawkins 1989).

With respect to recommendations for how local governments should handle fiscal stress, Levine's work examining the New York City fiscal crisis of 1973–74 is particularly useful (Levine, Rubin, and Wolohojian 1982). He and his coauthors adapt research on organizational decline in the private sector to government and use this to identify six preconditions for managing contraction that determine government capacity to make the necessary changes to maintain financial condition. These preconditions are listed below.

1. Authority to make and implement decisions about organizational structure and resources including adjusting budgets, reducing services, and terminating employees.
2. Continuity in top management to maintain consistency in retrenchment strategies over several years.
3. Rapid and accurate feedback to gauge the effectiveness of decisions.
4. Budget flexibility and slack resources, which allows resources to be redirected and buys time for innovation.
5. Existence of incentives for conserving resources and improving performance.
6. The capacity to target cuts according to goals and priorities.

With the exception of items 3 and 4, none of these preconditions have much to do with strategic problem solving as conceptualized here. Item 3 identifies feedback as a precondition for successful retrenchment during fiscal stress, which is an important factor in decision making and learning to deal with any threat. Slack resources, as identified in item 4, provide a strategic advantage for managing many kinds of threats and for entrepreneurs who want to take advantage of opportunities. The other items, however, focus on conditions in the institutional environment within which decisions take place, which is the focus of analysis in the next chapter.

Qualitative Methodology and Preliminary Evidence

Much of the data used to document the financial problems of Chicago municipal governments and their methods of problem solving is qualitative and is described in this section. This section also presents preliminary evidence on fiscal stress in these governments and their responses to such threats from the qualitative sources.

Data and Methods

There are two sources of qualitative data—interviews and news reports. Interviews were conducted with the chief financial decision maker in sixty-two municipal governments in the spring and summer of 2003. In most cases this person was the finance director, but oftentimes the interviewee was the mayor or CAO. The interviews were open ended but structured and focused on current and long-term causes of fiscal stress, especially with respect to the 2001 recession, strategies for dealing with fiscal stress, financial policies, and financial management practices.[11]

The tremendous variation in sources of fiscal stress, contextual factors, and approaches to financial problem solving among Chicago suburbs required that a relatively large number of governments be interviewed to obtain a broad understanding of these events. In this case, it made more sense to choose governments specifically to reflect a broad distribution of factors relevant to causes of financial condition and ways of solving financial problems than to use random sampling. A random sample with a low number of cases can result in samples with little variation on important variables. However, the fact that the sample was not chosen randomly raises the possibility that observed trends and findings will be the result of sampling bias. Thus an important question is whether the sample looks like the population.

Appendix 2 describes the sampling methodology in detail and provides tables showing the distribution of key features of municipalities that were interviewed compared to those not interviewed and the entire population of municipalities in the region. The joint distribution of the revenue wealth and spending need indices in appendix 2 shows that these variables are distributed similar to the total population, with some oversampling of poor and high-need municipalities and undersampling of wealthy, low-need governments. Home rule governments were also oversampled to get an adequate number of municipalities that were home rule but had populations below twenty-five thousand, which allows one to observe the separate effects of these highly correlated factors in the interview data. Appendix 3 describes the interview methodology and focus of questioning in more detail. It should be noted that many of the persons interviewed volunteered a great deal of information about economic development events, financial management practices, and fiscal strategies during the interview.

The sixty-two interviews were transcribed and coded according to the two schemes shown in appendix 4 using qualitative data analysis software, which allowed for both inductive and deductive coding methods.[12] First, all interview statements were coded according to twelve broad themes at the top of the appendix that reflect the four categories in table 3.2. Second, interview statements were also coded according to specific content, much of which corresponds to particular practices, policies, or issues noted in table 3.2. Notice that economic development, which does not appear in the table, has been added as an area of policy and practice due to its prevalence in the interviewees' comments. Statements about municipal governance and fiscal stress were other broad themes coded here.

The second major source of qualitative evidence of financial decisions and conditions in municipalities in the region are news reports from seventy local newspapers in the Chicago metropolitan region. Available articles about most of the region's municipalities were collected for all years from 2001 to 2006, although some newspapers were not available electronically prior to 2003. The articles collected focused on municipal elections, changes in elected and appointed personnel, governing and institutional features, and financial management practices and policies (usually with respect to the budget). News reports were collected for a total of 229 municipalities, and the sample excludes very small municipalities with no news and others with particular characteristics.[13]

Statements in the news reports were coded using the same qualitative data analysis software methods as the interviews. In this case, deductive coding is driven by theory or prior expectations using sophisticated search and relational coding retrieval, compared to inductive coding that modifies existing coding structure based on ideas and evidence developing during initial coding. Appendix 5 shows the coding structure for the news articles, which contain many similar codes as the interviews but demonstrate better coverage of politics and governance in the municipalities.

The problem with newspaper articles as a source of evidence is that coverage of governments and these topics is likely to vary widely in ways that are not representative of the entire population of municipalities or their experiences (MacManus 2004). Indeed, there seems to be little formal news coverage of local governments in the southwest part of the region within Cook County. These governments tend to be more politically governed and less reformed in terms of having appointed, professional managers or administrators. Of the 229 governments with at least one news report, 15 governments have reports that are fewer than 200 words total, and the combined reports in 47 governments are fewer than 500 words. A total of 92 governments have news reports with more than 2,000 words. Correlations of word counts of news reports with different variables and frequencies of coded statements in the news reports suggest greater news coverage in governments that are larger, wealthier, and corporate, but also those with greater conflict, turnover, and election challenges.

In this case, the generalizability of data from the news reports to the larger population of all municipal governments in the Chicago metropolitan region is very suspect. However, numerous news reports on events and conditions exist over time for many types of municipalities in the region and exemplify a broad range of socioeconomic, demographic, governing, and financial features that is very informative. It is also important to note that journalists are trained observers, which increases the reliability and validity of observations of individual municipalities with respect to the standards of reporting methodology.

The news reports on Chicago municipalities also supplement the interviews in a very useful way. Not surprisingly, most interviewees talked very little about the politics and governance of their municipality, which have significant effects on the financial policies and practices of these governments. By comparison, news reports tend to focus on politics and governance issues to a much greater degree. Unlike the interviews, however, news reports say little about financial management practices other than those that are found to be illegal or become particularly problematic. The interviews also document both near-term and long-term strategies, but news reports tend to focus on long-term strategies and broader sources of financial problems than the 2001 recession.

Another source of qualitative evidence used in this book is open-ended and structured interviews with executive directors in nine of the eleven councils of government (COGs) in the Chicago region in December 2009 and January 2010. The primary purpose of the interviews is to inquire about how the Great Recession was affecting municipal governments' finances and financial problem solving at that time. The interviews also queried these agencies about the history of collaboration and coordination between member governments and other local governments to resolve financial problems. Appendix 6 shows the list of COGs interviewed. Additional information from news reports and online budget documents about the impact of the Great Recession was collected in fall 2010 on the sixty-two municipal governments interviewed in 2003.[14] The interviews with the COG directors were taped but not transcribed, and neither these interviews nor the news reports and budget information on the Great Recession were coded or systematically analyzed with the qualitative software.

Evidence of Fiscal Stress and Responses

Table 3.4 shows a summary assessment of the level of fiscal stress that the interviewed governments were experiencing as a result of the 2001 recession and other threats using the following five categories: none, progressing, low stress, medium stress, and high stress. These assignments were based on my assessment of statements in the interviews and news reports that were coded as *fiscal stress—yes* and *fiscal stress—no* and the coded causes of fiscal stress in the interviews.[15] Although only one person was interviewed in most governments and there was only one interviewer, which does not

TABLE 3.4 Near-Term Fiscal Stress in Interviewed Municipalities, 2003

	No. of Municipal Governments	Percent of Governments
None	8	13.3
Progressing	5	8.3
Low stress	9	15
Medium stress	18	30
High stress	22	35.3
Total interviewed	**62**	**100**

allow these observations or interpretations to be verified, the news reports and quantitative data do allow for triangulation of information from different sources to arrive at conclusions about the level of fiscal stress experienced by the sixty-two interviewed governments during the period of study.

The table shows that fifty-one governments expressed that they were feeling some level of fiscal stress, but the largest percentage of the interviewed governments seemed to be experiencing medium or high levels of fiscal stress. Municipalities listed as progressing were actually better off in 2003 than they were in the late 1990s primarily because their financial condition and long-term solvency were so poor prior to 2003 due to low revenue wealth and high spending needs. Not surprisingly, most governments classified as having low or no short-term fiscal stress have high, long-term solvency, according to the quantitative data described in appendix 1. But about half of the governments with high, short-term fiscal stress due to the 2001 recession or other events have high, long-term solvency. The other half have low, long-term solvency, which indicates that governments with high fiscal stress due to the 2001 recession are just as likely to be fiscally wealthy as fiscally poor. It should also be noted that this assessment of fiscal stress does not apply to governments' water and sewer funds that were rated very differently in some municipalities. Of the forty assessments of water (and sewer) funds offered by interviewees, twenty-two (37%) of them described these enterprises as in good shape or experiencing no fiscal stress, twelve (20%) of them described their fiscal condition as OK, and only five (8%) described these funds as not doing well.

Tables 3.5 and 3.6 document the number of municipalities with statements coded for different sources of fiscal stress, fiscal problems, and strategies for handling fiscal stress and more pervasive fiscal problems as reported in the interviews and news reports respectively. With respect to the interviews, most municipalities (74%) reported that insurance costs (health, liability, or both) and pension liabilities were up significantly and were a significant source of fiscal stress. Other often-reported sources of fiscal stress were a decline in sales taxes (50%), state or county actions (often delayed payments of taxes), and the fiscal limitations created by tax caps (34% discussed tax caps in their government or others). Many interviewees also reported handling their fiscal stress by cutting spending (63%), increasing or adding revenues (77%), and using short-term borrowing and subsidizing from the other sources (75%).

It should be noted that short-term borrowing includes borrowing externally (e.g., tax anticipation notes), borrowing from other funds within the government, and even charging more to funds that share personnel. For instance, a higher proportion of the finance director's salary might be charged to the water, sewer, or tax incremental finance district (TIF) funds—which were often in better financial shape—to help alleviate stress on the general fund. Concerning long-term strategies or policies for managing finances and maintaining financial condition, 56 percent of interviewees claimed to be fiscally conservative, 44 percent claimed to have a policy of low or no property taxes, but 44 percent also claimed to value high-service levels. Of the forty-nine municipalities that discussed privatizing or contracting (80%), most of these indicated that this applied to few or none of their services.

With respect to the news reports, documenting the percent of municipalities in which events, conditions, or actions are reported is less meaningful due to the correlation

TABLE 3.5 Statements about Fiscal Stress Sources and Strategies: Number and Percent of Interviewed Municipalities, 2003

	Number of Municipal Governments	Percent of Governments Interviewed		Number of Municipal Governments	Percent of Governments Interviewed
Sources of fiscal stress			**Fiscal Strategies: All themes**		
Growth	6	10	Balance services and revenues	9	15
Income tax down	17	27	Export taxes	5	8
Insurance up	46	74	Fiscal conservatism	35	56
Low spending flexibility	11	18	Pursue grants	21	34
Mandates	14	23	Low or no property tax	27	44
P-tax appeal board	14	23	Low or no other tax	11	18
Pension funding	44	71	Maximize property tax levy	7	11
Revenues down	13	21	One-time revenue	8	13
Sales tax down	31	50	Contract out (most do not)	49	80
State or county actions	19	31	Rely on sales tax	9	15
Tax caps	21	34	Save during good times	11	18
Tax delinquents	7	11	Spend during good times	16	26
Strategies for managing fiscal stress			Special census	12	19
Cut spending	39	63	**Miscellaneous: All themes**		
Defer/delay hiring	19	31	Special assessment district	6	10
Defer/delay capital spending	27	44	Court businesses	10	16
Fund balance	30	48	Value high service levels	27	44
Increase or add revenue	48	77	Flooding and drainage	13	21
Reduce taxes, charges, or fees	12	19	Lawsuits	15	24
Borrow, subsidize, charge	43	75			
Total interviewed	**62**		**Total interviewed**	**62**	

TABLE 3.6 Statements about Fiscal Problems and Strategies: Number and Percent of Municipalities with News Reports, 2001–6

	Number of Municipal Governments	Percent of Governments with News Reports		Number of Municipal Governments	Percent of Governments with News Reports
Fiscal problems			**Fiscal strategies**		
Elastic revenue	7	3	Conservative spending	12	5
Flooding and drainage	52	23	Conservative taxes and fees	16	7
Growth	27	12	Court businesses	19	8
Insurance	61	27	Create or dissolve special district	4	2
Lawsuit	81	35	Export taxes	13	6
Mandates	19	8	High service levels	12	5
Pension	45	20	Obtain grants	33	14
Tax caps	13	6	Privatize and contract out	20	9
Unions	14	6	Rely on risky revenue	26	11
Water provision	53	23	Special census	22	10
			Special assessment district	16	7
Total municipalities with news reports	**229**		**Total municipalities with news reports**	**229**	

between percent of coded statements for a municipality and the degree of news coverage in that municipality. In this case, zero or few coded statements do not necessarily mean that the municipality has not experienced the events represented by the coded statements. Rather, it could indicate lack of news coverage. In this case, it is more important to focus on the number of municipalities with particular experiences and features associated with their experiences.

That said, the figures in table 3.6 show that lawsuits were reported to be a problem in eighty-one municipalities, which is a large amount, and more than fifty municipalities had news reports documenting problems with flooding or drainage, pension obligations, or water provision. By comparison, there are relatively few reports about fiscal strategies and policies. Only thirty-three municipalities were reported to obtain grants, and even fewer reported any of the other fiscal strategies shown here. Chapter 5 explores in more detail what created fiscal stress and opportunities for municipal governments in the Chicago region and their reactions to these events as reported in the 2003 interviews and news reports from that time period. It also documents effects and responses to the Great Recession by specific municipalities.

Listening to the taped interviews with COG directors and reading the news reports about the effects of the Great Recession shows it is having a more negative impact on municipal governments than the 2001 recession, but the severity of its effects also varies greatly among the sixty-two governments interviewed in 2003. Some governments have instituted radical options with respect to the hierarchy in table 3.3, such as levying the first ever property tax in the history of the municipality, but others expect modest increases in sales taxes and other revenues and even small surpluses in the latter half of 2010. Many expect the effects of the Great Recession, which officially ended in June 2009 according to the National Bureau of Economic Research, to linger for at least several years beyond that date because of the lagged impact of assessments on property values. However, as explained further in chapter 5, property taxes in Illinois are focused on levies, not rates, so declines in property assessments do not necessarily reduce the total property tax collected by local governments. However, all local governments in Illinois face the common threat posed by the state of Illinois' fiscal crisis, which may greatly reduce state aid or other revenue distributed to them by the state sometime in the future.

This recession also has added a new source of fiscal stress to the municipal governments in this region that were experiencing high levels of population growth and commercial development. As reported by the COG directors and in news reports, building literally stopped in many places in the region, leaving unfinished projects and bonds to repay. Pension liabilities also continue to increase for municipal governments in the state due to state mandates and poor returns on investments. Furthermore, the Great Recession has been longer than prior recessions, and many city governments around the United States report having to fundamentally reassess the provision of services in their communities (Hoene and Pagano 2010). All of this points to the fact that many, but not all, governments in the region have used up easy options for managing fiscal stress by late 2010—those further down the hierarchy in table 3.3—and are moving toward implementing more aggressive cutting and smoothing strategies. There also appears to be more of an emphasis on collaboration for service delivery in the news reports about the Great Recession and, as reported by the COG directors, especially for fire services. This suggests that collaboration and joint production are not perceived to be low-level, benign options for managing fiscal stress by these suburbs.

Conclusion

This chapter has presented a conceptual framework for describing and explaining, in part, how and why government officials make fiscal policy decisions and pursue particular financial management practices. This approach uses the metaphor of problem solving and incorporates concepts from strategic management to emphasize the importance of four factors in government choices. These factors are (1) professionalization in the area of financial management and knowledge of professional financial management standards and sustainable financial policies (policies that maintain or improve government solvency at all levels); (2) the role of threats and opportunities in evoking decisions and directing searches for solutions (narrowing consideration of options in the fiscal toolbox), (3) the hierarchical structure of options in the fiscal toolbox based on the aggressiveness and disruptiveness of solutions to financial problems, and (4) government officials' entrepreneurialism and approaches to managing and handling risk. With respect to the first factor, the variable FDS is used to measure how professional financial problem solving is likely to be in the Chicago suburban municipalities. Finally, the chapter describes the qualitative data and methodology used in this study, and it presents a preliminary description of sources of fiscal stress for the suburbs and their responses to the 2001 recession and the Great Recession. The next chapter presents two other conceptual frameworks for describing and explaining financial decisions that focus on the macro- and microlevel institutional and government environments.

Notes

1. He won the Nobel Prize in economics in 1978 for his work on bounded rationality.
2. Governments can designate municipal managers with executive and administrative powers via local ordinance rather than formally adopting the state-designated, council-manager form. Municipal managers in these positions may not have complete authority over the hiring and removal of some departmental heads, such as the police chief.
3. See www.gfoa.org/index.php?option=com_content&task=view&id=118&Itemid=130 for revised and up-to-date recommended practices.
4. Other participants in this initiative included the Association of School Business Officials International, Council of State Governments, International City/County Management Association, National Association of Counties, National Conference of State Legislatures, National League of Cities, and the US Conference of Mayors.
5. Other groups that establish standards of financial management policy and practice for local governments are the Association of Government Accountants (AGA), the Institute for Management Accountants (IMA), and the Governmental Accounting Standards Board (GASB).
6. Technically, local governments in Illinois do not have to adopt a budget unless they have passed an ordinance requiring them to use a budget format in place of an appropriations

ordinance. An appropriations ordinance specifies maximum spending levels for line items or objects of expenditure and may not contain revenue estimates. An appropriations ordinance also does not have to be adopted until the end of the first quarter of the fiscal year (65 ILCS 5/: Illinois Municipal Code; 50 ILCS 330/: Illinois Municipal Budget Law).

7. It should be noted that the strategies in table 3.3 are not what governments should do, but what they are likely to do when faced with fiscal threats.

8. The Fiscal Austerity and Urban Innovation (FAUI) project developed similar surveys on causes and impacts of fiscal stress that were distributed in 1983 to officials in US municipalities with populations of more than twenty-five thousand residents or more (more than one thousand cities). The survey was based on the permanent community sample (PCS), a national sample of sixty-two US cities monitored over twenty years that was initiated in 1966. Several hundred articles and books have used the PCS; Clark and Ferguson (1983) is the most comprehensive.

9. The survey was sent to each city/village hall with no stipulation about who would respond, and evidence indicated that more than one person often responded to the survey. A second round of surveys was sent to governments that did not respond to the first round. A special effort was then made to contact suburban officials in smaller suburbs and in suburbs with high rates of poverty in 1980 and 1990, as these governments' response rate was lower than other governments. Also, municipalities who responded to the survey were larger and tended to have more reformed governments, but a test of more than thirty-five financial and external environmental variables showed no significant difference between the survey and the population (Hendrick and Lindstrom 2002).

10. The method used was principal component analysis with varimax rotation and a loading criteria of .5 or greater. The strategy questions asked respondents to indicate strategies they have used for the past three years. Responses of the importance of each strategy ranged from 1 (least important) to 4 (most important). Each strategy group was computed as the average of all strategies associated with that group.

11. Approval of interviews in 2003 and 2009 by the Institutional Review Board at the University of Illinois at Chicago prevents identifying interviewees with particular comments. Because interviewees must remain anonymous, there are no citations to quotations from interviewees in the book.

12. QDA Minor is the software used to code, retrieve, and analyze all qualitative data in this study (www.provalisresearch.com/QDAMiner/QDAMinerDesc.html).

13. The four satellite cities in the region were excluded (Aurora, Elgin, Joliet, and Waukegan), as were other special cases such as Rosemont and Bedford Park that exist to serve nonresidents.

14. News reporting on suburban governments overall declined greatly after 2006.

15. Statements coded as *fiscal stress—yes* often applied to conditions during the fiscal good times of the late 1990s or revenue increases from population growth and development.

Chapter 4
Suburban Fiscal Governance

This chapter presents two additional frameworks for understanding the financial decisions that municipal governments make to adapt their fiscal structure to their fiscal and political environments. It also describes how the governments in the Chicago metropolitan region fit into these frameworks. Both frameworks are about governing structure and institutions and are intended to supplement the problem-solving/ strategic management framework presented in chapter 3. The first framework examines governing structure and institutions at the micro level, and the second focuses on governing structure and institutionalized rules about local finance and financial management at the macro level.

The micro level in this case is comprised of institutional arrangements at the local level that determine the role of government officials in financial decisions and acceptable solutions to financial problems. These institutionalized arrangements can be formal, as codified in village statutes, for instance, or less formal, such as the historical predominance of one party over another. The macro level in this case includes state-level financial rules that directly affect the external fiscal capacity of municipal governments in Illinois, which have already been discussed to some degree in chapter 2, and the regional governing structure. The regional governing structure is very important to municipal government financial decisions because it configures how governments interact with each other and how their decisions are related. No government is an island with respect to their financial decisions. Rather governments make financial decisions in an environment that includes many other local governments. Although the macrolevel institutions do not vary across municipal governments in the Chicago metropolitan region, this study must recognize how regional and state environments may affect government financial choices as a point of reference for interpreting its findings.

Institutions are formal and informal constraints, rules, and expectations about behavior and decisions that structure interaction among government officials and their relationship to citizens and other stakeholders. Institutions establish incentives for the behavior of government officials and limit or direct their choices with respect to each other and persons outside of government. Institutions provide order to government processes and the exchanges between individuals associated with government (North 1991). Institutions are commonly recognized by officials, often sanctioned, and fairly stable over time. Governing institutions also exist at different governing levels.

For instance, the US Constitution specifies a role for state governments in our federal system that gives them the authority to establish local governments. At the macro level state governments stipulate many rules for local governments including what services they provide, how they fund services, and their relationship to each other (e.g., ability of local government to enter into agreements). Thus, state rules greatly affect the policy options available to local governments to solve their financial problems and, in effect, determine the contents of the local fiscal toolbox. At the micro level, voters within local jurisdictions elect officials with the expectation that officials will conduct themselves in a particular way and make decisions about services and revenues that are consistent with the interests and values of the community. In this case, financial decisions occur within a set of governing arrangements that are specific to the local government, but that can be changed by local officials. For instance, officials decide how their government is structured, how authority is distributed, and whom to hire.

Also at the macro level, many local governments are part of a metropolitan region, which means they share a fiscal environment and some financial problems with other governments in the region. They also have many neighbors and their boundaries may overlap numerous other local governments. These conditions offer opportunities for collaboration and contracting with other governments to deliver services and generate revenue, but the conditions also create competitive pressures that can push governments toward particular financial choices. The region may even have its own institutions of governance, such as formal laws enacted by regional planning authorities that regulate local decisions and informal rules of cooperation between local governments that are promoted by subregional COGs.

The first section in this chapter describes the view of microlevel governing structure and institutions that is adopted here and how the 264 municipal governments in the Chicago metropolitan area are distributed on some of the important dimensions at this level. In effect, it describes how these governments look with respect to important factors that explain which choices they make from their fiscal toolbox to solve financial problems. The second section of the chapter examines the macrolevel institutional factors that affect both the size of the toolbox and the choices officials make from available options. The third section combines the frameworks in chapters 3 and 4 to present the basic model used to guide the investigation and explain events in subsequent chapters.

Microlevel Governing Structure and Institutions

The Institute of Governance defines governance as "the traditions, institutions, and processes that determine how power is exercised, how citizens are given a voice, and how decisions are made on issues of public concern" (http://iog.ca/en/about-us/governance/governance-definition). The concept is broader than government or governing structure alone, as it includes formal and informal norms and practices about governing and spontaneous and intentional systems of control of the governing processes. Governance can also include arrangements or processes at higher levels of government (Williamson 1996). Lynn, Heinrich, and Hill (2001, 7) define governance in the public sector as "regimes of laws, rules, judicial decisions, and administrative practices that constrain, prescribe, and enable the provision of publicly supported goods and services." They emphasize that governance links authoritative decisions at the policy or administrative levels to performance in service delivery and other areas including financial management and maintenance or improvement of financial condition. Defined in this way, governance encompasses managerial activities that contribute to governmental performance, not just policy decisions by elected officials. Lynn and colleagues also recognize that managers can design and change governance regimes at the administrative level.

Regimes are institutional in that they are a stable and commonly recognized set of formal or informal rules and configurations that establish governing process, structure interaction among government officials, constrain choices, create expectations about outcomes, and determine the roles and responsibilities of officials in the political, administrative, and managerial realms. The five categories of FDS shown in table 3.1 represent different institutional arrangements for the governance of municipal financial affairs, but also different administrative capacities in the fiscal area. Other important institutional arrangements for *fiscal governance* might be whether the treasurer is elected or appointed, whether the chief financial officer (CFO) is part time or full time, and the authority and responsibility of the CFO as specified in the statutes and commonly recognized by all officials. With respect to rules governing financial decisions, governments often have written and unwritten policies that constrain options or direct choices to certain options, such as policies against raising property taxes or expectations that year-end fund balances should be 30 percent of general fund expenditures. In this case, the degree of professionalization at the managerial level will influence financial governance regimes, but political institutions will have as big or even bigger effect on many government rules and processes. Political institutions will also affect officials' preferences and values toward options in the fiscal toolbox.

Institutional Structure

Three forms of government are widely recognized as constituting different institutional arrangements of municipal governance. These forms are council-mayor, council-manager, and commission. Differences between council-mayor and council-manager forms are recognized by the FDS variable, which also incorporates financial management institutions more specifically, but does not distinguish governments that have adopted the managerial form according to Illinois statutes. As used in most research on local government, the council-mayor/council-manager distinction does not recognize that many council-mayor governments have strong chief administrative officers, which gives these governments many institutional qualities of the council-manager form. Thus, a simple council-mayor/council-manager distinction is not likely to be sensitive enough to the kinds of institutional structures that could affect financial policies and practices in municipal governments.

Many recent studies of local government recognize hybrid forms of council-manager and council-mayor governments (Ebdon and Brucato 2000; DeSantis and Renner 2002; Frederickson, Johnson, and Wood 2004; Folz and French 2005; Nelson and Svara 2010), but the majority of studies distinguish only between council-mayor and council-manager types as defined by the International City/County Management Association (ICMA).[1] In practice, council-mayor and council-manager governments represent ideal types at different ends of a continuum of unreformed (political) and reformed (administrative) institutional regimes. Unreformed governments separate executive and legislative powers, and the mayor is the chief executive and administrative officer (CEO and CAO).

In Illinois, unreformed governments are also cities in which members of the council are elected by district. Mayors of cities have the power to appoint all officers and boards not covered by civil service and veto council ordinances. More reformed cities in Illinois have weak mayors who have no veto power and sometimes share appointment powers with the council or city manager. The most reformed municipalities in Illinois are villages in which the CEO is the president of the board, board members are elected at large, and the CAO is a municipal manager who has authority over the budget and power to hire and remove all departmental heads. On the other end of the continuum are villages in which the CEO is the CAO (often called mayor in this case). In between these two ends of the continuum are governments in which the mayor shares administrative authority with a CAO (Keane and Koch 1990).

Table 4.1 shows different institutional and structural arrangements that exist among the municipal suburbs in the Chicago metropolitan region and some demographic and socioeconomic characteristics of these governments. Assignment of municipalities to these categories was determined by examining ordinances, electoral records, and other secondary sources and contacting municipal clerks in some cases. The categories are weakly arrayed in the table from most reformed structures (A) to least reformed (E), although the level of reform of governments in category B relative to C is unclear. Also a municipality with an appointed treasurer will be more reformed compared to one with an elected treasurer, but it is not clear, for instance, how to rank a council-manager city with an elected treasurer to one with a weak mayor form and an appointed treasurer (categories C2 and D1).

There is even variation in levels of reform within the main categories. Structures B and D include municipalities in which the mayor appoints and supervises all personnel, and weaker mayors that share authority with the council or administrator. Structures C and A include municipalities where managers have the authority to hire and remove all or most directors and departmental heads, but both categories contain governments that have not adopted the full council-manager form as specified in state statutes.[2]

The median values for the demographic and socioeconomic variables show that council-manager villages and cities (A and C) tend to have the highest population density, income per capita, percent of managerial and professional population, and property values, but council-manager cities tend to have the highest population. Cities also have a higher percentage of commercial EAV than villages.[3]

The complexity of such structural arrangements and the lack of precision in their measurement may explain why research that attempts to link only two categories of form of government (council-mayor and council-manager) to fiscal performance (e.g., taxes, spending, and fund balance) shows little impact or impacts in the wrong direction (Morgan and Kickham 1999; Stumm and Corrigan 1998; Schneider 1989, 108; Hayes and Chang 1990; Deno and Mehay 1987; Farnham 1987; Morgan and Pelissero 1980). Other research demonstrates that council-manager governments implement more innovative and rational managerial practices (Poister and Streib 1989, 2005), but there is little research that directly links this form to improved service delivery or performance (Folz and French 2005). Thus the four variables used here to represent these institutional or structural features of municipal governments allow for greater variation than what is

TABLE 4.1 Structural Features of Municipal Governments in the Chicago Region: Median Values, 2000

Primary Structure		Secondary Structure	Number of Governments	Population	Population Density	Income per Capita	Manager and Prof. Population (%)	EAV per Square Mile	Commercial EAV (%)
A Village, council-manager (Weak mayor, appt. treasurer, managerial form)			53	23,276	4,191	30,467	42.9	9,391,324	18.2
B Village, council-mayor (Weak mayor, appt. treasurer)	B1	Manager	14	8,302	1,977	27,534	36.3	3,850,470	12.0
	B2	Administrator	71						
	B3	Mayor only	73	2,900	1,766	22,178	25.1	2,488,313	12.2
C City or commission, council-manager (Weak mayor, managerial form)	C1	Appointed treasurer	12	40,381	3,704	29,097	42.7	9,716,040	20.1
	C2	Elected treasurer	2						
D City or commission, council (Weak mayor form)	D1	Appointed treasurer	7	15,688	2,321	23,747	27.8	4,102,670	20.0
	D2	Elected treasurer	14						
E City or commission, council (Strong mayor form)	E1	Appointed treasurer	3	25,680	4,263	19,018	23.9	5,486,276	20.1
	E2	Elected treasurer	15						
Total			**264**						
				26.5	8.7	5.7	13.0	17.8	4.1

F values for all variables are significant at .000

possible with only two categories and one continuum. The four variables are financial decision structure, city or village, strong or weak mayor, and elected or appointed treasurer. However, elected treasurers and strong mayors only exist in cities.

Other Institutional Arrangements

Reformed and unreformed governments also vary according to political and cultural regimes and other institutional features that are not represented by governing structure alone. Table 4.2 presents different governing characteristics associated with formal and informal institutional arrangements linked with the reformed and unreformed ideal types of municipal government in Illinois. This table represents an elaboration of the two ideal types of government that Frederickson, Johnson, and Wood (2004, 8–10) described as political versus administrative or corporate. In addition to different forms of government, political versus administrative governments have different electoral processes, cultures, values, operational processes, and decision-making criteria as shown in the last four rows of the table.

Villages and cities in Illinois have the authority to run partisan elections with local parties (e.g., Good Government or Reform Party) appearing on the ballot, unless they pass a referendum that requires nonpartisan elections.[4] True council-manager forms of government are nonpartisan, unless they establish different provisions by referendum. Many governments with the authority to run partisan elections, however, have not done so and maintain a tradition of nonpartisan elections. In addition, governments that are nonpartisan can be informally partisan with officials running together under a slate (e.g., antigrowth) that is not on the ballot (Gove and Nowlan 1996).

Table 4.3 shows how partisanship of elections and government structure are distributed together for all municipalities in the Chicago region. Here partisanship is

TABLE 4.2 Institutional Features of Local Governments in Illinois

Political	Corporate/Administrative
Council is elected by wards or districts and is purely legislative.	Council is elected at large and mayor is president of the board.
Mayor is the chief executive and administrative officer and has veto power.	Village manager is the chief administrative officer with authority over budget and departmental heads.
Partisan elections	Nonpartisan elections
Departmental heads appointed based on patronage; elected official involved in administration	Departmental heads appointed based on merit; elected officials focus on policy
Distribution of benefits and rule enforcement based on favoritism, clientelism, and expediency	Distribution of benefits and rule enforcement based on equity and neutrality and is rule-based
Government culture of targeted responsiveness, particularistic interests, secrecy, and trust	Government culture of efficiency, inclusiveness, transparency, and professionalism

TABLE 4.3 Partisanship and Structure of Municipal Governments in the Chicago Region, 2003–7

	Village, Council-Manager/ Percent of 264	Village, Council-Mayor and CAO/ Percent of 264	Village, Council-Mayor, no CAO/ Percent of 264	City, Council-Manager/ Percent of 264	City, Council-Weak Mayor/ Percent of 264	City, Council-Strong Mayor/ Percent of 264	Total/ Percent of 264
Nonpartisan	12/23	11/13	7/10	11/79	8/38	6/33	55/21
Partisan-Independent	17/32	37/43	29/40	2/14	11/52	5/28	101/38
Partisan	24/45	37/43	37/51	1/7	2/2	7/39	108/41
	100	100	100	100	100	100	
Total/Percent of 264	53/20	85/32	73/28	14/5	21/8	18/7	264

determined by examining election results (canvas reports) for consolidated elections in 2003, 2005, and 2007 for all six counties in the region. These reports indicate municipal candidates' parties (for mayor, trustee, clerk, or treasurer) or whether the candidate is running as an independent. Municipalities with authority to run partisan elections in which all candidates ran as independent for all three elections were classified as partisan-independent. Municipalities with no party affiliation in these reports are classified as nonpartisan. Looking across the column percentages in the table shows that cities, and especially those with a council-manager form, tend to have nonpartisan elections compared to villages. Villages tend to have partisan elections, especially those without a separate CAO or that do not have a council-manager form. Cities with weak mayors tend to have partisan-independent elections followed by villages with a council-mayor form. Thus the level of reform of government structure does not follow the level of reform of elections in these municipalities, which makes it difficult to classify these governments neatly along the continuum of political versus corporate or administrative.

Less formally, the ideal political government on the left-hand side of the continuum in table 4.2 appoints key government officers based on patronage and distributes services according to voter and interest group support and political preferences. This government also applies operational rules such as awarding of contracts and regulatory enforcement (e.g., building codes or budgetary compliance) based on expediency and the power of clienteles and relies on informal political networks to develop policy and deliver services in many cases. In contrast, the ideal reformed government appoints based on merit, distributes services according to standards of equity, enforces regulations in a neutral manner, operates according to recognized standards and statutory restrictions, and relies on formal structures to conduct business and deliver services (Clark 2000; Frederickson, Johnson, and Wood 2004; Abney and Lauth 1986).

To a great extent, differences in operations and decisions in these two ideal types of government are derived from a different set of cultural values and decision-making heuristics that each type promotes. According to much research in the field, reformed or administrative governments will be more professional, more responsive to a broader set of interests, more transparent, and value efficiency and performance. Unreformed or political governments will value trust and familiarity of relationships, responsiveness to particular interests or specific requests, and secrecy (Hansell 2002; Dunn and Legge 2002; Svara 2001; Schilling 1995; Nalbandian 1992). In addition, the characteristics of reformed governments will tend to promote cooperation and arrest and reverse conflict when it arises (Svara 1990).

Unfortunately, the conditions in the last three rows of table 4.2 cannot be observed systematically for all municipalities in the region. For instance, some municipal codes specify that the CAO and other departmental heads are appointed based on merit, but most codes do not specify this, although the government may have a policy of conducting extensive searches for qualified CAO candidates when the position is vacant. Also terms such as *merit* and *qualified* are not very precise, which gives mayors and council members a lot of leeway in assessing candidates and allows for political appointments even in governments that require merit appointments. The only way to assess these nuanced conditions for individual governments is through the interviews, news reports, or other secondary sources such as municipal websites, budgets, and annual financial reports.[5] As indicated, the interviews did not provide a great deal of information about political processes, values, and conflicts, but the news reports did in many cases, which broadened the assessment of political and corporate governance features to more governments than those interviewed.

Table 4.4 shows the number and percent of municipal governments with news report statements that reference particular areas of politics and governance in the 229 municipalities for which news reports were collected. Statements and quotes were coded into to these categories if they demonstrated the features indicated. For instance, if the report or a quotation talked about how well the board members get along or how the mayor and board worked together to solve problems, these statements were coded as "board cooperate." Any form of conflict between officials or between residents and officials were coded under "conflict." The code "election challenge–high" designates elections in which competition and opposition between the candidates seemed particularly intense during an election, or where there were many challengers for the offices. Statements are coded as "governance–political" or "governance–

TABLE 4.4 Statements about Politics and Governance in the News Reports, 2001–6

	Number of Municipal Governments	Percent of Governments with News Reports
Politics and governance		
Board cooperate	28	12
Conflict	83	36
Election challenge–high	65	28
Election challenge–low	55	24
Governance–political	72	31
Governance–corporate	78	34
Long-term CAO (12 or more years)	26	11
Long-term mayor (12 or more years)	62	27
Turnover in administration	65	28
Turnover in elected officials	85	37
Governing role of attorney	9	4
Governing role of board	48	21
Governing role of CAO	43	19
Governing role of finance director	14	6
Governing role of mayor	49	21
Governing role of fire or police chief	12	5
Miscellaneous		
Whether to hire a CAO	17	7
Whether to hire other professional	15	7
Total municipalities with news reports	**229**	

corporate" if they demonstrated any of the features in the last three rows of table 4.2. For instance, "election rebound," as referred to by one interviewee, is considered to be an indicator of patronage and favoritism in the political form of government and is reported in many municipalities. It refers to the replacement of department heads, including the administrator or village manager, after a new mayor or slate is elected to the board.

As with the figures in table 3.6, the number and percent of governments for each code may be higher in reality, as news coverage does not exist for some governments and is uneven across the region. Nevertheless, the table shows that conflict is prominent, election challenges occur frequently, and there is much turnover in elected officials and administration. However, many mayors and CAOs also stay in the same government for twelve or more years.

All interviewed governments also are classified into several categories representing corporate or political governance, as shown in table 4.5, based on information in the interviews, news reports (governance–political and corporate codes), and secondary sources. Their financial decision structure is taken into consideration in classifying them, but so is evidence of how officers are appointed, how benefits are distributed, government culture, and the prevalence of high-powered or low-powered incentives. The categories were assigned to each government using an "artistic method of classification" that is somewhat subjective (Frederickson, Johnson, and Wood 2004, 153). The one government classified as having "political values" is close to the political end of the political-corporate continuum but is undergoing significant change toward corporate due to one individual. Governments that are political-corporate are basically political, but have some corporate features. Governments that are corporate-political are basically corporate, but have some political features.

Evidence from many governments in both hybrid categories in the table demonstrates the extent to which the political and corporate approaches and values clash, create conflict, and lead to turnover in elected and appointed officials. Most of the six governments that are classified as having corporate values are small but sometimes operate in a political manner due to their size. For instance, one of these governments is very wealthy, has board members who are highly trained professionals (doctors, lawyers, bank presidents), and offers few services (no water/sewer, garbage, fire). Highly paid, professional administrators are not needed to run these governments, and board members often get involved in administration in areas that match their training and experience, but the government is open, service delivery is rule based, and there is no electoral rebound.

One other caveat about the classifications of governments in table 4.5 is that they reflect conditions within a relatively narrow time period (2002–4). One important characteristic about form of governance and governing structure that is apparent from the qualitative data is that it is not constant. Although governance tends to evolve toward the corporate end of the continuum over time, as is apparent from the qualitative information (see table 4.6; and for evidence of changes in form of government nationwide, see Frederickson, Johnson, and Wood 2004, 102–3), oftentimes the progression is not linear. Governments can be more corporate than political in one elected administration, and more political than corporate in the next, especially as they experience growth and development.

TABLE 4.5 Form of Governance in Interviewed Municipalities, 2003

	Number of Municipal Governments	Percent of Governments Interviewed
Political	13	21.0
Political values	1	1.6
Political-corporate	10	16.0
Corporate-political	8	13.0
Corporate values	6	8.0
Corporate	24	40.3
Total interviewed	**62**	**100**

With respect to institutional arrangements that affect financial practices and policies more directly, there are several to consider here. One is whether the government operates under the Illinois Municipal Budget Law (50 ILCS 330/1) or under the appropriations ordinance (65 ILCS 5/8-2-9). At a minimum, all municipalities in the state must adopt an appropriations ordinance within the first three months of the fiscal year that specifies maximum expenditures for the current fiscal year, including reserves for employee pensions, which is filed with the county clerk. The ordinance does not require any additional financial information, including revenue projections. By comparison, if governments follow the budget act they must adopt and file a combined budget and appropriations ordinance.

Because the appropriations ordinance is difficult to alter, most municipalities significantly pad these numbers to avoid having to formally change the appropriations in case of unforeseen spending increases. However, many governments that have not adopted the budget act will operate with a realistic and comprehensive budget from which they devise the appropriations ordinance. But based on the qualitative evidence there also are many municipalities in the Chicago region that do not adopt a budget, either formally or informally, and some do not pass the appropriations ordinance until well after the fiscal year has begun. Some even rely on the annual financial report, assembled by the external auditors and delivered to them six to nine months after the end of the fiscal year, to obtain good information about their current financial position.

TABLE 4.6 Financial Decision Structure of Municipal Governments in the Chicago Region, 2003 and 2009

	Manager and Finance Director Percent of 264	Administrator and Finance Director Percent of 264	Administrator or Manager, No Finance Director Percent of 264	Finance Director, No Manager or Administrator Percent of 264	No Finance Director, Manager, or Administrator Percent of 264	Total
Count, 2003	75/28	40/15	56/21	18/7	75/28	**264**
Count, 2009	79/30	53/20	51/19	24/9	57/21	**264**

Levels of Governance

The concept of governance also applies to the administration of policies and practices, not just the political structure or process. Lynn and colleagues distinguish between institutional, managerial, and technical levels of governance in the public sector (Heinrich and Lynn 2000; Lynn, Heinrich, and Hill 2001; Hill and Lynn 2004; Ingraham and Lynn 2004). Prior discussion of governance has focused mostly on the institutional level, which encompasses the government's policymaking structure and lines of policy authority in the legislative and executive realms. The institutional level of governance also is affected by the relationship between citizen preferences and legislative choice, the prominence of business interests in the affairs of municipal government, and the relationships among members of the board in terms of their level of agreement or ability to work cohesively.

With respect to citizens' preferences and legislative choice in the municipal governments examined here, two measures may be useful in gauging these factors—percent vote for Bush in 2004 and percent population with manager and professional occupations. The presidential vote is an indication of the extent to which citizens in the jurisdiction identify and agree with Republican or Democratic values, and the occupational status of citizens (blue collar or white collar) indicates how likely they are to demand corporate and administrative governance.

The managerial and technical levels of governance, by comparison, are concerned more with the impact of governing relations between administrators and staff on the quality and level of government performance. The bureaucracy is the primary target of observation and analysis at these levels and focuses on explicit and implicit contractual relationships between legislators and administrators regarding the implementation of policy (at the institutional level), and between administrators or managers and staff regarding performance (at the managerial and technical levels).

One primary research question about governance at both levels is to what extent does the legislature (administrators) influence and control the decisions of administrators (staff) to ensure that policies are implemented as intended (a high level of performance)? Another is how can incentives or methods of control be structured at the institutional level to better ensure that administrators do the bidding of legislators, in accordance with the belief in the separation of politics and administration, and that the work is performed at a high level? High levels of government performance generally mean achieving intended outcomes (political and service goals) and operating more efficiently. On the financial side, good performance can be defined as maintaining the long-term and short-term solvency of government.

Two caveats are important when applying the governance model developed by Lynn and colleagues to the municipalities in this study and their financial performance. First, most of these governments are not bureaucracies as generally conceptualized. There are many definitions of bureaucracy and different associated features, but most people think of bureaucracies as relatively large organizations with many subunits. The work occurring within the subunits tends to be homogenous but differentiated when compared across them. Some might also claim that bureaucracies have significant levels of administrative personnel to manage and direct staff, are complex, and have a hierarchical structure (Scott, 1998, 260–84).

Looking at the number of full-time employees in all municipal governments in the Chicago region in 2000 and examining the organizational structure and employee lists of some of these governments more recently show that 65 percent have fewer than 100 employees, and 30 percent have fewer than 30 employees. Even governments with up to 175 employees have relatively flat structures with few personnel supervising many employees. Not surprisingly, fire, police, and public works departments tend to be more bureaucratic than others, but other departments share managers and personnel, especially in smaller governments.

As a result, the distinction between the managerial level and technical level of governance may not be very clear in these governments. This may be especially true for finance and administration departments that tend to be small and where the CFO and CAO are responsible for implementing financial policies and practices at an operational level. Furthermore, the technical nature of many financial decisions means that both the CFO and CAO, if they exist, are likely to influence fiscal governance at the institutional level. In other words, the relationships between the legislators and the CFO or CAO in many suburban governments may not be strictly top-down, but are also likely to be bottom-up in terms of the impact these administrators have on policy decisions and the institutional arrangements that affect all financial decisions (Feldman and Khademian 2002).

From a different perspective, the political nature of many financial decisions and their effect on financial outcomes, which are often central to the contractual relationship between elected officials and constituents, gives elected officials incentive to be involved in financial decisions at all governance levels. The ideal according to the philosophy of the separation of politics and administration is that elected officials make policy and administrators implement it (Wheeland 2000). But if the government does not have a CAO or CFO, or if institutional arrangements do not preclude or even support elected officials' involvement in financial decisions at the operational level, the ability to distinguish between different levels of fiscal governance in suburban municipalities according to the model proposed by Lynn and his colleagues will be muddled further.

More important is the second caveat in applying the Lynn model to the financial performance of government—good financial performance may not be consistent with the basic incentive structure of governance at the highest institutional levels. The nature of the contractual relationships between elected officials and constituents gives the former incentive to spend too much, tax too little, and eliminate financial controls, which will threaten government financial condition in the long run. In other words, to satisfy voters and supporters, elected officials may have more incentive to worsen than maintain or improve government financial condition. Thus financial performance is not just a matter of the contractual relationship between administrators and technical staff but also depends on the financial policies that elected officials want implemented, how and to what extent the policies are implemented by administrators, and the financial management practices of administrators and staff.

Transaction Risk and Trust

The nature of the contractual relationship between elected officials and the CAO and the transactions that establish this relationship are particularly critical areas of governance for suburban municipalities as observed from the qualitative data. Although 35 percent of the municipalities in the Chicago metropolitan area had no CAO in 2003 and therefore no such contractual relationship existed at that time, some of these governments may have had a CAO in the past, and many others probably had considered hiring a CAO. In addition, some of the fifty-six municipal governments with a CAO at the time may have chosen to do without a CAO sometime in the future. Comparing the frequencies for FDS in 2009 and 2003 in table 4.6 shows that the trend is toward these governments becoming more reformed with respect to financial governance over time, especially as their population increases, pressure for development increases, and government administration becomes too time-consuming or complex for the mayor alone. However, the movement toward reform is not always smooth. The qualitative evidence demonstrates that governments often wrestle with whether to hire a CAO because of the nature of the contractual relationship between elected and appointed officials.

The frequencies in table 4.4 show that seventeen governments reported wrestling with whether to hire a CAO during the time period of news reporting. The coded statements also show that the role of the attorney and fire or police chief in governing as the CAO was discussed in nine and twelve governments, respectively. Closer examination of these twenty-one governments shows that some governments are using their attorney as their CAO, others appoint their fire or police chief as interim CAO, and some make the latter arrangement permanent. Fire and police chiefs in several municipalities changed jobs to become CAOs in other communities, and the CAO in several governments was the police or fire chief in another government at the same time.

Tangential to the costs of hiring an administrator, the primary concern of elected officials in hiring a CAO chosen from a pool of outside applicants is that this person doesn't know or care about the people in the municipality. Many elected officials simply do not trust that such an individual, with significant authority over government operations, will act for the benefit of citizens. They feel that accountability will be lost once the mayor relinquishes administrative power and authority to a hired CAO, even one that is a professional, and that their elected position could be jeopardized if the CAO makes bad decisions. Many officials would rather hire someone they know, someone who lives in the jurisdiction, or even a relative of the mayor than the most qualified person for the job of CAO. These sentiments are what drive the electoral rebound discussed previously.

The lack of trust in a hired CAO is another manifestation of the basic problem with the contractual relationship between *principals* and *agents*. That problem is to ensure that the agent fulfills the contract according to the interests of the principal. In municipal governments the principals are the elected officials, and the CAO and CFO are the agents. More generally, the problem is one of aligning the agents' actions with the principals' goals, which becomes even more difficult when the parties' goals conflict. Aligning principals' goals and agents' actions is problematic because the institutional regimes and governance structure do not give the principal adequate control over the agent. In this case, the principal lacks information on which to judge the agent's actions fully after the fact (*ex post*), and/or the organizational limitations on the agent's discretionary and opportunistic behavior before the fact (*ex ante*) are not adequate.

Also establishing contracts, developing ex ante and ex post control mechanisms, and enforcing cooperation and compliance can be very costly for the principal. These costs are called *transaction costs* by economists, and having trust is one way that principals reduce the transaction costs of contracting with agents. Thus, it is not surprising that moving to a professional CAO is such a hard decision for some municipal governments in the Chicago region. From a problem-solving perspective, trust is a type of heuristic or rule of thumb that conserves cognitive resources in determining the qualifications of agents and their rate or likelihood of compliance with the contract (McEvily, Perrone, and Zaheer 2003).

The concept of risk, which is contrary to trust in this context, is also important here although the term *risk* is applied somewhat differently from that noted previously (Ring and Van de Ven 1992). With respect to contracts between principals and agents, risk applies to transactions rather than environmental outcomes. Instead of uncertainty over external events, such as the payoffs of investments in economic development, transaction risk applies to the likelihood that the agent will be opportunistic contrary to the contract due to the structure of incentives, the availability of opportunities, and the agent's propensity for opportunism (Nooteboom 1996). Transaction risk and trust will vary according to several factors, including the frequency of transactions between the principal and agent, the importance of socially embedded relationships inherent to governing and institutional regimes (such as greater trust of fellow party members than nonparty members), and either party having a reputation for compliance and equity (Ring and Van de Ven 1992).

The concepts of high-powered and low-powered incentives are another very useful way to think about the institutional structure within which transactions costs occur as it applies to corporate versus political forms of governance. *High-powered incentives* exist in situations where the benefits from transactions flow directly to the parties transacting, such as in a marketplace or an election. In elections, candidates trade decisions for votes and electoral resources from supporters, which are powerful motivations for candidates to deliver more benefits directly to a greater number of individuals and to take advantage of any opportunity that facilitates this outcome. *Low-powered incentives* exist in situations where the benefits of transactions do not flow directly to the parties transacting. Under such conditions appointed officials get no personal gain from implementing the desires of elected officials or the policies enacted by the legislative side. Rather appointed officials gain benefit through raises, promotions, and professional reputation and satisfaction. These incentives are much less powerful and less likely to facilitate opportunistic and exploitive behavior that is contrary to the rules of governance and of benefit to a limited constituency (Williamson 1985; Frant 1996).

In this case, political forms of government tend to promote high-powered incentives throughout the levels of governance, and low-powered incentives will be more prevalent in corporate or administrative forms. These different incentives explain many of the characteristics of political and corporate governance identified in the last three rows of table 4.2 and are especially important in explaining municipal decisions about development. Development and population growth offer politicians opportunities for direct benefit in the form of contributions from developers and businesses, increased government revenue due to building and impact fees, and very visible and positive changes in the physical and economic infrastructure (Feiock and Kim 2001).

Thus, development and population growth provide high-powered incentives to elected officials and so they pursue these outcomes to achieve their financial and political objectives.

Macrolevel Fiscal Institutions and Governance

Unfortunately, the effects of macrolevel fiscal institutions and governance cannot be determined in this study because there is no variation in these conditions among the governments examined here. All Chicago municipalities are in the same state and metropolitan region, which precludes assessing the effects of state-local or interlocal governing relations on these governments. However, potential factors at this level need to be recognized, as theory suggests their effects on financial decisions are significant. Moreover, the state of Illinois and the Chicago metropolitan region are relatively unique on some factors. Thus some discussion of macrolevel institutions and governance, especially in the financial area, is warranted, and findings from analyses must be interpreted with macrolevel conditions in mind.

State-Local Governing Relations in Illinois

Some important state-level fiscal rules that affect municipal governments in Illinois have already been described in the section on the unique features of Illinois and the Chicago region because of their importance to external fiscal capacity and how it is measured in this study. As is discussed in chapter 2, Illinois allows municipalities to collect a broad range of taxes and other revenues. Home rule privileges, which vary among municipalities in the Chicago region, also greatly broaden options for handling fiscal threats and opportunities because governments are not subject to tax and debt limitations.[6] Although state law constrains and dictates taxation for non–home rule municipal governments, home rule governments in Illinois have other privileges that are considered to be among the most liberal found in state constitutions (Wandling 2001). Analysis by Krane, Rigos, and Hill (2001, appendices) shows that incorporation is easy in Illinois compared to other states, but annexation is difficult, and there is limited extraterritorial jurisdiction with respect to zoning, regulation, and service provision.

The state also grants local governments in Illinois broad authority to cooperate, but also allows citizens to create special districts, which seems to be a favored approach to delivering local services in this state (Flickinger and Murphy 1990; Wandling 2001). Indeed, Illinois has more local governments than any other state. As of 2007, the Census of Governments reports that Illinois had almost 6,994 local governments compared to Pennsylvania, Texas, and California, which had the next highest number of local governments at 4,871, 4,835, and 4,344, respectively (www. census.gov/govs/cog/GovOrgTab03ss.html). Illinois also gives broad authority to municipalities in the area of economic development with respect to public-private partnerships for the creation of developmental corporations, enterprise zones, business districts, TIFs, and the use of tools such as tax abatements.

For the most part it seems that these state-level institutional arrangements will increase the size of the fiscal toolbox of municipal governments in Illinois relative to other states. This trend was supported by Pagano and Hoene (2010), who categorized all fifty states according to five different levels of state constraints on the fiscal policy space of municipal government. The municipal fiscal policy space, as defined by Pagano and Hoene but conceptualized here, represents the set of state-level parameters within which municipal officials create fiscal policy, and it can be thought of as the state-determined portion of the municipal fiscal toolbox. According to Pagano and Hoene, Illinois ranks in the first cluster of states with local governments that have the most autonomy.

Being home rule also facilitates financial problem solving in other ways. It gives municipal governments more functional authority (e.g., power to regulate) and personnel autonomy (e.g., hiring and termination of employees). Alternatively, non–home rule governments in Illinois are much more limited in authority and autonomy, which impedes their financial problem solving and results in creative solutions by some governments and interesting effects overall.[7] Illinois laws also affect municipal accounting practices, methods of property assessment, purchasing procedures, requirements to adopt and balance budgets, and a requirement to implement an audit (Hill 1978; ACIR 1993).

It is also very important to note how property taxes in Illinois are determined because it greatly affects the local fiscal toolbox and how local officials think about and make decisions about property taxes. Specifically, property taxes are based on the total levy that local governments extend, not the rate. However, non–home rule governments have maximum rate limits on particular services and spending purposes that do not exist for home rule governments.

States also distribute general aid to local governments and grants for specific programs in areas such as education and transportation, and more generally for capital improvements. These revenues are described in detail for Illinois municipal governments in chapter 2. It also should be emphasized that state income and motor fuel tax are distributed to municipal and other local governments as general aid according to population as a proportion of the total state population, but sales taxes are distributed based on point of sale. Many state grants to local governments require matching funds, which places positive pressure on local spending. Unfortunately, the matching requirements for grant dollars are unknown for the governments examined here.

On the spending side, state mandates can require local governments to provide certain services or to fund services at particular levels (e.g., employee pensions and entitlements). Such mandates often target environmental issues such as disposal of solid wastes, water quality, flooding, and pollution remediation (ACIR 1990). State-mandated increases to local pension benefits was one problem mentioned often in the interviews with COG directors in 2009 and noted by many news reports from this time period. Although Illinois passed the States Mandate Act in 1981 that required reimbursement to local governments for mandated services and tax exemptions that affect localities, it was one of four states classified as having ineffective legislation by Kelly (1994) due to its tendency to exclude mandates from reimbursement. States also pass tax expenditure mandates, such as property tax exemptions, that cost local governments revenue and limit their authority to raise taxes on certain populations.

The state's custodial role in the affairs of local government is one critical area of state-local fiscal relations that is not fully recognized in earlier discussions. Illinois has passed a wide range of laws that govern how local governments conduct their financial business, including laws that affect personnel and financial management functions, and the state monitors the finances of local government, especially education. However, it is the author's opinion that enforcement of such laws and state oversight of local governments that are not school districts is very lax in Illinois. The state also provided advice and training to local officials in different areas of financial management, especially budgeting and basic accounting, at one time through several departments, but those units no longer exist.

In extreme cases of fiscal stress, states often intervene directly in local government operations through regulation and appointed control boards to oversee financial decisions and they may even directly manage the financial affairs of local governments (Berman 2003). But Illinois' oversight of and involvement with local governments in this respect is ad hoc and hands-off by comparison to other states, mostly because the state has to be asked by the local government to intervene (Honadle 2003). The Financially Distressed Cities Law (65 ILCS 5/Art. 8 Div. 12) that applies to home rule municipalities and the Local Government Financial Planning and Supervision Act (50 ILCS 320/) that applies to other non–home rule governments, except school districts, do not allow the state to unilaterally intervene in the fiscal affairs of the local governments.[8] Rather, the state must be invited in by the local government via the passage of a local ordinance or a supermajority vote of the governing body, respectively.

The state-local relations described here can be summarized as a continuum of state control versus local autonomy (Stephens 1974). On one end of the continuum, state-local relations are *centralized,* in which the state limits local discretion in the different areas discussed previously and assumes greater responsibility for financing local government. On the other end of the continuum, state-local relations are *decentralized,* in which the state gives local government greater discretion over their structure, functioning, finances, and other matters but also more responsibility for delivering and financing local services and resolving their own problems. On one end, state governments are paternalistic and intrusive toward local government; on the other end, they have a hands-off approach and allow local government many privileges. In between, state-local relations take a variety of forms that mix centralized and decentralized features to achieve a balance of power that meets citizens' needs and reflects political and socioeconomic historical trends within the state.

Although this continuum simplifies the nature of state-local relations greatly, it does provide a basis for expectations about the effects these two opposing systems have on local financial policies and practices. First, economic theory states that there will be a better fit between local services and constituent needs and demands (called allocative efficiency) in decentralized systems to the extent that the economies of scale are appropriate to the services being delivered, and there are no significant positive or negative spillovers associated with them. In contrast, a centralized system is more likely to deliver a uniform package of goods and services across a broader area (Oates 1977, 2006). Second, decentralized systems have greater flexibility in adapting service and fiscal policy to changes in local conditions and adopting innovative approaches to solving problems. Third, civic participation is likely to be higher in decentralized systems where citizens are better able to monitor government activities and thus better able to hold local politicians accountable for their decisions (Dowding and Mergoupis 2003). Citizens are less likely to misperceive the relationship between costs and services if their services are provided and funded locally rather than centrally. Thus, fiscal decentralization also promotes "fiscal equivalence" (citizens "get what they pay for and must pay for what they get"), which reduces the perception of getting something for nothing and tempers demand for services (Oakerson 1999, 112).

On the other end of the spectrum, arguments against state-local decentralization include the following: (1) small, local governments are unable to realize economies of scale with many types of services and cannot prevent or compensate for the spillovers in costs and benefits that will occur among decentralized jurisdictions; (2) decentralized systems will not be able to compensate for fiscal disparities and inequalities in local service provision; and (3) local governments in decentralized systems are likely to be more corrupt, be of lower quality, and lack good financial management systems (Kee 2004).

With respect to financial problem solving, the size of the local fiscal toolbox is more likely to be constrained by state limitations and control in centralized state-local systems, but more likely to be constrained or enhanced by the local fiscal environment in decentralized systems. Relatively wealthy governments in decentralized systems will have the largest toolbox, compared to poor, high-need governments in decentralized systems that will have the smallest toolbox. All other things being equal, local governments in centralized systems will have more moderate-sized toolboxes. Because local financial policies and practices will be more constrained and dictated by state government in centralized systems, there should be less variation in the financial condition of local governments in these systems. By comparison, local governments in decentralized systems may also have greater variation in fiscal policies and practices, and those in states with little financial oversight should have a higher incidence of unsound or less than optimum financial management practices.

Where does Illinois rank on the centralization-decentralization continuum compared to other states? Table 4.7 shows how Illinois ranks on three measures of fiscal decentralization of state and local governments in 2007. The first column shows local government spending for operations (not capital or construction) as a percent of total local and state operational spending, and the second column shows local revenue as a percent of state and local revenue minus state and federal aid. The last column shows how much local governments in each state rely on state-shared revenue to deliver local services. Mathematically, the first and second measures are opposite of measures of state centralization developed by Stephens (1974) that focused on centralization of service distribution and financial responsibility, respectively. The table also shows that Illinois is relatively decentralized compared to other states. In fact, Illinois ranks seventh from the top if you add the rankings of all states across the three indicators. In this case, state-local fiscal decentralization should be recognized as a potential factor in the financial problems and solutions implemented by municipal governments in this study.

Interlocal Governing Relations in the Chicago Region

The system of interlocal governing relations is another contextual factor that should be considered to understand the financial pressures and options local governments face in controlling their financial condition and to explain their choice of fiscal policies

TABLE 4.7 Fiscal Decentralization of State-Local Governing Relationships, 2007 (%)

	Local Operational Spending of State + Local		Local Revenue of State + Local Revenue (Minus state aid)		Local Revenue from State (Not own-source)	
1	Nevada	69.7	Florida	51.6	Hawaii	7.5
2	California	66.8	Colorado	51.0	Nebraska	17.6
3	Florida	66.7	Nebraska	49.7	Tennessee	20.2
4	Tennessee	64.8	Nevada	48.7	Colorado	20.5
5	Colorado	64.6	Texas	47.2	South Dakota	22.4
6	Nebraska	63.1	Tennessee	46.4	Texas	22.5
7	**Illinois**	**61.8**	Georgia	45.7	Florida	22.7
8	Georgia	61.7	**Illinois**	**45.6**	Missouri	24.4
9	Texas	61.7	New York	44.7	South Carolina	25.7
10	New York	61.5	Washington	44.4	Georgia	25.9
11	Wisconsin	61.1	Arizona	42.9	Maryland	25.9
12	Arizona	61.0	California	42.6	**Illinois**	**26.4**
13	Michigan	60.2	Kansas	41.7	Washington	26.5
14	Kansas	59.6	Missouri	41.6	Utah	26.6
15	Indiana	59.4	Ohio	39.2	New Jersey	27.3
16	Wyoming	59.2	Oregon	39.2	Connecticut	27.7
17	Ohio	59.1	Alabama	39.2	New Hampshire	28.2
18	Oregon	58.4	Maryland	39.1	Louisiana	28.8
19	Virginia	57.7	South Dakota	39.1	Rhode Island	28.8
20	Minnesota	57.6	Iowa	38.6	Alabama	29.8
21	Missouri	57.3	Virginia	38.3	North Dakota	29.8
22	Washington	56.6	Indiana	38.1	New York	29.8
23	North Carolina	56.5	Pennsylvania	38.1	Kansas	29.9
24	Alabama	56.3	North Carolina	37.3	Iowa	30.2
25	Iowa	56.2	New Hampshire	37.3	Maine	31.0
26	Pennsylvania	55.7	New Jersey	37.3	Alaska	31.1
27	Idaho	54.9	Utah	36.7	Virginia	31.3
28	New Jersey	54.7	Wisconsin	36.0	Oregon	31.3
29	Maryland	53.4	South Carolina	36.0	Indiana	31.8
30	New Hampshire	53.2	Wyoming	35.7	Arizona	32.3
31	South Dakota	52.2	Michigan	35.2	North Carolina	32.4
32	Utah	50.4	Minnesota	34.8	Nevada	32.8
33	Connecticut	50.2	Connecticut	34.5	Oklahoma	32.9
34	Massachusetts	50.1	Massachusetts	33.4	Kentucky	33.3
35	Oklahoma	49.7	Idaho	33.4	Massachusetts	33.6
36	South Carolina	48.9	Louisiana	32.5	Pennsylvania	33.7
37	Louisiana	48.6	Oklahoma	31.2	Montana	34.3
38	Mississippi	48.6	Rhode Island	31.2	Ohio	34.6
39	Montana	47.9	Kentucky	29.4	Wyoming	35.3
40	Arkansas	45.9	Mississippi	29.3	Mississippi	37.0
41	Rhode Island	45.7	North Dakota	28.7	Idaho	37.4
42	North Dakota	45.3	Maine	28.4	Wisconsin	39.3
43	New Mexico	42.1	Montana	28.2	California	39.5
44	Kentucky	42.0	New Mexico	23.6	West Virginia	39.9
45	Maine	41.7	Arkansas	23.5	Minnesota	40.1
46	Vermont	41.5	Delaware	21.7	Michigan	40.1
47	West Virginia	41.5	West Virginia	21.5	Delaware	41.5
48	Delaware	37.2	Hawaii	20.8	Arkansas	48.0
49	Alaska	34.5	Alaska	20.3	New Mexico	48.1
50	Hawaii	19.6	Vermont	15.7	Vermont	60.4

Source: Calculations based on downloadable data available from the US Census Bureau, *2007 Census of Governments*, State by Type of Government—Public Use Format (www.census.gov/govs/estimate/historical_data_2007.html#state_local).

and practices. The continuum of centralized versus decentralized governing structure usually applies to different tiers of government (local, state, and federal) or different tiers of authority and responsibility within the same government. The continuum of fragmented versus consolidated governing structure is often applied to governments at the same level within a metropolitan region.

For instance, one can characterize local governance structure in the Nashville metropolitan region as more consolidated than many other metropolitan regions. The City of Nashville and Davidson County merged to become one government in 1962 with two service districts (one for county and one for municipal services). Since then the combined government has expanded beyond the original boundaries of Nashville to provide services to all areas of the county, thus eliminating the need for other local governments within Davidson County (Stephens and Wikstrom 2000, 70–75). The Minneapolis–St. Paul metropolitan region is also less fragmented than many other regions because of the Twin Cities Metropolitan Council. This planning agency encompasses seven counties, has authority over the plans and projects of special districts within the region, and may mediate conflicts between conflicting municipal plans. The council also operates regional transit and waste services, and implements and enforces metropolitan sharing of regional tax benefits from economic growth (Stephens and Wikstrom 2000, 95–99).

Both regional governments are in contrast to the Chicago metropolitan region, which has many local governments, many different types of overlapping local governments, and no formal structure or method for coordinating or controlling their actions and interactions.[9] Not only does Illinois have the most local governments of any state in the United States, but the region is likely to have more local governments than any other region in the country. Compared to the largest fifty metropolitan regions in the United States according to population, as of 2002, the Chicago area had 1,451 local governments compared to the New York metropolitan region, which was second highest with 1,321 local governments.[10] However, if you examine number of local governments per capita, Chicago ranks sixteenth from the highest in this group with Pittsburgh, Louisville, and Indianapolis ranked first, second, and third, respectively. Number of local governments per capita is often used as a measure of political fragmentation based on the argument that residents vote (Logan and Schneider 1981), and number of local governments per square mile might be considered a measure of spatial fragmentation. Illinois ranks second highest on spatial fragmentation, with New York first, and Philadelphia, St. Louis, and Pittsburgh third, fourth, and fifth, respectively.[11]

Many of the arguments about centralization or decentralization of state versus local government discussed previously also apply to fragmentation versus consolidation of local governments within a metropolitan region. Governments in fragmented systems tend to be smaller and therefore unable to realize economies of scale in production, which increases their per unit price of goods and services (Oakerson 1999). The numerous and oftentimes overlapping local governments that exist in fragmented systems also lead to duplication of service delivery efforts, especially in administrative areas. Consolidated systems, by comparison, can share administration and other production inputs (indirect and direct costs), which gives these systems better "economies of scope" and reduces per unit costs (Boyne 1992; Foster 1997).

A large number of small governments in an area will create more interjurisdictional externalities or spillover effects in which the actions of one government affect the welfare of governments nearby (Musso 1998). Externalities, or spillover effects, can be either positive, such as when one community's road improvements benefit residents and firms in neighboring jurisdictions, or negative, as when improving police protection in one community drives criminal activity across the border. Proponents of consolidated local government claim that goods and services that generate positive externalities are likely to be underprovided by governments within a decentralized region because of the problem of free riders, which gives governments less incentive to contribute their fair share of local goods and services to a region (Lowery 2000). Governments in fragmented systems also may have less motivation to collaborate to provide goods and services that generate positive externalities, or to reduce services that generate negative externalities (Oakerson and Parks 1989; Stephens and Wikstrom 2000).

In contrast, consolidated governments have the authority to regulate and the resources to compensate for these problems at a regional level, especially problems associated with uneven development, regional decline, and urban sprawl (Hawkins, Ward, and Becker 1991; Downs 1994; Rusk 1995). Proponents of consolidated government argue that citizen's knowledge of the costs of government and their service demands will be less accurate in fragmented systems because the systems are more complicated compared to consolidated systems where the link between services, taxes, and governments is clearer. Governments in fragmented systems, therefore, are better able to inflate revenues and service levels beyond what is efficient due to lack of consumer oversight (Brennan and Wagner 1977).

The case for fragmented and decentralized government is based on the seminal work by Charles Tiebout (1956) that views the metropolis as a marketplace where residents and businesses shop for local governments that best satisfy their preferences for public goods and services and their ability to pay (Oates 1972; Oates and Schwab 1991; Wilson 1999). The existence of numerous governments within a region (offering different service and revenue packages), the mobility of residents and businesses, and their knowledge of the contents of revenue and spending packages combine to create a competitive public market (Stein 1987; Dowding, John, and Biggs 1994). In the long run, competition to attract customers compels governments to produce and allocate goods and services more efficiently and sorts the population into homogenous groups within that market (Kenyon 1997).

Competition promotes productive efficiency of public services because governments attract businesses and residents by providing higher quality goods and services at a cheaper price. Competition also promotes allocative efficiency, which means citizens and businesses are more likely to get the level and quality of services they prefer as they move to the location that best satisfies their service preferences and financial capabilities.[12] Assuming citizens and businesses within a region have very different preferences for goods and services, a related argument for fragmentation is that citizens will benefit from having many different governments to choose from (Stein 1987). Thus metropolitan regions that are larger and offer more government options to residents and businesses will have more competition. Greater competition, in turn, means higher allocative and productive efficiency of local public goods and services in a region.

Competition also is facilitated by citizens comparing the quality of services and tax burden in their government to others in the region and pressuring elected officials to deliver better goods and services or lower taxes. Over time, government officials become sensitive to the level of services delivered by their neighbors or other comparable group (called "comps") and, more important, governments pay close attention to comparable governments' tax levels and charges. This is the *voice* mechanism of competition in which voters and other stakeholders directly pressure their government to look like what they observe in other governments in the region. In contrast, residents and businesses also create competition by relocating to new jurisdictions, or "voting with their feet," which is the *exit* mechanism (Hirschman 1970).

The varying claims about the effects of fragmented local government on financial decisions and the state's reputation of having very fragmented local government indicate the importance of determining the level of local fragmentation in the Chicago region. In effect, the fragmentation of the Chicago region may make the financial incentives, threats, opportunities, and even contents of the fiscal toolbox very different for municipal governments in this region compared to other regions. For instance, if local governance in the region is highly fragmented, competition may be higher and coordination to resolve regional problems may be more difficult. Higher competition may also increase pressure on local governments to lower taxes and charges and offer tax incentives to attract economic development. Alternatively, the competition created by fragmentation puts people at upper income levels and businesses that generate high levels of local revenue in the driver's seat of local policymaking as governments compete to attract these property owners to their jurisdiction (Schneider 1989).

Some have even argued that competition can be destructive because it will lead to public goods and services being underprovided or underfunded as competing governments engage in a race to the bottom with their tax rates (Rork 2003). It will also lead to the proliferation of tax incentives (tax expenditures) to the point where the costs are greater than the benefits (McGuire 1991). An overabundance of overlapping governments that share the same tax base may constrain shared government's ability to increase taxes through referenda or result in overgrazing of the tax base if local governments have authority to act independently (Berry 2007). Fragmentation may also increase spillover effects, which increases direct conflict between governments but may also provide increased opportunities for contracting, collaboration, and networking (Thurmaier and Wood 2002; Post 2004; Boyne 1992).

To the extent that population sorting and restrictions in population mobility occur more widely in fragmented than consolidated systems, one would also expect greater variation in fiscal capacities among local governments in fragmented regions. Thus fragmented regions are likely to have a higher proportion of local governments that are extremely poor with no capacity to provide necessary services and a higher portion of governments that can afford to spend lavishly, especially for education or unique services preferred by their voters (e.g., horse trails). In other words, variation in financial condition is likely to be greater in more fragmented local systems than consolidated ones, and systems that are more fragmented and more competitive are less likely to adopt policies that redistribute wealth and more likely to focus on development policies that maximize their competitive edge (Peterson 1981).

Fragmentation may also promote greater specialization among local governments in terms of some governments providing services and jobs for others (Howell-Moroney 2008; Orfield 2002). For instance, the Village of Rosemont in the Chicago region, which is near the region's largest airport, faces somewhat unique financial problems, because

TABLE 4.8 Combined Indicators of Fragmentation and Fiscal Dispersion in the Fifty Largest Metropolitan Regions, 2002

Sum of Rankings of 12 Indices[a]		Sum of Z Scores of 12 Indices[b]	
Pittsburgh	128	*Chicago*	*12.48*
Chicago	*139*	Pittsburgh	10.71
St. Louis	147	Philadelphia	8.80
Philadelphia	175	St. Louis	8.67
Houston	201	Houston	6.52
New York	206	Indianapolis	5.05
Atlanta	218	Denver	4.51
Boston	222	Louisville	4.44
Denver	224	New York	4.35
Indianapolis	229	Kansas City	4.26
Kansas City	236	San Francisco	4.24
Minneapolis	236	Boston	4.21
Cincinnati	239	Cleveland	4.04
Hartford	245	Cincinnati	3.87
Louisville	246	Los Angeles	3.82
Grand Rapids	247	Seattle	3.72
Cleveland	250	Atlanta	3.56
Seattle	250	Portland	3.43
Salt Lake City	253	Minneapolis	3.27
Detroit	259	Hartford	3.11
Milwaukee	259	Milwaukee	3.11
Columbus	261	Salt Lake City	3.09
Sacramento	266	Detroit	3.05
Portland	267	Columbus	2.91
Dallas	269	Dallas	2.68
San Francisco	270	Grand Rapids	2.54
Los Angeles	272	Rochester	2.35
Birmingham	287	Sacramento	1.69
Rochester	295	Birmingham	1.31
Orlando	300	Phoenix	1.11
Phoenix	316	Buffalo	0.13
San Antonio	323	San Diego	0.13
Oklahoma City	327	Orlando	−0.26
Buffalo	331	Oklahoma City	−0.64
Miami	336	San Antonio	−0.84
San Diego	365	Miami	−2.29
Austin	382	Tampa	−3.96
Tampa	393	New Orleans	−4.59
Jacksonville	413	Jacksonville	−6.91

TABLE 4.8 *(Continued)*

Sum of Rankings of 12 Indices[a]		Sum of Z Scores of 12 Indices[b]	
Nashville	420	Washington, DC	−7.63
Washington, DC	431	Richmond	−7.86
Las Vegas	437	Nashville	−8.33
Memphis	441	Austin	−8.50
New Orleans	444	Las Vegas	−8.79
Charlotte	456	Charlotte	−9.00
Richmond	457	Raleigh	−10.08
Norfolk	464	Baltimore	−11.55
Raleigh	466	Norfolk	−12.56
Baltimore	491	Memphis	−12.74
Greensboro	511	Greensboro	−14.61

[a]Smaller numbers are higher fragmentation

[b]Higher numbers are higher fragmentation

Source: Calculations based on downloadable data available from the US Census Bureau, *2002 Census of Governments*, Directory Information File—Individual Units (www.census.gov/govs/estimate/historical_data_2002.htm).

most of its land area is devoted to convention centers and hotels. Few people live there, so its constituency is not just the voting population. Other suburbs in the region may cater to industry and warehouse distribution facilities for large retail operations, and many suburbs are predominately residential with little commerce or industry.

Where does Illinois rank on the fragmentation-consolidation continuum compared to other states? Readers are referred to the working paper by Hendrick (2011) for details about how local government fragmentation and consolidation were constructed for the fifty largest metropolitan regions in the United States using 2002 Census of Governments data. Twelve indices of local government of fragmentation and fiscal dispersion were calculated for each region and then combined by adding the rankings and Z scores for all measures.[13] These combined indices are shown in table 4.8, which illustrates that local government in the Chicago region is indeed highly fragmented and fiscally dispersed.[14]

A Model of Financial Problem Solving

As described thus far in chapters 2 and 3, government financial decisions are the outcomes of strategic problem solving that takes place within a set of internal and external governing arrangements and a financial environment that can be relatively stable or dynamic. In this case, the strategic problem is to maintain or improve government financial condition or performance even while trying to achieve other objectives. Figure 2.2 shows that financial policies, practices, and reactions to changing financial condition are choices made about short-term and long-term revenues, services, assets, and liabilities. Possible choices that government officials could make might be thought of as a toolbox of fiscal options. The content of the toolbox is determined by the government's current fiscal structure and fiscal environment. Which options or tools officials choose from the toolbox depends on their heuristics and perspective toward risk or entrepreneurialism. It also depends on the values promoted and incentives structured by internal and external governing arrangements. In effect, the tools chosen by governments reflect how they resolve conflicts between the pursuit of good financial performance and the pursuit of objectives contrary to this outcome.

Figure 4.1 presents a picture of the primary factors affecting fiscal problem solving and financial condition as identified thus far. The diagram also shows how these factors are related in a basic way and is not meant to represent magnitudes of particular

FIGURE 4.1 Model of Financial Problem Solving

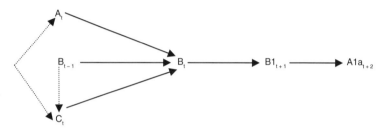

Context ($A_{current}$): Exogenous
  (1) External fiscal capacity:
      (a) Revenue wealth and spending needs
      (b) State institutions: Fiscal rules (e.g., home rule) and financial aid
  (2) Administrative capacity in fiscal area (financial problem-solving heuristics)
  (3) Governance (internal institutions and preferences)
  (4) Regional system of local government (competitive pressures) and state-local relations (decentralization)
Context (B_{past}): Endogenous
  Current financial structure, financial condition, and internal fiscal capacity (as determined by prior financial decisions)
Contextual events ($C_{current}$): Exogenous
  Fiscal Threats and Opportunities:
  • Events (e.g., recession or fiscal boom) or circumstances (assets and liabilities) that change or can change financial condition in a positive or negative way. Negative events or circumstances create fiscal stress.
  • Growth and development (special case of threats and opportunities)
Fiscal toolbox is a function of $A1_{current}$, B_{past}, and $C_{current}$.
$B_{current}$ financial decisions and strategies:
  (1) Δ Fund balance$_t$ − Borrowing$_t$ = Revenues$_t$ − Spending$_t$ All ≥ 0
  • Responses to fiscal stress and opportunities (e.g., change revenues, change spending, or use of slack resources)
  • Fiscal policies (e.g., tax rates, slack levels, debt levels, revenue burden)
  • Fiscal practices (e.g., use of fund balance, financing of capital investments, managing cash flow, contracting, earmarking)
Future financial condition: Short-term, service-level solvency (B_{future}), and fiscal capacity, long-term solvency ($A1a_{future}$)

effects. The symbol A_t ($A_{current}$) represents four sets of contextual factors within which financial decisions take place in the current time period: (1) fiscal capacity or long-term solvency, which is a function primarily of revenue wealth and spending needs (chapter 2), and state institutions or rules such as home rule or spending mandates and state financial aid (see sections on the unique features of Illinois and the Chicago region and on state-local governing relations in Illinois); (2) administrative and financial problem-solving capacity (chapter 3); (3) internal governing structure (see the section on microlevel governing structure and institutions); and (4) external governing structure (see the section on the unique features of Illinois and the Chicago region). All four factors are considered to be exogenous to financial decisions because they are not affected by financial decisions in the near term.

The symbols B_{t-1} (B_{past}), B_t ($B_{current}$), and B_{t+1} (B_{future}) represent government financial decisions in the past, current, and future time periods. These decisions demonstrate long-range fiscal goals, such as policies against levying a property tax, relying on sales taxes for most revenue, and funding police services at a high level. Financial decisions also demonstrate near-term objectives, such as the decision to raise tax rates, incur more debt, delay hiring, or cut travel budgets to deal with threats (such as economic recessions) or opportunities (such as matching grant programs from the state). Financial decisions can also refer to financial management practices or strategies such as use of fund balances, methods of managing cash flow and financing capital spending, and the earmarking of revenues for particular purposes.

The B symbols can also represent two other events: (1) government financial condition in the short run and with respect to service-level solvency when these decisions are viewed in the aggregate and across assets and liabilities, and (2) government fiscal structure, which is the product of past financial decisions that determine many options in the current fiscal toolbox. For instance, if a government has used up its fund balance in prior years, then that option will not be in its fiscal tool box in the current year. Likewise, if it has underfunded pension liabilities and capital investments in prior years, then claims on its current and future revenue streams will limits its ability to use that revenue for other purposes.

Current fiscal capacity ($A1_t$) and fiscal structure (B_{t-1}) are the most important and rigid boundaries of the fiscal toolbox examined here. When faced with resolving a financial problem, governments can utilize only the revenues, slack, or other assets available to them in the current time period. Chapter 2 identifies and discusses some of the most important financial boundaries that affect the size of the local government fiscal toolbox and options available to them. Some boundaries are a product of the external fiscal environment and include the wealth of its revenue bases, state statutes that limit access to these bases, and resources distributed from other governments through grants or shared revenues. Other boundaries of the fiscal toolbox are established by past fiscal decisions.

On the expenditure side, governments must deal with their liabilities and obligations. They cannot simply decide not to do certain things. They must provide the minimum level of services over which they have responsibility and pay their debts. Here too there are boundaries that limit their options for solving fiscal problems and pursuing fiscal goals. State and federal governments often mandate that local government provide particular goods and services that require a high level of expenditures, which obligates a portion of available resources and limits their ability to use those resources for other purposes. Other financial obligations are generated internally, such as when a government decides to borrow money to pay for capital infrastructure. Higher debt means higher debt service, which obligates resources and limits the size of the fiscal toolbox.

Administrative capacity and governing arrangements ($A2_t$ and $A3_t$) affect the tools that are chosen from the fiscal toolbox and are less rigid than the boundaries of the toolbox. Institutional rules, guidelines, and incentives established by governing arrangements can simply be ignored or worked around. For instance, having a council-manager form of government does not preclude an elected official from pressuring the city manager to hire certain individuals, but it does mean that the manager must approve the hire if it has established a managerial form of government according to Illinois law. Having good internal controls does not preclude someone from stealing government funds if they figure out a way to thwart the system. Making it clear to your elected representative that he will not get your vote if he votes for a tax increase does not ensure that he will vote according to your wishes.

As described previously, governing arrangements are simply rules, traditions, and structures that weakly limit options in the fiscal toolbox and move choices in a particular direction. In this case, whether the municipality has a political or corporate approach to governance can make certain tools or fiscal decisions more desirable than others. Similarly, interlocal competition for residents and businesses and the independence fostered by state-local decentralization can induce governments to make certain financial decisions or react to threats and opportunities in particular ways. Heuristics and attitudes toward risk and entrepreneurialism also move financial choices in a particular direction in the toolbox, but they are properties of the decision maker (and governing arrangements indirectly), not the fiscal toolbox or the environment.

The symbol C_t ($C_{current}$) represents exogenous threats and opportunities in the current time period that alter the size of the fiscal toolbox and influence the choice of particular tools. These events also motivate governments to make decisions or compel them to adapt to different circumstances. Many financial decisions are required at particular time periods, such as the decision to pass a budget or to pay debt service. But many decisions occur because of changes in the fiscal environment that actually or potentially create threats and opportunities that reduce and expand the fiscal toolbox. Economic recessions are one of the most common fiscal threats that motivate governments to lower spending or increase revenue in order to adapt or manage these conditions. Grant programs at the state or federal levels, such as the American Recovery and Reinvestment Act, motivate many governments to make investments in the capital equipment and infrastructure that they would not make otherwise.

Growth and development is another exogenous event that will be examined in more detail here because of the high number of fiscal opportunities and threats it presents to many municipalities, especially those in the outer ring of the region farthest away from the City of Chicago. These governments are usually very small, rural, and have few full-time or professional staff. They face enormous challenges in adapting their fiscal and governing systems to the changes brought about by the urban growth machine. As one mayor commented in an interview, "These developers know more about my town than I do." Although the subjects of population growth and economic development are somewhat beyond the focus of this book, these events are a significant factor in many governments' financial decisions, which in turn have a profound effect on their financial condition in future years.

The dotted lines between components A_t, B_{t-1}, and C_t demonstrate their complex relationship. For instance, the level of fiscal stress experienced by a municipality (C_t) is a function of how much it depends on revenue sources that are declining (B_{t-1}) and fiscal capacity ($A1_t$). Also governments with higher fiscal capacity ($A1_t$) are more likely to have corporate or administrative forms of governance ($A2_t$ and $A3_t$). Growth and development (C_t) can precipitate dramatic changes in administrative capacity and governance ($A2_t$ and $A3_t$) and also alter the effects of other exogenous conditions such as interlocal competition and collaboration. As described here, these effects are nonadditive (nonlinear) or indirect, but many factors can have additive (linear) or direct effects on financial decisions and financial condition.

For instance, home rule can directly affect revenues collected by dictating a government's ability to collect revenues from different sources (changing the size of the fiscal toolbox), or it can alter the extent to which governments come to rely on particular revenue sources (fiscal structure), which affects the extent to which fiscal structure must be changed to adapt to recessionary threats. Similarly, governments with political governing structures may react differently to growth and development or other fiscal threats and opportunities than governments with administrative governing structures. These types of relationships are well known but not always documented in research on local governance and government finances (Clingermayer and Feiock 2001; Feiock, Jeong, and Kim 2003; Lubell, Feiock, and Ramirez 2005).

Irrespective of context and contextual events, current financial decisions and strategies (B_t) for all funds, including many financial management practices, are subject to equation (1) shown in figure 4.1. The formula shows that change (Δ) in fund balance, which is the sum of past deficits and surpluses (revenues − spending), is a function of the deficit or surplus in the current fiscal year plus borrowing. The equation also shows that if an operating deficit occurs on the right-hand side, it must be countered on the left-hand side by either reducing the fund balance or borrowing. For instance, if spending increases dramatically due to pension mandates, revenues could remain the same if fund balances were reduced or borrowing increased. Similarly, if officials decide to lower taxes and reduce revenues, then spending or surplus resources must be decreased, or borrowing increased, to compensate.

With respect to figure 4.1, the primary research question investigated by chapter 5 is what fiscal threats and opportunities most impact municipal government financial condition in the Chicago region and how? The chapter focuses on explaining the effects of fiscal capacity ($A1_t$), fiscal structure (B_{t-1}), and particular threats and opportunities (C_t) on the change in financial condition ($B_t - B_{t-1}$ and $B_t - B_{t+1}$). Particular attention is focused on population growth and economic development as both threat and opportunity.

Chapter 6 investigates four primary research questions. The first two focus on how Chicago municipal governments respond to fiscal threats and opportunities, and what accounts for their responses. The second two questions focus on factors that determine the tools available to these governments and their choice of available tools. This investigation also distinguishes between financial or policy tools (category D in table 3.2) and practice tools (categories A, B, and C in table 3.2). The chapter pays particular attention to the relative effects of fiscal capacity ($A1_t$) in determining the size and content of the toolbox, administrative capacity ($A2_t$), and governance ($A3_t$) in the choice of tools used to manage fiscal stress and financial condition and the contingent effects of home rule on these relationships.

Finally, chapter 7 assesses the effects of fiscal capacity, governance, and other events on financial condition more generally by examining why governments with high fiscal capacity (long-term solvency) have low, short-term solvency (budgetary and service-level solvency) and why governments with low fiscal capacity have high, short-term solvency. This chapter also examines whether and how financial condition varies in governments with different administrative capacities and governance structures within different categories of similar municipal governments. The similarities of these governments help to factor out other events that might be affecting financial condition and allow the analysis to focus on the problem-solving and institutional factors that affect municipal government fiscal policies and practices.

Notes

1. Most studies drop the commission form due to its obsolescence in many parts of the country or include these forms with council-mayor governments.
2. Technically, managers in governments with true council-manager form have the power to appoint and remove all directors of departments. However, many governments are classified as council-manager if the manager is the CAO and can appoint and remove all directors except some, such as police and fire chief (65 ILCS 5/5-3-7).
3. It might also be useful to know whether the CFO is full-time, part-time, or contractual and to know whether the CAO and/or CEO (mayor or president) is full time or part time. However, the qualitative data revealed that many part-time mayors work full-time hours on mayoral duties, so this may not be a good measure of their level of involvement.
4. Prior to 1992, all villages could conduct partisan elections unless they adopted nonpartisan elections by referendum. After that date, municipalities are presumed to have nonpartisan elections unless they pass a referendum adopting partisan elections. However, municipalities that conducted partisan elections prior to 1992 may continue to hold partisan elections without conducting a referendum (65 ILCS 5/3.1-25-20).
5. Student groups in my budgeting classes have completed projects in four of the governments interviewed and other municipalities that were not interviewed, which provides additional information about these governments' finances and governing features.
6. Home rule is granted to municipalities with populations of twenty-five thousand, as certified by the US Census, but smaller municipalities can become home rule via referendum.
7. For instance, the designation of alternate revenue debt is one creative solution to the GO debt limits imposed by property tax limitations on non–home rule government.
8. School districts are handled much differently through (105 ILCS 5/) school code, which is the School District Financial Oversight Panel and Emergency Financial Assistance Law. www.ilga.gov/legislation/ilcs/ilcs3.asp?ActID=802&ChapterID=14.
9. The US Census Bureau and many other sources recognize five basic types of local governments: municipalities, counties, school districts, townships, and special districts. Special districts also have many different forms, but their usual purpose is to provide a single or narrow set of services, such as fire, library, and water reclamation.
10. Calculations based on downloadable data available from the US Census Bureau, *2002 Census of Governments*, Individual Unit File— Public Use Format (www.census.gov/govs/estimate/historical_data_2002.html).

11. How these data were collected and organized and how metropolitan regions were defined is explained in detail in Hendrick (2011).

12. Businesses and citizens often choose their location based on other factors such as access to customers or jobs, which weakens the claims that allocative efficiency is tied to the bundle and costs of services provided by local government.

13. The following measures, which examine fragmentation and dispersion in both horizontal and vertical dimensions, are used in this analysis: number of local governments, number of local governments per one hundred thousand population, number of local governments per ten square miles, percent special purpose governments, percent population in the central city, percent of local government spending by special purpose governments, percent of local spending by the central city, percent of local spending by the county, Hirschman-Herfindahl indices of number of governments of each type, spending by type of government, spending by each government, and spending by municipalities only.

14. Hendrick (2011) also shows that municipal populations in the Chicago metropolitan region are relatively varied and sorted on six social and economic measures compared to the other forty-nine regions.

Chapter 5

Fiscal Threats and Opportunities

What Creates Fiscal Stress and Munificence

This chapter focuses on identifying the events that promote fiscal stress and munificence in municipal governments in the Chicago metropolitan region. Using the strategic management metaphor, it describes the exogenous threats and opportunities municipalities faced from the mid-1990s to the mid-2000s in detail, and in the current recession more generally. In response to the first research question identified in the introduction, this chapter documents how threats and opportunities promote fiscal stress and munificence, focusing on changes to financial condition in the short term or near term. This chapter also examines how threats and opportunities vary with government external fiscal capacity and fiscal structure using the qualitative and quantitative data described in previous chapters. Thus the chapter also provides some preliminary answers to the third research question and begins to specify the relationships between fiscal capacity, fiscal structure, and changes in financial condition in municipal governments in the Chicago metropolitan area.

In figure 4.1 (C_t), fiscal threats and opportunities are conceptualized as events or circumstances that directly change or have the potential to change government financial condition if either acted upon or not acted upon. As discussed in chapter 2, financial condition is a state of being, whereas fiscal stress and munificence are more dynamic. Fiscal stress and munificence represent a negative and a positive change in financial condition respectively. Recessions and the loss of a major taxpayer are obvious threats. The launching of a large capital grant program by a higher level of government (Illinois First in 1999 and ARRA in 2009), a major taxpayer moving into the jurisdiction, and valuable physical assets such as lakes or nearby expressways are examples of opportunities to be exploited and leveraged to improve financial condition.

The time period examined for most quantitative data is from 1994/1995 to 2005/2006. The municipal interviews conducted in spring 2003 focused on the 2001 recession and other financial problems the governments were facing. Interviews with executive directors of the Chicago regional COGs in December 2009 focused in part on to the Great Recession of 2007 and differences between the earlier and latter recessions. News reports collected from 2001 to 2006 were examined to assess how many governments in the region were being affected by the earlier recession and other fiscal threats, and news reports were collected from 2009 through 2010 for all governments interviewed in 2003 that focused on extent of and reactions to the latter recession by these governments.[1] The interviews in 2003 also asked how the municipal governments reacted to the fiscal good times of the late 1990s when the economy was booming and state-shared income tax with municipalities was relatively high.

This chapter documents these threats and opportunities for municipal governments in the Chicago metropolitan region and focuses on their impacts or potential impacts on revenue and spending. Qualitative data also reveal that population growth and development create a unique set of exogenous threats and opportunities for governments that, if not managed correctly, can have negative effects on financial condition in the short run and long run. Governments in municipalities that are experiencing growth and development are examined in more detail to better understand what kind of fiscal problems these conditions create and how such pressures are likely to impact financial policies and practices. It should be noted that comments from COG directors in 2009 noted that the intensity of growth and development may be depressed permanently throughout the region because of the Great Recession, making the findings about these events somewhat tenuous and applicable only prior to this recession.

Some of the evidence to determine how fiscal threats and opportunities lead to fiscal stress and munificence in the short term, in conjunction with fiscal capacity and fiscal structure, comes from the quantitative data in the form of graphs of revenues, spending, and other aspects of financial condition of these governments overtime. Quantitative evidence is also presented using statistical regression analyses that combine important features of fiscal threats, opportunities, and capacity into the same model to assess their independent and conditional effects on fiscal stress.

Three approaches are used to document fiscal threats and opportunities with the qualitative data and establish linkages to fiscal stress and munificence. First, patterns of capacity and events (primarily growth) are examined across levels of near-term fiscal stress experienced by the interviewed governments (as defined in table 3.4) to look for within-group similarities coupled with intergroup differences. Second, outliers in these categories with respect to fiscal capacity and events are examined in more detail. A third approach that is used here, but more so in chapter 7, is a type of experimental design that looks for patterns of outcomes among detailed groupings of municipalities on some of the same factors used to choose municipalities for the interview sample and other factors considered to have a primary effect on financial practices, policies, and financial condition, or alter the effect of these factors. This classification is presented in appendix 7. Commonalities in the nature of exogenous threats and opportunities that governments deal with are examined within the groups in the appendix.

Threats and Opportunities on the Revenue Side

What revenue threats and opportunities have Chicago suburban municipal governments experienced since the mid-1990s? Most have been in the form of changes to different revenue bases, which creates fiscal stress or munificence for these governments. Figure 5.1 shows trends in median changes in per capita revenue sources in the 264 municipal governments from 1994 to 2005 and compared to changes in the consumer price index (CPI) for Midwest urban consumers. The changes are presented as ratios of future and past years, with a ratio of 100 indicating no change from a prior year. The gray line represents ratio changes in the CPI, and the three solid black lines represent EAV, sales receipts, and income tax per capita (state-shared revenue). The

FIGURE 5.1 Median Ratio Change in per Capita Revenue Sources

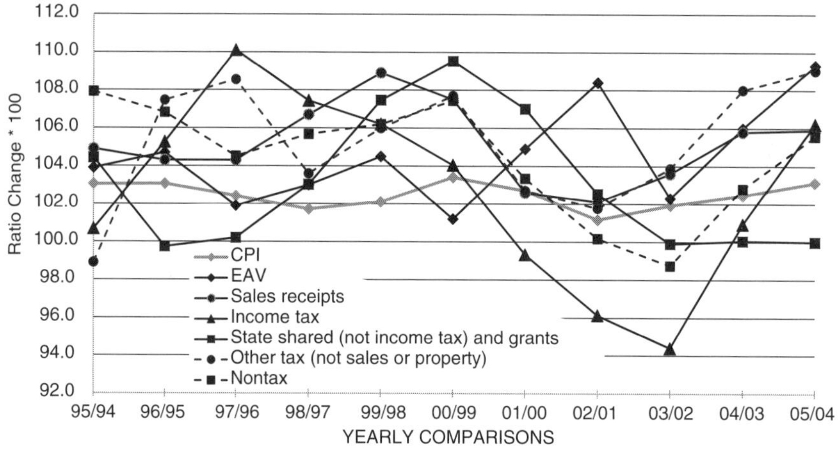

Note: Per capita values are not weighted by percent EAV.

three dashed lines represent nontax sources (fees and charges), other own-source tax sources (not sale or property tax), and state intergovernmental revenue (state-shared and grants) per capita excluding income tax.[2]

The figure shows that these governments were better off in the late 1990s than the early 2000s. The rate of increase in most revenues in the 1990s was significantly greater than the rate of increase in the CPI at this time. With the exception of EAV, the rate of increase in most revenues began to decline in 1999 up until 2002 or 2003 depending on the revenue. Income tax actually declined for three years consecutively beginning in 2000, increased modestly in 2003, and then surpassed the CPI in 2004. But income tax is only 10 percent of total revenue for the median municipal governments in the region, while sales taxes represent about 20 percent of own-source revenue. Recall from table 3.5 that income and especially sales tax reductions were often mentioned as primary sources of fiscal stress in the interviews, which is consistent with the trends shown here.

The increase in sales receipts and especially other taxes climbed beginning in 2002, and nontax sources of revenue increased beginning in 2003. Because changes in nontax and other tax sources of revenue are controlled in part by municipal governments when they alter tax rates and charges, it is likely that the governments initiated these increases in response to the recession as reported in the interviews and news reports.

Although the figure shows that many governments had recovered from the 2001 recession by 2005, the situation changed dramatically for them in the first six months of 2009 when sales receipts fell by a record $5.8 billion, or 11.5 percent, in the Chicago metropolitan region compared to the same period a year prior. This information was documented in a report by Melaniphy and Associates Inc. based on data released from the Illinois Department of Revenue as reported in the *Chicago Tribune* (Jones 2009). According to the report the decline ranks as the biggest percentage decrease in local retail sales in the region in at least twenty years. However, by September 2010, sales receipts increased in the Chicago region by 2.1 percent from the same period in 2009, according to a later report by Melaniphy and Associates (Jones 2010). The later report also noted that "no one is celebrating yet" due to the "snail's pace" of the rebound. Consistent with both reports, interviews in 2009, and news reports from that period, declines in sales taxes were particularly deep at that time. Many municipal governments also underestimated income and sales taxes, and some dramatically, for 2009 (FY 2009 or FY 2009–10), although some governments were expecting a slight increase in sales taxes in 2010.[3]

The higher rate of increase in state intergovernmental revenue that is not from income tax from 1997 to 2000 is another interesting trend in figure 5.1. Much of this trend is probably due to the massive infrastructure grant program initiated in 1999 by then governor Ryan. The grant program known as "Illinois First" distributed $6.3 billion to local governments in Illinois for investment in capital infrastructure. Consistent with the economic good times of the late 1990s, rates of increase in sales receipts, nontaxes, and other taxes were also getting larger from 1996 to 2001.

The unique story about the Great Recession for many local governments in the United States is the decline or expected decline in property taxes due to many residential and commercial foreclosures and, especially, declines in assessed value of property. These taxes are normally relatively immune from recessionary effects and are considered to be the most stable of all local taxes. According to the US Census of Governments for 2007, property taxes represent about 27 percent of own-source revenue (taxes and charges) for all municipalities in the United States, and only 9 percent of municipalities had no property taxes. Thus, it is probably accurate to say that most municipal governments rely to a great extent on property taxes to fund their operations, so the recessionary effects on local governments that began in 2008 or later could affect this important revenue stream for some time.

Indeed, as noted by Hoene and Pagano (2010) in their annual report on city fiscal conditions nationwide, the full effects of this recession on property tax revenues may not be seen until 2012. It takes time for assessments to catch up with market changes in most states, and Illinois is no different. In Illinois assessments are the responsibility of townships (coordinated by counties), and only one-third of the townships in each county are assessed each year. In addition, the state uses a three-year moving average to value assessments, which also delays and lessens market effects on assessed property values. However, foreclosures, weak home sales, a halt to commercial and residential development, and the tremendous increase in property tax appeals from all property owners have reduced property taxes and related revenue streams for many municipal governments in the Chicago region, as reported by the COGs in the 2009 interviews.

Weak home sales also have hit hard home rule municipal governments that rely on real estate transfer taxes, and the halt in development has hit municipal governments in the outer areas of the region harder than other parts of the region, especially those that were undergoing high levels of development prior to the recession. As discussed later in this chapter, high growth creates somewhat unique revenue and spending streams that will be radically disrupted when growth stops abruptly.

Similar to the nation as a whole, property tax for the median municipal government in the Chicago metropolitan region is about 25 percent of total revenue. Thus, future declines in assessed value could have profound effects on total revenues on top of the declines in sales and income taxes they have already experienced. However, Illinois municipalities are somewhat insulated from property tax changes due to changes in the assessed value because of how property tax is determined in the state. As discussed in chapter 4, property taxes are based on the total levy that local governments extend, not the rate, although non–home rule governments have maximum rate limits on particular services and spending purposes that do not exist for home rule governments. Indeed, several governments in the 2009 news reports claimed that their property tax rate had risen even though their tax levy remained below the non–home rule property tax constraints (PTELL).[4] The question is whether non–home rule and home rule governments will lower their tax levy in the future as assessed value shrinks to maintain the same tax burden or rate on property owners.

The degree of revenue decline is not the only financial challenge for municipal governments in Illinois during recessions. They must also deal with revenue uncertainty. This theme was not discussed much in the news reports, but interviewees often commented on this problem in the context of particular events. The most common event discussed here was property tax appeals, primarily from large commercial or office enterprises. Of the fourteen interviewees who discussed property tax appeals (see table 3.5), twelve of these noted that the appeals had a significant effect on their revenues and created anxiety about the level of property tax revenues they will receive from the county. The problem in another municipality was an inflation of EAV due to errors of classification of the property on the part of the county, but the effect on municipal revenues is the same as a property tax appeal.

Property tax appeals and errors in assessment are particularly onerous because compensation is retroactive. The county reduces the current year's property tax distribution to municipalities by the total revenue lost from multiple years of lowered EAV. One interviewed finance director noted, "We're getting banged on. Every municipality and taxing body is witnessing these appeals. We're getting hit by the PTAB [property tax appeals board] decisions, which are killing us, because they're going back two or three years. If we projected to bring in $4.1 million, it makes up about 25% of our overall revenue coming in, we might only get $3.5 because we just lost $300,000 on an appeals decision back a couple years." Another finance director noted, "The village has been hit very hard just recently because many of our major retailers in the mall appeal every year. It's a standard policy. They protest their taxes and their assessments through the county." A third finance director talked about the high transaction costs associated with property tax appeals because they "always have to send an attorney to fight for the city in these cases."

The current recession has produced even more property tax appeals than the earlier one because of the lag in assessed values relative to market values. Many property owners did not understand why their assessed value had not gone down, or even increased in 2008 and 2009, so they appealed. Many appeals must be resolved before the county can issue tax bills to their residents, which delays the county's collection and distribution of property tax revenue to local governments.

Lateness of revenue distributions from the state is another major source of revenue uncertainty for these governments, which had become particularly problematic by 2008 due to the state's fiscal crisis. Five of the interviewed governments in 2003 complained about delayed sales and telecommunications tax and grant payments from the state and its effect on their cash flow. Many interviewees in 2003 commented that revenue delays were worse due to the recession, and almost all interviewees from 2009 talked about a significant delay of revenues from the state of Illinois in the prior year.[5] Many municipalities also expressed a high level of uncertainty in 2003 about whether the state would reduce the municipal proportion of the state sales and income taxes to help balance the state's budget during the recession.[6] News reports and other sources indicate that these problems of delayed revenue and the threat of declines in state-shared revenue have become worse due to the state's current fiscal crisis and cash flow problems.

On the opportunity side, population growth and development is probably the biggest source of munificence for these governments. As one finance director noted about the effects of growth and the good times of the late 1990s, "We were living large. I mean we were having million dollar surpluses. The money was just rolling in buckets. We started to get a lot of political stuff in the paper about how the village was stashing way too much money away." Another opportunity many municipalities in the Chicago region have is a function of their "participation in the deep and diverse Chicago economic base." This is a standard refrain in Standard & Poor's assessment of the bond rating of Chicago suburban municipalities in their RatingsDirect research summaries, and seems to contribute to higher bond ratings for many governments in the region (www.standardandpoors.com/products-services/RatingsDirect-Global-Credit-Portal/en/us).

Fiscal Structure as a Contingency: The Curse and Promise of Sales Taxes

Although income tax represents a small percentage of total revenues in Chicago suburban municipal governments, at the median they experienced a 12.4 percent decrease in income tax between 2001 and 2004 according to figure 5.1. By comparison, the median municipality experienced less than .1 percent decrease in sales taxes at the lowest point between 2001 and 2002 (not shown in figure 5.1), yet sales tax decline was mentioned more often in the interviews as a significant source of fiscal stress. This is likely due to the fact that sales taxes comprise a larger percentage of total revenue in most municipalities than income tax. Mathematically, the effect of a 2 percent decline in sales taxes on a government that gets 40 percent of its revenue from this source will be bigger than the effect on a government that gets only 10 percent of its revenue from sales taxes. Similarly, a municipality with 40 percent of its revenue from sales taxes will get a bigger boost from a 2 percent increase in sales taxes than one with only 10 percent of its revenue from sales taxes. Another way of viewing this is that the volatility of sales receipts has a greater impact on municipalities that depend more on sales taxes.

Empirically, however, there is no correlation between percent of own-source revenue from sales taxes and change in own-source revenue among the Chicago municipalities for any years of data. Furthermore, municipalities with greater dependence on sales taxes were more likely to have lower levels of near-term stress as assessed from the interviews. These contrary effects may explain comments from interviewees in 2003 regarding significant increases and decreases in revenues as a result of changes in sales receipts due to the economy or the closing or opening of major retailers, especially dealerships that generate a significant amount of sales receipts for some governments. Dealerships were discussed in twenty-two of the sixty-two municipalities that were interviewed and in twenty-three municipalities in the news reports. Most valued them as revenue generators, courted them through incentives such as sales tax rebates, bemoaned their loss, or fretted about losing them. However, one municipality stated in the interview, "A lot of communities love car dealers in terms of the sale tax they produce, but give me a grocery store any day."

High sales-tax generators, whether it is dealerships, malls, or big box stores, present both opportunities and threats for municipalities. They offer opportunities to grow revenue, which is especially important if the government is not home rule and therefore limited in increasing property taxes or levying many of the taxes accessible to home rule communities. Discussions of commercial development in the news reports and interviews demonstrate the importance of high sales-tax generators to municipalities to improve the government's "economic picture" and "prevent deficits." Thirty governments reported using tax incentives, primarily sales tax rebates, in the news articles to attract or keep large commercial enterprises, and twenty-two governments reported the same in the interviews. Many governments interviewed also used other incentives to attract commerce such as special property classifications, tax rebates, or infrastructure improvements. But five municipalities in the news and interviews reported having a policy of not offering tax incentives to businesses under any circumstances. Most of these governments believed that their attractiveness as a location for commerce did not require them to offer such incentives.

More important, higher sales taxes provide municipalities an opportunity to export taxes to nonresidents and move away from the property tax. News reports about fourteen municipal governments document how sales taxes and commercial development allow them to rely less on the property tax. Reports about sixteen other governments document their financial and development objectives of moving their tax burden to nonresidents and the importance of "creating a tax base that no longer forces residential property owners to bear all the burden." As demonstrated here, sales taxes probably are the primary alternative to property taxes for most governments, but some governments, especially home rule ones, pursue a host of other taxes that export revenue burden to nonresidents. Some municipal interviewees did acknowledge the importance of having a diversified revenue structure more generally to combat national and local economic trends (and diversification of sales tax base also), but even here the value of diversification was discussed in the context of relying less on property taxes.

Moving revenue streams away from property tax toward taxes that can be exported to nonresidents makes particular sense for non–home rule governments where levy increases are limited. But why do home rule governments also pursue this objective so aggressively? First, residents are voters, and if taxes on them can be reduced or not increased while services are improved, then elected officials are more likely to get reelected. Second, property taxes and their burden may be more visible to property owners than other taxes. If you ask homeowners how much of their income they pay in property tax, most will know the answer. If you ask them how much of their income they pay in sales or utility taxes, most will not know the answer. Because sales and utility taxes are paid incrementally, taxpayers are unaware of the true rates or burden that these taxes place on them. Payment of property taxes, by comparison, is often in one or two lump sums, which makes these rates or burdens far more visible to taxpayers.

The third reason for pursuing sales taxes over property taxes is that the former is more agreeable to voters, as evidenced by the results of property and sales tax referendums put forward by non–home rule municipal governments in the region. In all elections from 2001 to 2006, thirty-eight sales tax and thirty-six property tax referendums were put forward by non–home rule municipalities (twenty-seven and twenty-two different governments, respectively). The property tax referendums were to raise the property tax levy or tax rates beyond the statutory limits, and the sales tax referendums were to initiate or raise non–home rule sales tax. With respect to the sales tax referendums, twenty-seven passed (71%) with an average rate of 60 percent yes votes. By comparison, only sixteen of the property tax referendums passed (44%), with an average rate of 47 percent yes votes. News reports about referendums in some municipalities also show that municipal officials emphasize the exportability of sales taxes to nonresidents in promoting sales tax referendums, which appears to be a successful marketing claim.

Consistent with these observations, governments in both the interviews and news reports often bragged about having no property taxes, or having the lowest rate compared to their neighbors or other governments with similar characteristics. These claims remind one of the fictitious town of Lake Wobegon, Minnesota, where all children are above average, and the frequency of claims demonstrates what economists refer to as *yardstick competition*. *Yardstick competition* occurs when governments compare their politics and practices to other governments, which appears to be common with property taxes (Kenyon 1997). The political sensitivity of property taxes is further demonstrated by the popularity of property tax rebates. Five municipalities in the news reports and interviews routinely abated property taxes to homeowners from operational surpluses with much fanfare from the mayor. Rebating property taxes makes sense for non–home rule communities that will lose future property taxes under the property tax levy limitations, if they reduce the property tax levy or rate, but this is not true for home rule communities. However, two of the five communities that rebated property taxes are home rule.

Although large sales-tax generators create benefits for municipal governments where such businesses are located, relying on sales taxes also threatens these governments' financial health due to the volatility and uncertainty of these revenues streams. Government officials from seventeen different governments in the news reports and interviews discuss the problem of being sales tax dependent and how this creates financial risks for them due to being vulnerable to economic downturns and the closing or moving of major retailers. Many government officials also acknowledged the risks of giving incentives in the form of tax expenditures to sales-tax generators because they may go out of business or move to other jurisdictions. In these cases the foregone taxes plus any infrastructure improvements made by the government to attract businesses may not equal the revenues generated during their time in the jurisdiction.

The finance director quoted earlier who likes the certainty of grocery stores over car dealerships also talked about the costs of tax incentive wars over dealerships in the following way: "I thank God I don't have to play that game. It's ridiculous. Up here it's [this community] versus [that community]. I think all of them are killing each other to get a car dealer to locate a block further north or south." Another government with a policy against offering tax incentives to commercial enterprises described the situation similarly: "Super Target, Kohl's, Home Depot, we joke we got the dancing stores. First they're going on [this community's side], and then they're going on [our] side. Then we deny them on [our] side, so they go back to [the other community] which can't get the development approved. So they're back in another spot on [our] side. It's back and forth, and you're chasing the same thing, sales tax."

Despite the sometimes intense competition among municipal governments to attract or retain commercial enterprises and the risks associated with relying on this revenue, most municipal governments appear to have concluded that these risks are worth the potential benefits. As discussed later in this chapter, competition for commercial enterprises and other development becomes more pronounced among growing municipalities and manifests in other ways, such as annexations. One interviewee from a growing community with annexable land described the problem of attracting commercial enterprises and diversifying the tax base in the following way: "The concern is that our neighboring communities are kind of in a race to gobble up as much land as possible before the other guy gets it. [This community] is looking to establish a retail center, right at our boundary agreement with them, at the southern part. Our concern is if they get that established, we will become [a] donut hole where there's so much retail all around us, that nothing will ever get built within our borders." Another growing community described the threat associated with not being competitive in attracting commercial enterprises in this way: "You're chasing the sales tax dollars. In our community, and of course in other communities, there's a logic that if you're going to have it on your border, you're foolish to think that it's not going to impact you, so why not control it and get value from it."

The boom-and-bust effect of sales taxes on municipal governments that depend highly on these revenue sources may explain comments by interviewees in 2009 that it is these municipalities that appeared to be most affected by the 2008–9 recession. As explained more in chapter 6, many governments that depend heavily on sales taxes maintain higher reserves to compensate for the volatility of their revenue, but the reserves were used up in 2008. As a result, these governments faced big cuts to balance their budgets in 2009 and 2010. One interviewee in 2009 noted that poorer municipalities and those less dependent on sales tax did not really become "used to having a lot of money," as did wealthier governments that are more dependent on sales taxes. In 2010, Schaumburg, which relied on sales taxes for 60 percent of its own-source revenue in 2006, imposed its first municipal property tax in its fifty-three-year history to solve its financial problems with the Great Recession.

Home Rule and Tax Caps as a Contingency: It's Not Just about Revenues

As discussed in chapters 2 and 4, home rule privileges in Illinois greatly affect the size of the government's fiscal toolbox. It expands their ability to collect additional sales taxes beyond the state shared rate and increases options to export revenues through the real estate transfer tax (to buyers), the hotel-motel tax, and other entertainment taxes. Due to PTELL, non–home rule governments cannot increase their property tax levy by more than 5 percent or the rate of inflation, whichever is less, and they have specific property tax rate limits for seventy-five different services and funding areas, including the general fund.[7] Non–home rule governments also have limited ability to issue GO debt, impose impact fees on developers, enter into agreements with contractors and other governments, and impose many regulations (e.g., property maintenance; see chapter 2).

The effect of home rule on fiscal policies and practices will be examined in more detail in chapter 6, but it will be useful to assess some of the effects of this exogenous condition on financial strategies and the municipal toolbox in the context of critical fiscal threats and opportunities. With respect to changes in revenues, many non–home rule municipalities in Illinois are limited in their use of and reliance on property taxes to fund services as compared with home rule governments.

A study by Dye and McGuire (1997) on the effects of PTELL in the six counties in the Chicago metropolitan area shows the dramatic effects of the new law on tax revenues in municipalities and other local governments. Comparing per capita and total tax rate changes in local governments in Cook County, which were not subject to PTELL in 1991, and the other five counties in the metropolitan region, which were subject to PTELL beginning on that date, shows a tremendous decline in total property taxes in the capped counties after 1991.[8] But from 1991 to just before 1993, the growth in property taxes remained the same for municipalities and school districts in Cook County and the capped counties. Also interesting is that the growth rate in the capped counties prior to 1991 when they were not capped was much higher than Cook County (14.6% and 9%, respectively) that did not become capped until 1994.

Figure 5.2 shows the median ratio for change in total property taxes and property taxes per capita for home rule and non–home rule municipal governments in the

FIGURE 5.2 Median Ratio Change in Total Property Taxes and Property Taxes per Capita for Home Rule and Non–Home Rule Municipalities

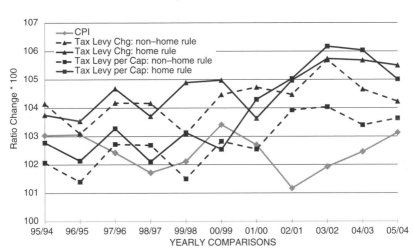

Note: Per capita values are not weighted by percent EAV.

Chicago region between 1994 and 2006, with the CPI for comparison.[9] The figure shows there is little systematic difference between home rule and non–home rule governments until after the recession of 2001–2 when property taxes increased at a slightly faster rate for home rule governments. However, the rate of increase in property taxes in both home rule and non–home rule governments is faster than the rate of increase in the CPI (inflation) after 2000, which demonstrates the extent to which property taxes in Illinois are immune to recessions due to the focus on levies and not rates to determine property taxes collected. The consistently higher values of change in total property taxes compared to per capita values, especially for non–home rule governments, reflect the fact that new growth is exempt from property tax caps, which allows the overall levy to grow far above the CPI rate in these governments.

One reason for the similarity in rates of increase in property taxes between home rule and non–home rule governments is apparent from the interviews and news reports. Of the twenty-eight home rule communities interviewed, ten claimed to operate as if they are not home rule with respect to levy increases. These governments are a mix of wealthy, poor, large, small, residential, and commercial, which suggests that this strategy is not exclusive to home rule governments that have access to other revenue sources and therefore can afford not to raise property taxes.

Consistent with the lack of success of property tax referenda, voters' attitude toward property taxes is evident from news reports about governments that are trying to become home rule through referendum. Whether home rule passes depends on voters' trust that government will not abuse home rule privileges by raising property taxes or debt that must be guaranteed by property tax. One way these governments gain this trust is to promise "fidelity to property tax caps" as claimed by officials in six of the municipal governments that went to referendum during the time period examined. Consistent with the success of sales tax referenda, governments also argue that being home rule allows them to raise taxes that can be exported to nonresidents, and many promise to dedicate new home rule tax revenues to particular purposes.

Surveys of home rule municipalities in Illinois in 1983 and 2002 by James Banovetz (2002) also shows that municipalities generally did not use home rule powers to levy higher property taxes in either 2002 or 1983. Only 18 percent and 16 percent of respondents, respectively, reported using home rule for this purpose. By comparison, 57 percent of the municipalities reported levying other home rule taxes in the first survey, and 83 percent reported doing so in 2002. The most common home rule taxes levied in 2002 were sales taxes and hotel/motel taxes (60% for both), but only 5 percent and 35 percent reported levying a home rule sales and a hotel/motel tax, respectively, in 1983. In fact, use of all home rule taxing privileges other than for increasing property taxes was reported to be much greater in 2002 than 1983.

Responses to these surveys suggest that home rule governments have taken advantage of their status to diversify their revenue beyond the property tax since 1983. These effects were articulated in more detail in both the interviews and, to some extent, the news reports. As one official noted, "There are other advantages [to home rule], not necessarily just in taxes, but legislatively, that allow home rule communities to function more efficiently." Another official from a very wealthy but small municipality stated, "Well I think it [home rule] gives you flexibility to do things. There was a period of time when we weren't home rule. We had financial troubles, and the home rule gave us the flexibility to solve those problems." Still another official from one of the poorest municipalities in the region commented, "Home rule has given the board and the mayor autonomy to use creative means and methods to maintain [fiscal solvency], and more autonomy to do innovative, legal things, things they wouldn't be able to do if we weren't home rule. Without home rule they would have to use templates to resolve problems."

Of the municipalities that were not home rule at the time of the interview, officials in three that are fairly wealthy stated that they were managing well without increased home rule revenue privileges, but one saw significant threats on the horizon to their financial condition due to the property tax levy being consumed by increasing pension and health care costs. Three other wealthy municipal governments, two of which were interviewed, ran very high-profile campaigns either before or after 2003 to pass referendums for home rule. All three were facing financial problems at the time, but two of the governments focused their arguments for home rule on nonrevenue privileges, such as home rule governments not having to comply with the state affordable housing mandate. The referendums passed in both of these municipalities, but not in the other municipality that emphasized raising the sales tax to take advantage of non-residents shopping in their many commercial enterprises. Four of the poorer non–home rule governments interviewed talked about tax caps and lack of home rule as having a terrible effect on them and as being a big disaster financially and their biggest source of fiscal stress. The high-growth municipalities that were not home rule at the time of the interview talked about it mostly in terms of having limited abilities to issue contracts with developers and impact fees (except through annexation), impose property regulations, and facilitate economic development.

Several other municipalities talked about the problems of not being home rule more from an operational level. When asked why a home rule referendum recently passed in their municipality, the finance director commented on the constraints posed by having separate levies for different services. "There are a lot of sharp professional people here [on the board and in town]. [Passing the referendum for home rule] wasn't very controversial. If you're not home rule you have to dedicate that money to tourism, or promoting of this kind of thing or that kind of thing. If you are home rule that [revenue] just goes into the coffers, and you can use it for anything." This official said the board thought the earmarking was "kind of silly" and that home rule better fit their approach to governing and operating. Another finance director from a much poorer and more blue-collar municipality noted that "the board is less frustrated by [lack of home rule] than the staff is, because they don't see [the problems] as much as we do."

Lack of home rule also creates challenges for municipal governments issuing GO debt. Because property tax is the pledge for GO debt in Illinois, PTELL tax caps on levy increases in non–home rule governments also limit their ability to issue GO debt. According to state statute, estimated repayment of GO debt (debt service) cannot increase the tax levy beyond what existed to repay debt at the time PTELL was adopted by or imposed on the county. Thus if a non–home rule government wants to issue GO debt beyond the PTELL level, then it must do so through referendum. In this case, a non–home rule government that had higher GO debt at the time PTELL took effect would have more flexibility in issuing GO debt in the future than a government that had little GO debt prior to adoption of PTELL. It also means that non–home rule governments, especially those with lower credit quality, will have to resort to other types of bonds that often impose higher costs on the government. Several finance directors talked about this problem, and one believed it contributed significantly to an even lower bond rating for their government. Such problems beg the question of whether being non–home rule leads to other inefficiencies and transaction costs that increase the cost of providing municipal services and solving financial problems for these governments.

The PTELL statute that governs GO debt also has a provision that exempts debt service from PTELL rate limits in some cases. This provision was discussed in interviews with five non–home rule communities who used accounting and debt abatement practices to maximize their access to GO debt: "Abate debt service, not property taxes because it doesn't go against your tax cap calculations [levy limits]." One government referred to the provision as creating the opportunity for a backdoor referendum to increase debt and higher property tax liability. Another somewhat popular strategy for dealing with the constraints of tax caps is to always raise your levy to the maximum, "even if you don't need it. You never leave dollars on the table because it doesn't go back into the next year's compilations."

The evidence presented here demonstrates the extent to which being home rule in Illinois broadens municipalities' options for solving financial problems, especially on the revenue side of the financial toolbox. As a result of limitations on their financial toolbox, non-home rule governments seem to engage in and develop more creative strategies for handling their fiscal problems. As described in chapter 3, being strategic with respect to financial condition is about positioning the government to be financially successful. In this case, many non-home rule governments appear to make decisions that maximize their financial options within the smaller toolbox. But governments also position themselves to satisfy voters, which often leads to revenue choices that put the government at greater risk of financial success. Another general observation about revenue decisions in response to fiscal threats and opportunities is that municipalities with home rule status appear to be less revenue driven than non-home rule governments, where revenue seems to be the anchor around which spending and other financial decisions must orbit.

Threats and Opportunities on the Spending and Cost Side

What sources of fiscal threats and opportunities exist for municipal governments in the region on the spending and cost side as reported in the interviews and news reports? Most municipalities interviewed mentioned pensions as a source of current or future fiscal stress and of concern (forty-four municipalities according to table 3.5), but ten of these indicated that their pension funds were fully funded in 2003 due to conservative investing that avoided the precipitous drop in the stock market in the years just prior to the interviews. Five more municipalities indicated that their pensions were fully funded prior to the bear market in 2000 to 2002. Several other municipalities noted that their unfunded pension obligations were not significant due to the age of police and fire employees and the relatively few current retirees. More recent interviews, however, noted that declines in pension worth seemed to be a bigger problem in 2008 than in 2000 to 2002, given that these investments have experienced two strong bear markets in seven years, with the second being slightly more severe in terms of percent decline in the Dow Jones Industrial Average than the first (Ritholtz 2009).

However, investment losses were not the only source of pension problems for those interviewed in 2003 and 2009. As noted by eight interviewees and news reports in different municipalities, the state had increased police and fire retirement benefits just prior to 2003, which increased local government obligations to these funds. Several interviewees in governments without home rule noted that this mandate was particularly threatening to them because they have fewer revenue options and are constrained by PTELL from increasing property taxes to fund these new obligations. Since then, the state of Illinois has continued to increase pension benefits for local public safety employees, making this the greatest source of fiscal stress mentioned in the 2009 interviews, just behind declines in revenue.

To the extent that pension liabilities increase due to mandates or the declining value of investments, services currently funded by the property tax in non–home rule governments must now be funded from other sources. In this case, pension obligations will continue to take up greater proportions of the total property tax levy than they did in the past in these governments. As one interviewee noted, "When we have to double our pension levy, it [spending for other services] has got to come out of other revenue sources. At some point, you may have to give up police officers to pay for the remaining officers' pensions." Reports from both the Civic Federation (2009) and the Illinois Municipal League (2007) note these trends in the governments they examined. Another demonstration of the effects of pension increases on dedication of property tax revenue over time is observed from Villa Park's six-month analysis of revenues and spending in 2009. This document shows that retirement as a percentage of property tax levy was 22.2 percent in 1996, but increased to 39.5 percent by 2009.[10]

The other significant source of mandates that affect the finances of municipalities in the Chicago metropolitan region is the Environmental Protection Agency (EPA—US and Illinois). In conjunction with the Metropolitan Water Reclamation District (established in 1989), all three agencies issue numerous mandates that affect water and sewer services and infrastructure construction in the region. They also have significant oversight of municipal actions in these areas and sometimes file lawsuits against municipalities that do not comply with regulations and orders.

These threats go hand in hand with the flooding problems experienced in many municipalities in the region primarily due to poor drainage and management of storm water and sanitary sewers rather than the flooding of waterways. However, the Fox River that runs north and south through many suburbs on the western side of the region sometimes floods, which creates financial problems for these municipalities. Flooding and attendant problems of pollution of drinking water were mentioned together in fifty-two different municipalities in the news reports, and eight interviewees discussed problems with flooding, although only a few of these mentioned it as a significant source of fiscal stress.

However, the costs of dealing with flooding as noted in the news reports, even in small communities, are often in the millions and are funded primarily through debt (general obligation and revenue bonds), special service area assessments, and TIF property improvements. Thus dealing with flooding and drainage can create significant obligations for current and future revenue streams. Reported impacts of flooding on citizens is often thousands of dollars of damage to many homes, and mayors often publicize their accomplishments in reducing and controlling flooding in their jurisdictions, especially during elections.

Thus it is not surprising that many municipal governments in the region have significant water and sewer (sanitary) enterprises that account for or precipitate many financial decisions. The financial condition of these funds was sometimes reported by interviewees in 2003 to be worse than governmental funds, but they were most often reported to be in better shape. Also the news reports and interviews revealed that many municipalities sell water to other municipalities, which sometimes subsidizes their operating funds. According to the quantitative data for 2005, water and sewer activities comprise approximately 18 percent of the total budget of these governments on average, and over 25 percent of the total budget in one-fourth of the municipalities in the region.

Increasing insurance rates was another significant spending threat discussed in the news reports and interviews for 2003. Of the sixty-one and forty-eight municipalities in the news reports and interviews respectively that claimed higher insurance costs were a major source of fiscal stress (see tables 3.5 and 3.6), most focused on health insurance. However, increases in liability insurance were also mentioned quite often, due to major losses in the insurance industry, including the events of 9/11, that were somewhat unique to this time period. Many governments in the interviews also noted that health insurance increases were a constant problem for them and had been especially significant in the years prior to 2003, with 25 percent to 50 percent increases in costs. The following phrases were used to describe health insurance increases and their effects on government finances: "going to kill this community," "been brutal for the last few years," "primary cause of fiscal problems," "gone berserk recently," and "will drive you up a wall."

Lawsuits

Lawsuits are another significant financial threat that deserves special mention. Lawsuits were identified as problems for eighty-one different municipal government in the news reports, and fourteen of these incidents are associated with fiscal stress according to the qualitative coding scheme in appendix 5. Lawsuits were mentioned by interviewees in fifteen different municipalities and, of these, five indicated they were a significant source of fiscal stress. Analyses of lawsuits from both the news reports and interviews show a variety of causes, many of which can be classified into three categories.[11]

First are work-related lawsuits, such those associated with the death or serious injury of a municipal employee while on the job or actions by employees that kill, hurt, or offend someone else (e.g., charges of racism and sexual harassment). Second, many lawsuits are related to development and growth in municipalities. Indeed, almost half of the eighty-one references to lawsuits in the news reports are linked with one of the development and growth codes in appendix 5. Among these codes, lawsuits are associated most with goals disputes, usually involving developers but also residents and other local governments. Development and growth lawsuits are associated more with commercial than residential development and are sometimes linked to annexations and TIFs. These lawsuits also arise from intergovernmental agreements or contracts (regarding TIFs, water provision, drainage, and sewers), problems with drainage and sewerage, underfunded pensions, and insurance.

Last, many lawsuits involve political conflict between government officials. Usually the lawsuits are between elected officials (e.g., mayor versus board or between board members) but also occur between elected and appointed officials (village manager or department head versus elected official or municipal government). In fact, lawsuits are associated more with the politics and governance codes in the news reports (especially political conflict) than with work and growth or development codes combined. Of course, news reports are likely to focus on political conflict to a greater extent than other topics affecting municipal financing and governance, but the extent to which political conflict involves lawsuits is noteworthy. Particularly striking examples of such lawsuits covered in the news reports during the period of time examined occurred in the villages of Barrington and Wadsworth, where the mayors of both towns (or reported allies of the mayor) were involved in several simultaneous lawsuits with board members at different periods of time. Most cases of politically driven lawsuits can be thought of as a by-product or a type of spillover cost from political conflict, which is discussed in more detail later in this chapter.

Costs of lawsuits can involve monetary settlements, but municipalities are often insured for these events, especially if they are work related (e.g. workers' compensation). However, dealing with lawsuits—either successfully or not—creates significant transaction costs for municipalities usually in the form of legal and lawyer fees, which are in addition to insurance (risk) costs. A news report in March 2005 indicated that Bensenville, with a budget of $19.3 million, spent more than $1 million a year in legal fees, not including its protracted legal fights with the City of Chicago over O'Hare Airport. "At any [board] meeting you will have as many as seven attorneys present and no fewer than two. The village is suing the Illinois Insurance Commission, the Bensenville Park District, the police, firefighters, an attorney, scores of local business and residents too" (*Daily Herald* 2005). In 2001, village officials in Antioch warned that "residents could face up to $20,000 in individual property assessments to pay off legal fees if the massive Neumann Homes development is rejected (*News Sun* 2001). News reports in 2005 of South Barrington's ($4 million budget) legal battles with developers also note the following: "In just two years, the attorney bills mounted to more than $1 million, a figure current board officials blame for last year's property tax hike of nearly 36 percent, to nearly 60 cents per $100 of assessed valuation. The jump was one of the steepest in the Northwest suburbs" (Ryan 2005).

Political Conflict

Even if political conflict does not generate lawsuits between government officials, it creates other negative spillovers that increase the transaction costs of delivering services and doing business with the government and thus poses a threat to municipal finances. These spillovers are a particular problem in municipalities undergoing development or trying to collaborate with others. High levels of political conflict between government officials, referred to as the "crazy period" of infighting by one interviewee, can slow policymaking decisions and focus attention on the conflict to the exclusion of other concerns. It can also make government dysfunctional. The news reports contain many editorials about different municipalities that call for compromise between government officials to restore a sense of professionalism to the government and to "end the infighting that sometimes has paralyzed the City Council" (Flynn 2005).

Close examination of the news reports shows concern about the transaction costs of political conflict. For instance, in 2005 the Village of East Dundee was reported to be a party in the "Cambridge fiasco," which involved a 432-home subdivision in which developers pulled the plug because of a conflict between a new president and board members (Carr 2005). One board member "felt there wasn't a true team effort going on between the board, administration and staff," and that "village trustees were not involved in the planning or negotiations with Cambridge" because the board "didn't have all their oars in the water, yet alone rowing in the same direction" (Elejalde-Ruiz 2005a). Conflict in the Village of Island Lake in the same year notes the struggle "to get village business on track." "The constant quarrels meant that the monthly list of agenda items grew like a weekly grocery list. Nothing was getting done. Sometimes it felt there were arguments just to prevent the village from getting things done." Although the board managed to approve a 222-home subdivision, the plan "nearly got buried in the bickering" (Kuczka 2005).

Although pull factors are often the reason appointed local government officials change jobs, the effects of conflict as a push factor on turnover of administrative and elected officials is well documented in the literature (McCabe et al. 2008). Whitaker and DeHoog (1991) and DeHoog and Whitaker (1990) found strong evidence of city manager turnover due to political conflict between elected officials or between elected officials and the city manager in their qualitative study of 133 municipalities in Florida. Feiock and Stream (2002) show that turnover of managers is more likely when there is council turnover. Using survey data from the International City/County Management Association, findings from Clingermayer and Feiock (2001) suggest that turnover reduces long-term commitments and shortens the time horizon of fiscal policy decisions. This is likely to reduce planning for capital spending, economic development, and other areas of financial policy and practice, and it will hamper consistent implementation of strategies in these areas. In addition, the uncertainty (risk) created by political conflict will increase the costs of dealing with a government and establishing agreements with it (transaction costs). These problems will decrease the likelihood of establishing and maintaining long-term arrangements between the municipality and other parties such as developers, contractors, and even other governments.

Political conflict that results in turnover of city or village administrators or managers will also make it more difficult to hire qualified persons to replace individuals who leave. For instance, the Village of Oak Brook, a well-known Chicago suburb, lost its manager in late 2003 due to "the deteriorating relationship between the village board and staff," as noted by the village president, and that relationship "is [also] hampering the search for a new village manager." "There's fairly common knowledge in the DuPage [County] area that we've got some problems here." The fact that only twenty-one people had applied for the post at that time surprised industry experts, who expected the number of applicants to be "more in the area of 40 or 50" (Groark 2002).

Political conflict and turnover occur in governments in all sampling categories of interviewed governments in appendix 2 and groupings of all governments in the Chicago region in appendix 7 but are very prevalent in governments that are growing and developing. News reports and interviews demonstrate the extent to which rapid growth and development can generate political conflict about the future of the community and how to achieve that vision. Growth and development can also generate conflict over the governing roles of elected and appointed officials. Conflict over roles often exemplifies broader disagreements among officials and voters over whether their governing institutions should be closer to the political or corporate end of the continuum shown in table 4.2. Such disagreements seem to be a normal part of the process of adapting their fiscal and governing structure to these physical and financial changes.

Often described as "growing pains" in the news reports, there is much documentation of board turnover in developing municipalities as voters attempt to elect new board members to reduce conflict, create better planning for development, and increase diplomacy with developers and other external parties. Some news reports note the chilling effects of board conflict and indecision on commercial development, and the level of concern in communities that increasing board conflict will create such problems for them in the future. Noteworthy examples of these problems in the early 2000s occurred in the villages of Plainfield, Marengo, Mokena, Carpentersville, Hoffman Estates, Matteson, and Wadsworth.

Of the fifty-one municipal governments in the sixtieth percentile of population growth between 2000 and 2005 in the Chicago metropolitan area, thirty-five have statements coded as goals disputes in the news reports. Most statements demonstrate disagreements between elected officials, candidates for election, and residents over the level of commercial and residential development. Many residents want to limit development to maintain a rural character, but fighting development is often costly and not successful. Other factions want to promote different residential and commercial mixes, believing that not having commercial development within their boundaries and not controlling growth in nearby unincorporated areas will depress or even threaten the future financial condition of the government. Not surprisingly, these disagreements will manifest as election challenges and turnover in administrators and elected officials in such governments.

Conflict is also very discernable between government officials in high-growing municipalities as their approach to governance shifts from political to corporate, especially with respect to the issues of whether to hire a CAO and the role of elected and appointed officials. Examining the available history in news reports and interviews of municipalities who are beginning to experience growth or who realize they are in the path of the growth machine show they indeed wrestle with whether to hire their first CAO, what role that person will have, and whether the person will be a professional or political appointee. However, once the town hires its first CAO, the transition may not be smooth. The town may continue to debate the necessity of such a costly employee, choose to leave the position vacant for an extended period of time, or combine the position with another department head to save money. Mayors who are retired from their regular jobs often argue and demonstrate they have the period to devote to dealing with growth and development, but the strain on elected officials without an administrator during this period is very evident.

The usual evolutionary path of municipal governance in rural jurisdictions that experience growth and development is that governments without a CAO (mayor only) eventually retain a full-time CAO. Most then hire an assistant CAO or director of community or economic development to focus on managing the growth and development. Unless the municipality remains small, almost all municipalities will eventually hire a finance director, as is evident from comparing the fiscal governing structures of governments that are in early stages of growth to those in latter stages. However, conflict over the role of the CAO and mayor may still exist after the municipality has been built out. Even in governments where a council-manager form is established by ordinance or referendum, it does not prevent elected officials in such governments from behaving as if they have a council-mayor form, which leads to political conflict and turnover of staff.

Citizens in at least three governments in the Chicago region successfully passed referenda that required their governments to adopt a managerial form due to problems of political conflict and the desire to reduce political control over administrative decisions.[12] However, that did not dissuade the mayors in two interviewed municipalities from sponsoring future referenda to revert back to the mayoral form, or board members in Maywood, where no interview occurred, from attempting to override the village manager's decisions or policies and authority to appoint departmental heads. Several news reports and editorials in 2005 about Maywood also documented board members' efforts to influence departmental operations and how this affected financial condition and operations. One finance director, who left Maywood in August 2005, explained the reasons for her departure to the news in much detail. She discussed the disputes over governing roles between elected and appointed officials in the municipality and how this led to staff turnover, reduced revenue, and higher service costs (Pollard 2005; *Westchester Herald* 2005).

Coded news segments on political conflict in eighty-three different municipalities show a great deal of tension over the adoption and maintenance of political versus corporate/administrative institutional features associated with the roles, responsibility, and authority of elected officials and the CAO in governments irrespective of level of growth and development. Statements coded for either political or corporate governance according to whether they demonstrate characteristics on either side of the continuum in table 4.2 show that conflict and struggle often exists within governments over the values and expectations represented on each side of the continuum. Turnover of appointed officials, especially the election rebound described in chapter 3, may move a corporate government more toward the political end of the continuum for a period of time until a new set of board members moves the government back toward the corporate end.

Growth and Development

Previous discussions in this chapter have described some of the opportunities and challenges municipalities face when the growth machine arrives. There are opportunities for political gain by elected officials, and both opportunities and challenges for securing the government's financial future. Often, municipalities cannot prevent growth from happening within their boundaries. Rather, they can only control it to some degree and manage it in such a way that it yields more benefits for the government and citizens than costs. They have even less control over growth and development outside of their boundaries unless the land is unincorporated and they can annex. All of this requires government officials to be proactive and strategic, both managerially and competitively, to avoid financial pitfalls and with respect to what other governments are doing to advance desirable growth and development within their boundaries. It also requires them to have a vision for the future, the time horizon to plan for and implement long-term strategies, and enough entrepreneurialism and administrative capital to identify and successfully exploit opportunities that come along.

One might say that rapid growth and development create a different set of threats and opportunities for governments compared to those that are built out or not undergoing major development or redevelopment. Each situation requires a different set of governing and financial strategies (tools from the toolbox) to be successful overall and to maintain government financial condition in the short run and long run. Many governments that are experiencing rapid growth and development are small and rural and may not have the administrative or fiscal capacity to deal with these pressures. These governments must adapt to a new environment, which often requires fundamental changes to their governing institutions to make them more supportive of sustained and strategic approaches to managing growth and development.

The interviews and news reports suggest four stages or phases of growth and development with respect to the types of financial threats and opportunities governments face and the kinds of economic development strategies they pursue to retain long-term financial condition. These phases are loosely described as *growth initiation* in which a sleepy town is awakened to residential developers knocking at their door, and it becomes evident the jurisdiction is in the path of future growth. Under *rapid growth* municipalities are adding residents and sometimes commercial enterprises at a high rate through development of existing land and annexation in conjunction with agreements with developers and other governments. In the third phase, *built out,* the growth rate declines and municipalities anticipate the day when they have no room to annex and few undeveloped parcels of land. The last phase of *redevelopment* occurs when governments are not adding population, or where population is declining, and most new development is on previously developed land. To some extent, the last phase is not mutually exclusive with the others because governments that are in the process of rapid growth or being built out may be redeveloping significant portions of the jurisdiction, especially downtown areas.

Reading portions of the news reports and interview transcripts that deal with growth and development, the concept of a growth machine seems very descriptive of events in some municipalities. Molotch (1976) first proposed this term to describe the coalition of government officials and local business elites that promote and pursue economic development within a jurisdiction. He described the growth machine as hegemonic over local politics almost to the exclusion of other concerns, which often leads to clashes between pro-growth (businesses) and anti-growth sentiments (residents) among constituents. His claims of hegemony may oversimplify policymaking in many governments and not apply to others. But the qualitative evidence examined here shows that governments that are experiencing growth initiation or rapid growth can be inundated with development pressures and incentives and that business interests are often central to their policymaking and politics.

Separating Chicago suburban municipalities into the four categories of growth identified here to examine the threats and opportunities they face is not possible, but the municipalities as categorized in appendix 7 can be used to examine municipal governments in growth initiation or the early stages of rapid growth versus those in later stages of rapid growth or those in early stages of being built out. Governments in the first category are smaller and tend to be rural and in the outer ring of the region. Those in the second category are larger and more likely to exist in the middle ring of the region.

Growth Initiation and Rapid Growth

Unfortunately, there are few news reports of municipalities in the early stages of growth initiation, as their small size deters reporting. Also prior studies of development tend to focus on governments that are in the last two rather than the first two phases of growth (Peterson 1981; Schneider 1992; Clingermayer and Feiock 2001). But what news reports that do exist focus on the political conflict that growth initiation creates. Also no interviewed governments could be characterized as experiencing growth initiation, but some officials did talk about it retrospectively from what they remember or what was generally accepted as historical record in their municipalities. The comments tend to focus on residential development happening first, the government not being prepared to deal with growth administratively, and not controlling events according to municipal interests, especially in dealing with developers. One interviewee commented that the developers are sometimes "like amateurs, they just don't know how to pull all their facts together." Another interviewee, however, described dealing with developers in an entirely different way.

> The developer probably knows a lot more about your community than you do most of the time. They not only understand the economic, they understand the social aspect. So when the developer approaches a community, they know pretty much what they're getting into. And this one developer, he understands our infrastructure history. So it's not really like oh my God you don't have water. They're like okay you need water, that will be another $200,000, you need a sewer, that's another $1.5. They also know the more economically feasible ways of making it happen, and they're tied into everybody. They're tied into the state. They understand the processes and procedures to get funding. They understand that we necessarily don't have the staff to do the research. In fact we had one developer said hey you guys can get a grant, they got the grant. We had an engineer who came in and said hey, there's a street and road grant that you guys are possibly eligible for based on your socio-economic condition. Six months later they had 3 something million-dollar grant for our street.

As residential development increases, municipalities need to be much more proactive and strategic about their financial future than they have been in the past. The quality of residential development and other factors such as housing density and balance with commercial or industrial land uses will determine future revenue and spending streams, fiscal structure, and, ultimately, the long-term financial condition of these municipalities. These governments will need sustained strategies for controlling and directing growth if they are to obtain the future they envision and maintain financial strength. This assumes, however, that most stakeholders agree on what the future looks like. Disagreement over this vision often creates enormous political conflict among elected officials and constituents.

To use the metaphor of strategic planning, municipalities will need an agreed-upon vision of what their community will look like after growth and development to increase the chances of achieving these outcomes rather than outcomes that generate more costs than benefits for the government. Governments have particular physical characteristics that will affect the kinds of development that is likely to occur within their boundaries, and they have administrative or governing strengths and weaknesses that will affect their ability to intervene in the development process. Governments facing growth will need to reasonably assess their strengths and weaknesses and the challenges and opportunities that growth brings to the municipality in order to devise successful strategies for managing it and achieving financial objectives. As growth initiation moves into the next phase of rapid growth, municipalities will need to monitor the environment continuously and adjust strategies accordingly, as conditions often change quickly at this time. More generally, the government must be supportive of strategy making during rapid growth and implementation of strategies across the first two phases.

Examining governments in categories A, B3, B4, and E in appendix 7 that exhibited high growth between 2000 and 2005 (or between 1995 and 2000) and that are small or were very small prior to high growth shows some common challenges (n = 33).[13] Many governments in this group recognized the need for comprehensive growth and land use plans, and some acknowledged that planning for growth and development must account for future revenue and spending streams, the capacity of government to handle growth, and how new capital infrastructure will be financed.

Of the four governments interviewed in this group (population 4,000 to 7,000), three had professional CAOs, and two of these three also had a finance director. Both the news reports and interviews indicate that growth was managed in a proactive manner in all three cases. These governments engaged in planning for growth using strategic planning and/or developing or updating their comprehensive plan, and they assessed conditions to inform courses of action using tools such as citizen focus groups, marketing studies for economic development, or surveys of businesses. They also developed and implemented strategies in anticipation of growth, such as building infrastructure prior to development or establishing zoning and building standards in line with their vision and position in the development market.

Table 5.1 shows other strategic issues and goals of a financial nature regarding growth and development that were evident from the news reports on this group of thirty-three municipalities. The table also shows problems and solutions that are associated with these issues and goals.[14] One strategy, intermunicipal boundary agreements, is particularly noteworthy here because of its frequency in both the news reports and interviews. All seven governments interviewed with population growth greater than 30 percent between 2000 and 2006 discussed the significance and role of boundary agreements to their development strategy. News reports on thirty-two different municipal

TABLE 5.1 Development-Growth Issues in Small and Very Small, High-Growth Municipalities: Initiation and Early Rapid Growth (n = 33)

Strategic Financial Issues and Goals	Problems and Solutions
Bring in more commerce to offset residential	▾ Higher competition with neighbors ▾ Diversify revenue to be less dependent on property taxes in the future ▾ Being a "donut hole" with retail in neighboring towns with no room for commerce within own boundaries; becoming a bedroom community ▾ "Too many municipalities fail to understand the dynamics of rapid growth until too late and find they are not much more than a place where residents sleep, eat, and overburden districts and other services."
Pursue boundary agreements and coordinate developer rates (impact and building fees) and standards with neighboring governments	▾ Reduces *competition* by limiting annexation, land use, and the ability of developers to "play off one town against another" ▾ Reduces *transaction costs* by lessening disputes with other municipalities over annexation (border wars) and the need for negotiation with neighboring and overlapping jurisdictions over development ▾ Reduces unwanted *spillovers* from neighboring jurisdictions (e.g., traffic)
Annexation	▾ "Gobble up more land before the other guy gets it." ▾ Development and land use control in unincorporated areas nearby to obtain control, reduce negative spillovers, and gain benefits ▾ Greater revenue from annexed areas but higher service needs, especially capital infrastructure (unless private well and septic)
How to finance growth and meet new service needs	▾ Determine charges, impact fees, and in-kind payments on developments and mix of private/public responsibility (e.g., roads in new subdivision) to reduce impact of growth on existing residents and businesses ("development should pay for itself") ▾ Anticipate upgrades to major service systems (esp. water, sewer, and roads) so not overwhelmed, and ensure adequate systems are installed ▾ Increased transactions with developers regarding annexation and infrastructure agreements ▾ Monitor the quality of developers' work and compliance with contracts
Increase opportunities by changing the financing rules	▾ Pursue home rule via referendum ▾ Referenda to alter non–home rule rate limits ▾ Special census
Increasing the capacity of government to attract commerce and manage growth	▾ Hire development director (community or economic) ▾ Create economic development corporation ▾ Hire a CAO ▾ Hire staff or contract for legal, engineering, permits, and inspections to handle increasing workload

TABLE 5.1 *(Continued)*

Strategic Financial Issues and Goals	Problems and Solutions
Increased complexity of financial management	▼ Hire a professional finance director ▼ Hire financial consultants
Impact of growth on schools and overlapping governments	▼ "The growth is here. We can't stop it, but we can try to work together to manage it." ▼ Meetings with overlapping schools and special districts: fire, water authority, library, and park districts (sometimes more than one of each—boundaries not coterminous) ▼ Disputes and lawsuits with schools over TIF

governments discussed the importance of boundary agreements in managing growth and annexation, and several noted that they do more than control boundary lines for annexation. These agreements also can stipulate future land use and zoning requirements for unincorporated areas after they are annexed. Overall, an assessment of statements in both the news reports and interviews demonstrates that these agreements are highly valuable because they reduce competition, transaction costs, and negative spillovers from growth and development.

It should also be noted that chasing commerce and embracing economic development is not typical of some governments where growth is initiating or rapid, or others that were in the path of the growth machine at one time but dramatically limited its impact on their jurisdiction. These governments and their residents seem willing to pay for the privilege of not having commercial development through higher property taxes, and many choose to rely almost exclusively on property taxes according to the quantitative data. Many of the smaller communities in category B4 of appendix 7, and those that are white-collar and residential communities in category E13, fit this description. The broader purpose of strategies in these fifteen communities is to maintain a particular community image and culture associated with characteristics such as "quality living in a natural setting," preserving the "wide expanses of natural lands and development planned to nurture the flora and fauna native to the area," or even "preserving our equestrian nature and reputation." At least three of these communities have five-acre minimum lot sizes, and most are rural.

The one government out of the four total that were interviewed in the larger group of thirty-three small and growing municipalities that did not have a professional CAO is particularly noteworthy because of its poor financial condition and the significant fiscal threats it was facing at that time. The government did little planning for growth, and it did not appear to be proactive or strategic in its decisions to handle growth. It had a part-time financial professional who acted as its finance director and whose advice and influence on elected officials seemed to be limited to dealing with the financial consequences of growth after the fact. At the time of the interview the government was dealing with major lawsuits from citizens and the Illinois EPA concerning its sewerage system, and its old water system was very inefficient at "50 percent line loss" on pumped water that was burning out one pump a year. These problems posed great threats to the government's financial solvency, which then limited its options to take advantage of population trends and opportunities for development.

News reports of other municipalities in this group of thirty-three that were not interviewed show additional short-term consequences of not managing the strategic issues listed in table 5.1, including the following:

▼ Instituting a housing freeze (cooling off period) to take stock, upgrade building and zoning codes, and assess the development process to date
▼ Instituting damage control from growth effects
▼ Financial chaos and uncertainty (due to improperly documented financial transactions and incomplete financial reports, for example)
▼ Dropping the ball with developers and losing development to neighboring towns
▼ Dramatic increases in water/sewer rates and taxes to service existing residents because of failure to plan for needed upgrades to system due to growth
▼ Backlog of permits and inspections

One important question that this list and table 5.1 raise is what factors affect these governments' ability to adapt successfully to growth and development from a financial perspective? The answers to that question are beyond the scope of this book, as this would require an extensive case study of several governments over a period of time. However, the most obvious set of factors to examine in such a study are those associated with the governing structure of the municipality (e.g. reformed or unreformed) because of the different type of heuristics (political or corporate) that are likely to predominate in governments with different forms. Different forms of government also have different approaches to governance that affect the policy time horizons of officials (e.g. long-term planning) and choice of strategies.

Rapid Growth and Built Out

What are the primary strategic financial issues for larger governments that are firmly in rapid growth or in the early phases of being built out? Governments in the early stages of being built out are experiencing a lessening of growth and a decline of the revenues associated with growth through mechanisms such as building fees and developer charges. Table 5.2 shows the strategic issues and goals that were evident from the news reports of thirty-five different municipalities (and interviews in nine of these governments) that are moderate to very large in population and experienced high growth from 1990 to 2000. These governments are in sections F and I of appendix 7 and represent governments that have "been around the block" a few times with developers and financial issues related to growth compared to the thirty-three governments represented in table 5.1.

Because revenues often outpace operating expenditures by a wide margin in rapidly growing governments, managing finances in these governments can be very different from managing those in governments that are not growing. The median ratio of revenues plus fund balance to spending for high-growth ($\geq$40% population increase) and low growth (<5% population increase) governments each year from 1998 to 2005 is about 192 to 245 and 152 to 167, respectively. In other words, revenues plus fund balance in growing governments is more than 90 percent to 145 percent greater than spending, but

TABLE 5.2 Development-Growth in Moderate to Very Large, High-Growth Municipalities: Rapid Growth and Early Built Out (n = 35)

Strategic Financial Issues and Goals	Problems and Solutions
Continue to bring in commerce, work to retain existing commerce, and diversify land use to light industrial	▼ Larger and more aggressive economic development, less emphasis on community development ▼ Work more with chamber of commerce and businesses groups ▼ Development of business parks ▼ Use of rebates and tax incentives ▼ Competition more intense, riskier and larger projects, "lots at stake"
Pursue boundary agreements and annexation	▼ Less annexable land and emphasis on boundary agreements than small governments ▼ Moratorium on annexation versus "growing the village" to provide more revenue ▼ Transactions with developers and others (schools esp.) concerning projects and annexation continue at high levels ▼ Formalization of earlier informal agreements with neighboring and overlapping governments
Financing growth and meeting new municipal service needs	▼ Higher demand from residents for amenities like parks and recreation and better basic services ▼ More infrastructure to maintain and service; more flooding and drainage problems ▼ Determine appropriate mix of financing for infrastructure improvements: (a) debt (GO or other), (b) charges on existing residents (including special assessments and taxing districts), and (c) incentives to developers, including use of TIFs ▼ Assess charges to developers and new residents and businesses to ensure growth is paying for itself; assess zoning and building standards; rework or tweak comprehensive plan
Increased complexity of financial and capital management	▼ Hire a professional finance director ▼ Capital planning and long-term financial planning ▼ Project management ▼ Frequent assessment of costs, benefits, and rules for growth and development ▼ Increased competition and strategic interaction with other governments in the region ▼ Developers, residents, and businesses demand more efficient, streamlined, and reliable transactions with the government; "bring a businesslike atmosphere" to the government
Changing the financing rules	▼ Pursue home rule via referenda or annexation ▼ Referenda to alter non–home rule rate limits ▼ Special census
Impact of growth on schools and overlapping governments	▼ "The growth is here. We can't stop it, but we can try to work together to manage it." ▼ Meetings with overlapping schools and special districts: fire, water authority, library, and park districts (sometimes more than one of each—boundaries not coterminous) ▼ Disputes and lawsuits with schools over TIF

TABLE 5.2 *(continued)* Development-Growth in Moderate to Very Large, High-Growth Municipalities: Rapid Growth and Early Built Out (n = 35)

Strategic Financial Issues and Goals	Problems and Solutions
What to do with downtown and establishing or maintaining an image	▼ Maintain small-town and Mayberry charm ▼ Find and develop the "gateway to our community" ▼ Distinctive, upscale, unique, and in search of a positive image
Prepare for transition to built out in revenue and spending streams	▼ Revenues will no longer outpace spending ▼ Revenues generated from new growth, building fees, and development charges (nonrecurring) will no longer be available ▼ Growth will no longer be the driver of expenditures

only 52 percent to 67 percent higher than spending in governments that are not growing. In addition, that ratio also is consistently less for governments in table 5.1 (170 to 237) compared to those in table 5.2 (197 to 261) for the same years, which indicates that governments in the early stages of growth are not generating revenues and fund balances to the same degree as governments in the latter stages of growth.[15] Also interesting is that the ratio for the interviewed government that was discussed previously in table 5.1, which was dealing with major lawsuits from the Illinois EPA, was never higher than 140. While not the lowest ratio in this group, the value confirms the interview observation that this government was not benefiting financially from its population growth.

Table 5.3 presents another view of the impact of development and population growth on municipalities. It shows the average ratio change of different revenues and taxes for all pairs of years between 1994 and 2000 (fiscal good times) and between

TABLE 5.3 Average Ratio Changes in Revenues for Municipalities in First and Last Quintiles of Population Change: 1994 to 2000 and 2000 to 2006

	All Pairs of Years Between	Municipalities in Lowest Quintile of Population Change	Municipalities in Highest Quintile of Population Change
Average ratio change property taxes	1994–2000	105.7	109.5
	2000–2006	105.1	110.9
Average ratio change sales taxes	1994–2000	105.1	112.8
	2000–2006	102.4	108.1
Average ratio change other taxes	1994–2000	108.8	130.1
	2000–2006	108.0	113.5
Average ratio change nontax revenues	1994–2000	109.8	114.2
	2000–2006	106.4	111.6
Average ratio change state-shared revenues	1994–2000	108.5	117.2
	2000–2006	103.8	108.5
Average ratio CPI	1994–2000	102.6	
	2000–2006	102.3	

2000 and 2006 (fiscal bad times) for municipalities in the highest quintile (eightieth percentile) and lowest quintile (twentieth percentile) of population change for the two sets of years. The table demonstrates the effects of population growth on all revenues collected by municipalities under different economic conditions.[16] Table 5.3 shows that growth drives up all own-source revenue, even sales tax revenues during times of fiscal stress compared to governments that are not growing. Income tax and motor fuel tax, which are both state-shared revenues, are distributed by population and so also increase as municipal population grows relative to other governments.

The increase in state-shared revenue that municipalities receive due to population growth is one reason why many conduct special censuses—they need to prove this growth to state government to receive higher levels of income and motor fuel tax. The other reason to conduct a special census is to determine if the population is greater than twenty-five thousand, which gives the municipality home rule status. The qualitative data show that a special census is an important fiscal tool for many municipalities that have experienced any growth or that may be near the twenty-five thousand population target. Twelve of the governments interviewed (19%) and twenty-two governments in the news reports had recently conducted or were going to conduct special censuses. Three of these governments reported conducting two special censuses within a year of each other, which can cost from $25,000 to more than $100,000. However, revenue benefits from special censuses are reported to range from $100,000 to $600,000 per year.

Another significant difference between governments in tables 5.1 and 5.2 is apparent from looking at the distribution of FDS for each. Among the thirty-three governments in table 5.2, only five (15%) had a finance director, and ten (30%) had no CAO. By comparison, of the thirty-five governments represented in table 5.3, twenty-eight (80%) had both a finance director and a CAO. Not surprisingly, more municipalities in table 5.2 have home rule (34%) than in table 5.1 (15%). Also, municipalities in table 5.2 are relatively evenly divided between the six counties, but those in table 5.1 are concentrated in Lake County with none in either Cook or DuPage counties. Finally, growing governments tend to rely much more heavily on nontax sources of revenue for operating expenses, which includes building fees and developer charges. Not shown here, the median reliance on nontax sources of revenue is consistently ten to twenty points higher for governments in table 5.2 than for those in table 5.1 for most years between 1998 and 2006.

Comparing problems and solutions in tables 5.1 and 5.2 shows that as governments move out of growth initiation and through rapid growth, there is greater emphasis on economic development and more aggressive pursuit of commercial enterprises and developing business parks for light industry. There is also evidence of governments investing more of their own resources, including land, into larger and riskier retail or combined retail/commercial projects than in the earlier stages of growth, and somewhat less emphasis on annexation and boundary agreements. A moratorium on annexation was discussed by four governments in table 5.1, but several others admitted to using annexations to implement the strategy of "growing the village" to provide more revenue.

Revenue streams are very different when governments are growing and developing, but so are spending streams. As one government official from table 5.2 commented, "Growth has diverted the village government from everyday services." Table 5.2 also shows that the level of service and capital needs or demands, and the methods of financing growth, are somewhat different than for governments in table 5.1. With respect to capital financing, larger governments seem to take advantage of more funding options. Although developer charges, impact fees, and in-kind payments are still important, news reports and interviews for governments in table 5.2 show a greater discussion of use of debt (GO or other form) to fund capital development, special assessments or taxing districts, and TIFs. Three governments from table 5.2 boasted that developers pay for or construct all new infrastructure that is created by the growth, including water systems, sewers, and roads.

It is also evident from many news reports that new growth creates spillover effects or costs on existing infrastructure, including flooding, drainage, and traffic problems. Governments in table 5.2 also have more infrastructure to service and maintain than those in table 5.1. Officials from governments in both tables also claimed that growth and new residents create higher demand for amenities such as parks and recreation services, better water quality, and government-provided water, sewer, and garbage pickup. "The more a city fuels its retail and residential growth, the more its residents expect in government services." All of this begets greater need and demand for infrastructure spending, which leads to the use of different financing tools for capital items as growth becomes more rapid.

Thus, although revenues are still outpacing expenditures by a large margin for most of the governments in table 5.2, they are discussing fiscal stress more than governments in table 5.1. These discussions are primarily in the context of the 2002–3 recession, but also in anticipation of the end of growth when revenue increases slow and expenditures begin to outpace revenues. Five of the ten governments interviewed in table 5.2 talked about the financial changes that will occur when the municipality becomes built out, and three others noted the artificially high surpluses created by current growth revenues. One government admitted that "at the moment we're trying to keep ourselves from becoming dependent on the growth related fees." Two of the interviewed governments that were approaching the built-out stage noted that they did not plan well enough for commercial development (they are too residential), and a third was attempting to reverse the focus on residential development somewhat late in the game.

The need to redevelop or create a downtown area was another growth-related event that was discussed much more by governments in table 5.2 than those in table 5.1 in the news reports and interviews. In many cases, the character of the downtown area was considered to be integral to developing or maintaining a community image and sustaining retail sales and property values. More broadly, many governments discussed the importance of their image to the region, the need to change their image, and developing or solidifying their image through marketing and tools such as gateways. Oftentimes the stated image was associated with small-town or rural charm, and three governments referred to their Mayberry image.

Correlations of the frequency of statements coded as fiscal stress—yes and fiscal stress—no in the news reports with all statements about growth and development from appendix 5, and controlling for word count, shows that many development and growth codes are negatively associated with fiscal stress—yes and positively associated with fiscal stress—no. In other words, the growing and developing governments are reported to be less fiscally stressed. The only exception here is for the TIF and built-out codes, which are positively associated with fiscal stress—yes and negatively associated with fiscal stress—no.

It should also be noted that of the ten governments interviewed in table 5.2, all except one claimed to have benefited financially from the growth and were either claiming or demonstrating that they were handling growth and economic development strategically to some degree. A visit to that dissimilar municipality for the interview with the mayor (they had no CAO, finance director, or economic development staff) showed numerous new residential developments, mostly higher density, and many vacant commercial buildings. The mayor, who had been in office twenty-two years, confirmed these problems, but he expressed no plan for future population growth when asked, nor did the government have an active economic development program. Furthermore, the mayor perceived no need for TIFs, although many sections of the city would have qualified for this fiscal tool.

The mayor was considering doing a special census and recognized that permit fees were "up due to growth" and sales taxes were down ("retirees are not buying"), but his primary financial response to the growth was to "lower property taxes." He also called the police chief into the interview to answer many of the financial questions asked during the interview. According to news reports, the long-term mayor lost the election two years after the interview due to lack of commercial progress in the city. One citizen complained in an editorial, "I'm frankly tired of watching the property values in other cities surrounding [City X] skyrocket, while the value of my home is static" (Ruffatto 2003). The new mayor promised to "aggressively seek out business opportunities," "install a strategic plan," and "pull out the red carpet for businesses to come to this city." Other candidates in the election also promised to focus more on economic development and hire a professional city manager or administrator (Malone 2005).

Levels and Causes of Fiscal Stress

Much of this chapter is devoted to identifying different financial threats that create fiscal stress or munificence for municipal governments in the Chicago metropolitan region. Recall that fiscal stress is defined as a change (even expected change) in government financial condition. On the spending side, some of the common sources of fiscal stress observed here are lawsuits, flooding and drainage problems, increasing insurance costs (medical and liability), and higher pension liabilities associated with the recession. Political conflict and disputes also appear to create higher fiscal stress, especially in developing municipalities, due to the higher transaction costs of doing business with and governing within such governments.

On the revenue side, having a strong commercial base presents opportunities to improve financial condition and reduce reliance on property taxes (which is politically popular), but it can also become a factor in fiscal stress during recessions because the tax base tends to shrink faster and to a greater extent than other revenue bases. Income tax, which is a significant part of state-shared revenue, also shrinks more during recessions and threatens governments that rely more heavily on this source for basic operations. The conditional effects of home rule status on fiscal stress and munificence also were examined, although this feature does not really constitute an opportunity or threat. Rather it affects how the government is able to respond to threats and opportunities and the fiscal tools available to it.

This section examines how levels of fiscal stress or munificence vary by causes of fiscal stress in conjunction with government fiscal capacity to respond to threats and opportunities. These events are examined for all municipal governments in the Chicago metropolitan region using regression analysis and observation of trends and they are examined for the interviewed governments using qualitative methods. Based on prior discussions and analyses, subsequent analyses assume that revenue wealth, population growth, and home rule are the most critical factors in determining the size of the fiscal toolbox and sources of threats and revenue.

General Trends and Outliers

The ratio of revenue plus fund balance as a percentage of spending is an indicator of short-term fiscal stress in all governments (see appendix 1). That ratio represents the resources that government has immediately available for meeting service needs and so is a measure of budgetary solvency or balance with the environment. Changes to this ratio thus represent fiscal stress or munificence in the short term rather than changes to long-run financial condition. Figure 5.3 shows this ratio for 1998 to 2005 for municipal governments in the highest and lowest quintile (twentieth and eightieth percentile) of the revenue wealth index, governments with percent population change in the highest and lowest quintile between 2000 and 2005, and home rule and non–home rule governments. Changes in this ratio over time as demonstrated by the slopes

FIGURE 5.3 Median Revenue plus Fund Balance as a Percentage of Spending for Municipalities in the Highest and Lowest Quintile of the Wealth Index (2000), Highest and Lowest Quintile of Percent Population Change (2000–5), and Home Rule and Non–Home Rule (1998–2005)

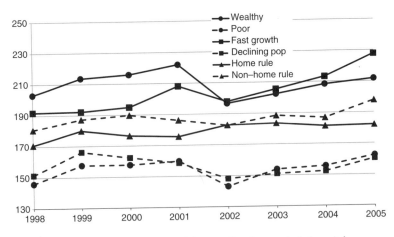

Note: Revenue and fund balance includes capital, but spending does not include capital.

of the trend lines reveal the immediate effects of fiscal threats on government. The gap between the lines for different types of governments reveals variations in short-term financial condition due to fiscal capacity and growth.

Consistent with the discussion of this ratio for high-growth versus low-growth governments earlier in this chapter, figure 5.3 shows that the median values for governments in the first and fifth quintiles of population change are significantly different. The dotted line demonstrates that municipalities with the lowest change in population (less than −2.5%) have a declining or stagnant ratio of revenues plus fund balance relative to spending from 1999 to 2004. The figure also shows that this ratio or percent for all years is much lower than for municipalities in the highest quintile of population change (greater than 18%). Compared to governments in the lowest quintile of population change, those in the highest quintile experienced greater increases in revenue resources relative to spending from 2000 to 2001, and then again from 2002 to 2005.

Figure 5.3 also shows that revenues and fund balances increased faster than spending from 1998 to 2001 and from 2002 to 2005 for wealthy governments, but dropped dramatically for them in 2001 as a result of the recession. By comparison, there was little change in resources to cover spending in poor governments prior to 2001, and these governments did not experience the consistent recovery that wealthy governments did after the recession. In other words, wealthier governments were more likely to improve their financial condition during the good times but fall further during the bad times. Revenue wealth and poverty also show similar effects on fiscal stress and munificence as high population and low population growth.[17] In contrast, there is little difference in budgetary solvency or changes in budgetary solvency for home rule compared to non–home rule governments.

The link between fiscal stress and financial condition is also observed in the interviewed governments. As presented in table 3.4, these governments are classified into five different categories of short-term fiscal stress according to statements in the interviews and news reports. Of the twenty-two governments that were classified as high fiscal stress in the table, five are very wealthy (wealth index in the ninetieth percentile), six have more moderate wealth, and the rest are some of the poorest governments in the region (wealth index in the fifteenth percentile). According to the interviews and news reports, the most common cause of high fiscal stress in the poor governments is the economy, as it is for many others in the region. But events such as the loss of five auto dealerships, successful property tax appeals that require retroactive repayment of property taxes, and lawsuits and mandates to upgrade water and sewer systems also contributed to fiscal stress in these municipalities. It is clear from the interviews that all these governments operate on the edge with little slack to absorb even a small amount of fiscal stress.

That governments with low wealth are likely to experience and report higher levels of fiscal stress is not surprising. More interesting is why wealthier governments were experiencing high fiscal stress, especially the five that were very wealthy according to the index. Figure 5.4 shows the revenue plus fund balance to spending ratios for these five governments from 1998 to 2005 with the home rule governments presented as dashed lines. All governments except Lake Forest show declines in these ratios, and some declines are quite dramatic. News reports and interviews confirm these problems. The two home rule governments, which had the steepest declines in

FIGURE 5.4 Revenue plus Fund Balance as a Percentage of Spending for Municipalities That Have High Wealth and High Fiscal Stress, 1998–2005

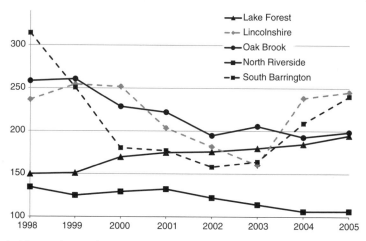

Note: Dashed lines are home rule governments.

these ratios, experienced specific incidents unrelated to the recession that caused high fiscal stress. Lincolnshire experienced the relocation of a major retailer that accounted for most of their sales tax, and, as described previously, South Barrington fought very expensive development-related lawsuits during this period of time.

It is also noteworthy that the ratios for most of these governments either improved very quickly after 2003 or grew more slowly. Both North Riverside and Oak Brook rely very heavily on sales taxes, as over 60 percent of their own-source revenue comes from this source, and interviews and news reports both discuss how heavily these governments were hit by the recession that reduced sales receipts. Conversely, Lake Forest, with 60 percent of its own-source revenues from property taxes, did not appear to be highly stressed based on their ratios in figure 5.4. However, the city had very high spending levels, in part because of the high demands of citizens (spending per capita is more than 300% of the median for all municipalities in the region).[18] In this case, its perceived level of stress is due to the recession in conjunction with high spending levels and the lack of home rule that limits access to its primary tax base.

The causes of high fiscal stress in the six moderately wealthy governments that were interviewed with high fiscal stress according to table 3.4 also include the loss of major retailers, and many cite higher spending needs and spending expectations of citizens combined with lower fiscal capacity due to not being home rule. With respect to the twenty-seven governments that had none, low, or medium levels of fiscal stress, the news reports and interviews show that the sources of fiscal stress for these governments were similar to those for governments with high fiscal stress, but there is less discussion of financial problems overall. The exceptions here are that more high-stress governments cite reductions in income taxes and delinquent taxes as causes of fiscal stress, and more governments with moderate and low levels of fiscal stress cite declines in sales taxes and increases in insurance costs. Discussions of lawsuits and political conflict are also more prevalent in high-stress governments than in those with low or moderate levels of fiscal stress.

In contrast to the prior governments, the ratios of resources to spending for all moderately wealthy and wealthy governments with moderate and low levels of fiscal stress were quite high, even during the recession. The two exceptions here are Indian Head Park and Wilmette. In this case, Wilmette's lower ratio may reflect the fact that it is home rule and has little dependence on elastic revenue sources, so it does not accumulate surplus revenues. Indian Head Park, however, appears to have much lower budgetary solvency at that time than all other interviewed governments in this category, as its ratio of resources to spending was quite low between 1999 and 2005.[19]

All governments with moderate or high levels of wealth that were interviewed were still doing capital spending at that time according to the interviews and news reports, but many governments with low wealth were cutting back significantly on capital spending. Most of the governments with moderate levels of fiscal stress have home rule, which may explain why they were not worse off, and most of those that are not home rule in this group tried to become home rule via a referendum at some time. Other trends in the fiscally stressed, lower-wealth, low-growth governments that were interviewed suggest the extent to which being very poor magnifies the effects of fiscal stress, or makes governments more vulnerable to fiscal threats. In addition, having some wealth and growth helps to insulate governments from fiscal threats. There are no truly poor governments with low or no fiscal stress, but wealth does not necessary insulate governments from high levels of fiscal stress either.

Figure 5.5 shows trends in the ratio of resources to spending for the five interviewed governments that were in better financial condition during the 2001 recession than prior to it. In fact, all of them were in bad fiscal shape in the good times of the late 1990s for similar reasons, including poor wealth, high need, and, for most, high levels of political conflict. The figure demonstrates that several governments had

FIGURE 5.5 Revenue plus Fund Balance as a Percentage of Spending for Municipalities with Financial Condition Reported as Better Off Than Prior Years, 1998–2005

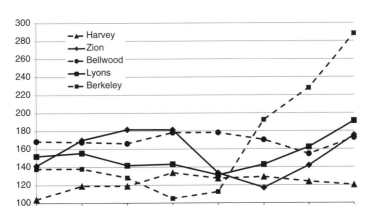

Note: Dashed lines are home rule governments.

resources that were barely able to cover spending, but all show increasing budgetary solvency some time prior to 2003 or shortly after 2003. And three show some very dramatic increases in solvency after 2002.[20] Three of these governments had recently acquired entrepreneurial finance directors or administrators with much financial knowledge who became change agents in improving these governments' financial condition. These individuals could be described as prospectors (risk-seeking) rather than defenders (risk-averse). They admitted that they enjoyed the challenge of trying to improve their governments, and their mayors, who were their primary supporters, seemed to have the political capital to make things happen. As noted in chapter 3, entrepreneurs tend to see opportunities more than others, and four of the interviewees talked at length about the importance of opportunities such as growth.

Reports of fiscal stress and the link among fiscal stress, fiscal capacity, and growth were not assessed as systematically with the qualitative data from 2009 and 2010 as with the qualitative data for the 2001 recessions. As noted previously, news reporting on these governments dropped dramatically after 2006, which created a bigger sampling problem of overreporting on wealthy and larger governments. But some trends seem apparent from the qualitative sources on the Great Recession and informal discussions with many finance directors at various functions in 2009 and 2010.

First, many governments have not been affected as negatively by the Great Recession as others. According to all interviews with COG directors, every municipal government in their organizations had been highly affected by the 2009 recession, and to a greater extent than the 2001 recession. According to one interviewee, "No one has been spared." However, other sources indicate that some governments are doing well despite the dramatic and sustained declines in sales and income taxes since 2008. In fact, New Lenox (group F15 in appendix 7) rebated 40 percent of the village's portion of the property tax to homeowners in late 2009, which was higher than the 33 percent rebated in the prior year. In some cases, good financial condition as reported by officials is assisted by deep reserves, but other governments that appear to be less affected by the Great Recession are not highly dependent on elastic revenues and have a diversified revenue structure.

Regression Analyses

One way of corroborating the trends in fiscal stress observed from the qualitative data is to examine the causal effects of key factors identified in the prior analyses using more sophisticated methods. Similar to figures 5.3 to 5.5, this section assesses the causes of fiscal stress with regression analysis using change in the ratio of revenue plus fund balance to spending as a measure of fiscal stress and munificence. This measure of fiscal stress also reflects changes in budgetary solvency or balance and is calculated as the ratio of budgetary solvency in the current year (t) relative to the prior year (t – 1).

Table 5.4 shows the results of regression analyses that examine the linear and conditional impacts of causal factors or independent variables identified previously on the level of government fiscal stress in municipal governments in the Chicago region from 1999 to 2005. Some of these factors are measured as change and calculated as ratios of current to prior years similar to the dependent variable. Change is measured

TABLE 5.4 Regression Analysis Estimating the Effects of Different Factors on Change in Budgetary Solvency (Fiscal Stress)

Change Ratio: [(revenue + fund balance)/spending (t)]/(t − 1); 1998–2005	A coeff./prob.[a] All municipalities	B coeff./prob.[a] Poor[b]	C coeff./prob.[a] Wealthy[c]	D coeff./prob.[a] Declining population[d]	E coeff./prob.[a] High growth[e]	F coeff./prob.[a] Not home rule	G coeff./prob.[a] Home rule	H coeff./prob.[a] Low reliance on sales tax[f]	I coeff./prob.[a] High reliance on sales tax[g]
Change ratio sales receipts (t/t − 1, log)	−.005/.82	.112/.008	−.029/.57	.151/.005	.004/.82	.017/.71	−.025/.19	−.041/.16	.068/.21
Change ratio intergovt. revenue (t/t − 1, log)	.075/.001	.098/.014	.047/.23	.098/.002	.159/.000	.046/.14	.104/.000	.099/.003	.021/.61
Change ratio population (t/t − 1, log)	.083/.001	.052/.096	.166/.003			.088/.002	.089/.12	.052/.22	.14/.01
Population (t − 1, log)	.011/.000	.009/.068	.011/.048	.009/.022	.014/.018	.017/.000	.005/.28	.014/.02	.017/.002
Home rule (t − 1)	.0008/.92	.008/.49	−.0004/.97	.003/.71	−.014/.36			.014/.37	.0008/.93
Revenue wealth, 2000	.005/.24			−.001/.81	.017/.061	.006/.21	.004/.62	.013/.17	.009/.12
2000	−.025/.01	−.032/.074	−.027/.18	−.030/.028	−.009/.56	−.011/.40	−.050/.002	−.022/.30	−.036/.02
2001	−.013/.26	−.006/.77	−.023/.25	−.029/.071	.018/.37	.003/.85	−.042/.014	.002/.94	−.042/.009
2002	−.067/.000	−.069/.001	−.088/.000	−.062/.000	−.045/.012	−.065/.000	−.070/.000	−.071/.002	−.101/.000
2003	−.015/.23	−.002/.94	−.037/.066	−.028/.11	−.0007/.97	−.020/.22	−.009/.61	−.013/.62	−.049/.003
2004	−.002/.89	−.006/.77	.006/.78	−.008/.59	.008/.69	−.004/.76	−.002/.93	.028/.21	−.057/.000
2005	.031/.005	.043/.026	.017/.42	−.0004/.98	.060/.002	.044/.003	.006/.73	.063/.002	−.010/.61
Intercept (1999)	3.80/.000	3.31/.000	3.68/.000	3.37/.000	3.72/.000	3.75/.000	3.80/.000	3.98/.000	3.41/.000
R²	.08	.11	.12	.11	.11	.08	.12	.10	.14
Chow test, F =		2.20[h]		2.0[h]		1.97[h]		2.63[i]	

[a] Probabilities are calculated from robust standard errors.
[b] Lowest tercile of wealth index, 2000.
[c] Highest tercile of wealth index, 2000.
[d] Lowest tercile of population change, 2000–5.
[e] Highest tercile of population change, 2000–5.
[f] Lowest tercile of percent sales tax, 2000–5.
[g] Highest tercile of percent sales tax, 2000–5.
[h] Significant at .05.
[i] Significant at .01.

as a ratio of X_t to X_{t-1} (*100), instead of the more common percent change of (X_t − X_{t-1}) to X_{t-1} (*100), because some changes are negative and cannot be logged. Most variables are transformed using logarithms to control for the high level of skewness that often exists in change variables, which creates problems for estimating regression models. Slope coefficients for variables in which both the independent and dependent variables are logged are interpreted as elasticities (the percent change in the dependent variable for a 1% change in the independent variable) and so are comparable.[21] The year designations in the model represent different years of change, so 1999 represents changes from 1998 to 1999 and so on.

The independent variables examined here are change in sales receipts (sales tax), change in intergovernmental revenue (income tax), change in population (growth and development), population (size of government), home rule, and revenue wealth (long-term solvency). The model also includes fixed effects (binary variables) for each year to estimate the impacts of state, regional, and national fiscal conditions that are common to all municipalities in the region for each year, but which vary by year.[22] The recession of 2001, with effects felt in 2002 and 2003, is the most obvious event that would show similar effects on all municipalities and would not have an impact in all years.

The municipalities are then divided into quintiles for revenue wealth, change in population, home rule, and reliance on sales taxes (percent sales tax of own-source revenue), and the models are rerun for the same independent variables for governments in the highest and lowest quintiles for each variable. The purpose of this secondary analysis is to examine the conditional effects of these factors on change in budgetary solvency. The interviews and graphs shown in this chapter strongly suggest that home rule and revenue wealth (fiscal capacity) and population change (opportunities and threats) do not alter government budgetary solvency in a straightforward manner. Rather these factors change the size of the fiscal toolbox for solving financial problems, which changes a government's ability to adapt and the effects of other factors on changes to government financial condition. Previous analyses also showed that the effects of the recession in terms of generating fiscal stress varied according to how dependent the governments were on sales taxes, which is also examined here.

The first number in each cell of table 5.4 is the coefficient for the independent variable showing its effects on the dependent variable, and the second number is the probability associated with that coefficient, which designates its statistical significance. Lower probabilities mean that the coefficient is less likely to have occurred at random and more likely to reflect the true effect of that independent variable on the dependent variable. The intercept for this model represents the average change in budgetary solvency for all municipalities in the region in 1999 from 1998. The coefficients for the other years represent average changes in the change in budgetary solvency from 1999. The R^2, which ranges from 0 to 1, shows how much total variation in budgetary solvency is explained by the model.[23] The R^2 values are fairly low, which is not unusual for change data, but the purpose of this analysis is not to explain budgetary solvency completely. Rather, it is to corroborate and elaborate on the trends identified previously. The F values for the Chow test show whether differences between models for governments in the highest and lowest quintiles of the different factors are statistically significant (Chow 1960). The highlighted cells are of greatest interest here.

Column A in the table presents the results of the model for all municipalities. It shows that changes in intergovernmental revenues and population have a positive effect on change in budgetary solvency. In other words, increases in intergovernmental revenues and population lessened fiscal stress, and smaller increases or declines in these variables increased fiscal stress. Larger governments also had greater increases in budgetary solvency during the time period, but home rule status, change in sales receipts, and revenue wealth had no linear effect on change in resources relative to spending. The variables that represent different years of data (with 1999 as the intercept) show that resources relative to spending declined significantly from 2001 to 2002 compared to changes in that variable in 1998 and 1999. This result reflects the increase in fiscal stress that occurred for many municipalities due to the 2001 recession.

Although revenue wealth has no linear effect on fiscal stress according to the first set of results, the results for columns B and C show that long-term solvency has conditional effects on fiscal stress by changing the impact of other variables. In this case, change in the budgetary solvency of poor municipalities (those in the lowest quintile of the revenue wealth index) is positively affected by changes in sales receipts, but wealthy municipalities are not affected. The budgetary solvency of wealthy governments is also less positively affected by changes in intergovernmental revenue than poor governments. Conversely, wealthy governments are more positively affected by increases in population than poor governments. Wealthy governments also experienced a greater decline in budgetary solvency in 2002 and 2003 than poor governments, but experienced no increase in budgetary solvency in 2005.

Columns D and E in table 5.4 show that municipalities with declining population also are affected differently by some of these factors than municipalities with fast growing populations. Similar to poor versus wealthy governments, the budgetary solvency of governments with declining populations is positively affected by changes in sales receipts, but governments with fast growing populations have little change in fiscal stress due to changing sales receipts. However, unlike wealthy governments, those with high growth experienced greater changes in budgetary solvency in response to changes in intergovernmental revenue. Governments with declining populations also experienced greater fiscal stress from 2000 to 2002 compared to high-growth governments, which experienced a noticeable decline in budgetary solvency in 2002 only.

The results here show that poor municipal governments and those with declining populations are less able to absorb declines in sales taxes and intergovernmental revenue and so have greater fiscal stress when this happens. But financial condition improves more in these governments when commercial activities increase. Wealthy and growing governments, however, experienced more fiscal stress due to the recession overall than poor governments and those with declining populations. Unlike wealthy versus poor governments, governments with high growth experienced greater fiscal stress and munificence in response to changes in intergovernmental revenue than governments with low growth. This impact is likely due to the fact that the level of state-shared income tax revenues received by municipalities is a function of their population. Population increases, which tend to be documented better than population decreases, reduce fiscal stress and increase munificence more directly in governments with fast-growing populations. High-growing governments also are more reliant on nontax sources of revenue than governments with little growth, which gives the former another source of revenue to manage fiscal stress.

Columns F and G in table 5.4 show the effects of fiscal capacity, financial threats, and opportunities on fiscal stress in home rule and non–home rule governments. According to the coefficients and probabilities, home rule governments experienced a significant decline in budgetary solvency from 2000 to 2002, but non–home rule governments were affected only in 2002. Changes in intergovernmental revenue also more greatly affect fiscal stress and munificence in non–home rule governments than home rule governments, but home rule governments are not particularly affected by changes in sales receipts. Among non–home rule governments, size of government more greatly affects fiscal stress than in home rule governments. Greater size may give non–home rule governments a bigger, less constrained toolbox than smaller governments, but size is not as relevant to fiscal stress in home rule governments.

The last two columns in table 5.4 show how the effects of these factors on fiscal stress or munificence vary by whether governments are highly dependent or nondependent on sales tax revenue. As expected, change in sales receipts across all years has no effect on fiscal stress if you are controlling for the reliance on sale taxes, but notice that those with high reliance on sales taxes experience much more negative and long-term effects of the recession than wealthy governments or those with declining populations. Governments with high reliance on sales tax also are more greatly affected by change in population due to its effect on sales receipts and other revenues that are correlated to growth and development.

Conclusion

This chapter covers a lot of material in terms of identifying the kinds of threats that create fiscal stress for municipal governments in the Chicago metropolitan region and also some important opportunities that these governments can take advantage of to improve financial condition. Although the analyses focused on the 2001 recession, the more recent interviews presented here suggest that many types of fiscal problems are not likely to change in the more recent recession. What is different is the severity and persistence of these problems. For instance, dealerships were noted to be highly valued by municipal governments in the early 2000s because of their ability to generate a large amount of sales taxes, but governments who rely on them to fund much of their operations run the risk of experiencing greater fiscal stress during any recession than governments that do not rely on this source of funds. The Great Recession was especially hard on auto dealers due to the debt crisis that led to a precipitous decline in auto sales and subsequent near bankruptcy of GM and Chrysler. All other things being equal, governments that rely heavily on sales taxes from dealerships will be hurt even more by this recession than the recession of 2001, and governments without dealerships will not be affected by this particular threat in either case. Similarly, reductions in sales receipts due to the Great Recession appear to be more severe than in 2001, but governments that do not rely on sales taxes will not be affected as greatly by either recession.

Some of the other important and exogenous fiscal threats identified here, such as flooding and drainage problems, are not linked to recessions and are specific to the region or even certain areas of the region. But they occur irregularly and are not likely to be any different today than in the past. Property tax appeals and mandates that affect pensions also are specific to the region and state and may be loosely linked to recessions or other exogenous events, but they are widespread among the municipal governments examined here. Other threats such as the closing of a retailer or the exit of a major property taxpayer also are irregular and widespread, but not infrequent.

This chapter also identified four categories of population growth and development as a means of identifying the different threats and opportunities these governments are facing, and it discussed many of the choices that high-growth and development governments make to adapt to their new situation. It is apparent from the financial problems of high-growth and development governments that they are very different from other governments, and the size and content of their fiscal toolbox also are likely to be different. These features are investigated further in the next chapter.

The declines in real estate values, housing sales, and residential and commercial development are very important threats to many Chicago municipalities and unique to the Great Recession. This recession also has produced many property foreclosures that have reduced property tax revenue for local governments. The chapter explained, however, why a decline in real estate values and housing sales is not likely to affect the level of property taxes collected by municipal governments in Illinois. Conversely, a decline in housing sales will affect home rule municipal governments that levy real estate transfer taxes. Although these taxes do not usually represent a significant portion of total, own-source revenues for any government in the region, they have probably declined greatly in all jurisdictions that choose to levy such a tax.

More profound effects of the Great Recession on some governments in this region are due to the literal freeze of all development in the region. It is not clear how widespread these problems are in the Chicago region or their range of effects on particular governments, but the revenue and spending streams for many of the small, high-growth governments described here have undoubtedly changed fundamentally as a result of the decline in the housing and development market. This may be especially true for governments that are in the rapid growth phase or even the early stages of being built out, as much of their fiscal structure is geared toward collecting and using development-related revenues (e.g., building and tap-on fees) and delivering development-related services (e.g., economic development department and building inspectors). These revenues and the need for such services have probably declined greatly and may be depressed permanently according to initial reports, which could alter the level of threat and opportunity posed by high growth and development in the region in the future.

One lesson that can be derived from the analyses presented here is that fiscal stress (a decline in government financial condition) due to exogenous threats is a function of how exposed government fiscal structure is to them or the risk of such events occurring. As described here, exposure to risk is, in part, a function of government fiscal structure. The choices governments make regarding how to reduce their exposure or compensate for their exposure with slack (internalized risk) or other means such as insurance (externalized risk) is the subject of the next chapter, but this chapter indentified some threats that are more risky for municipal governments. For instance, exposure to declines in sales receipts or the closing of an auto dealership can be managed by diversifying one's revenue sources or by maintaining enough slack to absorb the effects of the threat until the government can adapt more permanently. But it is more difficult to reduce municipal exposure to events such as state mandates on pension obligations or property tax appeals, as the probabilities of these events are less known.

Political conflict is another type of threat that is difficult to predict or manage and that can be a source of fiscal stress. Political conflict often leads to negative spillovers, such as lawsuits between government officials and higher transaction costs for persons trying to transact business with the government. This chapter also talked about how political conflict is very common in municipal governments with high population growth and development, but it is not necessarily more disruptive than in poor governments with declining populations. It is important that political conflict in governments with high growth and development is often accompanied by and focused on changes to their internal, institutional structure. In addition, how the fiscal threats and opportunities of growth and development are handled by the government, which can improve or weaken its financial condition in the long run or the short run, is linked to changes in governance.

The analyses presented here also show that home rule increases the options the government has for managing fiscal stress and maintaining financial condition. In fact, the regression results reported in table 5.5 show that the budgetary solvency of home rule governments changes more dramatically in response to changes in sales receipts and intergovernmental revenue than that of non–home rule governments. This finding suggests that governments with home rule have chosen to expose themselves more to fiscal threats and opportunities than non–home rule governments, probably through greater reliance on sales taxes and other volatile revenue sources. However, home rule governments also are in a better position to take advantage of opportunities that are not merely financial, especially with respect to growth and development.

Finally, it is apparent from the analyses in this chapter that government fiscal stress and change in financial condition are in part a function of its reactions and policies in response to threats and opportunities. In other words, it depends not only on the size of its fiscal toolbox but also on the choices it makes from that toolbox. The next chapter focuses on explaining the tools that Chicago municipal governments use given the set of tools available to them.

Notes

1. Unfortunately, news reporting on municipal governments declined dramatically in 2006, and the reporting that does exist is mostly for wealthier and larger governments.
2. All figures in this chapter exclude revenues for enterprise funds, primarily water and sewer.
3. There is no consistency in fiscal year time periods for municipal governments in Illinois, however; most have a calendar fiscal year, and many others are on a May to April schedule.
4. Because property tax decisions are based on the levy, the property tax rate floats for home rule and non–home rule governments to the extent that the latter meets PTELL and is within the statutory rate limits.
5. This problem became worse later as the state's fiscal condition deteriorated further. According to the October 2010 quarterly report on the state's financial position by the Illinois state comptroller, the backlog of unpaid bills and fund transfers stood at $6.4 billion at the

end of the fiscal year (June 30, 2010). This amount represents almost 23 percent of general fund revenues in FY 2009–10. Furthermore, the state had accumulated more than $3.5 billion general fund obligations since the beginning of 2011, further delaying payment of state vendors and local government transfers.

6. Although the municipality owns the sales receipts generated within its boundaries, the rate at which that base is taxed is controlled entirely by state government for non–home rule municipalities and partially for home rule governments.

7. As of 2009, the rate limit on the general fund for non–home rule municipalities is .25 percent, or the rate limit in effect on July 1, 1967, whichever is greater. The rate limit may be increased up to .4375 percent by referendum (DCOE, Illinois).

8. Currently PTELL is adopted countywide outside the Chicago metropolitan region through referendum. Once PTELL is adopted, then the county and all local governments in the county are subject to caps on property tax levies. PTELL was imposed on all local governments in the Chicago metropolitan region, except those in Cook County, by the state legislature in 1991 and then imposed on Cook County in 1994. PTELL does allow the tax levy to be increased beyond the statutory level to cover debt service in the event that revenues do not come in as expected and it excludes EAV increases generated by new growth.

9. Total property tax levy includes property taxes collected for pensions and enterprises.

10. www.invillapark.com/UserFiles/File/Finance/FY0910/FY10_analysis_11-16-09.pdf.

11. The material effects of lawsuits on the finances of eight governments where the lawsuits were reported to be a significant source of fiscal stress were examined in the notes to CAFRs available online or through interviews. Most of CAFRs did not indicate material effects, which shows the extent to which CAFRs focus on future risk, not past events; underreport the financial impact of lawsuits; or focus only on the direct costs of lawsuits.

12. Officials in two of the three governments were interviewed, but officials in the other—Maywood—declined to be interviewed.

13. Population ranges of small and very small governments are indicated in appendix 7. High or rapid growth is defined here as population changes over 25 percent (eighty-sixth percentile). Maximum percent population change between 1990 and 2000 was close to 1,500, and the maximum for percent population change between 2000 and 2005 was estimated at 280.

14. Tables 5.2 and 5.3 are constructed from examining coded statements for most development and growth codes from appendixes 4 and 5.

15. Seventeen of the governments in table 5.2 are medium sized (48%) and fifteen and are large (43%). Only three governments are very large with populations above forty thousand.

16. New growth is excluded from property tax caps that affect non–home rule governments, which allows their levies to increase beyond the capped levels.

17. Although similar in effect, revenue wealth (capacity) and population change (opportunity) are not related in a linear manner. Wealthy governments tend to have moderate growth, and poor governments tend to have either high or low growth.

18. Oak Brook had also invested heavily in capital infrastructure improvements just prior to the recession, which exacerbated their fiscal stress and led to the political conflict mentioned earlier.

19. There is little news on Indian Head Park, so there was no way of confirming the interviewee's perceptions that the government is moderately stressed, but other fiscal indicators suggest that it was having significant financial problems during this time.

20. The dramatic decline in budgetary solvency seen in Zion from 2001 to 2003 was due to the close of a nuclear power plant that removed $36 million of assessed value from the jurisdiction.

21. The wealth index contains negative values, so logarithms cannot be computed for this variable.

22. Fixed effects for municipalities would add more than 250 binary variables to the model. Although there are methods of accommodating this form, a simpler model was used here as the variable revenue wealth approximates fixed effects because it is constant across all years for each municipality.

23. For instance, the value of .031 for 2005 in column A shows that the change in (revenue + fund balance)/spending for 2004–5 was .031 higher than the change for 1999–2000.

Chapter 6

Financial Problem Solving

Tools for Managing Threats and Opportunities

This chapter focuses on answering the second question in the introduction: What tools do municipal governments in the Chicago metropolitan region use to respond to threats and opportunities and maintain or improve financial condition in the near term? This chapter also examines some of the contextual factors from figure 4.1 that can affect the availability of policies and practices to these governments and their responses to threats and opportunities in the short run, which is the focus of question three from the introduction. More generally, this chapter examines how contextual factors affect the contents of governments' fiscal toolboxes and their choice of tools to resolve immediate fiscal threats and opportunities. This chapter explores answers to the second question more comprehensively than chapter 5 by examining the effects of more factors on the toolbox and choice of tools, including fiscal governing structure. Recall from chapter 3 that governing structure is considered to affect how governments solve financial problems and their preferences for professional and corporate solutions.

Although the tools for managing threats, opportunities, and financial condition in the long run and short run are part of the same toolbox and are not necessarily mutually exclusive, this chapter focuses on tools used to solve new financial problems and those that require an immediate response from the government. Chapter 7 focuses more on the strategies governments use to maintain financial condition over the long haul: how municipal governments maintain or improve financial condition more generally and adapt to their environment. If short-run tools constitute tactics, long-run tools constitute strategies with broader and longer time horizons. Fiscal strategies to maintain financial condition overall can be financial policies or practices that municipal governments claim to follow, such as maintaining a certain level of fund balance or not levying a property tax, and that therefore place soft constraints on available tools. For instance, home rule governments in this region that claim to follow PTELL will not be as likely to raise revenue beyond this cap as those with no such policy, all other things being equal. However, governments with this policy can change or ignore it to deal with financial problems more easily than they can change or ignore harder constraints such revenue wealth.

The first three sections of this chapter examine the financial tools that municipal governments in the Chicago metropolitan region used to manage the 2001 recession primarily and the Great Recession secondarily. Examination of these tools is structured according to equation (1) in figure 4.1, which shows that, within the current time period, governments' decisions about revenues minus spending must equal change in fund balance minus borrowing. In effect, each component of equation (1) represents a different set of tools to respond to fiscal threats, opportunities, and financial problems. These sections use qualitative data to document the financial tools these governments employed and corroborate some observations using descriptive quantitative data presented here and in the last chapter. The descriptive quantitative data also reveal some strategies these governments pursued during this time period to maintain financial condition in the long run.

 Compared to the news reports, the interviews provide much more detail about governments' responses to threats and opportunities. Unfortunately, neither the interviews nor news reports for the Great Recession are comprehensive enough to document anything other than general trends in responses to that event. As noted previously, the sample of governments from this recession in the news reports are probably more biased than the sample from the 2001 recession, and so news reports from the later recession were not coded or assessed as systematically as reports from the earlier recession. In addition, quantitative data are not yet available to corroborate qualitative observations about the Great Recession. However, it is apparent from the limited evidence that the fiscal toolbox of many Chicago municipal governments had shrunk considerably more in the latter recession than the earlier one because the latter has been longer and more severe. In effect, many governments had used up the easier and more desirable fiscal tools (those higher in the hierarchy of table 3.3) by the end of 2009 as compared to 2002. This required many governments to make more radical changes to the balance equation (1) in 2010 than in 2003.

The last section of this chapter uses regression analysis to explain the financial tools these governments used to manage financial problems from 1999 to 2005 as a function of key factors identified in figure 4.1. These factors are (1) fiscal capacity, especially revenue wealth, spending needs, and home rule; (2) administrative capacity and governance, especially fiscal governance (fiscal decision structure); (3) fiscal structure (e.g., fund balance and revenue diversification); and (4) exogenous fiscal threats and opportunities, especially change in fiscal capacity and growth. As discussed in chapter 4, the fiscal tools governments use to solve financial problems are a function of the content of the government's fiscal toolbox and the choice of tools. The content of the fiscal toolbox is determined by factors (1), (3), and (4), and the choice of tools is determined by factors (2) and (4).

Spending

Table 3.5 shows that spending cuts, in addition to increasing and adding revenue, were discussed most often as ways of dealing with fiscal stress in 2003. The executive directors of the COGs also reported that governments were doing far more cutting than raising revenue as of late 2009. But closer examination of the interview statements in 2003 on strategies for managing fiscal stress shows that actual cuts in services are one of the least preferred options. Rather, governments prefer to cut spending slack or what they consider to be surplus spending. More specifically, they make cuts that will not affect services immediately or directly. They push off current spending into the future, especially capital items; delay hiring for vacant positions; underfund pensions;

and cut travel or other nonessential expenditures such as work-force training. There is the inescapable problem, however, that 70 percent to 80 percent of the budgets for most municipal departments and services are for personnel items (salaries and benefits), which have a high level of fixity relative to capital, travel, and other line items. Many governments also are subject to contractual agreements with unions and state statutes that limit their ability to underfund pensions too much.

Interviewees and news reports in 2003 also indicate that once the easy and undisruptive options for reducing spending are used up (once all the fat or fluff has been cut), governments will then focus on scaling back rather than eliminating services by cutting overtime, reducing hours of operation, eliminating pay raises, and pushing off costs to employees (e.g., increase employee health benefit contributions). Greater reductions in spending are achieved using across-the-board cuts and eliminating targeted services while maintaining a priority of not cutting core public safety services. Pay cuts and layoffs, especially for core public safety services, are the least desirable methods of dealing with fiscal stress. Several governments mentioned using furloughs and early retirement as a means of handling their fiscal problems in 2003, claiming that this was more desirable than firing people.

By comparison, news reports from 2009 and 2010 and interviews from 2009 report that furloughs, early retirement, and firing people were much more common than in the earlier recession as many governments were facing their second or third years of depressed and declining revenues. But even during the Great Recession, many municipalities reported being able to "meet basic service needs" and "continue to provide the highest quality of services." Many governments also continued to aggressively pursue economic development, and some saw "the first sign of recovery on the horizon" for their 2010 budget. But there are other municipalities in the news reports that warn if things do not improve in the economy or if state government reduces state-shared revenue to "manage their $11.5 billion debt," then future lean budgets will mean "reduced staffing and reduced services" that will "impact the public health, safety, and welfare of the community" (*Daily Herald* 2010a, 2010b). Much smaller municipalities in the Chicago region seem to be targeting payroll for spending cuts, as this is the biggest portion of their budget, using such threats to gain concession from the unions.

Eight governments interviewed in 2003 mentioned having to lay off employees, although more governments considered it. One larger government ($38 million budget) laid off thirty part-time employees in 2003 according to news reports (Calumet City), and a wealthier one of similar size laid off twelve full-time and part-time employees (Downer's Grove). Three of the smaller interviewed governments ($4–$17 million budgets) laid off only a few or one employee, which clearly was painful for them nonetheless (Forest Park, Prospect Heights, LaGrange Park, Berkeley). A very wealthy government (Wilmette, $25 million budget) also laid off several employees.

Interestingly, none of these eight governments could be described as having very poor long-term solvency—what Schick (1980) would describe as total scarcity. In fact, the fiscal capacities of the two poorest governments, Berkeley and Calumet City, were in the thirtieth percentile of the revenue wealth index, and the fiscal capacities of Wilmette and Downer's Grove are in the eightieth percentile of this index. Downer's Grove was highly dependent on sales taxes (almost 40% of their own-source revenue) and took a big hit in the 2003 recession, but it also was dealing with property tax appeals from major retailers that reduced property tax levies from prior years. Reliance on sales taxes in Berkeley was more than 50 percent below the median of all governments in the Chicago region. But its reliance on intergovernmental revenue was much greater than the median, which made them vulnerable to the dramatic decline in income tax that occurred at that time. Prospect Heights and LaGrange Park also relied heavily on intergovernmental revenue for operations.

From reviews of all qualitative evidence on spending cuts, the Village of Broadview stands out as particularly fiscally stressed. Standard and Poor's downgraded the village's bond rating from A to BBB− (four levels) in 2005, and news reports in 2006, which was not a recession year, stated that it had to lay off "almost half of its workforce" to offset a budget deficit that had been accumulating since 1999. According to one report, the cuts included one-third of the police and firefighting forces. The article also reported that the government had a $1.7 million deficit ($19 million spending in 2006). The severity of the cuts appeared to be driven by the government's inability to meet payroll in the not-too-distant future. The report also notes that a resident who ran unsuccessfully for the village board in the prior year suggested that the financial condition of the government was so bad that it should ask the governor to appoint a commission to oversee the village's finances.[1]

Surprisingly, the wealth index for Broadview in 2000 was 30 percent above the median for municipalities in the Chicago region, primarily because of its high sales taxes, but it is not home rule, which makes its access to that revenue base limited. Instead, it was highly dependent on property taxes, with spending per capita in the ninetieth percentile compared to all other municipal governments in the region at that time. In conjunction, these reports, data, and timing of the crisis suggest that this government isn't necessarily experiencing a high level of fiscal stress as this concept is defined here. Rather its current financial problems are due to poor financial condition that has developed incrementally over a long period of time. Unfortunately, there are no subsequent news reports on this municipal government to show how or whether this situation was resolved, or whether it was able to improve its financial condition.[2]

One contingency about spending cuts that was evident from the interviews is that, all other things being equal, large governments have greater spending surplus or slack than small governments, especially for personnel expenditures. One interviewee noted that because of the size of his government, "I'm lucky, I can ask for a seven percent across the board cut from most of my departments." In contrast, a very small government noted that across-the-board cuts in departments and cuts in personnel expenditures are not options because indirect spending and personnel are so tightly coupled across functions: "We couldn't [cut personnel], there's only four people running the village, so we wear many hats. As far as the police department goes, there are three shifts, so you need three sergeants, you need night patrolmen, and you need six dispatchers. We have absolutely the bare minimum for what we need to deliver our services. We could not cut personnel." Thus, the tools for cutting spending may be fewer in smaller governments than larger ones, which may alter the order in which types of spending cuts are pursued in governments of different size. Smaller governments may have to move more quickly toward cutting services at the same level of negative fiscal pressure as a large government.

The majority of the cutting strategies discussed thus far help government maintain budgetary and service-level solvency by reducing the spending side of the equation. However, the Broadview example demonstrates that these strategies sometimes can be used to maintain solvency in the short run, such as laying off employees to meet payroll. Other spending strategies that were identified in the qualitative data are more strictly for managing fiscal stress in the short term. One such strategy, delaying payment to vendors, was mentioned by four governments in the interviews, two of which were not poor according to their revenue wealth index. The revenue wealth indices for the two poor governments, however, were in the tenth percentile, and one of them describes very clearly how this strategy was a normal financial management practice:

> We generally run probably 60 days behind on all billing. We've always been that way. Some companies won't put up with it, and others will, so you go to the ones that will, as long as there's no late fees involved with it. So if you get a few phone calls now and then, you're late on this, you're late on that, and there's certain times of the year where we know we're always going to have that money crunch. But I'm always able to find a way to where we never have any major shortfalls. We've never missed a payroll, that's the big thing. I make sure everyone gets paid, but every now and then the attorney or the auditor or the engineer, they might wait a couple months.

Professional standards of financial management practice would not recognize delaying payments to vendors or others as a good method of cash management. While it does not directly reduce their service-level or long-term solvency, it does reduce their short-term solvency and flexibility for coping with threats, which places them at higher risk of a declining financial condition in the future.

Alternatively, finding ways to operate more efficiently is a highly valued strategy for reducing spending in government, especially from a political perspective. The problem, however, is that this strategy is not conducive for dealing with fiscal stress quickly or with high levels of fiscal stress. Its popularity is demonstrated by the high number of elected officials and candidates for public office who advertise their abilities to eliminate wasteful, fraudulent, and abusive spending. A great deal of literature in public administration also is devoted to improving government efficiency. However, an examination of statements in the interviews coded for monitoring, cost assessment, and other efficiency-related financial management practices shows that governments do not use this strategy to manage fiscal stress.

Most of the spending strategies identified in the qualitative data to deal with fiscal stress can be implemented quickly and focus on reducing liabilities in the near term rather than the long term as a first step in adapting to new conditions. By comparison, strategies for increasing efficiency cannot be implemented quickly as they often require monitoring and analysis to determine where costs or spending can be reduced to achieve the same level of benefit. Thus, many popular spending strategies, such as reducing health care coverage of employees or slowing capital equipment replacement schedules, reduce the operating level of government rather than increase efficiency. The impacts of strategies for increasing efficiency also require a longer time horizon to implement than the strategies or tactics normally used to manage fiscal stress. In this case, one cannot increase efficiency simply by eliminating the waste, fraud, and abuse line-item in the budget.

One interviewee in 2003 noted, "We shop the markets very carefully on liability, and we try to negotiate reasonable things in our contracts. We used our GO obligation to fund enterprise revenue debt, so saved some money there." Another government noted that increasing efficiency is "basically just looking for new suppliers, always trying to find people that'll give us quality work or quality materials at a lower cost." A third government interviewee noted that "we've done just about everything to reduce costs. We've switched telephone companies. We switched insurance companies. We go out for bids now on everything." The annual financial report from a fifth government stated that they increased efficiency in 2002 by switching insurance brokers, restructuring investments, distributing bid documents electronically, and automating employee travel and mileage reimbursements. A sixth government noted that they reduced costs and increased service levels by franchising and not just outsourcing their garbage hauling services. A seventh government talked about how its centralized purchasing reduced costs, and an eighth government talked about reducing insurance costs through better risk management.

These are not one-shot strategies with individual, dramatic effects. Rather, they reduce spending incrementally and must be implemented continuously over time to have an impact. Some governments commented about the low payoffs and high costs of efficiency strategies. One claimed they are "maxed out on productivity," and another explained that "there's nothing we can do [to increase efficiency]. How can we get smarter, wiser, better, by just making people work harder? We don't sell a product so we can't get more efficient in delivering the product. Our product is service. It takes X amount of time to respond to a fire call, to deal with the police issue, to patch a pothole, and those things aren't going to change." Another government representative stated, "We know when we have to make improvements to get better, but at the same time in order to make improvements, we got to spend money, and sometimes we don't have the money. So we think we can get a little savings there, but it costs some money up front, and we struggle to find out where that money's going to come from."

Discussions of increasing efficiency were often in the context of cost analyses, as governments must know what their costs are to know if they are increasing efficiency. However, cost analyses were associated more often with governments trying to determine if their fees and charges are covering costs and to justify raising fees and charges than with trying to increase the efficiency of their operations. Vehicle sticker operations were targeted by many governments as being a very inefficient way of raising revenue (and not very politically popular). One government noted in the interviews, "We get $900,000 a year for our vehicle sticker program and it costs us $200,000 to do it, very labor intensive. We figured out that we collect 89 cents on the dollar, but only 20 cents on the dollar for delinquent stickers." Several other governments even noted that they eliminated the vehicle stickers because it was costing more to collect the fees than they were making in revenue from that source.

Interviews where knowledge of costs were mentioned in conjunction with assessing costs, monitoring, and other financial management practice codes show that governments also assess efficiency when considering contracting or outsourcing services. Although many governments noted that outsourcing saved them money, and quite a few relied on that strategy heavily, many also noted that it was not more efficient or cost-effective:

- ▼ "We took a look at the numbers and found out that we could be saving money by bringing it in house, which is kind of the reverse of what you would think, but that's the numbers [we] came up with."
- ▼ "But we're always looking to do those kind of things [joint services]. Right now we're looking at joint dispatch, but you don't necessarily save money. In fact, the people that looked at this have said you're not going to save money doing this."
- ▼ "We had considered privatizing this stuff [as part of the negotiations]. However, it appeared that the cost would be greater than what we spent—for example, maintenance of our parks and common grounds area. We also went out and got a couple of bids on that, and it was higher than what we were paying."
- ▼ "We would end up paying a lot more by outsourcing, but see, you got to keep looking at that, because that can change tomorrow."

One notable difference between responses to the 2001 recession and the Great Recession is the extent to which Chicago municipalities are now exploring greater collaborative methods with other local governments, including consolidation of public safety services and departments, to reduce the number of public safety employees on their payroll. The interviews in 2003 asked specifically about cooperation, interlocal agreements, and collective action with nearby and overlapping local governments and how such interactions were affecting financial decisions in their government. Interviewees' comments ranged from "there is no communication," "it's all very independent," and "no one wants to give up control" to descriptions of a wide variety of arrangements. The collaborative arrangements listed below were culled from both the interviews and news reports from that time:

- ▼ Regular meetings with overlapping taxing districts
- ▼ Coordinating bonding and referenda
- ▼ Contracting for services with other municipalities for building inspection, police, computer services, and ambulance
- ▼ Sale of water
- ▼ Joint ventures—dispatch, engineering studies, solid waste, waste treatment and water reclamation, insurance and risk management, and bonding
- ▼ Sharing of TIF revenues and impact fees
- ▼ Donation of land or subsidizing security and public works services to other governments
- ▼ Participation in councils of governments
- ▼ Mutual aid and sharing of fire equipment
- ▼ Membership in COGs

The COGs, many of which sponsor some of the joint ventures listed previously, were the most common interlocal arrangements mentioned in the interviews. These joint ventures help member governments increase efficiency by providing local services at a level that increases economies of scale or by providing services that reduce the cost of service delivery by member governments. There are eleven councils of governments in the six-county Chicago metropolitan region if you include the regionwide Metropolitan Mayors Caucus (see appendix 6). All governments in the region belong to at least one COG, and many interviewees in 2003 noted that these organizations were important to their governments.

Compared to states such as Georgia and Michigan where COGs have evolved over time to deliver economic development, transportation, work-force development, and human services, those in the Chicago region and Illinois function primarily as organizations for networking, information sharing, coordination, informal cooperation, and lobbying (primarily state government). Some deliver internal services to their members (e.g., purchasing pools, surplus equipment auctions, IT, and employee training), and several sponsor health insurance cooperatives and bond banks. But several appear to do very little to support structured collaboration and joint services, and membership in one, the Southwest Conference of Mayors, is limited to mayors only. Four COGs describe themselves as facilitators of shared service networks in the core areas of mutual aid, building inspection, and public works, but none of these networks are managed per se by the COG.

Outside of the COGs, municipalities in Chicago participate in a multitude of bilateral cooperative arrangements, some of which are provided by COGs, in different parts of the region. Groups of municipalities in different parts of the region have formed liability and risk management cooperatives, and the annual financial reports of many governments show numerous joint ventures in waste and water facilities. These types of efforts and the COG activity support the conclusion that many interlocal cooperative arrangements exist in the region, but three characteristics about these arrangements are apparent from all the evidence. First, very little operational spending is for collaborative activities. Second, most of the arrangements are not in the core service areas of public safety. Third, the arrangements are all voluntary and decentralized. In this case, the motivation for collaborating to deliver local services is completely with the individual governments.

The interviews with the executive directors of the COGs in 2009, however, revealed a potential new trend in collaborative arrangements among Chicago municipalities in response to the Great Recession. The combined factors of the length and depth of this recession, mandated increases in pension contributions to police and fire by state government since 2000 (discussed at length in the section on threats and opportunities on the spending and cost side), and the high proportion of municipal spending for public safety and personnel seemed to have made collaboration in these areas more attractive. For municipal governments specifically, the benefits to these governments from collaboration for core services have now become greater than the costs due primarily to the reduction in personnel that results from these arrangements. Consolidation of fire services across fire districts or municipal governments, which has an improved economy of scale in larger spatial areas, is now being openly discussed and actively promoted.

The transition and transaction costs of collective action, however, are still formidable, as noted in a study conducted by the Metropolitan Mayors Caucus (MMC) in late 2009, which was one of the COGs interviewed in 2009.[3] This study was discussed by several of the other COG executive directors in the interviews as it had been released just prior to the interviews, but these interviewees confirmed that many of the concerns and claims about collaboration in the study were being expressed by their member governments. Municipal governments in the Chicago region are looking for more dramatic ways to cut costs to cope with the recession and rising pension costs, and combining fire services is being perceived as a logical way to significantly reduce spending.

Revenues

Table 3.5 shows that most interviewees in 2003 reported increasing or adding new revenue as a way of managing fiscal stress, which was also common in 2009 according to the news reports but somewhat contrary to claims by interviewees in 2009. Figures 5.1 and 5.2 provide some insight into the importance of different revenue options to Chicago municipalities from 1994 to 2006. Figure 5.1 shows that municipal governments likely countered the effects of the 2001 recession by increasing other taxes and nontax sources of own-source revenue (primarily fees and charges). Figure 5.2 shows that home rule governments increased property taxes more than non–home rule governments during and after the recession. However, even non–home rule governments increased property taxes at a greater rate after the recession than before the recession, and they increased the property tax levy by more than the change in the CPI.[4] Thus the revenue tools municipalities in this region use to manage fiscal stress depend greatly on their home rule status.

In total, the interviews, news reports, and quantitative data suggest that these governments prefer to increase taxes, fees, and charges that can be exported to nonresidents rather than to increase revenues that place a greater burden on property owners within their jurisdiction. Increasing general sales taxes is probably the most popular and readily available option among exportable taxes for most municipalities, but many initiate or raise other exportable taxes such as hotel-motel, food and beverage, and real estate transfer (tax on the buyer). The most popular fees and charges to increase seem to be building fees, impact fees, and tap-on charges to capture more money from development and support services to new development. Increasing property taxes is the least preferred option for raising revenue, followed by vehicle stickers, utility taxes, and water and sewer charges. But which options governments choose also depends on the options available to them and the payoffs associated with the options. Instituting a hotel-motel tax may not be a very productive way for a municipal government to generate revenue if there are few hotels or motels within its boundaries. A government that has reached the maximum rates for all utility taxes no longer has these tools in their fiscal toolbox, and many of those interviewed noted that they were at their maximum rates for utility taxes, especially telecommunications.

Evidence of government attitudes toward raising property taxes is apparent from statements by twenty-three of the sixty-two governments interviewed emphasizing that raising property taxes was not an option for managing fiscal stress. Of the twenty-eight home rule communities interviewed in 2003, seven claimed to have a policy of operating as if they are not home rule with respect to limits on levy increases mandated by PTELL. In other words, these home rule governments will not raise the property tax levy more than 5 percent or the rate of inflation, whichever is less. As one interviewee from a home rule government stated, they "live by the [non–home rule] tax cap." Seven interviewees in home rule governments also claimed that property tax levies had not increased at all for many years, due in part to the good times of the late 1990s that allowed them to rely on more elastic revenue sources during this time. Another interviewee in a government without a property tax talked about the competitive advantage that not having a property tax gives them in attracting commercial enterprises, and four others bragged about their low property taxes ("the property tax badge," as one interviewee referred to it). Three interviewed governments (as confirmed in the news reports) rebated property taxes to homeowners more than once during the period of study, and one interviewed mayor in another municipality had proposed this policy to the board.

Among the forty-five governments in the news reports in which property taxes were discussed, officials in four home rule governments claimed to have a policy of following the tax cap law, one mayor bragged that his government had no property tax, and two more governments were reported to have rebated property taxes to homeowners. Many other governments, as reported in the news, marketed increases in exportable taxes to constituents during the recession years as property tax relief.

From 2002 to 2005, fourteen municipal governments in the Chicago metropolitan region had zero property taxes or property taxes that were less than 5 percent of total own-source revenues. Figure 6.1 shows how property taxes as a percent of own-source revenues, averaged for all years from 2002 to 2006, are distributed in 256 municipal governments in the Chicago metropolitan region. It shows a wide range of dependence on this primary revenue source. According to the Illinois Department of Revenue, the median property tax rate among all Chicago municipalities during this time for regular fund was only .84 and seventeen had rates that were zero or less than .1.[5] In this case, property owners at the median pay $840 for every $100,000 of equalized assessed value, or $2,100 for a home and property worth $250,000 of assessed value, which is a market value of $750,000, as residential property in Illinois is assessed at 33 percent of market value.[6]

However, this relatively low rate of property taxation at the median and claims about not raising property taxes from interviewees belie a wide range of property tax levels and many decisions to raise property taxes among municipal governments in the region. Indeed, figure 5.2 shows that many of these governments do raise property tax

FIGURE 6.1 Frequency Distribution of Average Percent Property Taxes of Own-Source Revenue, 2002–6

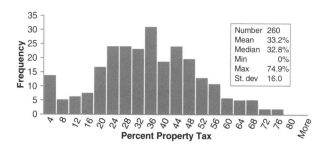

FIGURE 6.2 Median Property Tax Rate for Regular Funds for Home Rule and Non–Home Rule Municipalities, IDOR, 1994–2005

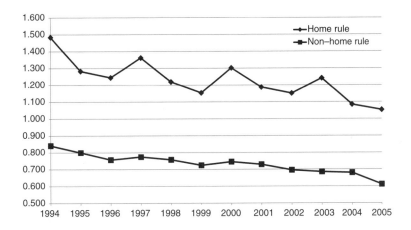

levies to deal with fiscal stress, and data on tax rates show that 15 percent (n = 40) had an average total regular funds tax rate that was greater than 2 percent of EAV from 2002 to 2005. Figure 6.2 shows the median tax rate for all regular funds for home rule and non–home rule municipalities from 1994 and 2005 and demonstrates that property tax rates tend to be more than 50 percent higher in home rule governments. The median average regular funds tax rate for home rule governments from 2002 to 2005 was 1.17, but .66 for non–home rule governments.

More interesting is the fact that, while tax levies may have increased during this time period, median property tax rates have declined for all governments since 1994, but especially for home rule governments. This pattern of falling tax rates in municipalities, due to EAV increasing faster than inflation, was observed generally in northeastern Illinois (Civic Federation 2008) and in Cook and DuPage counties (Illinois Department of Revenue yearly publications, www.revenue.state.il.us/AboutIdor/TaxStats/index.htm). It also demonstrates why property tax rates are likely to increase in these governments as EAV declines due to the Great Recession.

Although most governments may prefer to increase revenues other than property taxes, or at least to make claims to that effect, several interviews suggest that raising property taxes may be no big deal for exclusive and wealthy communities. One mayor from such a community commented that raising property taxes is insignificant and equal to a normal dinner at a restaurant. Another interviewee from a municipality with very wealthy residents noted that they would rather raise property taxes than fees or other taxes because of residents' ability to itemize their property taxes on federal tax returns.

One factor to keep in mind in assessing claims about property taxes in the news reports and interviews is that it is hard to judge how much such taxes are really changing or how property taxes compare in different municipalities because the noted increases, decreases, or comparisons are being discussed in three different ways. First, property tax levels or changes in levels can refer to the tax levy, which is the amount of property taxes collected by the government.[7] Second, property tax levels and changes can be discussed in terms of the homeowners' tax bills. Third, comments about property tax levels or changes can refer to the tax rate. Thus, when individuals talk about property taxes increasing, decreasing, or being lower or higher than those of other governments, it is often not clear what ruler they are using.

It is also somewhat difficult to compare property tax rates across municipalities as many of them have varied rates within their borders due to special assessment areas or districts (special funds rate), which are popular tools for funding capital infrastructure. Although 97 governments (37%) did not levy for a special district from 1994 to 2005, 136 governments (52%) levied for them for six years or more, and 57 municipal governments (22%) had special levies for all years from 1994 to 2005.

By comparison, increases in most other revenues, but especially sales taxes, are discussed in the news reports and interviews in terms of changes in rates. The greater popularity of increasing sales taxes compared to property taxes was discussed in chapter 5, and the finding here that governments prefer to raise sales and exportable taxes over property taxes supports that discussion. In the context of managing fiscal stress, forty-seven of the interviewed governments reported increasing sales tax rates or pursuing increases through referenda, and twenty-six of these were not home rule. Fifty-two governments in the news reports either increased sales tax rates or pursued rate increases, and twenty-six of these are not home rule.

Figures 6.3 shows how sales taxes as a percent of own-source revenue were distributed for the municipalities in the Chicago region from 2002 to 2006. Compared to the distribution of percent property taxes in figure 6.1, sales taxes comprise less of own-source revenue than property taxes, but dependence on sales taxes varies as widely as dependence on property taxes according to the standard deviations of these distributions. In addition, the distribution for sales taxes is bimodal as indicated by the two peaks in the bar graph in the figure that show dependence on sales taxes among the municipalities aggregates between 12 percent and 16 percent and between 28 percent and 32 percent of total own-source revenue.

Figure 6.4 shows the median sales tax effort for home rule and non–home rule governments separately for all years from 1995 to 2005. Technically this value is not the sales tax rate, as there are different sales tax rates for general merchandise, food, drugs, and vehicles, but most municipal sales taxes come from general merchandise.

FIGURE 6.3 Frequency Distribution of Average Percent Sales Taxes of Own-Source Revenue, 2002-6

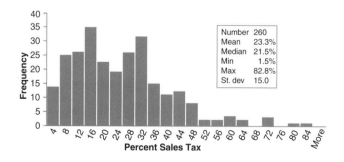

FIGURE 6.4 Median Sales Tax Effort (Sales taxes/sales receipts) for Home Rule and Non–Home Rule Municipalities, 1995–2005

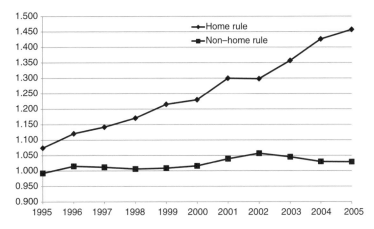

Note: Excludes sales taxes devoted to pensions and enterprises.

Thus sales tax effort represents an aggregation of total sales tax generated from all those sources and does not include sales taxes they sometimes devote to pensions or enterprises. The figure demonstrates very well that the sales tax effort for home rule governments has increased consistently since 1995 but has remained relatively stable for non–home rule governments. In 1995, the median sales tax effort rate was .99 for non–home rule and 1.075 for home rule governments. But by 2005 the sales tax effort for the former increased only to 1.029 after declining from a high of 1.057 in 2002, while sales tax effort in the latter ballooned to 1.457 by 2005. Home rule governments may add to the state rate at will, but non–home rule governments must do so by referendum. Thus home rule governments have used sales taxes to enhance revenues during this time period.

Figures 6.5 and 6.6 show the average percent of own-source revenues from other taxes and nontax sources respectively from 2002 to 2006. At the median, percent of

FIGURE 6.5 Frequency Distribution of Average Percent Other Taxes of Own-Source Revenue, 2002–6

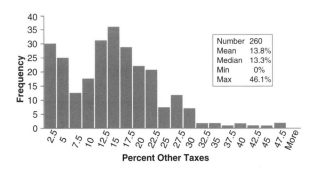

Note: Primarily utility and replacement taxes, but there are many other taxes, especially for home rule governments.

FIGURE 6.6 Frequency Distribution of Average Percent Nontax Revenues of Own-Source Revenue, 2002–6

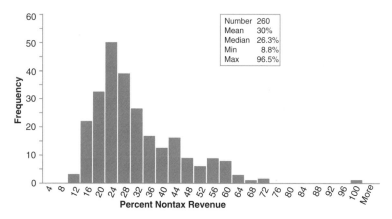

Note: Primarily fees and charges. Excludes charges associated with water, sewer, and other enterprises

other taxes (primarily utility and replacement taxes) is only 13 percent of own-source revenues, but dependence on this revenue among all municipalities ranges widely from zero to almost 50 percent. Median percent nontax revenue (fees and charges not for water and sewer), and therefore dependence on nontax revenue, is higher at 26 percent of own-source revenue for the same time period. Figure 6.7 shows that the distribution of nontax revenues per capita, as a measure of tax burden, is also quite varied with a median of 171 and standard deviation of 338. The need to remove six governments with rates greater than 1,000 from this distribution is evidence of the problem of using population to standardize fiscal measures as discussed in chapter 2. In this case, per

FIGURE 6.7 Frequency Distribution of Average Nontax Revenues per Capita, 2002–6

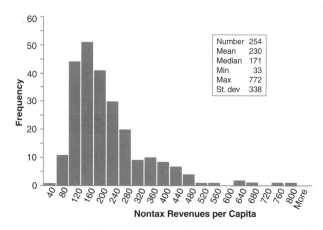

Note: Excludes charges associated with water, sewer, and other enterprises. Per capita values are not weighted by percent EAV. Six municipalities were excluded from this graph with rates greater than 1,000: Bedford Park, Rosemont, McCook, Volo, Elwood, and Hodgkins.

capita values distort the true impact of fiscal and other events on municipal residents, especially for municipalities with very few residents relative to commercial and industrial activities.

Figure 6.8 shows the median for other tax and nontax revenue and enterprise charges per capita for all municipalities from 1994 to 2005 with a comparison to CPI values (2,000 = 100). Both nontax and other tax revenues increase faster than the CPI, especially nontax revenue. But enterprise charges per capita, which are primarily for water and sewer, actually decrease from 1998 to 2000 and remain stable after that date. In this case, municipalities' attitudes and actions toward charges and fees for water, sewer, and nonenterprises as documented in the interviews and news reports fit the pattern in this figure.

As discussed previously, some interviewees claim that raising fees and charges, especially vehicle stickers, are not efficient methods for raising revenue. As one finance director noted, "The way the mayor and the board looked at that, they said, you know, we could raise 32 different fees and not generate much new revenue." Yet about half of the sixty-two governments interviewed and sixty governments in the news reported raising fees and charges during the time period examined. However, one should distinguish between raising fees and charges as a way of dealing with fiscal stress and raising fees and charges to cover expenses and maintain financial condition.

Most discussion of raising fees and charges in both the news reports and interviews centered on the water and sewer funds, and increases in these rates must be devoted to those services. Thus raising water and sewer fees does not really provide the government with general relief from fiscal stress. In most cases governments talked about raising water and sewer rates to cover maintenance and installation of capital infrastructure for these systems rather than as a way of dealing with a decline in their overall financial condition.

FIGURE 6.8   Median Other Tax, Nontax, and Enterprise Revenues or Charges per Capita, 1994–2005

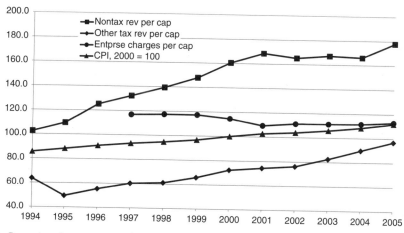

Note: Per capita values are not weighted by percent EAV.

Water and sewer systems are expensive and have significant health and quality of life impacts on citizens, businesses, and visitors to the municipality. Clean water is essential, and good sewers help prevent wastewater flooding and inadequate drainage of precipitation that plague this region. But there is much evidence in the interviews, combined with the news reports, of governments' reluctance to increase water and sewer fees as demonstrated in figure 6.8. There is also much evidence of governments getting into trouble for underfunding these systems and then having to raise water and sewer rates significantly in a short period of time to square up liabilities that have built up in these systems. As one finance director noted in the interview: "In the past there was a period where the board went nine years without raising water rates at all. We're still recovering from that. We just got behind the eight ball. There were some maintenance things that weren't getting done, so we've phased in water rate increases over the past five years. The farther you fall behind, the more expensive it gets."

Long delays in water and sewer system improvements can lead to lawsuits or mandates from either the Illinois or the federal EPA. At least four municipalities interviewed talked about having to raise water and sewer rates to make improvements to water or sewer systems as mandated by either the federal or Illinois EPA. Another interviewed government was forced to triple water rates in 2008 to finance capital projects to prevent sanitary sewer backups and overflows that resulted in a notice of violation from the Illinois EPA and court action from the regional water reclamation district. Four other governments talked about wanting to or having recently gotten their boards to consider or agree to annual increases in the water and sewer rates to alleviate the problems of not raising rates over an extended period of time, and then having to raise rates significantly to catch up. One finance director noted that his board went ten years without raising the water and sewer rates, which drew down reserves substantially in those funds, and that he wanted to get the board "thinking about the notion of indexing all fees on an annual basis to cover expenses." Another finance director talked about regular increases in charges and fees to "make services [such as building permits] stand on their own."

It was apparent from interviews and news reports that government officials often do not think of the water and sewer fund as a capital-intense enterprise but as another governmental fund in which level of services provided and funding are determined, in large part, by political considerations. This underlying theme is demonstrated clearly in several news reports that document the difficulty government officials have in raising water and sewer rates to meet significant revenue shortfalls and capital needs as determined by outside consultants. A study by one consultant on the rates charged by the suburb of Carpentersville in 2005 noted that the village would have to raise water and sewer rates by 40 percent and 26 percent, respectively, in order to cover the expenses of these services in the future and necessary infrastructure improvements. Although the rates had not been changed in more than five years, one trustee stated, "Nobody wants to raise rates at this point." Another wondered if such a large increase and the infrastructure improvements were really necessary, and the village president noted that there was an $11 million surplus in those funds that could be tapped before "shifting the burden to residents" (Elejalde-Ruiz 2005b).

The suburb of Wauconda had a similar experience in the same year with a consultant's report on their water and sewer rates and the financial condition of these enterprises. The consultant noted that the village's "expenses are going up but your revenues are hardly changing," which has put it "millions of dollars behind in structural improvements and maintenance." The consultant's report determined that the base rate for water and sewer would have to increase by more than 30 percent, and the additional rates for higher levels of usage would have to change by more than 85 percent to prevent further deficits and meet the needs of the department "without borrowing from Wauconda's general fund." The consultant also noted that the village was "not alone in its reluctance to adopt annual rate increases" and that many communities go through this struggle. "They wait until they get into a deficit (before raising rates)" and should "consider automatic annual rate increases starting with at least a three to five percent increase each year" (Schmidlkofer 2005).

The interviews also send the message that many times fees and charges not associated with water and sewer also do not get assessed regularly to determine whether they are covering costs or whether costs are increasing. The concern here is that some general fund enterprises are being increasingly subsidized by the general fund revenues. Fees and charges that were mentioned most often in this regard are garbage, ambulance, building fees, and tap-on or impact fees for developers.

Contrary to reports by most executive directors of the COGs in 2009, the trend toward raising all forms of taxes and charges was very evident among the news reports about interviewed governments in 2009 and 2010. As noted previously, the well-known suburb of Schaumburg, with over 60 percent of own-source revenue coming from sales taxes in 2005, imposed its first municipal property tax in its fifty-three-year history thereby dropping its membership in the exclusive club of governments in the region with no property tax. Its level of commercial activity is high with $41,868 sales receipts per capita in 2005, but it is not the highest—twenty-eight other municipal governments in the region having higher levels. The new property tax was expected to generate almost $24 million, with approximately $80 million in operating expenses in the general fund in the 2009–10 budget (www.ci.schaumburg.il.us/SiteCollection-Documents/2010-11%20Budget.pdf), and cost the owner of a $250,000 home $252 a year. However, more than half of the total property tax in Schaumburg is expected to come from commercial property owners (Graydon 2009).

Fund Balance and Borrowing

According to equation (1) in figure 4.1, governments have other options than raising revenues or reducing spending to adapt to fiscal threats at budget time or during the fiscal year. They can transfer money from the fund balances, or they can borrow. Most municipal governments in this region have two sets of funds for which they account for all operations and capital spending. These fund sets are labeled as government and enterprise funds, with a separate capital fund in the set of governmental funds. It is often the case that one fund will borrow from another fund in the same set or in another set according to the qualitative information. Governments also shift funds from one set to another through higher "charge-backs," which are charges that one fund makes to another (e.g., to pay some portion of the finance director's salary). Municipal governments also borrow externally to increase cash flow or to improve budgetary solvency

(Bunch and Ducker 2003). Forty-three of the governments interviewed talked about increasing charge-backs to other funds, or engaging in some form of short-term borrowing externally or from other funds to handle fiscal stress at budget time. As one finance director noted, "If we're sitting with $1 million in our TIF fund, and we don't have any money in our corporate fund, you better believe, I'm going to say, let's look and find out what we can charge to the TIF or police protection [funds]. The difference [between communities] is how aggressively they utilize their TIF revenues. Some communities charge TIF districts for a lot of things—salary items and things like that. Other communities are just very strict. It depends on how much they need the cash."

It was clear from comments from three finance directors that short-term borrowing from external sources to balance the budget (e.g., tax anticipation notes or lines of credit) is not a desirable financial tool, and five other finance directors expressed the opinion that interfund borrowing also is not desirable. But comments from four mayors reflected the opposite opinion about short-term borrowing. In fact, one mayor expressed some pride in using the line of credit for cash management and for capital equipment purchases when necessary. In effect, this government was using the line of credit as surplus funds. Three governments also noted that, at that time, it was more efficient to borrow money than pull surplus funds out of investment for short-term needs.

Of the thirty interviewed governments that talked about their fund balances or surplus funds, most agreed that they go to these sources first to manage fiscal stress, especially in the short run. As one finance director noted, "Fund balances allow us to do fast changes without the effort of thinking things through." In other words, fund balances buy government time to think about the best ways to manage fiscal stress and adapt to changing conditions, which is especially helpful if they anticipate that solving these fiscal problems will involve more drastic measures later on. Three governments viewed the fund balance also as an opportunity fund that allows governments to take advantage of grants with matching provisions and provide seed money for worthwhile projects. However, lines of credit can function the same way. Other governments are more protective of their fund balance and look first for spending cuts to manage fiscal stress. In contrast, a small percentage of governments interviewed claimed to maintain little or no fund balance, preferring instead to balance the primary fiscal equation by borrowing.

How or whether governments use their fund balance or reserves for managing fiscal stress depends on how they think about it and its connection to the financing of capital equipment and infrastructure. When asked about the use of their fund balance in the interview, ten governments considered the fund balance to be primarily for cash management, not a rainy day fund, and several maintained only the minimum amount to pay their bills. One mayor described his policy toward the fund balance in this way:

> Money's like manure. It doesn't do you any good unless you spread it around. To stockpile money for a rainy day fund is a great idea, but then that money is just sitting there and it's not doing any good for anybody. So rather than have that money stockpiled, I would rather invest that money in infrastructure, because that's the same thing. A lot of towns build up reserve funds, we never have built up a reserve fund, because [the utility tax] acts as our reserve fund. If we run into a problem then we would just suspend the infrastructure improvements and use that money.

Other governments use surpluses and the fund balance to save for capital equipment and infrastructure spending, as suggested in the previous quote. In this case, there is a direct connection between fund balance levels, current surpluses, and capital spending. Many governments use the fund balance and current surpluses to buy capital equipment or undertake infrastructure projects when times are good, and some devote an entire tax or some portion of a tax to capital projects when times are good. When times are bad and they are experiencing fiscal stress, they use the fund balance or revenues dedicated to capital spending to solve their fiscal problems. In effect, the revenues dedicated to capital spending act as a source of surplus funds that help them balance equation (1) for operations.

Three interviewees talked about how their board was more comfortable with a large cushion in the fund balance, primarily because of their exposure to volatile revenues. In fact, interviewees in five governments with relatively high reliance on sales taxes talked about the link between the fund balance and bond ratings. One official from a government with more than 50 percent of own-source revenue coming from sales taxes commented that it was the bond rating agencies that were driving their high level of fund balance that was in the seventy-eighth percentile of average fund balances as a percent of total spending for all governments from 2002 to 2006. Another official stated that having a steady fund balance is good for bond ratings, and a third talked about increasing their fund balance to raise their bond rating. The following paragraph from a news report on Vernon Hills in 2001 documents the reporter's education on local government financial management from the village's finance director and demonstrates the link among fund balance, capital spending, and debt in dealing with fiscal stress (Lenhoff 2001).

> As of December, Vernon Hills had about $20 million in surplus, which is expected to decline in the next three years to about $9 million. The $9 million represents about 40 percent of their operating costs, debt service and base infrastructure maintenance. In order to maintain the current desirable AA bond rating, Vernon Hills will need to keep that surplus percentage in place. This is also important because sales tax is the village's main source of revenue (50 percent), rather than property tax or other taxes. Also, because Vernon Hills is getting closer to being build-out, the dramatic increases in sales-tax revenues are expected to level off, rather than continue to increase due to the growth. As for where the $11 million in the surplus will go over the next three years, approximately $7 million is slated for development, another $1.3 million will be loaned to the school district for development, then $6 million will go to build infrastructure, and more than $3 million will go to build roads. Now, if you're a financial genius (like the new and budget-improved me), you'll notice that those figures don't add up to $11 million, but to a higher figure ($18.3 million). The extra money will come from acquired debt.

Figure 6.9 shows municipal government trends from 1998 to 2005 for the three structural features just discussed with one feature measured in two ways. One trend line shows the median fund balance as a percent of total expenditures including capital spending (governmental funds). Another trend line shows the median fund balance as a percentage of total expenditures excluding capital spending (only available from 2001 to 2005). A third trend line shows the median percent deficit or surplus as a percentage of total expenditures (governmental funds only without capital spending),

FIGURE 6.9 Median Fund Balance (with and without capital), Deficit/Surplus, and Capital Spending as a Percent of Total Spending, 1998–2005

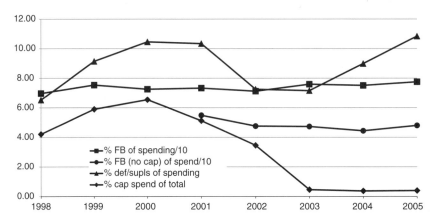

Note: These trend lines show totals for the general fund, special revenue funds, and debt service fund. Deficit/surplus is without capital. Fund balance percent is divided by 10 to show easily on this graph and compare to capital spending and deficit/surplus amounts. Thus the true level of the fund balances is ten times higher than what is shown here.

and the fourth trend line shows capital spending as a percent of total expenditures (governmental and enterprise funds). Percentages for both fund balance trends are presented as one-tenth of their original amounts to better show how these trends compare to capital spending and deficits/surpluses in the same graph. (See figure 6.10 for the distribution of average fund balances as a percentage of expenditures—no capital funds—from 2002 to 2006.)

FIGURE 6.10 Frequency Distribution of Average Fund Balance as a Percent of Total Spending, 2002–6

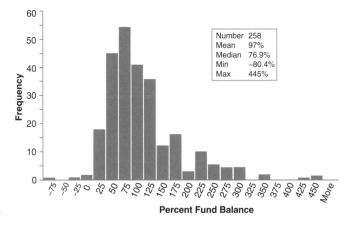

Note: Includes the general fund, special revenue funds, and debt service fund but no capital spending.

Figure 6.9 shows that municipal fund balances remained relatively stable during the time period, but surpluses increased during the late 1990s, declined during the recession, and then rose after 2003. Capital spending also rose in the late 1990s, in part due to the Illinois First program discussed in chapter 5, declined during the recession, and then remained close to zero after the recession ended. According to this graph the recession appeared to have a significant effect on capital expenditures, a modest effect on fund balances without capital funds, and a temporary effect on deficits/surpluses. Interestingly, capital spending had not yet recovered for these governments by 2005, although surpluses were increasing, and the increasing surpluses appear not to have gone into the fund balances. Thus one could predict that the surpluses available in 2005 were likely to be used by these governments to increase capital spending after 2005.

Regression Analyses

What determines which fiscal tools municipal governments use to manage fiscal stress and how do they take advantage of fiscal munificence? This chapter has discussed numerous tools that governments use on both sides of equation (1). The qualitative evidence presented here suggests that which tools governments use to manage fiscal stress depends on what tools are available in their toolbox. Generally speaking, the better government fiscal capacity and financial condition, the bigger the toolbox.

In the spending category, all other things being equal, governments prefer solutions that have less profound effects on services, especially core services, but they will progress toward these solutions as fiscal stress increases or continues over time. In other words, they will progress toward less desirable options as the toolbox shrinks. Likewise, on the revenue side, governments prefer to increase revenues that have less visible impacts on taxpayers, especially residents who are voters, but will progress toward more visible sources as other options are used up or become less effective in maintaining financial condition. On the other side of the primary fiscal equation, fund balances are often the most preferred method of managing fiscal stress early on, in part because they allow government to maintain taxes and spending at the same level for a short period of time. In accordance with professional standards of good financial management, borrowing is the least preferred method to deal with fiscal stress for most governments, but not for other governments.

The qualitative evidence also shows that fund balances and surplus resources are linked to capital spending, which is shown to be a preferred target for spending reductions. In fact, many governments reported that they retract capital spending and/or surplus resources during fiscal bad times and expand capital spending and/or surplus resources during fiscal good times. Many governments reported that surplus resources are a primary source of capital funding in addition to debt. Thus responses to fiscal stress and munificence that involve capital spending, fund balances, revenue, and operational spending will be related. The important question in this case is how are these responses to threats and opportunities affected by capacity, governance, and fiscal structure?

This section examines how municipal governments' responses to fiscal stress and munificence are related and affected by these events using regression analysis that estimates a system of three equations. The dependent variables are ratio change in own-source revenue, operational spending, and capital spending. The independent variables in each equation vary according to what is relevant to government responses in each area as theorized here and deciphered from the qualitative evidence.

Table 6.1 shows the variables included in this analysis. All dependent variables are considered to be a function of (a) exogenous events that can be opportunities or threats (change in population, EAV, sales receipts, and intergovernmental revenue); (b) fiscal capacity (revenue wealth, home rule, and spending needs, and debt); (c) fiscal governance (whether there is a CAO and a finance director); (d) surplus resources (fund balance and deficit or surplus); (e) past revenue burden or spending effort (per capita own-source revenue, operational spending, and capital spending); and (f) the other dependent variables. Items (d) and (e) represent features of government fiscal structure that can constrain or broaden the fiscal toolbox. For instance, governments with a high revenue burden will be less able or likely to increase revenue burden to solve fiscal problems, and governments with a low fund balance will not be able to use these funds to avoid revenue increases.

Fund balance and surplus/deficit were included in the model as separate independent variables rather than combining them into a measure of short-term solvency (fund balance plus deficit or surplus/spending) because of the complex nature of their relationship to each other and the other dependent variables. Also both variables have been used frequently to indicate short-term fiscal solvency in prior research (Hendrick 2006; Marlowe 2005; Poterba 1994; Hou 2003).

The model is estimated for the years 1999 to 2005, which includes both fiscal good times and fiscal bad times for many municipalities, for all three dependent variables using two-stage least squares (2SLS).[8] The system of equations also is estimated separately for small and large governments (spending less than or greater than $10 million) and for home rule and non–home rule governments. The qualitative and quantitative evidence presented thus far present strong confirmation that the range of causes and responses to fiscal threats and opportunities is fundamentally different in home rule and non–home rule governments. There is much less evidence of significant differences between small and large governments, but because home rule is linked to size of government in Illinois, comparing results for size and home rule status will help to distinguish the effects of government size from size of the fiscal toolbox.

The data are combined cross-sectional and time series, so binary variables are added that represent different years to create a fixed effects model similar to the regression analyses conducted in chapter 5. However, specific year variables were included only if they were found to be significant in regression analyses of individual equations using ordinary least squares.[9] Fixed effects for the different municipalities are approximated by the wealth and spending needs indices and the fiscal governance variable as their values vary by municipality but are fairly constant across years. Also as in the regression analyses, change is measured as a ratio of X_t to X_{t-1} (*100) instead of the more common percent change calculation because most of these variables are logged. This transformation helps to control for the high level of skewness that often exists in change variables and creates many problems for estimating regression models.

TABLE 6.1 System of Equations for Responses to Fiscal Stress and Munificence

(1) Ratio change own-source revenue	Log (OSR t/OSR t − 1)
Ratio change population	Log (population t/population t − 1)
Ratio change equalized assessed value	Log (EAV t/EAV t − 1)
Ratio change sales receipts	Log (sales receipts t/sales receipts t − 1)
Ratio change intergovernmental revenue	Log (IGR t/IGR t − 1)
Revenue wealth, 2000	Revenue wealth index (see appendix 2)
Home rule	0 = not home rule; 1 = home rule
Fiscal governance, 2003	0 = mayor, finance director, or CAO only 1 = CAO and finance director
Percent fund balance in base year	Log (fund balance/operational spending) t − 1
Percent deficit or surplus in base year	Log ([revenues − spending]/op. spending) t − 1
Own-source revenue per capita base year	Log (own-source revenue/population) t − 1
Years	0 = 1999, 2001, 2002, 2004 1 = 2000, 2003, 2005
Ratio change operational spending	
Ratio change capital spending	
(2) Ratio change operational spending	Log (OS t/OS t − 1)
Ratio change population	
Ratio change intergovernmental revenue	
Spending needs, 2000	Spending needs index (see appendix 2)
Fiscal governance, 2003	
Percent fund balance in base year	
Percent deficit or surplus in base year	
Operational spending per capita base year	Log (OS/population) t − 1
Years	0 = 1999, 2002 1 = 2001, 2003, 2004, 2005
Ratio change own-source revenue	
Ratio change capital spending	
(3) Ratio change capital spending	Log (CS t/CS t − 1)
Ratio change population	
Ratio change intergovernmental revenue	
Total debt per capita base year	Log (total debt/population) t − 1
Fiscal governance, 2003	
Percent fund balance in base year	
Percent deficit or surplus in base year	
Years	0 = 1999, 2001 1 = 2002, 2003, 2004, 2005
Ratio change own-source revenue	
Ratio change operational spending	

Tables 6.2, 6.3, and 6.4 present the results for the 2SLS regression analysis. The equations were also estimated using ordinary least squares (OLS) for purposes of comparison, but these secondary results are not presented here. Because the dependent variables are endogenous and are estimated as independent variables in the other two equations, estimating all equations separately using OLS can produced biased and inconsistent parameter estimates. However, Hausman tests of differences in variances between equations estimated with each method (Pindyck and Rubinfeld 1990, 176–77) show mixed results for the presence of endogeneity with some tests being significant (tests with capital spending) and others not significant.

The overall fit of the capital spending equation is not very good, due to the very high deviation of this variable, even when it is logged. Capital spending can change dramatically from one year to the next compared to spending and revenue, which makes accurate estimation much more difficult. Such variability also creates additional problems for estimating 2SLS compared to OLS. Also the R^2 reported by 2SLS really has no statistical meaning as the actual values of the endogenous variables are used to calculate this statistic, although the model is estimated with the instrumental variables. Thus the residual sums of squares can be greater than total sums of squares, as they are here, which yields negative values for R^2. Again, for comparison, the 2SLS R^2 is reported first for each equation, followed by the OLS R^2.

The regression analysis confirms the effects or lack of effects of key factors identified in the qualitative analysis about the tools governments use to manage fiscal threats and opportunities. The model shows that population growth raises revenues and spending in these governments, and change in sales receipts alters revenue, as one would expect. That change in EAV has no effect on revenue changes is not surprising given the emphasis on property tax levies in Illinois rather than rates in determining the level of property taxes collected. Revenue wealth and spending needs, which are capacity factors, appear to have no immediate impact or weak positive effects on changes in revenues and spending during this time period. By comparison, home rule governments appear to use their increased capacity to increase revenue more than non–home rule governments.

All other things being equal, governments that are more corporate (have both a CAO and a finance director) are more likely to increase own-source revenue and reduce spending than are noncorporate governments. To the extent that increasing spending and reducing revenue, which is the pattern for noncorporate governments during this time period, results in revenue deficits, corporate governments will have better solvency overall. This result also demonstrates the extent to which noncorporate governments may give in to pressure to underfund high levels of service.

The regression results also show that surplus resources have a negative effect on revenues, but a positive effect on spending. When applied to periods of fiscal stress, this pattern suggests that governments with surplus resources are less likely to increase revenues and decrease spending. In other words, they are able to use slack to solve financial problems rather than revenue or spending options, which—as noted in the interviews—are less desirable and are often less strategic options for adapting to threats and opportunities. The effects of prior revenue and spending effort are weak in these equations but show that governments with higher spending effort tend to reduce spending in subsequent years. This could reflect preferences for spending cuts when

(Text continues on p. 182.)

TABLE 6.2 Responses to Fiscal Stress and Munificence: Two-Stage Least Squares Regression Results for Change in Own-Source Revenue, 1999–2005

Ratio (Change) Own-Source Revenues, t/t − 1

	All Govts N = 1501 R² = .28/.37		Small Govts N = 801 R² = .27/.38		Large Govts N = 700 R² = .21/.39		Non–home Rule Govts N = 890 R² = .32/.39		Home Rule Govts N = 604 R² = −.06/.48	
	Coeff.	Z	Coeff.	Z	Coeff.	Z	Coeff.	Z	Coeff.	Z
Ratio population	0.143	8.2***	0.143	6.4***	0.149	6.6***	0.148	8.4***	0.165	2.4**
Ratio EAV	−0.016	−0.8	−0.007	−0.1	−0.020	−1.3	−0.033	−1.4	0.011	0.3
Ratio sales receipts	0.098	5.4***	0.080	3.3**	0.180	4.8***	0.071	3.1**	0.150	4.8***
Ratio IG revenue	−0.024	−1.8*	−0.038	−1.9*	−0.014	−1.1	−0.080	−4.7***	−0.005	−0.3
Home rule	0.015	4.0***	0.027	3.5***	0.017	4.0***	0.004	1.0	−0.001	−0.1
Revenue wealth 2000	−0.004	−1.2	−0.007	−1.5	0.004	0.8	0.015	2.9**	−0.005	−0.7
Fiscal govern	0.009	2.1**	0.017	2.6**	−0.005	−0.9	−0.011	−3.2**	−0.011	−1.6
Fund balance, t − 1	−0.012	−4.2***	−0.012	−2.9**	−0.001	−0.2	−0.047	−5.8***	0.008	0.7
Deficit or surplus, t − 1	−0.032	−4.9***	−0.043	−4.2***	−0.030	−3.7***	−0.015	−2.5**	0.012	1.7*
Own-src rev per cap, t − 1	−0.001	−0.3	−0.005	−0.7	0.007	1.3	−0.015	−2.5**	0.012	1.7*
Ratio operate spending	0.326	3.0**	0.363	3.0**	−0.031	−0.2	0.501	4.5***	0.217	1.0
Ratio capital spending	0.019	2.5**	0.021	2.0**	0.001	0.1	0.010	1.1	0.049	4.1***
2000	0.012	2.2**	0.016	1.8*	0.014	2.0**	0.014	2.0**	0.002	0.3
2001										
2002										
2003	−0.011	−1.9**	−0.009	−1.0	−0.013	−2.2**	−0.014	−1.9*	0.004	0.5
2004										
2005	0.033	4.5***	0.036	3.0**	0.021	3.0**	0.039	3.9***	0.039	3.7***
Intercept[a]	2.3	5.5***	2.3	5.3***	3.5	5.3***	2.1	5.0***	1.9	2.6**

Note: All variables logged except home rule, fiscal governance, revenue wealth, spending needs, and years.

*Probability of .10 ≥ Z ≥ .05; ** probability of .05 ≥ Z ≥ .001; *** probability of .001 > Z.

[a]Intercept is fiscal govern = 0 and years = 1999, 2001, 2002, and 2004.

TABLE 6.3 Responses to Fiscal Stress and Munificence: Two-Stage Least Squares Regression Results for Change in Operational Spending, 1999–2005

Ratio (Change) Operational Spending (no capital), t/t − 1

	All Govts N = 1501 R^2 = .19/.29		Small Govts N = 801 R^2 = .30/.31		Large Govts N = 700 R^2 = .08/.24		Non–home Rule Govts N = 890 R^2 = .28/.29		Home Rule Govts N = 604 R^2 = .28/.39	
	Coeff.	Z	Coeff.	Z	Coeff.	Z	Coeff.	Z	Coeff.	Z
Ratio population	0.058	2.1**	0.023	0.6	0.080	2.4**	0.018	0.4	0.226	3.8***
Ratio IG revenue	0.081	6.4***	0.097	5.5***	−0.001	−0.1	0.107	6.1***	0.006	0.3
Spending need 2000	0.015	2.0*	0.007	0.6	0.020	1.9*	0.012	1.1	0.021	1.8*
Fiscal govern	−0.014	−2.9**	−0.016	−2.3**	−0.013	−2.2**	−0.015	−2.2**	−0.016	−2.5**
Fund balance, t − 1	0.012	3.4**	0.013	2.5**	0.009	1.6	0.010	2.0**	0.023	4.3***
Deficit or surplus, t − 1	0.019	2.0*	0.034	2.4**	0.018	1.7*	0.027	1.8*	0.008	0.6
Op. spending per cap, t − 1	−0.013	−2.3**	−0.016	−1.9*	−0.014	−1.9*	−0.015	−1.6	−0.010	−1.4
Ratio own-srce revenue	0.323	2.5**	0.475	3.0**	0.096	0.6	0.411	2.2**	0.227	1.2
Ratio capital spending	−0.024	−2.2**	−0.001	−0.1	0.011	0.6	−0.012	−0.8	−0.002	−0.2
2000										
2001	−0.025	−3.0**	−0.033	−2.7**	−0.035	−3.6***	−0.037	−3.2**	−0.022	−2.1**
2002										
2003	−0.022	−2.9**	−0.028	−2.5**	−0.011	−1.3	−0.023	−1.9*	−0.014	−1.5
2004	−0.030	−4.1***	−0.034	−3.3**	−0.001	−0.1	−0.029	−2.4**	−0.016	−1.6*
2005	−0.057	−7.4***	−0.074	−7.1***	−0.016	−1.2	−0.066	−6.1***	−0.033	−2.7**
Intercept[a]	2.6	4.9***	1.8	2.8**	3.8	5.4***	2.2	2.6**	2.5	4.0***

Note: All variables logged except home rule, fiscal governance, revenue wealth, spending needs, and years.

*Probability of .10 > Z ≥ .05; ** probability of .05 > Z ≥ .001; *** probability of .001 > Z.

[a]Intercept is fiscal govern = 0 and years = 1999, 2000, and 2002.

TABLE 6.4 Responses to Fiscal Stress and Munificence: Two-Stage Least Squares Regression Results for Change in Capital Spending, 1999–2005

Ratio (Change) Capital Spending, t/t − 1

	All Govts N = 1501 R² = −.12/.08		Small Govts N = 801 R² = −.04/.08		Large Govts N = 700 R² = .10/.11		Non–home Rule Govts N = 890 R² = −.35/.11		Home Rule Govts N = 604 R² = −.65/.07	
	Coeff.	Z	Coeff.	Z	Coeff.	Z	Coeff.	Z	Coeff.	Z
Ratio population	1.219	2.5**	0.688	1.3	−0.158	−0.3	2.256	2.2**	0.060	0.0
Ratio IG revenue	0.517	1.9*	0.347	0.9	0.426	1.8*	−0.478	−0.7	0.484	1.4
Total debt per capita, t − 1	0.122	4.0***	0.121	3.4**	0.074	1.4	0.083	2.2**	0.233	3.1**
Fiscal govern	0.026	0.3	0.128	1.1	−0.125	−1.3	0.188	1.4	0.145	1.0
Fund balance, t − 1	0.020	0.3	−0.078	−0.9	0.199	2.4**	0.006	0.1	−0.354	−1.8*
Deficit or surplus, t − 1	−0.336	−1.9*	−0.261	−1.1	−0.186	−1.0	−0.743	−2.1**	−0.121	−0.5
Cap. spend per cap, t − 1	−0.025	−1.0	0.008	0.2	−0.078	−2.2**	0.000	0.0	−0.092	−1.8*
Ratio own-source revenue	−5.872	−1.7*	−5.067	−1.4	3.784	1.0	−11.419	−1.8*	−14.038	−2.0**
Ratio operate spending	−1.045	−0.4	2.070	0.6	−4.076	−0.9	2.144	0.5	12.110	1.7*
2000	−0.241	−2.2**	−0.449	−2.9**	−0.024	−0.2	−0.203	−1.2	−0.401	−1.9*
2001										
2002	−0.567	−3.5***	−0.505	−2.7**	−0.184	−0.8	−0.717	−2.5**	−1.089	−3.3**
2003	−0.504	−3.8***	−0.297	−1.6	−0.312	−2.0**	−0.701	−2.6**	−0.641	−3.0**
2004	−0.613	−5.2***	−0.411	−2.2**	−0.713	−5.4***	−0.859	−3.9***	−0.365	−1.8*
2005	−0.558	−3.4**	−0.278	−1.1	−0.817	−5.1***	−0.516	−2.1**	−0.356	−1.3
Intercept[a]	30.2	3.2**	15.1	1.5	5.3	0.4	42.8	2.5**	12.9	0.7

Note: All variables logged except home rule, fiscal governance, revenue wealth, spending needs, and years.

*Probability of .10 > Z ≥ .05; **probability of .05 > Z ≥ .001; ***probability of .001 > Z.

[a]Intercept is fiscal govern = 0 and years = 1999 and 2001.

prior spending is high, or that governments with high spending simply have more places to cut.

The regression results in table 6.2 also show that home rule governments react very differently to factors than do non–home rule governments in both the revenue and spending portions of the equation. Moreover, the reactions for large governments are somewhat similar to home rule governments, and non–home rule governments are similar to small governments. The results show that home rule governments are less affected by population change on the revenue side, but more affected on the spending side, and they are affected very little by changes in intergovernmental revenue. By comparison, non–home rule governments reduce own-source revenue but increase spending when intergovernmental revenue increases. In this case, revenue and spending in non–home rule governments seem to be affected more by threats and opportunities than in home rule governments. In fact, non–home rule and smaller governments are affected to a greater extent by all factors in the equation than home rule and larger governments.

The equation for change in capital spending is not as robust as the others, but it shows that capital spending increases when there is debt and increases in population and intergovernmental revenue. Capital spending also declined throughout the early 2000s, but especially in 2004. Results for change in own-source revenue also show trade-offs with capital spending, which is how the link between these events was described in the qualitative evidence, but there is little evidence of a connection between surplus resources and change in capital spending.

Conclusion

Going back to the questions asked at the beginning of this chapter, some answers are now evident. With respect to the question of how do municipal governments in the Chicago metropolitan region respond to fiscal stress (threats of change in financial condition), it is apparent that important findings from studies of cutback management in governments in the late 1970s still apply (table 3.3). The qualitative evidence presented here shows that, as in an earlier era, Chicago municipal governments begin with delaying tactics that allow them to avoid more severe tactics in the near term, then move on to stretching and resisting, where they scale back noncritical operations and enhance revenues in ways that are less likely to be noticed by residents. In the last stage and under the most severe fiscal threats, governments make more dramatic cuts in services, curtail core services, and increase visible revenues to the extent that such tools are available in their fiscal toolbox.

In this case, the primary issue is not whether these governments are more likely to raise revenue or cut spending. Rather, it is about what options are generally available to them, how much fiscal stress they are experiencing and for how long, what options they have already used up, and how painful available options are on several dimensions. One dimension of pain identified here is political, in which the incentives to choose particular options, such as whether to cut spending or raise revenues, are enhanced when governments compete to attract sales enterprises or the right to claim having the lowest taxes and charges. The visibility of property taxes and the tendency to compare property tax levels among similar governments contributes greatly to the general unwillingness to raise property taxes instead of sales taxes.

Another dimension of pain is the impact of options on core services and operations. Although one can envision a strategy of cutting core services and operations to elicit more revenue from taxpayers, as the "greedy bureaucrat" is sometimes prone to do (Bartle and Korosec 1996), the municipal governments studied here seemed to protect their core services and operations for as long as possible.[10] They also avoided firing personnel overall, but this may change as the effects of the Great Recession continue for some governments. Collaborating in the delivery of core services or transferring services to special districts is one way these governments can mitigate the effects of personnel reductions, but these do not seem to be desirable options for many governments in the region.

The analyses presented here reveal additional information about how governments respond to fiscal stress that may reflect the unique qualities of municipalities in the Chicago region or represent an elaboration of findings from the earlier studies. First, municipal governments pursue more strategies of all kinds, not just more painful strategies, the greater their fiscal stress. Second, the solutions governments apply here for solving near-term financial problems are a function of their exogenous fiscal capacity, especially home rule with respect to revenues, and their fiscal structure, which reflects available internal options or those they have not used up.

As shown in the regression analyses in tables 6.2 to 6.4, the effects of fiscal capacity on revenue and spending responses seem to be more conditional than linear. For instance, wealth and spending needs have little direct effect on changes in revenues and spending respectively, but home rule alters revenues and spending both directly and conditionally. Specifically, home rule governments are more likely overall to increase revenues, and they have different revenue and spending responses to particular threats and opportunities, such as changes in population and intergovernmental revenue. The revenue responses of non–home rule governments also are more greatly affected by fiscal structure (fund balance, surpluses or deficits, and current revenue burden), which makes sense, as they have fewer revenue options by law than home rule governments. In this case, there are trade-offs between the munificence of the fiscal structure in non–home rules governments and their decision to increase revenues (once threats and opportunities are controlled for).

A third finding about how governments respond to fiscal stress is identified in the last row of table 3.3. Examining fiscal capacity and measures of financial condition for all municipal governments in the Chicago region shows four to seven with fiscal health that is so poor and that has remained low for so long that their fiscal toolboxes are totally empty. They literally have no options for coping with threats and opportunities, which puts them in perpetual fiscal crisis. These government's responses to fiscal stress do not progress in the same manner as other governments' and, in fact, do not progress at all because there is nowhere to go—not even down. Governments under such conditions engage in unrealistic, escapist, and even illegal activities as documented in East St. Louis. Assuming that in general, the application of professional standards of financial management will help governments improve their financial condition in the long run, such practices and policies are likely to have little impact, as they simply have no options for improving their financial condition.

Notes

1. According to the Local Government Financial Planning and Supervision Act (50 ILCS 320/).
2. A credit report by Standard and Poor's in 2007 discusses an upgrade in outlook from negative to stable because the village was able to pass a referendum that allowed it to increase its non–home rule sales taxes. The report also notes that the village's financial management practices are standard in that it maintains adequate policies in most but not all areas and that it has no capital planning or debt policy and estimates spending and revenues based on the prior year's budget.
3. Service Delivery Task Force first report to the full caucus, December 14, 2009.
4. This is the mandated limit of increase in property tax levy in non–home rule governments without a referendum (PTELL).
5. Excludes special funds such as special assessment areas that generally apply to only a small portion of the municipality.
6. Cook County residential properties are assessed at only 16 percent of actual market value. Forty-six percent of the municipalities, which represents over 50 percent of the municipal population in the region, are in Cook County.
7. Technically, the amount of property taxes collected by governments in Illinois is called the extension, not the levy. The levy is the property taxes requested by government, and the extension is the property taxes allowed by the county.
8. 2SLS is used rather than 3SLS because the latter method will propagate specification errors throughout the system.
9. Adding dummy variables for all years to all equations in the system greatly increased the problems of estimation associated with the system being overidentified, so insignificant year variables were removed from each equation.
10. There was more evidence of governments coping with fiscal stress by cutting core services out of frustration with unions than maneuvering additional money out of taxpayers.

Chapter 7

Financial Problem Solving
Tools for Managing Financial Condition

This chapter focuses on answering two questions. First, what do municipal governments do to maintain or improve financial condition and solve their financial problems in the long run? In other words, what are the broader strategies they use to achieve their financial goals rather than the tactics they use to manage fiscal stress in the near term? Such decisions can encompass a wide range of fiscal policies, such as not issuing debt and relying heavily on sales taxes. They can also include what many people consider to be financial management practices, such as whether governments implement a comprehensive budget or an appropriations ordinance and the internal controls they put in place to protect assets. Second, what factors most affect financial condition in municipalities, and does implementing strategies that are more consistent with corporate forms of governance result in governments having better financial condition overall?

Table 3.2, which shows categories of fiscal tools that were examined in the 2003 interviews, is useful for understanding the difference between financial tools and practice tools for managing fiscal stress and maintaining financial condition. Category D represents tools that have the most direct effect on financial condition, some of which were discussed in chapter 5 and are analyzed here in more detail. Some of these tools, such as the fund balance, are associated with both tactics and strategies. For instance, using the fund balance to maintain spending in the near term is a tactic that was investigated in chapter 6. The decision to maintain a particular level of fund balance for cash management and as a rainy day fund is a longer-term strategy and is investigated in this chapter. By comparison, tools that are not in category D of table 3.2 affect financial condition more indirectly. They represent the methods governments use to assess, solve, and control financial problems more generally rather than the solutions or tools used to solve particular problems. The tools in categories A, B, and C would be better described as financial management practices rather than fiscal policies or strategies.

The first section of this chapter examines the fiscal policies that Chicago municipal governments implemented in the late 1990s up through 2005–6 using the qualitative data. It also explains their policies using variables that represent the primary factors from the model in figure 4.1 including fiscal capacity, administrative capacity and governance, and fiscal structure using regression analysis. These policies have the most direct effect on the financial stability and health of municipal governments. The second section of this chapter documents the different budgeting and planning practices (category A) employed by the interviewed governments, and presents evidence of financial practices in the other two categories (categories B and C). Evidence is also provided on how the practices in all three categories change when governments change or attempt to change their fiscal governance from political to corporate. The third section of this chapter identifies the effects of key factors on overall financial condition by systematically examining Chicago municipal governments that are outliers on different combined dimensions of financial condition. This section also compares the financial condition of governments with different governing structures and fiscal administrative capacities within the municipal groups in appendix 7. Recall that appendix 7 shows how Chicago municipalities were grouped according to factors such as size, growth, and revenue wealth in order to hold these factors constant to examine events within groups (such as growth, as discussed in chapter 5). More specifically, this section provides some answers to the question of whether governing structure and good financial management can improve municipal financial condition overall.

Fiscal Tools for Managing Financial Condition

As discussed in chapter 6, fiscal capacity (e.g., wealth and home rule) has a prominent effect on the size of the fiscal toolbox. Fiscal structure, such as the level fund balances and cash solvency, also affects the size of the toolbox. A government with low fiscal capacity or fund balance will have fewer options to respond to exogenous financial threats than one with high fiscal capacity or fund balances. Other structural features, such as the dependence on sales taxes or intergovernmental revenue, also affect the impact of future exogenous events in terms of the severity of the financial problems these events create. In this case, government fiscal structure can affect both the size of the toolbox and the risk of exogenous events that have a negative impact on government financial condition. Some tools will work better than others to improve or maintain financial conditions given particular risks, and some tools may increase or reduce financial risks more directly, but which tools are actually chosen from among those available is considered to be a function of governance and administrative capacity. As described in chapter 4, governance and administrative capacity are linked factors that affect preferences for particular tools and heuristics associated with assessing what tools work better and which are more or less financially risky.

Spending, Revenue, and Fund Balance Strategies

Patterns of tool use described in chapter 6 show an order of operations in managing fiscal stress that is very similar to what is described in table 3.3 (Levine 1978). In effect, that order of operations constitutes a financial strategy or policy for managing fiscal stress. When faced with fiscal threats, Chicago municipal governments begin with near-term tactics that delay moving to tools that have more profound effects on services or that are more difficult to implement. If the problem remains and the first order of tools have been used up, or if the problem is severe enough and delaying tactics are not sufficient to maintain financial condition, governments will turn to stretching and resisting, and then to cutting and smoothing. This trend was seen across similar governments that experienced different levels of fiscal stress in the two recessions using the qualitative data.

Although one can quibble about how many categories of responses there are to fiscal stress, the order of operations is very evident. That order is based on ease of implementation, level of disruption to services (especially core services and operations), political desirability, and the tools available to the government. As discussed previously, subsidizing spending with surplus funds is the first choice for many governments to manage fiscal stress because it does not affect services, revenues, or other visible and fundamental aspects of their fiscal structure. Similarly, surplus funds can be readily used to take advantage of opportunities that require a financial commitment from the government.

From a problem-solving perspective, the use of surplus funds in the first stage of dealing with fiscal threats gives government the time to obtain more information about the threat and identify the best tools or strategies for maintaining financial condition in the future if the threat continues or becomes more severe. Thus, the order of operations for government coping with fiscal stress is not simply about government denying financial problems or looking for ways to avoid dealing with them, although that certainly happens, as documented here. Rather, the order of operations represents a broader policy for solving financial problems that facilitates government adaptation to the fiscal environment.

One important finding about the use of tools in 2003 and 2009, irrespective of which level of response a government was at, is that all governments chose a variety of tools in all areas of the primary fiscal equation in figure 4.1 to manage fiscal stress. The FAUI survey of municipal governments conducted just after the recession of 1991 that was discussed in chapter 3 shows that Chicago municipal governments pursued more strategies the greater their fiscal stress. The correlation between the sum of responses to twelve questions inquiring about the importance of different financial problems and the sum of responses to twenty-seven questions about fiscal strategies is .41. It demonstrates that the greater the severity and number of fiscal problems, the greater the importance of a larger number of strategies.

Figures 7.1 and 7.2 further confirm the effects of spending threats, revenue opportunities, and fiscal capacity on decisions about spending and revenue. Both figures show median spending per capita with and without capital spending and median own-source revenue per capita from 1998 to 2005 with all values corrected for the employment cost index. Figure 7.1 shows these trends for municipalities in the highest and lowest quintiles of the wealth index as calculated in 2000, and figure 7.2 shows the same trends for home rule and non–home rule municipalities separately.

The most obvious difference between the sets of trend lines in figure 7.1 is that spending and revenue per capita are much greater for wealthy governments (solid lines) than poor governments (dotted lines). Poor governments show a slight increase and then a leveling off of own-source revenues and spending during this time period, but basically there is little change in these three trends. By comparison, wealthy governments show a decline in spending and especially capital spending beginning in 2000, and like poor governments they show little change in revenues per capita over the entire period. All trend lines converge for wealthy governments by 2005, which indicates they did little capital spending and there is little difference between own-source

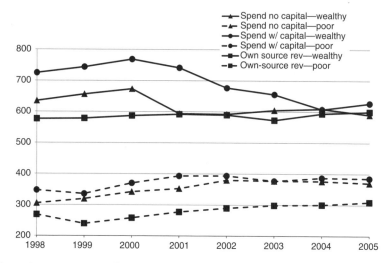

FIGURE 7.1 Median Spending (total and without capital) and Own-Source Revenue per Capita for Municipalities in the Highest and Lowest Quintiles of the Wealth Index for 2000, 1998–2005

Note: Per capita measures are weighted by the percent of EAV that is residential to correct for higher per capita measures in less residential municipalities. The actual per capita values are about 20 percent to 25 percent higher. Values are corrected for the employment cost index, 2000 = 100 ECI.

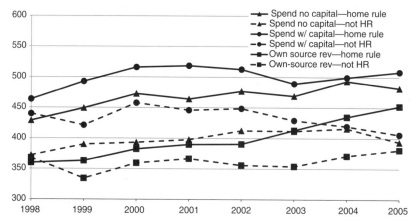

FIGURE 7.2 Median Spending (total and without capital) and Own-Source Revenue per Capita for Home Rule and Non–Home Rule Municipalities, 1998–2005

Note: Per capita measures are weighted by the percent of EAV that is residential to correct for higher per capita measures in less residential municipalities. The actual per capita values are about 20 percent to 25 percent higher. Values are corrected for the employment cost index, 2000 = 100 ECI.

revenue and operational spending in their fiscal structure. The difference between the lines with the box symbols and those with the circle and triangle symbols represents, to a great degree, the contributions of intergovernmental revenues to spending, and wealthy governments do not appear to be using this revenue to fund any operational spending after 2000. Poor governments, by comparison, rely consistently on this revenue as demonstrated by the similar spacing between these lines at all time periods. Also noteworthy is that poor governments consistently spend much less for capital items than wealthy governments.

Figure 7.2 shows the same trend lines for home rule (solid lines) and non–home rule (dotted lines) governments. Spending with and without capital items is greater for home rule than non–home rule governments, but as in figure 7.1, capital spending as a proportion of total spending is very low for all governments by 2003 (see figure 6.9 also). More interesting is the progressive increase in own-source revenue in home rule governments beginning in 2002 such that own-source revenue now seems to fund a much greater portion of total spending in home rule governments than in the past. As in figure 7.1, the difference between the lines with the box symbols and those with the circle and triangle symbols is mostly due to intergovernmental revenues. By comparison to non–home rule governments, home rule governments funded a great portion of spending with intergovernmental revenues until 2002. By 2005, however, both home rule and non–home rule governments were doing little capital spending and relied much less on intergovernmental revenue to fund either operational or total spending with capital.

One question that often arises regarding governments' reactions to fiscal stress is whether governments prefer spending cuts or revenue increases to manage fiscal stress. The answer to this question is not straightforward as the order of operations of tactics and the availability of reserves and borrowing complicates preferences for one strategy over another. However, preferences for these strategies were explored to some extent in the interviews in 2003. All interviewees were asked to assess where their governments could be located on a continuum of valuing low spending and being fiscally conservative versus valuing high service levels whatever the cost. Not surprisingly, most interviewees claimed that their governments were on the low tax and low spend end of the scale or in the middle, but eight claimed that their governments, most of which are home rule, would raise revenue before cutting services. Five interviewees noted that their board often contradicted themselves in this regard by not adequately funding spending increases or compensating for revenue declines and other fiscal threats with spending cuts.

The fund balance practices and policies discussed in the interviews were quite varied and often related to policies and practices associated with capital planning and debt as discussed more in the next section. Most governments that talked about fund balances expressed an opinion as to how much should be maintained in them, and industry standards were often referenced, but those standards are for cash management purposes and much less than the levels shown in figures 6.9 and 6.10. Some governments noted that their board debated and determined fund balance policy and levels, but several government officials noted that their board did not "totally understand" fund balances. Several other interviewees noted that they try not to draw the board's attention to them. News reports about two governments documented incidents in which the large amounts of money in their fund balances became a source of political embarrassment and conflict. Indeed, the impression given from news reports is that surpluses are not desirable and inefficient. Governments with surpluses and high fund balances sometimes experience attitudes of "gotcha" by news reporters and others. The political sensitivity of these funds is evident in the following quote from an interview with a mayor:

> My goal every year is to bring in a budget that's $200,000 deficit intentionally. Number one, if you have a surplus, everyone tries to find a way to spend it. If you start with a deficit, you're less likely of getting the pressure of spending extra money. We've done that year after year. I would not have a right to raise taxes if I had a balanced or a surplus budget, that's my opinion. If we always have a deficit, we have a reason for raising taxes. I sound illogical, but I could see the tax payers group suing a municipality or any taxing body that continually ran a surplus if they raise taxes.

How governments choose to raise funds for the fund balance is also quite varied. Some interviewees talk about building surpluses by underestimating revenues and overestimating expenditures. Others talked about loosely earmarking a portion of some tax for the fund balance or making spending cuts to replenish reserves. One government discussed at length that reserves must be planned ahead of time, and not just the result of what is left over at the end of each fiscal year. Demonstrating the link between fund balance and borrowing, one fairly common way of establishing a fund balance is by issuing special bonds to establish a "working cash fund." Seven interviewed governments talked about establishing such funds using bonds.[1]

Policies and practices regarding cash reserves and the fund balances among municipal governments in the Chicago region were discussed in the previous chapter in the context of capital spending and reliance on sales taxes. Figure 6.10 shows that the normal fund balance in Chicago municipal governments is close to 50 percent of total spending for the general fund, special revenue funds, and debt service fund (the percentage is slightly greater for general funds only). By comparison, the National League of Cities (NLC) reports that fund balance as a percent of expenditures in 379 cities nationwide with populations greater than 10,000 had risen from a norm of 18 percent in 2000 to 25 percent in 2007 (Hoene and Pagano 2010). The fund balance norm for municipalities in the Chicago region is clearly much higher. It is also much higher than the minimum of two months of general fund operating expenditures that is recommended by the Government Finance Officers Association (www.gfoa.org/downloads/AppropriateLevelUnrestrictedFundBalanceGeneral Fund_BestPractice.pdf).[2]

What accounts for the higher fund balances among Chicago municipal governments? One reason may be their greater reliance on more volatile taxes, especially sales taxes, than generally occurs in municipalities in other states. Few states allow municipalities to levy sales taxes or distribute state-shared sales tax revenue based on the point of sale in those municipalities, although 69 percent of the municipalities responding to the NLC survey had both sales and property tax authority. In this case, Chicago municipal governments seem to have adapted to their somewhat unique condition, driven in part by the bond rating agencies as observed in many credit reports for municipalities in the region from Standard and Poor's.

Another related explanation for the discrepancy between normal fund balances for municipalities in the Chicago region and in the NLC survey is the difference in the size of the governments for the two populations. Fifty-nine percent of the cities in the NLC survey have populations greater than fifty thousand, but only 8 percent of the municipalities in the Chicago region do. GFOA also recognizes that larger governments may not need fund balances that are as high as small governments' because the former can predict revenues more accurately, and larger governments tend to have more diverse revenue structures. It was also noted previously that larger governments tend to have more spending slack in their fiscal structure, which also reduces the need for revenue reserves.[3] Indeed, the correlation between government population and the size of the fund balance among the Chicago municipalities is $-.20$. Thus Chicago municipal governments may also have adapted their reserve structure to the risks associated with being smaller.

Capital Spending and Financing

Chapter 6 documents the link between existing revenues, fund balances, and borrowing in the financing of capital items and management of fiscal stress in chapter 6. Capital spending and revenue that is earmarked or dedicated to capital spending is viewed by many municipal governments as a source of surplus spending or revenues that can be tapped to handle fiscal stress in the short run, just as the fund balance can finance capital spending and be used to alleviate fiscal stress. In fact, many governments in the interviews admitted that their primary method of financing capital items was by generating surpluses during the good times to save for capital projects or budgeting for capital spending based on forecasted surpluses.

Although both strategies view capital spending as secondary to operational spending, the latter approach to capital investment is especially ad hoc and haphazard. It might be summarized as—invest in capital only when it is broken or when money and grants are available. An alternative approach is to plan and budget for capital spending each year on both the revenue and spending side of the equation (1) to insure that capital needs are met. This approach probably requires government to finance capital spending to some degree with debt or dedicated revenue, as it may be too difficult to maintain a consistent capital spending stream using savings, surpluses, and grants alone.

Interviewees in some governments with an ad hoc approach to capital investing claimed to not have the revenue streams to fund a planned capital program, but for others it seemed tied to a reluctance to issue debt and an unwillingness to raise taxes and revenues for this purpose. As noted previously, many governments claimed to be very fiscally conservative, and more than a few had experienced underfunded water and sewer systems. Some of this underfunding is due to water rates not keeping pace with inflation and capital needs, but many of the capital improvements to these systems are funded with general obligations bonds because they are cheaper than revenue bonds. General obligation bonds are guaranteed by the property tax in Illinois, and revenue bonds are guaranteed by the revenues from water and sewer charges, which are considered riskier by borrowers. Even though the water and sewer fund will repay the operating funds for its claim on the property tax from GO debt used to finance water and sewer improvements, some mayors interviewed seemed reluctant to increase the property tax levy for GO debt for any purposes.

One thing to keep in mind when assessing governments' attitudes toward their fund balance and the link between fund balances, surpluses, bond ratings, and capital expenditures is that many municipal governments in the Chicago metropolitan area do not go to the bond markets to issue debt, and so do not have bond ratings. In 2003, 57 percent of the 264 municipal governments did not have bond ratings through Moody's, and 55 percent had no Moody bond ratings in 2009.[4] Governments obtain and expire their bond rating as they choose to enter or exit the bond market. In total, the percentage of governments that did not have a bond rating in either 2003 or 2009 was 52. These governments probably did not issue debt in this manner during this time period and therefore did not have the same pressures on their fund balances as governments that issued debt through the bond markets. Some governments without bond ratings may have a policy of financing capital expenditures in other ways, as discussed previously, or had little capital spending during this time period.

According to the Illinois comptroller data, in 1998, 20 percent of the municipal governments in the Chicago metropolitan region had no bonded debt, and that percent had risen to 28 by 2006. In a reverse trend, 10 percent of the governments had no debt of any kind in 1998, but only 2 percent had no debt of any kind by 2006. Thus, an increasing number of governments relied on other forms of debt than bonds to fund capital spending between 1998 and 2006. Indeed, eighteen of the sixty-two governments interviewed talked about relying on installment contracts or local banks for capital financing rather than going to the bond market. One of the primary reasons for not bonding, as discussed in previous chapters, is that non–home rule governments are limited in issuing GO debt due to restrictions on the property tax levy, and new debt must be approved through referendum. As such, tools for financing capital spending are very limited for non–home rule governments.

Figure 7.3 shows general obligation, total bonds, and total debt per capita for home rule and non–home rule governments for 1998 to 2005.[5] All per capita values have been corrected for the CPI, with 2000 as the base year. The figure clearly shows a tremendous difference in levels and types of debt for the two types of governments. General obligation and total bond levels are much less in non–home rule governments and are a smaller proportion of their total debt compared to home rule governments that clearly take advantage of their status to issue more debt and a greater proportion of bonded debt. Home rule governments have another advantage over non–home rule governments in the bond market in that, all other things being equal, home rule governments have higher bond ratings. It is clear from bond rating comments from Standard and Poor's that being home rule does increase the bond rating, which lowers the cost of debt for these governments.[6]

Figures 7.4 and 7.5 show total debt and GO debt per capita, respectively, for the five quintiles of municipal wealth (2000) from 1998 to 2005. Interestingly, the level of total debt per capita across all years is progressively higher for each quintile of wealth, but GO debt shows a much different relationship with wealth. Specifically, the wealthiest governments' debt equaled that of governments with medium and high wealth in

FIGURE 7.3 General Obligation, Total Bonds, and Total Debt per Capita for Home Rule and Non-Home Rule Municipalities, 1998–2005

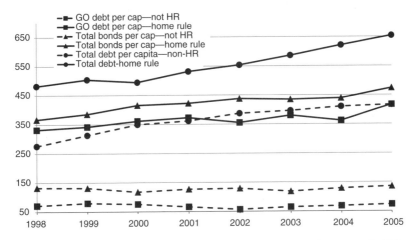

Note: Per capita measures are weighted by the percent of EAV that is residential to correct for higher per capita measures in less-residential municipalities. The actual per capita values are about 20 percent to 25 percent higher. Corrected for consumer price index (Chicago), 2,000 = 100 CPI.

1998, then declined dramatically to equal GO debt in low-wealth governments, and then increased dramatically after 2000 to again equal GO debt in medium and high wealth governments by 2005. In other words, there is a lot more variability in GO debt per capita in governments in the highest quintile of revenue capacity than in other governments in the Chicago metropolitan region.

FIGURE 7.4 Total Debt per Capita for Municipal Wealth Index Quintiles, 1998–2005

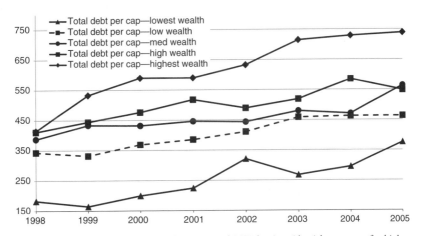

Note: Per capita measures are weighted by the percent of EAV that is residential to correct for higher per capita measures in less-residential municipalities. The actual per capita values are about 20 percent to 25 percent higher. Corrected for consumer price index (Chicago), 2000 = 100 CPI.

FIGURE 7.5 General Obligation Debt per Capita for Municipal Wealth Index Quintiles, 1998–2005

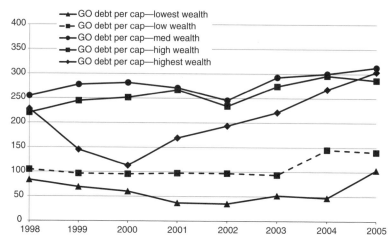

Note: Per capita measures are weighted by the percent of EAV that is residential to correct for higher per capita measures in less-residential municipalities. The actual per capita values are about 20 percent to 25 percent higher. Corrected for consumer price index (Chicago), 2000 = 100 CPI.

Several interviewed governments claimed to have zero debt, and five other interviewees talked about their governments' not being comfortable with taking on debt, wanting to pay off debt as quickly as possible, and residents saying that the government "should get away from debt and do everything pay-as-you-go." The impetus behind these sentiments is the cost of debt and especially bonding with all the consultant and underwriting fees. Furthermore, "building reserves to pay for capital items as opposed to issuing debt generates investment income."

Whatever the reason for not funding capital spending at the optimum level, be it low wealth, fiscal conservancy, or a lack of financing options, the problem of infrastructure deficiencies was noted numerous times in the news reports, and three interviewees mentioned "being several years behind on the capital plan" as a result of the recession.[7] Another interviewee who was a finance director noted the following about infrastructure deficiencies and their effects on financial condition:

> We're keeping up our water systems. I don't want to be like Town X, or some of these other towns, when they have 100 year old sewers, they don't know how they're going to pay for it. Because if you don't attend to your infrastructure, it becomes a massive crisis down the road and you never get out from underneath it. Then your whole town falls apart, industry moves away because everything's falling apart. We always replace some section of the water mains every year, because you've got to do it, you just can't ignore it and put your head in the sand.

Although twenty-six governments claimed to be mostly pay-as-you-go for capital financing (fund balance, surplus, or dedicated revenue source), most governments claimed to use multiple methods. In addition to pay-as-you-go, debt, and grants, growing governments can use resources generated by development to finance capital spending, such as impact fees and developer-constructed infrastructure, and they also use special assessments as discussed previously. In 2005, exactly 50 percent of the municipalities in the Chicago metropolitan region levied property taxes for special service areas according to the Illinois Department of Revenue. Non–home rule governments also do creative things with general obligation debt, such as issuing bonds continuously to maintain the debt portion of the property tax levy and to avoid future referendums to issue new debt after the old debt is paid off.[8]

Professional standards of financial management state that proactive strategies toward capital investment make the most sense, but preferences for low taxes and revenue burden and against debt may run contrary to this strategy. The graphs presented here also show that being non–home rule and of low wealth may also reduce tools for investing in and maintaining capital assets. However, many governments in the news reports and interviews talked about different proactive strategies for financing capital improvements. For instance, many talked about dedicating particular revenue sources to capital spending, including sales taxes, property taxes (not tied specifically to GO debt), vehicle stickers, and gasoline taxes. Others discussed their vehicle reserve funds and revolving equipment funds for capital equipment.

Dedicating sales taxes to capital spending, as promised by six governments in the news reports and interviews in their quest for home rule, makes a lot of sense from a risk standpoint as capital spending has more flexibility than operational spending for absorbing the effects of a recession. However, earmarking a certain portion of the stable property tax to capital spending ensures that capital spending will continue during periods of fiscal stress, and using gasoline and vehicle stickers may be a more equitable method of financing capital spending on highways in terms of who benefits most from the investments (those who use the roads). Only 22 percent to 24 percent of municipal governments had no dedicated revenue for capital spending from 2001 to 2005, and municipal governments with such revenue dedicated between 4 percent and 5 percent of their total revenue to capital purposes.

Regression Analyses

What factors determine which financial tools municipal governments use to manage financial condition for the long haul? Thus far this section has presented evidence of substantial differences in spending, revenue, and debt for governments that are wealthy versus those that are poor and home rule versus non–home rule. The qualitative evidence also suggests that these governments have very different policies regarding debt, capital investment, and fund balances. This section will examine the impact of important factors identified previously (and in figure 4.1) on these fiscal policies, which are also financial tools, using regression analysis and data from 1999 to 2005. This period of time includes both fiscal good times and fiscal bad times for municipal governments in this region. The relatively high levels of shared income tax, sales receipts, and capital grants from state government in the late 1990s allowed municipalities to do more capital investment, service growth, tax rebates, and general fund subsidies than in the past. However, by 2001 most governments were beginning to experience the effects of the recession, which was over for them by 2004.

Table 7.1 shows the basic model to be estimated for seven financial policy areas. These areas are own-source revenue per capita, operational spending per capita, capital spending per capita, dedicated capital revenue per capita, total debt per capita, budgetary solvency (fund balance + revenue as a percentage of operational spending), and reliance on sales taxes (percent sales tax of own-source revenue). The independent variables include all those used to estimate the revenue wealth index, plus grant and nongrant state-shared revenue per capita, and all variables used to estimate the spending needs index. Note that median age of housing and income per capita are only available for 2000 and 1999, respectively, making their values constant for all years within each municipality, and less accurate measures of infrastructure age and personnel wealth respectively. However, relative level of income per capita is not likely to change dramatically from 1999 to 2005. In this case, both variables function as cross-sectional, fixed-effects indicators.[9] Four additional variables are included in the model to reflect fiscal opportunities, events, or other conditions that could affect the size and content of the fiscal toolbox, including population growth.

Other factors examined here are size of municipality (population), how residential the municipality is, and miles from the city of Chicago.[10] The residentialness of the municipality may affect the weight given to voters by government officials in municipal decisions, the types of revenue and spending streams governments experience, and the burden of payment for services on residents. Miles from the city of Chicago reflects

---

TABLE 7.1   Model and Variables to Assess Fiscal Policies: Tools for Managing Financial Condition

Appendix 1 explains these variables in more detail.

Basic model to estimate with regression analysis:
FPFT = RW + SN + OV + FS + FG + YR.

FPFT =   Financial policies or financial tools: Own-source revenue per capita, operational spending per capita, capital spending per capita, dedicated capital revenue per capita, total debt per capita, budgetary solvency (fund balance + revenue as a percentage of operational spending), and reliance on sales taxes.

RW =   Revenue wealth: All items in revenue wealth index plus intergovernmental revenue: sales receipts per capita; EAV per square mile; income per capita; grants per capita; nongrant, state-shared revenue per capita; and home rule.

SN =   Spending needs: All items in the spending needs index: crime per capita; median age of housing; population density; square miles of roads; and whether municipality is in a fire district, park district, or library district.

OV =   Other variables that may affect fiscal capacity or present a threat or an opportunity: percent residential EAV, municipal population, ratio change in population, miles from the central city (city of Chicago).

FS =   Fiscal structure of the government: Revenue diversification, fund balance as a percent of spending (lagged), surplus or deficit as a percent of spending (lagged).

FG =   Fiscal governance: Financial decision structure: FDS (binary variables for all categories with mayor only as intercept), whether treasurer is elected, partisan elections (binary variables for all categories with partisan elections as intercept), whether government is a city with wards, whether government is a strong mayoral form.

YR =   Year of data with 1998 as intercept, 1999 to 2005.

level of spending needs or demands, especially for capital infrastructure. There were several comments from interviewees about how residents in rural areas expect and require fewer services due in part to lower expectations for services. But outer ring municipalities have much less capital infrastructure to maintain as more properties have private wells and septic systems. Infrastructure also becomes newer as you move away from the Chicago area according to a map of median age of housing.[11]

Three fiscal structural variables—revenue diversification, level of fund balance, and level of deficit or surplus (both as a percent of spending)—are included in the model where they are appropriate. To avoid endogeneity, deficit-surplus is measured for the prior year, and fund balance is measured for the two years prior as fund balance (t − 2) plus deficit or surplus (t − 1) equals the fund balance (t − 1) according to the rules of accounting. However, using lagged structural variables to measure deficit or surplus resources also makes sense logically. As shown in figure 4.1, fiscal structure is the outcome of financial decisions in prior years and defines many of the tools available to government to manage fiscal stress and maintain financial condition in the current year. Fiscal structure also can provide municipal governments a buffer for environmental threats and the resources to take advantage of opportunities, so whatever choices governments make regarding revenues, spending, and debt in the current year will be based on the fiscal toolbox in a prior year. Also the surplus–deficit variable reflects the level of fiscal stress the government may be experiencing as it is, in effect, a change variable that is equal to the difference between the fund balance in year t and t − 1.

The next set of explanatory variables included in the model measures fiscal governance using the fiscal decision structure variable (2003 only), the partisan elections variable, whether the treasurer is elected, and several categories of the structure of government variable (whether government is a city with ward elections and whether the mayor is strong). Because these variables are categorical, the categories must be entered into the model as dummy variables with one category left out. The null categories for all these variables are represented by the value of the intercept. As with income and age of housing, these variables are constant for all years within each government. However, some of these variables did not change in actuality between 1999 and 2005.

The last set of factors included as explanatory factors in the model are dummy variables for six of the seven years of data. These variables are used to account for the fixed effects of the different years and so reflects the common threats and opportunities experienced by the municipal governments during fiscal good times and fiscal bad times. Finally, the model is run for home rule and non–home rule governments separately based upon the tremendous differences in financial policies observed for these governments in many of the graphs in this chapter. The shaded results in the last four rows of each table indicate a difference of 50 percent in the coefficients for these two types of governments. The regression models are estimated using ordinary least squares, and the significance tests reported in tables 7.2 to 7.8 (values for t and ρ) are based on robust estimates of standard errors.[12] Unstandardized slopes are symbolized as β and the betas are standardized slopes that show the effects of all independent variables factors on fiscal policy in standard deviation units. All dependent variables and most independent variables, except those indicated in the table, are logged and so the values of β for these effects are interpreted as elasticities.[13]

(Text continues on p. 212.)

TABLE 7.2 Regression Analysis of Own-Source Revenue Per Capita, 1999–2005

Own-source revenue per capita	All Governments, R² = .50				Home Rule[b] R² = .61		Non–Home Rule[b] R² = .54	
	β	beta	t	ρ	β	ρ	β	ρ
Sales receipts per capita	0.275	0.53	19.3	0.00	0.297	0.00	0.262	0.00
EAV per square mile	0.078	0.13	3.6	0.00	-0.040	0.31	0.165	0.00
Income per capita, 1999	-0.019	-0.01	-0.6	0.56	0.021	0.69	-0.010	0.80
Grants per capita (fed and state)	0.074	0.16	7.2	0.00	0.076	0.00	0.073	0.00
Nongrant, state-shared revenue per cap	0.179	0.11	2.6	0.01	0.186	0.01	-0.059	0.57
Home rule	0.194	0.18	7.8	0.00				
% residential EAV	0.409	0.24	4.9	0.00	0.426	0.00	0.405	0.00
Population	-0.067	-0.16	-4.6	0.00	-0.060	0.01	-0.010	0.57
Ratio change population	0.093	0.03	1.2	0.24	0.136	0.60	-0.043	0.61
Miles from Chicago	-0.297	-0.25	-8.3	0.00	-0.533	0.00	-0.099	0.01
Crime per capita	-0.038	-0.09	-3.2	0.00	0.002	0.93	-0.052	0.00
Median age housing, 2000	1.119	0.01	0.5	0.64	-6.021	0.10	-1.565	0.55
Population density	-0.185	-0.29	-5.9	0.00	-0.306	0.00	-0.161	0.00
Square miles of roads	0.111	0.15	3.8	0.00	0.046	0.18	0.150	0.00
Fire district	-0.086	-0.08	-3.4	0.00	-0.133	0.00	-0.011	0.73
Park district	-0.079	-0.07	-3.4	0.00	-0.003	0.93	-0.140	0.00
Library district	0.111	0.10	4.9	0.00	0.211	0.00	0.010	0.75
Revenue diversification t − 1	-0.826	-0.18	-6.9	0.00	-0.261	0.09	-1.178	0.00

Fund balance as % of spending t − 2	−0.101	−0.06	−2.1	0.04	0.093	0.21	−0.117	0.02
Surplus deficit as % of spending t − 1	0.077	0.05	1.8	0.07	0.297	0.00	−0.038	0.41
Manager and finance director, 2003	0.151	0.13	4.4	0.00	0.093	0.09	0.154	0.00
Administrator and finance director, 2003	0.164	0.11	4.6	0.00	−0.117	0.04	0.264	0.00
Administrator only, 2003	0.032	0.02	1.1	0.29	−0.030	0.53	0.063	0.10
Finance director only, 2003	0.246	0.11	7.4	0.00	0.066	0.23	0.365	0.00
Nonpartisan elections	0.012	0.01	0.4	0.68	−0.178	0.00	0.036	0.28
Partisan authority but run nonpartisan	−0.016	−0.01	−0.6	0.56	−0.041	0.39	−0.019	0.58
Elected treasurer	−0.232	−0.14	−6.8	0.00	−0.414	0.00	−0.174	0.00
City with wards	0.147	0.11	4.4	0.00	0.273	0.00	0.063	0.23
Strong mayor	0.228	0.11	6.8	0.00	0.391	0.00	0.154	0.00
2000	0.027	0.02	0.8	0.44	0.018	0.71	0.039	0.38
2001	0.045	0.03	1.3	0.20	0.062	0.22	0.054	0.23
2002	0.060	0.04	1.7	0.09	0.100	0.06	0.056	0.19
2003	0.082	0.05	2.4	0.02	0.157	0.00	0.055	0.19
2004	0.124	0.08	3.6	0.00	0.209	0.00	0.087	0.05
2005	0.162	0.11	4.6	0.00	0.241	0.00	0.115	0.01
Intercept[a]	−5.3		−0.3	0.77	49.2	0.08	15.0	0.45

Note: All variables logged except binary (home rule, governance, and years) and revenue diversification.

[a] Intercept represents 0 for all binary variables.

[b] β for home rule and non–home rule have 50% difference in shaded areas.

TABLE 7.3 Regression Analysis of Operational Spending per Capita, 1999–2005

Operational spending per capita	All Governments, R^2 = .56				Home Rule[b] R^2 = 60		Non–Home Rule[b] R^2 = .65	
	β	beta	t	ρ	β	ρ	β	ρ
Sales receipts per capita	0.215	0.47	18.5	0.00	0.241	0.00	0.203	0.00
EAV per square mile	0.086	0.16	4.8	0.00	−0.006	0.84	0.156	0.00
Income per capita, 1999	−0.050	−0.04	−1.9	0.06	−0.009	0.83	−0.050	0.13
Grants per capita (fed and state)	0.089	0.22	10.4	0.00	0.100	0.00	0.086	0.00
Nongrant, state-shared revenue per cap	0.287	0.21	5.2	0.00	0.267	0.00	0.100	0.25
Home rule	0.169	0.18	8.0	0.00				
% residential EAV	0.346	0.23	5.1	0.00	0.400	0.00	0.295	0.00
Population	−0.086	−0.24	−7.3	0.00	−0.077	0.00	−0.044	0.00
Ratio change population	−0.038	−0.01	−0.6	0.56	0.041	0.86	−0.164	0.02
Miles from Chicago	−0.217	−0.21	−7.6	0.00	−0.413	0.00	−0.052	0.11
Crime per capita	−0.035	−0.10	−3.6	0.00	0.003	0.86	−0.049	0.00
Median age housing, 2000	−0.959	−0.01	−0.5	0.60	−6.149	0.05	−3.132	0.12
Population density	−0.138	−0.25	−5.4	0.00	−0.258	0.00	−0.105	0.00
Square miles of roads	0.062	0.09	2.6	0.01	0.029	0.31	0.076	0.04
Fire district	−0.079	−0.08	−3.8	0.00	−0.126	0.00	−0.013	0.61
Park district	−0.064	−0.07	−3.4	0.00	−0.015	0.61	−0.111	0.00
Library district	0.087	0.09	4.6	0.00	0.199	0.00	−0.018	0.48

Revenue diversification t − 1	−0.655	−0.16	−7.0	0.00	−0.125	0.31	−1.041	0.00
Fund balance as % of spending t − 2	−0.070	−0.04	−1.8	0.07	0.136	0.03	−0.110	0.01
Surplus deficit as % of spending t − 1	−0.347	−0.27	−12.3	0.00	−0.217	0.00	−0.418	0.00
Manager and finance director, 2003	0.127	0.12	4.6	0.00	0.069	0.11	0.131	0.00
Administrator and finance director, 2003	0.140	0.11	4.7	0.00	−0.109	0.03	0.212	0.00
Administrator only, 2003	0.037	0.03	1.5	0.13	−0.013	0.74	0.057	0.05
Finance director only, 2003	0.181	0.09	6.4	0.00	0.047	0.32	0.282	0.00
Nonpartisan elections	0.002	0.00	0.1	0.92	−0.146	0.00	0.016	0.56
Partisan authority but run nonpartisan	−0.010	−0.01	−0.5	0.65	−0.018	0.64	−0.020	0.47
Elected treasurer	−0.221	−0.16	−8.0	0.00	−0.354	0.00	−0.174	0.00
City with wards	0.148	0.13	5.3	0.00	0.242	0.00	0.080	0.06
Strong mayor	0.187	0.10	7.0	0.00	0.317	0.00	0.104	0.01
2000	0.028	0.02	1.0	0.33	0.037	0.36	0.030	0.41
2001	0.033	0.02	1.2	0.25	0.064	0.13	0.033	0.37
2002	0.089	0.07	3.1	0.00	0.133	0.00	0.083	0.02
2003	0.094	0.07	3.3	0.00	0.158	0.00	0.074	0.03
2004	0.101	0.07	3.5	0.00	0.174	0.00	0.072	0.04
2005	0.101	0.08	3.4	0.00	0.187	0.00	0.054	0.15
Intercept[a]	12.8		0.9	0.35	51.8	0.03	29.6	0.05

Note: All variables logged except binary (home rule, governance, and years) and revenue diversification.

[a]Intercept represents 0 for all binary variables.

[b]β for home rule and non–home rule have 50% difference in shaded areas.

TABLE 7.4 Regression Analysis of Capital Spending per Capita, 1999–2005

Capital spending per capita	All Governments, $R^2 = .34$				Home Rule[b] $R^2 = .36$		Non–Home Rule[b] $R^2 = .38$	
	β	beta	t	ρ	β	ρ	β	ρ
Sales receipts per capita	0.423	0.23	7.8	0.00	0.684	0.00	0.320	0.00
EAV per square mile	0.113	0.05	1.4	0.16	−0.311	0.07	0.197	0.05
Income per capita, 1999	0.224	0.05	1.8	0.07	−0.217	0.31	0.428	0.01
Grants per capita (fed and state)	0.243	0.15	6.3	0.00	0.206	0.01	0.257	0.00
Nongrant, state-shared revenue per cap	0.832	0.15	3.4	0.00	0.959	0.01	0.393	0.29
Home rule	0.213	0.06	2.1	0.04				
% residential EAV	−0.256	−0.04	−0.9	0.39	−0.492	0.27	−0.080	0.85
Population	0.166	0.11	3.1	0.00	0.174	0.07	0.390	0.00
Ratio change population	−0.064	−0.01	−0.2	0.87	−0.639	0.48	−0.289	0.48
Miles from Chicago	−0.112	−0.03	−0.8	0.41	−0.858	0.00	0.084	0.62
Crime per capita	−0.087	−0.06	−2.0	0.04	−0.165	0.07	−0.047	0.38
Median age housing, 2000	5.684	0.02	0.7	0.51	14.294	0.40	−12.804	0.22
Population density	−0.094	−0.04	−1.1	0.28	−0.319	0.06	−0.014	0.90
Square miles of roads	0.206	0.08	2.3	0.02	0.124	0.32	0.236	0.08
Fire district	−0.251	−0.07	−2.4	0.02	−0.568	0.00	0.267	0.04
Park district	−0.225	−0.06	−2.5	0.01	−0.112	0.51	−0.306	0.00
Library district	0.354	0.09	3.6	0.00	0.559	0.00	−0.019	0.88

Revenue diversification t − 1	−0.860	−0.05	−2.0	0.05	0.129	0.84	−1.320	0.01
Fund balance as % of spending t − 2	0.181	0.03	1.0	0.31	0.349	0.36	0.286	0.11
Surplus deficit as % of spending t − 1	0.529	0.10	3.0	0.00	0.826	0.00	0.335	0.10
Manager and finance director, 2003	0.420	0.10	2.9	0.00	0.685	0.01	0.240	0.16
Administrator and finance director, 2003	0.473	0.09	3.3	0.00	0.937	0.00	0.294	0.08
Administrator only, 2003	0.094	0.02	0.7	0.47	−0.231	0.33	0.368	0.02
Finance director only, 2003	1.344	0.17	8.0	0.00	1.172	0.00	1.739	0.00
Nonpartisan elections	0.082	0.02	0.7	0.46	−0.247	0.19	0.083	0.58
Partisan authority but run nonpartisan	0.127	0.03	1.3	0.20	0.260	0.19	0.019	0.87
Elected treasurer	−0.239	−0.04	−1.3	0.19	−0.815	0.01	−0.006	0.98
City with wards	−0.195	−0.04	−1.2	0.22	0.276	0.31	−0.418	0.05
Strong mayor	0.668	0.09	3.9	0.00	1.046	0.00	0.443	0.06
2000	−0.031	−0.01	−0.3	0.75	0.062	0.70	−0.076	0.53
2001	−0.604	−0.11	−4.7	0.00	−0.263	0.20	−0.782	0.00
2002	−0.934	−0.18	−7.4	0.00	−0.604	0.00	−1.101	0.00
2003	−1.803	−0.34	−13.9	0.00	−1.559	0.00	−1.924	0.00
2004	−1.896	−0.35	−14.5	0.00	−1.717	0.00	−1.977	0.00
2005	−1.893	−0.35	−14.0	0.00	−1.791	0.00	−1.945	0.00
Intercept[a]	−53.1		−0.8	0.41	−104.9	0.41	84.1	0.29

Note: All variables logged except binary (home rule, governance, and years) and revenue diversification.

[a] Intercept represents 0 for all binary variables.

[b] β for home rule and non–home rule have 50% difference in shaded areas.

TABLE 7.5 Regression Analysis of Dedicated Capital Revenue per Capita, 2001–5

Capital revenue per capita	All Governments, R² = .36				Home Rule[b] R² = .41		Non–Home Rule[b] R² = .43	
	β	beta	t	ρ	β	ρ	β	ρ
Sales receipts per capita	0.345	0.19	5.6	0.00	0.446	0.00	0.241	0.00
EAV per square mile	−0.099	−0.05	−1.0	0.31	−0.520	0.02	0.057	0.64
Income per capita, 1999	−0.084	−0.02	−0.6	0.57	−0.260	0.32	0.108	0.58
Grants per capita (fed and state)	0.361	0.23	8.2	0.00	0.297	0.00	0.366	0.00
Nongrant, state-shared revenue per cap	0.788	0.14	2.9	0.00	0.284	0.44	1.069	0.02
Home rule	−0.018	0.00	−0.2	0.87				
% residential EAV	−1.147	−0.19	−3.5	0.00	−0.207	0.63	−2.010	0.00
Population	0.406	0.28	6.5	0.00	0.446	0.00	0.581	0.00
Ratio change population	−0.104	−0.01	−0.3	0.80	−2.365	0.01	0.240	0.57
Miles from Chicago	−0.217	−0.05	−1.4	0.16	−1.060	0.00	0.182	0.37
Crime per capita	−0.101	−0.07	−2.0	0.05	−0.238	0.01	−0.025	0.70
Median age housing, 2000	−11.533	−0.04	−1.2	0.23	−3.647	0.83	−22.589	0.06
Population density	−0.046	−0.02	−0.4	0.67	−0.138	0.47	−0.028	0.85
Square miles of roads	0.264	0.10	2.3	0.02	0.000	1.00	0.396	0.02
Fire district	−0.065	−0.02	−0.5	0.61	−0.557	0.00	0.428	0.01
Park district	−0.242	−0.06	−2.3	0.02	−0.073	0.67	−0.305	0.02

Library district	0.229	0.06	2.2	0.03	0.224	0.19	0.060	0.69
Revenue diversification t − 1	−0.382	−0.02	−0.8	0.45	0.923	0.22	−0.437	0.44
Fund balance as % of spending t − 2	0.200	0.03	0.9	0.40	−0.208	0.64	0.597	0.02
Surplus deficit as % of spending t − 1	1.544	0.30	4.5	0.00	2.909	0.00	0.970	0.01
Manager and finance director, 2003	0.762	0.19	4.6	0.00	0.760	0.00	0.783	0.00
Administrator and finance director, 2003	0.822	0.17	5.2	0.00	1.026	0.00	0.763	0.00
Administrator only, 2003	0.409	0.09	2.7	0.01	0.087	0.73	0.557	0.00
Finance director only, 2003	1.069	0.14	5.2	0.00	0.333	0.33	1.526	0.00
Nonpartisan elections	0.331	0.07	2.5	0.01	0.081	0.72	0.418	0.02
Partisan authority but run nonpartisan	0.518	0.14	4.4	0.00	0.495	0.01	0.531	0.00
Elected treasurer	−0.017	0.00	−0.1	0.94	−0.019	0.95	−0.157	0.62
City with wards	−0.564	−0.12	−2.8	0.01	−0.500	0.12	−0.493	0.07
Strong mayor	0.823	0.12	4.1	0.00	1.156	0.00	0.667	0.02
2002	−0.042	−0.01	−0.3	0.76	0.024	0.91	−0.057	0.74
2003	−0.025	−0.01	−0.2	0.85	0.107	0.60	−0.063	0.72
2004	0.007	0.00	0.1	0.96	0.209	0.30	−0.075	0.68
2005	0.049	0.01	0.3	0.74	0.179	0.37	−0.045	0.82
Intercept[a]	80.076		1.1	0.27	36.562	0.77	157.905	0.09

Note: All variables logged except binary (home rule, governance, and years) and revenue diversification.

[a] Intercept represents 0 for all binary variables.

[b] β for home rule and non–home rule have 50% difference in shaded areas.

TABLE 7.6 Regression Analysis of Total Debt per Capita, 1999–2005

Total debt per capita	All Governments, $R^2 = .43$				Home Rule[b] $R^2 = .41$		Non–Home Rule[b] $R^2 = .43$	
	β	beta	t	ρ	β	ρ	β	ρ
Sales receipts per capita	0.516	0.28	8.2	0.00	0.829	0.00	0.423	0.00
EAV per square mile	0.013	0.01	0.1	0.89	−0.753	0.00	0.399	0.00
Income per capita, 1999	−0.581	−0.12	−4.9	0.00	−0.752	0.00	−0.442	0.00
Grants per capita (fed and state)	0.291	0.18	6.0	0.00	0.312	0.00	0.312	0.00
Nongrant, state-shared revenue per cap	0.379	0.07	1.3	0.20	0.213	0.37	0.537	0.24
Home rule	0.431	0.11	4.3	0.00				
% residential EAV	0.019	0.00	0.1	0.96	0.241	0.49	−1.025	0.04
Population	0.270	0.18	4.1	0.00	0.040	0.62	0.629	0.00
Ratio change population	1.213	0.11	3.1	0.00	1.031	0.18	0.780	0.04
Miles from Chicago	−0.436	−0.11	−3.0	0.00	−1.853	0.00	0.799	0.00
Crime per capita	−0.007	−0.01	−0.2	0.88	0.079	0.34	−0.079	0.21
Median age housing, 2000	10.946	0.04	1.3	0.20	6.545	0.61	1.234	0.91
Population density	−0.572	−0.26	−5.5	0.00	−0.353	0.03	−0.673	0.00
Square miles of roads	0.599	0.22	5.6	0.00	0.309	0.01	0.801	0.00
Fire district	−0.072	−0.02	−0.7	0.50	0.582	0.00	−0.105	0.45
Park district	−0.230	−0.06	−2.7	0.01	−0.107	0.42	−0.366	0.00
Library district	0.312	0.08	3.4	0.00	0.429	0.00	−0.064	0.62

Revenue diversification t − 1	−0.817	−0.05	−1.7	0.10	1.907	0.00	−2.151	0.00
Fund balance as % of spending t − 2	−0.578	−0.09	−2.7	0.01	−0.269	0.41	−0.424	0.08
Surplus deficit as % of spending t − 1	−0.464	−0.09	−3.0	0.00	0.504	0.04	−1.017	0.00
Manager and finance director, 2003	0.485	0.12	3.5	0.00	1.065	0.00	0.089	0.60
Administrator and finance director, 2003	0.550	0.11	3.8	0.00	0.551	0.02	0.606	0.00
Administrator only, 2003	0.340	0.07	2.7	0.01	0.377	0.07	0.359	0.03
Finance director only, 2003	0.245	0.03	1.5	0.15	0.523	0.03	−0.075	0.78
Nonpartisan elections	0.185	0.04	1.8	0.07	−0.131	0.46	0.395	0.00
Partisan authority but run nonpartisan	−0.347	−0.09	−3.2	0.00	0.035	0.84	−0.500	0.00
Elected treasurer	−0.172	−0.03	−1.2	0.22	−0.916	0.00	0.042	0.86
City with wards	0.379	0.08	3.3	0.00	0.754	0.00	0.228	0.24
Strong mayor	−0.208	−0.03	−1.3	0.18	0.839	0.00	−0.878	0.00
2000	−0.026	0.00	−0.2	0.85	−0.072	0.67	−0.030	0.87
2001	−0.025	0.00	−0.2	0.86	−0.018	0.92	−0.036	0.85
2002	0.029	0.01	0.2	0.84	0.039	0.83	0.068	0.72
2003	0.136	0.02	1.0	0.34	0.186	0.30	0.187	0.30
2004	0.163	0.03	1.1	0.26	0.265	0.15	0.157	0.40
2005	0.232	0.04	1.6	0.12	0.243	0.20	0.180	0.35
Intercept[a]	−77.0		−1.2	0.24	−35.2	0.72	−7.487	0.93

Note: All variables logged except binary (home rule, governance, and years) and revenue diversification.

[a] Intercept represents 0 for all binary variables.

[b] β for home rule and non–home rule have 50% difference in shaded areas.

TABLE 7.7 Regression Analysis of Budgetary Solvency, 1999–2005

Fund Balance + Revenue as a Percentage of Operational Spending	All Governments, R^2 = .55				Home Rule[b] R^2 = .57		Non–Home Rule[b] R^2 = .57	
	β	beta	t	ρ	β	ρ	β	ρ
Sales receipts per capita	0.039	0.10	4.4	0.00	0.047	0.02	0.039	0.00
EAV per square mile	0.055	0.12	3.8	0.00	0.031	0.21	0.046	0.03
Income per capita, 1999	0.117	0.12	4.4	0.00	0.042	0.25	0.172	0.00
Grants per capita (fed and state)	−0.025	−0.07	−3.8	0.00	−0.003	0.73	−0.027	0.00
Nongrant, state-shared revenue per cap	0.002	0.00	0.1	0.96	−0.010	0.87	−0.058	0.55
Home rule	0.060	0.07	3.7	0.00				
% residential EAV	0.039	0.04	0.7	0.49	0.058	0.39	0.108	0.28
Population	−0.053	−0.17	−6.1	0.00	−0.072	0.00	−0.045	0.00
Ratio change population	0.134	0.06	1.6	0.11	−0.065	0.68	0.114	0.19
Miles from Chicago	0.095	0.11	4.4	0.00	0.113	0.01	0.087	0.01
Crime per capita	−0.004	−0.01	−0.5	0.62	−0.017	0.14	0.006	0.56
Median Age Housing, 2000	2.926	0.05	2.1	0.03	12.128	0.00	−0.838	0.67
Population density	0.080	0.18	5.3	0.00	0.042	0.06	0.108	0.00
Square miles of roads	−0.057	−0.10	−3.3	0.00	0.037	0.08	−0.122	0.00
Fire district	−0.013	−0.02	−0.7	0.50	0.018	0.48	−0.027	0.36
Park district	−0.015	−0.02	−0.9	0.36	−0.003	0.91	−0.016	0.48
Library district	−0.008	−0.01	−0.5	0.65	−0.092	0.00	0.056	0.04

Revenue diversification t − 1	−0.433	−0.13	−5.4	0.00	−0.156	0.06	−0.604	0.00
Surplus deficit as % of spending t − 1	0.641	0.58	10.0	0.00	0.597	0.00	0.650	0.00
Manager and finance director, 2003	−0.001	0.00	−0.1	0.96	0.031	0.36	0.009	0.79
Administrator and finance director, 2003	0.002	0.00	0.1	0.94	0.045	0.26	0.007	0.84
Administrator only, 2003	−0.051	−0.05	−2.3	0.02	−0.057	0.13	−0.050	0.08
Finance director only, 2003	0.105	0.07	3.3	0.00	0.064	0.12	0.166	0.00
Nonpartisan elections	0.048	0.05	2.4	0.02	0.034	0.23	0.047	0.14
Partisan authority but run nonpartisan	0.058	0.07	3.4	0.00	−0.009	0.72	0.083	0.00
Elected treasurer	0.053	0.04	2.0	0.04	0.145	0.00	0.030	0.48
City with wards	0.002	0.00	0.1	0.93	0.004	0.90	−0.001	0.99
Strong mayor	−0.072	−0.05	−2.8	0.01	−0.178	0.00	0.014	0.70
2000	−0.037	−0.03	−1.5	0.14	−0.054	0.11	−0.022	0.53
2001	−0.041	−0.04	−1.5	0.13	−0.080	0.01	−0.014	0.72
2002	−0.107	−0.09	−4.1	0.00	−0.131	0.00	−0.094	0.01
2003	−0.075	−0.07	−3.1	0.00	−0.096	0.00	−0.069	0.04
2004	−0.057	−0.05	−2.3	0.02	−0.074	0.03	−0.053	0.12
2005	−0.033	−0.03	−1.3	0.19	−0.063	0.05	−0.009	0.80
Intercept[a]	−22.6		−2.2	0.03	−90.1	0.00	5.5	0.71

Note: All variables logged except binary (home rule, governance, and years) and revenue diversification.

[a] Intercept represents 0 for all binary variables.

[b] β for home rule and non–home rule have 50% difference in shaded areas.

TABLE 7.8 Regression Analysis of Sales Tax as a Percentage of Own-Source Revenue, 1999–2005

Percent sales tax	All Governments, R^2 = .68				Home Rule[b] R^2 = .75		Non–Home Rule[b] R^2 = .70	
	β	beta	t	ρ	β	ρ	β	ρ
Sales receipts per capita	0.525	0.70	30.2	0.00	0.471	0.00	0.559	0.00
EAV per square mile	0.041	0.05	1.6	0.12	0.248	0.00	−0.089	0.00
Income per capita, 1999	0.125	0.07	3.2	0.00	−0.101	0.10	0.243	0.00
Grants per capita (fed and state)	−0.048	−0.07	−4.3	0.00	−0.040	0.02	−0.062	0.00
Nongrant, state-shared revenue per cap	−0.146	−0.07	−1.9	0.05	−0.149	0.06	0.016	0.89
Home rule	0.058	0.04	2.1	0.04				
% residential EAV	−0.458	−0.19	−4.7	0.00	−0.423	0.00	−0.512	0.00
Population	0.059	0.10	3.4	0.00	0.045	0.09	0.009	0.68
Ratio change population	−0.508	−0.12	−5.5	0.00	0.475	0.07	−0.591	0.00
Miles from Chicago	0.457	0.28	10.6	0.00	0.568	0.00	0.303	0.00
Crime per capita	0.016	0.03	1.1	0.29	0.024	0.27	0.017	0.29
Median age housing, 2000	−3.648	−0.03	−1.3	0.21	14.587	0.00	−6.724	0.04
Population density	0.142	0.16	4.4	0.00	0.155	0.00	0.174	0.00
Square miles of roads	−0.075	−0.07	−2.2	0.03	0.080	0.06	−0.156	0.00
Fire district	0.073	0.05	2.6	0.01	0.085	0.03	0.016	0.64
Park district	0.153	0.10	5.8	0.00	0.110	0.02	0.170	0.00

Library district	0.005	0.00	0.2	0.83	−0.105	0.01	0.093	0.01
Fund balance as % of spending t − 2	0.001	0.00	0.0	0.99	−0.257	0.00	0.012	0.80
Surplus deficit as % of spending t − 1	−0.059	−0.03	−1.5	0.13	−0.120	0.09	−0.005	0.91
Manager and finance director, 2003	−0.217	−0.13	−5.7	0.00	−0.145	0.02	−0.268	0.00
Administrator and finance director, 2003	−0.188	−0.09	−4.9	0.00	0.021	0.76	−0.282	0.00
Administrator only, 2003	−0.101	−0.05	−3.1	0.00	0.028	0.65	−0.157	0.00
Finance director only, 2003	−0.232	−0.07	−4.6	0.00	−0.102	0.27	−0.320	0.00
Nonpartisan elections	−0.115	−0.06	−3.4	0.00	0.106	0.06	−0.167	0.00
Partisan authority but run nonpartisan	−0.050	−0.03	−1.6	0.10	−0.052	0.32	−0.071	0.05
Elected treasurer	0.200	0.09	4.8	0.00	0.496	0.00	0.200	0.00
City with wards	−0.042	−0.02	−1.1	0.27	−0.293	0.00	0.039	0.49
Strong mayor	−0.158	−0.05	−3.6	0.00	−0.317	0.00	−0.170	0.00
2000	−0.049	−0.02	−1.3	0.20	−0.048	0.40	−0.055	0.25
2001	−0.072	−0.03	−1.8	0.07	−0.082	0.15	−0.060	0.23
2002	−0.109	−0.05	−2.8	0.01	−0.126	0.03	−0.096	0.05
2003	−0.173	−0.08	−4.3	0.00	−0.196	0.00	−0.157	0.00
2004	−0.223	−0.10	−5.6	0.00	−0.228	0.00	−0.217	0.00
2005	−0.286	−0.13	−7.0	0.00	−0.288	0.00	−0.284	0.00
Intercept[a]	26.4		1.2	0.23	−116.2	0.00	50.8	0.04

Note: All variables logged except binary (home rule, governance, and years) and revenue diversification.

[a] Intercept represents 0 for all binary variables.

[b] β for home rule and non–home rule have 50% difference in shaded areas.

Tables 7.2 to 7.6 show that governments with more wealth and that are home rule collect more revenue, spend more, and issue more debt. Assuming that own-source revenue per capita is a simple measure of revenue burden on the population and spending per capita is a measure of spending effort, the results show that revenue burden is lower in larger governments, but spending effort is also lower. Sales receipts have the biggest effect on raising revenue burden according to the betas in table 7.2 and demonstrate preferences for exporting revenue sources. Thus, the actual revenue burden on municipal residents and the level of service effort they experience from governments with high retail sales is probably much less, as demonstrated by the significance of percent residential EAV in tables 7.2 and 7.3. As expected, governments in fire and park districts collect less own-source revenue and spend less, but governments with library districts spend and collect more revenue.

Although the effect is not pronounced according to the betas, governments with higher levels of revenue diversification also collect less own-source revenue and spend less for operations and capital. When one considers the number of variables included in the model to control for many factors that affect revenues and spending in these governments, these results suggest that those with more revenue diversification impose less revenue burden on their citizens and may operate more efficiently. Not surprisingly, higher surpluses and fund balances are associated with higher capital spending, dedicated capital revenue, and debt.

These results demonstrate the effects of fiscal stress and munificence discussed previously and how these decisions are related to policies about how capital spending is financed. Governments spend for capital during good times and retract capital spending in bad times, and governments that rely more on pay-as-you-go methods of financing rely less on debt. The coefficients for the two intergovernmental variables in tables 7.3 to 7.5 (grants and nongrant state-shared revenue) also show that governments take advantage of this revenue to increase spending. Grants are especially associated with the level of revenue dedicated to capital spending and the level of debt.

Higher surpluses, however, also are associated with higher revenue burden, especially in home rule governments, and both higher surpluses and fund balances are associated with lower spending effort, especially in non–home rule governments. This suggests that when controlling for revenue wealth and spending needs, governments that build surpluses have lower spending effort, and governments that maintain lower surpluses and fund balances use these resources to increase spending effort. This is contrary to the idea that the deficit-surplus measure indicates fiscal stress but is consistent with claims by many governments that they maintain lower fund balances and surpluses to deliver higher levels of service, especially during times of fiscal stress.

With respect to the governance variables, the results show that governments with mayors only (intercept) spend less and collect less revenue per capita than governments with finance directors (with or without a CAO), and mayor-only governments less debt. Governments with administrators or managers only collect similar amounts of own-source revenue and have a similar level of operational spending effort as governments with a mayor only, but the former have more dedicated capital revenue and debt than the latter. Again, considering that the model controls for capacity, size, and other factors, one can infer that government preferences and heuristics for different fiscal tools for maintaining financial condition vary according to whether govern-ments are corporate (CAO and finance director) or political (mayor only). The results for FDS remain the same even when variables measuring population and voter prefer-ences (e.g., education, vote for Bush in 2004, and percent of the population that are managerial and professional) were included in the model.

Municipal governments with elected treasurers also have less own-source revenue burden and spend less for operations and capital, but cities with wards and municipali-ties with strong mayors collect more revenue and spend more. Conversely, strong mayoral systems have more capital spending and dedicated capital revenue, but cities with wards have less dedicated capital revenue. It is also noteworthy that the effects of FDS on spending and revenue were greater for non–home rule governments in most cases (the effects of some categories of financial decision structure on capital spending, capital revenue, and debt were greater for home rule governments). However, the ef-fects of an elected treasurer, being a city with wards, and having a strong mayoral system were stronger for home rule governments. Partisanship did not have much of an effect on spending and own-source revenue, but governments with partisan elec-tions have less dedicated capital revenue and those with nonpartisan elections have more debt.

The broad picture painted by the results of the governance variables is that gov-ernments that are more corporate administratively collect more revenue to provide higher levels of service, they invest more in capital infrastructure, and they are more willing to pay for capital investment with debt. However, with respect to political institutions, the results are very mixed, with some governance structures (elected treasurer) mirroring those of mayor-only administrations, but other political struc-tures (strong mayor and city with wards) mirroring some of the choices of corporate administrative structures (e.g., strong mayoral governments spending more for capital, and cities with wards issuing more debt). In this case, the effects of the institutional features of political and corporate governance presented in table 4.2 on choice of fiscal policies and financial tools are not linear or consistent, which makes it difficult to develop an indicator of governance that measures only one dimension or con-tinuum. Most previous studies have used simple binary variables (usually council-manager versus council-mayor governments) to attempt to capture corporate versus political governance. These results demonstrate why the use of dummy variables has not often produced meaningful findings about the effects of governing structure in prior research.

The results for the budgetary solvency equation, table 7.7, probably say more about governments' policies regarding their fund balance and their use of this tool during fiscal stress than the level of stress they experienced. However, this dependent variable also could be interpreted as a measure of financial condition more so than revenue per capita (as a measure of revenue burden) and spending per capita (as a measure of spending effort). As with many of the fiscal policies discussed here, bud-getary solvency is higher in governments with more wealth and that are home rule, newer, and larger. As expected, governments with higher surpluses have greater bud-getary solvency, but those with more revenue diversification have less solvency, which probably reflects their policy of maintaining lower fund balances rather than financial condition per se. Financial decision structure has little effect on budgetary solvency or fund balance levels, but governments with partisan elections and strong mayors have lower solvency or fund balances, and governments with elected treasurers have higher levels. The year variables show that budgetary solvency in these governments has been consistently lower for all years since 1999, especially for home rule governments, but the greatest decline in solvency occurred for all governments in 2002, with gradual improvements since that time.

The last set of results in table 7.8 shows the factors that affect the extent to which governments rely on sales taxes. We know from the qualitative evidence that dependence on sales taxes exposes governments more to the threat of recessions, but it also gives them a windfall of revenue during fiscal good times that they are likely to spend on capital items or use to increase their fund balances in response to pressures from bond rating agencies.[14] Not surprisingly, governments with higher sales receipts tend to depend more on sales taxes, and this variable has the greatest effect according to the betas.

Home rule governments also depend more on sales taxes, but so do larger governments and those further from the city. Governments with more intergovernmental revenue per capita rely less on sales taxes as do growing governments probably due to the simple fact that growing governments have alternative sources of revenue. Governments with a more corporate administrative structure (according to results of the financial decision structure variables) rely less on sales taxes as do nonpartisan governments, but governments with a strong mayor and home rule cities with wards, which are associated more with political governance, also rely less on sales taxes. Although sales tax capacity is controlled for in the equation, it is likely that cities with wards and strong mayors have less opportunity to increase sales taxes than is accounted for by this control variable. The results for partisanship and financial decision structure suggest, however, that more corporate governments will reduce their risk and exposure to this volatile revenue source.

Earlier sections of this chapter focused primarily on the effects of fiscal capacity, structure, threats, and opportunities on the size of the fiscal toolbox. The regression analysis in this section examines the effects of governance on fiscal policies more systematically than has been done previously. The results show that corporate governments have different fiscal policies and use different financial tools than political governments, and these institutional differences are both administrative (fiscal decision structure) and political (partisan elections, strong mayor, city with wards) in origin. In terms of some of the important heuristics identified in chapter 3, corporate and political governments take on different risks with respect to sales taxes (political governments tend to rely more on sales taxes) and debt (corporate governments take on more debt). Politically administered governments also appear to underinvest in capital infrastructure in attempts to lower revenue burden and maintain lower spending effort, and governments with a more political governing structure (partisan election and strong mayor) have less budgetary solvency, although type of administrative structure (fiscal decision structure) has little effect on either the fund balance or the broader measure of budgetary solvency. The next section focuses on the differences in financial management practices that often affect the implementation of fiscal policies.

Practice Tools for Managing Financial Condition

What other tools do municipal governments use to manage their financial condition, and does this vary by governance structure? The previous section assessed the effects of different factors from figure 4.1 on fiscal policies and practices that are most directly linked to the government's financial health and stability as summarized in category D of table 3.2. Essentially these tools (e.g., revenue burden, spending effort, and capital investment) represent the strategies that governments have applied over a period of time to maintain or improve financial condition. By way of comparison, chapter 6 focused on assessing the tools (e.g., changes in taxes, spending, and capital investment) that governments use in the near term to cope with threats and opportunities. This section describes the policies or practices governments engage in to solve financial problems and maintain financial health and are represented in categories A, B, and C of table 3.2. Because many of the practices in these categories represent routine processes or government-wide approaches to financial decisions and activities, one would expect the routines or approaches to vary by the predominant financial heuristics of the government. As discussed in chapter 3, problem-solving heuristics should vary by governance structure and fiscal administrative capacity.

Budgeting and Planning for Capital and Operations

Examining the recommended fiscal practices and policies established by GFOA shows a long list of best practices for how to improve financial management and maintain financial condition in the long run.[15] We know from prior analyses that fiscal capacity is probably the most important factor in maintaining municipal government financial condition, but professional norms establish that particular financial tools will increase the likelihood that a poor government will have better financial condition and decrease the likelihood that a wealthy government will have poor financial condition. Closer examination of GFOA standards reveals three areas of policy and practice that contribute to financial condition: which financial choices governments make (category D), how governments solve fiscal problems (categories A and C), and how governments implement choices and solutions (category B). The professional recommendations for how governments should solve fiscal problems on the administrative or corporate side of the continuum in table 4.2 are very consistent with what many view as rational decision making, in contrast to boundedly rational decision making.

As generally known in the field of public administration, rational decision making involves a thorough investigation of options, assessment of their impacts, and choice of an option that maximizes benefits and minimizes costs. Less rational or more boundedly rational decision making relies on heuristics that simplify the process by reducing the number of options considered and investigated and easing the criteria used to evaluate options (Simon 1991). The GFOA-recommended practices and policies exemplify rational decision making with their strong emphasis on planning; analysis; informed decision making; accurate forecasting; consideration of risk; and assessment of costs, benefits, and impacts. For instance, the GFOA recommends that governments engage in strategic and long-term financial planning, assess operational performance, measure the costs of services, create a comprehensive risk management program, and closely monitor their financial condition. Overall the recommendations advocate financial decision making that is comprehensive, orderly, and systematic to be better prepared to handle future threats and take advantage of opportunities. This approach is in contrast to the rules of thumb, tricks, and shortcuts to financial management described by many interviewees here.

Budgeting and fiscal planning, especially for capital expenditures, is a central element of any financial management program at the local level and thus is the subject of numerous GFOA best practices. It was also the subject of numerous questions in the interviews. As described in chapter 3 (note 4), the state only requires local governments to pass an appropriation ordinance rather than a budget. Although many municipal governments in the Chicago metropolitan region have a formal budget, many do not, and some do little more than pass the appropriations ordinance. Relying only on an appropriations ordinance to guide financial decision making throughout the fiscal year is certainly not consistent with GFOA best practices nor is it a rational approach to maintaining financial condition. It is a very poor tool for fiscal planning, and it does not promote a proactive and directed method for achieving financial goals. It also makes government more vulnerable to threats and less capable of pursuing opportunities because it has not considered possible future events and therefore is less likely to build the capacity to deal with these events.

The picture of budgeting and financial planning painted by the interviewed governments is a continuum of rational, best practices on one end to approaches that are more ad hoc and reactive (financial decision making in the moment) on the other end. There is indeed a great deal of variation of government practices along this continuum, and almost all governments interviewed had some level of planning for operations in the coming fiscal year. However, one had done little budgeting or fiscal planning for a long time because whatever budget was established was understood to be inaccurate. This government is likely in the worst financial condition of all governments interviewed, and the tenuousness of their financial condition simply made planning impossible. As the interviewee claimed, "True departmental budgets don't make sense. We are surviving from one week to the next, from one month to the next. How do we manage from month to month? I think someone said once if you can work in [this town] and maintain at least some level of operation, you can go someplace else and just be a genius, because here you work with pretty much nothing, Again, I can't say it enough, it is pure surviving here."

These sentiments express almost exactly what was described by Caiden and Wildavsky in their book *Planning and Budgeting in Poor Countries* (1974) as "continuous budgeting." They found that poor countries could not really produce "comprehensive statements of governmental intentions for the coming year" because uncertainty and missing resources made that impossible. Budgeting in such situations must be "explicitly geared to making ad hoc decisions on resource allocations" (316). Cities like the one interviewed here and East St. Louis are in extreme survival mode all the time, as described in the last category in table 3.3. They face total scarcity and high levels of uncertainty, which makes financial planning meaningless.

No doubt there are other municipalities in the Chicago region that function in this manner, and those that come to mind from news reports and quantitative evidence all are very poor and small (e.g., Ford Heights, Phoenix, Dixmoor). Lack of capacity in the form of resources and little slack may give such governments no other choice but to be reactive and ad hoc in their budgeting and financial management practices. Such financial problems raise the question of which fiscal tools will best help these governments maintain or improve financial condition, as those on the rational and professional end of the continuum may not be appropriate. But given the public safety obligations of municipal governments in this state, maybe the more appropriate question is whether such governments should even exist and what the role of state government should be in monitoring and solving their financial problems.

Although poor but not in extreme survival mode, four other governments interviewed also used the appropriation ordinance as their budget and primary fiscal document. Five more interviewed governments had a very minimal budget that was not comprehensive or was for internal purposes only. In these cases, the appropriation ordinance was still the primary financial guiding document. Some of these governments would develop the appropriation ordinance from the budget, but most talked about developing the budget from the appropriation ordinance, and several admitted to not passing the appropriation ordinance until the end of the third month from the start of the fiscal year, as required by state statute. In about half of these governments the budget developed from the appropriations ordinance was not an operating budget but a cash budget targeted more on cash flow than cost of operations and sources of funding.

Of the nine governments that relied on the appropriations ordinance for budgeting and fiscal planning during the early 2000s, all except one are in the thirtieth percentile of the revenue wealth index for 2000, all except one have budgets less than $10 million, and all but one are assessed as having a form of governance that is political according to the classification system presented in table 4.5. That table shows thirteen of the sixty-two governments interviewed are classified as politically governed (with no CAO). Eight of these thirteen use the appropriations ordinance as a budget. It is also interesting that four of these eight governments had mayors who had been in office more than twenty years, which gave them political control and well-established heuristics for budgeting and financial management. Given that these mayors are not professional managers or finance directors, one can assume that their approach to budgeting and financial management is not consistent with professional standards or rational decision making as defined here. Rather, their approach to financial decision making and practice is more boundedly rational.

The one wealthy government that used the appropriations ordinance as the budget of the nine total is extremely small, with total spending less than $1 million. It is classified as having corporate values due to the high number of elected officials that are legal or financial professionals, but it has no CAO or finance director.[16] Of the five remaining governments from the thirteen that are classified as politically governed, three are fairly large governments with budgets greater than $25 million and they operate with a budget document. In this case, these governments may be too big to operate fiscally on the appropriations ordinance alone.

One heuristic or budgeting strategy on the ad hoc and reactive end of the continuum of budgeting practices is described by the following interviewee: "Well usually it's a deficit budget that gets passed, because the projected revenues are less than everybody's expenses added together. We budget a deficit, and then keep a close eye on the budget as to what's being spent. We'll give [the departments] what they want and then tell them you can only spend 89% of your budget. That's the way it works here."

Three of the interviewed governments described using this strategy of budgeting a deficit, monitoring spending and revenues through the year, and then making the necessary adjustments at the end to balance the budget, thereby forgoing the need to plan or forecast. A somewhat different strategy on the nonrational end of the continuum is exemplified by the following interviewee and has some of the attributes of process incrementalism (Wildavsky 1984). These attributes are exemplified by the following rules: Look at what you did last year in spending, guesstimate revenue change, and adjust spending to guesstimated revenues. "To begin, we go over all the previous year's budget, and look at whether we've gone over or under. We take a look at all the money that's coming in, and we guesstimate as to whether or not that amount is going to continue, or increase or decrease. From there we'll select different line items, as whether or not we can still afford them, or something has to be deleted, or consolidated."

Four of the governments also expressed that they rely heavily on their auditors to guide them with fiscal policy and planning, which is contrary to standards of probity in the profession of financial management.[17] The primary conclusion one can draw from these stories is that political governments that are small and poor are more likely to operate without a meaningful budget, which is contrary to some of the most basic best practices of financial management according to GFOA. They are also likely to use heuristics that are contrary to a rational approach to financial management and decision making. However, not all small and poor governments from the interviews relied on the appropriations ordinance or other less rational tools of financial management and decision making. Three interviewed governments that could be classified as low wealth and high fiscal stress (table 3.4) had comprehensive budgets with capital plans, and one of these had earned the GFOA Distinguished Budget Presentation award recently for the quality of its budget document.

It was also interesting that nine interviewed governments claimed to have recently moved away from relying on the appropriation ordinance as the budget document. Two of these governments were experiencing high growth, and the one small, wealthy government had recently acquired a major commercial district and believed it could no longer function financially in a reactive manner. Their part-time finance director admitted to being on a steep learning curve with developing an operating budget and a better means of monitoring spending and revenue during the fiscal year. Five of the other governments in this of nine were relatively poor but had recently undergone political transformations that facilitated the hiring of entrepreneurial change agents who seemed to value greatly the challenge of improving their governments' financial management practices. Some of these change agents discussed at length the financial management practices that existed prior to their employment and the kinds of changes they were attempting to make or had already made. Their stories will be used to assess financial management practices other than budgeting and planning in the next section.

Moving further toward the rational end of the continuum of budgeting and fiscal planning, there are numerous governments that develop a meaningful budget but do little capital planning. In fact, twenty-six interviewed governments do not have a capital plan or construct a separate capital budget, which includes the nine governments that rely on the appropriation ordinance. Four more interviewed governments do capital planning only for streets. The extreme survival mode government identified previously described its capital planning in the following way: "Pray that nothing burns down or breaks down to the point that we have to leave or do without. Right now we're in a building that if it wasn't as sunny outside, if it was raining or snowing right now, you wouldn't be sitting in that seat. We'd probably be over there doing the interview because the roof leaks over here. So you know, our capital improvement plan isn't that great. In fact, its non-existent." Another interviewee described capital planning in his government in this way: "People have asked me in discussions, why don't we do a five-year [capital] projection? I always tell them that would scare me to death. We get through it [capital spending] a year at a time."

One finance director in a highly political council-manager government who was working to institute a capital planning process claimed that, "There's no capital plan in place where certain things are bought each year. They kind of wing it, and there's been a lot of backwards things that have happened—like we'll replace a street and we won't replace the water mains or the water problems underneath it. So now to fix those water problems, we have to rip up the newer streets. A lot of half measures also have been taken, you know, short-term solutions to capital problems."

In effect, decisions about capital spending in governments without capital planning or budgeting mirror the operational budgeting decisions of governments in survival mode and also those of very small governments with few operational responsibilities. Whether governments engage in capital planning is a function of their level of capital responsibilities and whether they have enough resources to dedicate revenue each year to capital projects with some degree of consistency. Poor financial condition and fiscal stress get in the way of consistent capital spending in many governments because they often raid the dedicated capital funds to cover revenue shortfalls. In such cases the capital spending plan consists of "whatever is left over after operations are taken care of." But there is enough evidence in the interviews that lack of capital planning and budgeting is often less a matter of fiscal capacity and more a matter of professional inclination and corporate thinking. As one professional administrator and change agent noted in the interview, "We went through several years of basically having no money, and there were board members who were asking me why are we even going through a budget exercise when we have no money? My answer to them was, well, do you ever want to have money?"

On the rational end of the budgeting and planning continuum, nine of the interviewed governments do long-range financial planning and projections or multiyear budgets, or have governments engaged in some level of strategic planning. As one finance director noted, "The three-year financial plan has been an eye opener, especially for the board when we're saying, okay we're going to be a million and a half short next year with status quo, and we'll be three million dollars short in two years, what do you want to do? It's like strategic planning focused on the finances. Everything revolves around the projections for the future and the financial goals of the budget." Another finance director stated, "Our capital plan is presented to the board on a balanced basis as much as possible. So to say it's fully funded doesn't mean we have cash in the bank today, but what we would anticipate over a 5-year period to be able to fund that plan. So our capital plan is a fully funded document utilizing different sources of revenue to ensure that the plan is followed."

Clearly, the two governments represented in the last two quotes operate with a different set of heuristics or tools for budgeting than governments on the other end of the continuum, given the extent to which they embrace planning for fiscal, operational, and capital decisions. Twelve of the sixty-two governments interviewed had received both GFOA awards for their budget document and comprehensive annual financial report, which suggests an emphasis on rational approaches to fiscal decision making and corporate or professional governing more generally. In fact, eleven of these twelve governments are classified as corporate according to table 4.5, with one classified as corporate-political due to its history of the finance director and administrator being political appointments.

Conversely, fourteen governments are classified as corporate, but they have not won the GFOA budget award. Examining their budgeting documents and interview statements reveals that the majority have very comprehensive budgeting documents and a budgeting process that emphasizes planning, analysis, and assessment of outcomes. Moreover, many of these governments had won the GFOA award for the comprehensive annual financial report.

With respect to methods of planning and budgeting control at the managerial level of governance, the majority of governments interviewed had a bottom-up approach where the first stage is the departments submitting their wish lists to the mayor or chief budget officer (finance director or CAO). The first step in a top-down approach is the mayor or CAO telling departments what their spending targets and priorities will be, which has been referred to as target-based budgeting (Rubin 1992). Top-down approaches were claimed to be routine by four governments, all of which are corporate. It was also clear from the interviews, however, that the budget process became more top-down for many governments during the 2001 recession and other periods of fiscal stress. Several governments described it as being a "tighter budget process": "We've been hearing the departments complain about the new budgeting process. They have to do a lot more justifying, and providing details and analysis, than what they've been asked to in the past. In the past departments worked up a budget by taking last year's and crossing out this number and writing the new number. They would bring it in, sit down with the village administrator, go over it, make cuts here or there. Basically the departments came in with their wish lists, and the village manager would cut things out."

With respect to the actors' roles and interaction with others in the budget process at the institutional level of governance, there was interesting variation among governments as to the extent to which the board or trustees were involved in the budgeting process and financial planning. Interviewees from both corporate and political governments talked about the board being highly involved as a matter of practice more than institutional rule, or particular board members being critical to budget decisions and fiscal policies because of their expertise (e.g., financial officers of corporations). Ten administrators talked about strategies of bringing in board members more directly or earlier into the budgeting and planning process and working to educate board members about budgeting, planning, and fiscal issues. The purpose of this strategy is to facilitate agreement on the budget and fiscal policies and to "wean the board off of micro-managing and turn it into more of a policy making body." This strategy was implemented in a variety of governments, but none were administered by the mayor alone.

Other Financial Management Practices

This section documents other tools and strategies that are not in category A of table 3.2 that municipal governments in the Chicago region use to maintain or improve financial condition. Practices in category B emphasize fiscal and managerial control rather than finding solutions to financial problems. As shown here, the tools in category B present a variety of methods local government uses to implement and protect the financial solutions they pursue, such as auditing capital investments and instituting checks and balances on purchases. Many of the interviews also talked about insurance and risk management (in category D), as critical tools for protecting the government against events or threats that, if they occur, can increase government liabilities dramatically. Because such tools in categories B and D are more relevant to implementing solutions than solving problems, the tools chosen in this case are more likely to be a function of the governing (institutional) structure (Lynn et al. 2001) than the individual problem-solving heuristics. As noted previously, however, heuristics and governance structure are related.

By comparison, the tools in category C focus on finding financial solutions to problems using rational, analytical methods. Most of the governments interviewed here demonstrated that they were champions at monitoring cash and transactions during the fiscal year based on their statements or the contents of their budget and annual financial report. This is true even for some governments that do not pass a meaningful budget, which suggests how important monitoring cash flow is to maintaining financial condition in these governments. However, more than a few political governments were not very vigilant in cash management or used heuristics that most would consider contrary to the promotion of good financial condition. Several talked about relying on bank statements to manage cash and authorize spending, and one government consistently relied on their audited annual financial report to help them determine their current financial position: "If I look at the bank statements, I can tell if we have money or not. Maybe that's not good enough for the state or the public, but I can tell. The banks send me all kinds of letters if I spend too much, and I know when a fund is going to short, or if I have to move funds from one place to another, or quit spending."

One popular strategy or tool for managing cash, as was noted by many interviewees, is to underestimate revenue and overestimate spending. This helps to ensure there will be a balanced budget throughout the fiscal year, and also a surplus at the end of the fiscal year. Instead of accurately estimating future revenues and spending, rigorously monitoring cash flows, and incorporating this information into budget development and implementation, they use shortcuts that achieve the same objective. This practice is not necessarily undesirable and may even be more appropriate for small governments and those with poor fiscal capacity. Furthermore, this practice may actually help some governments that do not have the capacity or resources to adopt more rational practices to maintain their financial condition.[18]

Alternatively, there are news reports from several governments, including Maywood and Broadview, discussed previously in this chapter and others, that show what happens when governments are not very proficient with monitoring cash balances and budgets. Undoubtedly the use of shortcuts and unsound financial management practices in these governments probably contributed to their poor fiscal health. Other governments in the news demonstrated significant problems with monitoring cash and transactions, which usually coincided with problems of fiscal control and reporting. One of the most extreme and well-reported examples is Carpentersville, whose difficulties surfaced in 2003 when their financial problems were found to "extend beyond an incomplete audit." According to a newly hired finance director, the village violated several laws and regulations by not filing financial statements with the appropriate agencies, and the auditors found extensive errors within the finance department. He described the errors as "extraordinarily serious" and "indicative of extreme failure in internal control" (Carr 2003).

The interviewed governments with weak monitoring and reporting and problems of financial control were all classified as political according to table 4.5. However, Carpentersville has a professional village manager and a finance director, it is not a city with wards, elected officials generally run as independents (but they have the authority to run partisan elections), and its top administrative officials do not seem to be political appointments. Thus, Carpentersville is probably on the corporate end of the governing continuum, which does not coincide with its financial problems. In this case, evidence shows that its political culture and high conflict at the institutional level, due in part to its very rapid growth, likely clashed with the corporate culture at the managerial level to create high turnover of the CAO and finance director and dysfunction in fulfilling the duties of these offices. Antioch and Lakemoor are examples of two other growing municipalities with similar financial management problems and high levels of political conflict at that time.

Because the policies and practices in categories B and C in table 3.2 were not the focus of the interviews in 2003, the use of these tools by Chicago municipalities was not systematically investigated in all interviewed governments. Although many volunteered enough information to assess some practices in these areas, the lack of consistency in information across interviews makes it difficult to document trends and assess links to factors in the model in figure 4.1. However, interviews in nine governments provided a lot of information about financial management practices that existed prior to hiring the interviewee and how this person was changing or had changed these policies and practices. In five cases, the interviewees (finance director or CAO) were acting as entrepreneurial change agents to institute major reforms in financial management and government financial position. In four cases the interviewees were the first finance director hired by the government.

As described in chapter 5, five interviewees were encountered who could best be described as change agents. These individuals were either CAOs with lots of financial knowledge, or finance directors who acted as CAOs in order to get reforms instituted. They could be described as prospectors (risk seeking) rather than defenders (risk averse). They seemed to thrive on the challenge of trying to improve their governments, and they all elicited some bravado about their impact. They and their sponsor (the mayor) also seemed to have the political capital to make things happen at both the institutional and managerial levels of governance. Four of the change agents were still in their position at the time of this analysis, and according to the quantitative data financial condition had improved in three since the change agent had arrived.[19] The new finance directors in the other four governments, which all had CAOs, did not seem to be change agents. Rather their hiring seemed to be part of the normal evolutionary process of governments becoming more corporate as they grew and acquired more service responsibilities.

Table 7.9 summarizes the focus of practice changes by these nine interviewees and presents extensive quotes from five. The quotes demonstrate the kinds of financial

TABLE 7.9 Change in Financial Management Practices

A	Financial and internal controls, especially purchasing, overtime, and budget implementation. Also, increased attention to risk management.

"The village had not turned out a utility bill in eight months. It was two years behind on reconciling the checking accounts, it hadn't done an audit in over two years, and it hadn't filed a treasurer's report with the County in two years. I came up with about $700,000 that I couldn't reconcile, not that the money was missing, but they weren't keeping good track of transactions. Oh, that was another thing, they were doing manual checks using the computerized checks, so I couldn't even account for the numbers of the checks. It was chaos. I finally got a complete reconciliation right before Christmas so that I was able to have an ending figure for starting my fiscal year 2002 budget. We just about got the annual financial report completed for last year, and we're just starting to do the annual financial report for the current year." [The current fiscal year was almost done at the time of the interview.]

B	Financial planning and correct representation of costs and financial condition

"The first I asked for when I came here was a copy of their budget, and they handed me the appropriations ordinance. I said this can be burned as far as I'm concerned. We're still on the appropriations ordinance, but we now have a budget and we're moving towards the budget act. We've also consolidated a lot of funds, which obviously is another part of GASB 34, but there were something like twenty different funds, and some of the funds had amazing fund balances. We consolidated all of our bond issues last year, which resulted in quite a bit of savings. Another thing that we did is to increase fees to make building, garbage, water, and sewer stand on their own. Before the village was subsidizing basically the entire building department, I mean the fees were so low. We also started to shift some of the salaries of the public works guys [from the general fund to the water fund]. In the past when a water main broke, all salaries used to be overtime charged to the general fund."

C	Financial planning and controls

"The first two years I was here, we went through the appropriation process [ordinance only]. Those numbers just are not realistic. So we adopted the budget process in lieu of the appropriation ordinance, which makes us have to pass a budget before the fiscal year starts. A lot of the smaller towns have what I call ma and pa accounting, and that's what they had here. It was manual ledgers and stuff, and they had like twenty-five different checking accounts. We're down to one now. Then they went to a computer, and the young lady that was here just did not understand how to do it. She just didn't have the background and the experience. They had audit findings and other problems. They had problems paying their bills and some other things. We've put in procedures and policies and so on, accounts payable, cash receipts, all the things that the auditors, for internal control and all that stuff. Like I said, before I came here, we had a number of qualified findings in the audit."

D	Financial controls, especially purchasing and budget implementation

"Purchasing I've really honed in on since I've started, because when I came on, there were no policies, there were no set procedures. Each department was kind of doing their own thing. So I came in with a policy to fill out a purchase order. I sat down and went through, and kind of created some new rules. I'm also trying to get the departments to stick to their budget. I give them updates every other month on where they're at in their budget. I have to say that most of the department heads really did monitor spending, but they kind of did it in their own way. When I came on there were all these funds that were kind of sitting around, that we don't use anymore, so I did a lot of general ledger cleanup. I am feeling, since I've come, there's just a lot of things we'd like to improve on, and fix and clean up and it's just a matter of, it's going to be kind of slowly going through it all. Unfortunately, finding records has been difficult, and I'm curious about what they did with all that [bonded debt]. I know they've bought a few large water mains, but what else did they use that money for?"

TABLE 7.9 Change in Financial Management Practices

E	Financial controls and reporting

"When I got here, one of the major challenges was that we had twenty-three bank accounts. We had a ledger system that you had to make fifty entries to make the books balance at the end of a normal cycle. I spent a lot of time trying to figure out who we owed money to, putting the entries on the books, and all the work that goes into keeping track of this stuff. I reengineered the books and how things were posted, and closed all those accounts. Now there is one account spread all across the funds. Everything was delinquent as far as the comptroller's report wasn't filed until February. The audit was never done on time. The budget was never done on time. People never got financial reports on time—on a monthly basis. Now they get them five days after the month ends. It allows them to see where they're at, to make sure that they're within their budget."

management practices that existed prior to the new finance directors or change agents coming to the government, and the kinds of changes these individuals made or were attempting to make at the managerial level of governance. The practices that existed prior to their hire were not consistent with professional standards or a rational approach to problem solving. Rather they were based on expediency, which is more closely associated with political forms of governance, compared to professional practices that emphasize rules and procedures, which is more closely associated with corporate forms of governance.

It is important to highlight that the term rational does not mean better, and there is nothing necessarily pejorative about using boundedly rational approaches. It also cannot be established with certainty that instituting corporate financial management practices will improve government financial condition, although that is the broad subject of the next section. However, by definition, the practice changes instituted by these interviewees improved government accountability, which is another goal of professional budgeting practices. Notice that most of the perceived deficiencies in table 7.9 and changes instituted by the interviewees focus on having a more accurate picture of financial position and more control over solutions implemented, which lead to better financial reporting and accountability overall.

Once governments get beyond implementing basic corporate tools of financial management, they move on to practices that affect financial operations at a higher level This trend was observed in three of the governments in this group of nine in which the interviewees, who were new finance directors, talked about the following changes: establishing written fiscal policies and purchasing manuals, implementing a more top-down approach to budgeting, taking bids from financial institutions to manage the government's investments to maximize rates of return (instead of relying on the local bank), accurately assessing infrastructure needs and increasing infrastructure investments, raising water rates to match costs, creating an equipment reserve fund, doing a strategic plan or planning exercises with the board, and instituting a five-year capital improvement program.

It is not clear how many of all interviewed governments have written fiscal policies and financial management practices or whether the policies were comprehensive in their coverage of best practice areas such as the fund balance, purchasing, and investments. About 20 percent of the interviewed governments, all classified as corporate according to table 4.5, had some policies listed in their budget. Five other corporate governments claimed that they had informal policies in place of written policies, and most expressed a desire to have written policies. A news report from the Village of Lincolnwood demonstrates the opinions voiced by these governments on this matter. In this case, the mayor of Lincolnwood noted that the new policies, which were informal in the past, were not just "bureaucratic rules," but would "protect the village from any future financial damage" (Routliffe 2006). In this case, written policies help remove tools from political consideration and limit their use in the satisfaction of high-powered incentives.

Many of the tools and strategies in category C have already been discussed at some length in chapter 6 in the context of cost analyses and improving efficiency. It was noted that claims of managing fiscal stress by improving efficiency are popular with government officials, but the reality is that improving efficiency by assessing how productivity can be increased (not just from making spending cuts) is more the exception than the norm, and it is not a good tool for reigning in spending during times of fiscal stress. These strategies are not costless, and their benefits for maintaining financial condition are largely incremental and cumulative. Many of the interviewed governments assess the costs of providing services, but it is primarily for the purpose of determining fees and charges, not improving efficiency. Although three finance directors interviewed went to great lengths to assess their government's projected and current financial position, virtually none of the governments interviewed assessed operational performance beyond input and basic output measures.

The last area of financial management to be discussed here is risk management, because the interviews yielded some surprises. Risk management is generally defined as the management of risks and prevention of financial loss due to disasters, crises, illegal activities, lawsuits, and any threats that could severely impact the government or its assets. One of the biggest tools in risk management is insurance. Another is what municipality A in table 7.9 described as "worker's comp loss prevention program," which consisted of job safety training and the appointment of a departmental safety officer. Many of the interviewed governments talked about being members of one of six different insurance pools or cooperatives for liability, and a few governments participated in one of several pools mentioned for health insurance. The most common liability pool mentioned is run by the Illinois Municipal League (Illinois Risk Management Association), which requires that members meet particular standards of loss prevention practice. As noted by government D in table 7.9, "We'd love to be in IRMA. We met with them actually this month, and I highly doubt we'll get accepted, but we're going to go through the application process. But it's great, because once you're a part of it, you have to hold certain standards, it's a way to explain to your employees why they have to do things."

Although attention to risk by governments usually focuses on the spending side and finding ways to prevent dramatic increases in liabilities, at least three other governments thought about the risks their governments face on the revenue side. All three governments carried business or revenue interruption insurance to protect them against loss of revenue from particular sources. What was most surprising, however, was that at least twenty-two of the sixty-two governments interviewed were self-insured for health, liability, workers' comp, or some combination of all three. Generally, it was the larger governments that were self-insured for health, but not always, and many governments claimed that being self-insured was more cost-beneficial.[20]

However, several governments that were self-insured admitted to being hit by a significant number of health or liability claims that were creating a lot of fiscal stress for them. This is the obvious risk of being self-insured, but another risk of self-insurance has to do with accountability and security. The funds used to administer self-insurance programs are sizable and require good internal controls similar to pension funds. Even in governments where internal control of pensions is not good (e.g., San Diego), the unions may act as a watchdog of these funds. However, there is no such inherent check and balance on self-insurance funds. This problem was demonstrated in 2002 when Mayor Betty Maltese from the infamous Chicago suburb of Cicero, which many claim was once owned by Al Capone, was convicted for the loss of the town's self-insurance funds that were diverted for personal use by insurance executives who were business partners with her in several ventures.

Explaining Overall Financial Condition

Knowing which tools different governments use for managing fiscal stress and financial condition says little about which strategies and heuristics are better for maintaining financial condition. In fact, none of the analyses presented thus far have really examined whether and to what extent governing structure, fiscal structure, and fiscal capacity affect financial condition overall. The first section of this chapter uses many indicators of financial condition from chapter 2 to assess what factors affect different components of financial condition, but they are used sequentially and individually as dependent variables (see tables 7.2 to 7.8). In other words, the effects of governing structure, fiscal structure, and fiscal capacity are examined for different dimensions or areas of financial condition, not for financial condition as a whole. However, assessing financial condition comprehensively is difficult as its different dimensions, in conjunction with events that trigger fiscal stress and munificence, cannot be combined in a straightforward manner to yield one indicator of overall fiscal health. Rather, the dimensions of financial condition and change events (fiscal stress) must be examined according to their relevance and in a manner that allows them to relate in nonlinear ways.

This task is accomplished here in two ways. First, municipalities with extreme outcomes of different dimensions of financial condition are examined to determine if there is an explanation. For instance, governments with high budgetary solvency but low fiscal capacity are examined on other features such as governing structure, growth, capital investment, debt, and level of political conflict to determine why they have good short-term solvency despite their poor long-term solvency. Similarly, governments with high fiscal capacity but low budgetary solvency are also examined to determine likely causes. The second method assesses the effects of governance primarily and fiscal events secondarily on financial condition within most of the municipal groups in appendix 7. This second approach compares the quantitative indicators of financial condition and the qualitative information for corporate and political governments in the different municipal groups to evaluate the effects of governance structure on financial condition more comprehensively and generally.

Financial Condition in the Extreme

Table 7.10 shows governments that are outliers on different dimensions of financial condition, how outliers were identified, and some features of these governments. One thing to keep in mind with respect to outliers in categories 1 and 2 is that very high budgetary solvency and slack are not necessarily good, and low budgetary solvency and slack are not always inappropriate to the fiscal environment. That is why rural municipalities with populations less than one thousand and high growth are eliminated from group 1, and governments with very high wealth and that are home rule are eliminated from group 2. In the first case, very small and rural governments have very low revenue wealth, but their spending needs are also low, and growth is enhancing their surplus revenues greatly. Thus, these municipal governments are removed from the analysis. In the second case, several municipalities were removed that have populations with very high income and are what one might describe as exclusive. These municipalities, which were interviewed in 2003, have home rule and little sales tax, which makes them far less vulnerable to recessions and better able to handle them. Thus, their need for budgetary solvency and slack is far less than that of most governments.

Most of the municipal governments in the Chicago region with high budgetary solvency and slack generally have high fiscal capacity, and many experienced high growth from 1990 to 2000 and/or from 2000 to 2005. Most of these are not home rule, as they tend to have populations less than twenty-five thousand. There are four, however, in category 1 of table 7.10 with a revenue wealth-to-spending ratio that is in the thirtieth percentile, that did not have high growth, and were not home rule. In other words, these governments had low fiscal capacity at the time, yet they were able to maintain high budgetary solvency. Three of these governments have both a village manager and a finance director, which are somewhat unusual for governments of this size. Beach Park had an administrator only in 2003, and none had a strong sales tax base from 2000 to 2005. Flossmoor and Riverside have higher revenue wealth overall (60th and 55th percentiles); Beach Park and Richton Park have low revenue wealth (17th and 12th percentiles). Revenue burden in three of the governments is in the seventy-fifth percentile, which may help support the high budgetary solvency and slack in these governments, but capital spending in three governments completely stopped from 2002–3 to 2006. Debt burden is high only in one government in group 1.

News reports on all four governments and a student report on the budgeting process in one show little political conflict in all and attention to professional budgetary methods and strategic planning in two of them. One editorial by a newspaper on Flossmoor described it as a "well-run, stable town." It also stated that "the village has an AA bond rating, which is a good sign of its economic stability" (*Star* 2005). All governments run nonpartisan elections except Riverside, which has a very interesting feature in this respect. Riverside Community Caucus was established in 1927 by a group of residents who believed their village government should not be subject to the influence of major political parties. The sole purpose of the caucus is to find, nominate,

TABLE 7.10 Outlying Governments in Different Dimensions of Financial Condition

(1) High budgetary solvency and slack, low fiscal capacity. Governments in the highest quintile of budgetary solvency and governmental budgetary slack, but low revenue wealth to spending need ratio. Rural municipalities with population less than 1,000, high growth, and wealthy/exclusive are eliminated.

Beach Park (12,500, CAO)	Flossmoor (9,300, CAO and FD)
Richton Park (12,500, CAO and FD)	Riverside (8,900, CAO and FD)

(2) Low budgetary solvency and slack, high fiscal capacity. Governments in the lowest quintile of budgetary solvency and governmental budgetary slack with a high revenue wealth to spending need ratio. Governments with very high wealth and that are home rule are eliminated. Small, exclusive municipalities with very high personal income per capita and home rule are eliminated.

Bensenville (20,700, CAO and FD)	Merrionette Park (2,000, M)★
Beecher (2,033, CAO)★	Midlothian (14,300, M)★
Forest Park (15,700, CAO)	North Riverside (6,700, CAO and FD)★
Glencoe (8,700, CAO and FD)	Orland Hills (6,800, CAO)★
Island Lake (8,100, M)	South Chicago Heights (4,000, CAO)
Indian Head Park (3,700, CAO)	Westchester (16,800, CAO and FD)

(3) Low revenue burden relative to spending effort, low budgetary solvency and slack. Governments in the lowest quintile of revenue burden minus spending effort but budgetary solvency and governmental budgetary slack less than the median.

Antioch (8,800, CAO, P)★	Orland Hills (6,800, CAO, P)★
Darien (22,900, CAO)★	St. Charles (27,900, city)★
Downers Grove (48,700)★	Westmont (24,500)★
Indian Head Park (3,700, CAO)	Willowbrook (9,000)★
Lake Zurich (18,100, P)	Winfield (8,700, P)
Matteson (13,000)★	

(4) High revenue burden relative to spending effort, high budgetary solvency and slack. Governments in the highest quintile of revenue burden minus spending effort but budgetary solvency and governmental budgetary slack that is close to or above the median, and/or have high revenue wealth.

Berkeley (5,200, CAO)	Northlake (11,900, FD, city)
Calumet Park (8,500, M)	Park Forest (23,500, CAO and FD, NP)
Glenwood (9,000, CAO)	Riverside (8,900, CAO and FD)
Hanover Park (38,200, CAO and FD)	Thornton (2,600, M, NP)
Hazel Crest (14,800, CAO)	University Park (6,700, CAO and FD, NP)
Maywood (27,000, CAO and FD)	

Note: Budgetary solvency and governmental budgetary slack are averaged for 2001 to 2005.

★Dependence on sales taxes is high.

CAO: chief administrative officer; FD: finance director; NP: nonpartisan; M: mayor only; P: partisan.

and support the candidates for elected offices, and there has been little challenge to the caucus' candidates in past elections (Anthony et al. 2009).

With respect to group 2, governments in the region with low budgetary solvency and slack generally have low fiscal capacity, most had little population change since 1990, and they are a mixture of home rule and non–home rule. However, there are fourteen outlying municipal governments in this group with relatively high fiscal capacity, including three with very high median income per capita (more than 250 percent of the median of all municipalities in the Chicago region). In this case, government wealth does not prevent poor financial condition on the other dimensions. After removing two governments with home rule that do not require the same level of solvency and slack as those without home rule, the question here is why do the remaining twelve governments with high fiscal capacity have low solvency and slack?

First, five of these governments are fairly dependent on sales taxes, and closer examination of qualitative and other quantitative data shows that these five governments had low surplus resources prior to the recession and had not recovered by 2005–6. Not being home rule and having little surplus limited the size of their fiscal toolboxes and therefore probably reduced their capacity to manage the threat of the 2001 recession. In addition, all governments except two have partisan elections, and one of these is a commission form of government. Council members in commission governments act as departmental heads, which makes this form more political than corporate. The fiscal decision structures of these governments are a mixture of mayor only, administrator only, and CAO with a finance director. The three governments that were mayor only in 2003 might be classified as more political than corporate, especially given their partisan elections, but what can be said about the governing structures of the other nine governments in category 2 with a CAO?

No news is available from Beecher, and news reports from Forest Park and Orland Hills fit the pattern of a political government with respect to the roles of elected officials, the appointment of the CAO and others, electoral challenges, and a record of past problems with accountability and fiscal improprieties. South Chicago Heights and Westchester had long-term administrators and mayors (fifteen and twenty years respectively) in the early 2000s, and the village administrator in Indian Head Park is also the chief of police. Bensenville has a very outspoken mayor, very high debt, and has spent a great deal of money fighting lawsuits with the City of Chicago during this time period.

News reports about Glencoe and the interview in North Riverside show nothing unique about the institutional features of governance in these municipal governments other than high turnover of elected officials in Glencoe in 2004. The personal income of residents in this government is the third highest in the region, and it has very high debt. In this case, it seems that the high service demands of residents, the lack of home rule, and the government's push to use development to increase the tax base has placed it in a precarious fiscal condition. North Riverside, by comparison, depends on sales taxes for over 60 percent of its revenue, which probably explains its poor solvency and slack during this time period.

The level of government revenue burden relative to spending effort is the basis of the analysis of groups 3 and 4. When spending effort is subtracted from revenue burden, negative values indicate that governments are spending more than they need given the revenue they draw from their combined bases. Positive values suggest they are not spending enough yet draw a high rate of revenue from their combined bases. Although high values on both the positive and negative sides represent an imbalance with the fiscal environment, high negative values for this equation may not necessarily indicate poor financial condition. In fact, governments that spend more than they need, finance the spending using a smaller portion of their revenue base, and have high budgetary solvency and slack are probably in the best fiscal shape overall. They are able to provide high levels of service at low revenue rates and reduce their vulnerability to fiscal threats (or increase their ability to leverage fiscal opportunities). On the other hand, governments that spend more than they need yet have low solvency and slack are likely to be spending too much relative to the resources coming in. These governments are at risk of worsening financial condition in the long run.

The eleven outlying governments in group 3 of table 7.10 have low revenue burden relative to spending effort, and budgetary solvency and slack that is less than the median. In other words, these governments are spending a lot relative to the revenue burden on the population, but their short-term financial condition is not good. The political pressures to spend high, tax low, and rely on sales taxes have been noted here and in previous chapters, and it is likely that the financial condition of many governments in this group is the result of such pressures. Although none of these governments are mayor only, and only four hold partisan elections, news reports on all governments show that seven of them have high political conflict and turnover of officials, and two of these have seemingly significant financial management problems as noted by the audits. In addition, St. Charles is a city with council elections by ward, which moves it toward the political end of the continuum in table 4.5.

Governments in the region that spend little relative to their needs and draw high levels of revenue from their combined bases to finance services are probably in the worst financial condition overall because they cannot meet their spending needs with the revenues available to them. Indeed, if you examine governments in this group and remove those that are very small, have very high growth, have very high income, or are a satellite city, the revenue wealth of the majority that are remaining is in the thirtieth percentile. Furthermore, the budgetary and governmental solvency of most is less than the median. However, seventeen of these governments have budgetary solvency and slack that is close to or above the median, and six of these have revenue wealth that is above the fortieth percentile (Cary, Elmwood Park, Evanston, Hillside, Oak Park, and Richton Park), which probably accounts for their good financial position. The eleven outlying governments in group 4 of table 7.10 have revenue wealth that is in the thirtieth percentile, which makes it more challenging for them to maintain high budgetary solvency and slack. In this case, the important questions are what do these governments have in common, and how are they different from the twenty-six other governments in the larger group that have low budgetary solvency and slack?

First, all but two of the eleven governments in group 4 are home rule, only three are nonpartisan, two are mayor only, and all but one rely little on sales taxes. By comparison, eleven of the twenty-six nonoutlying governments with very poor financial condition are non–home rule, six are cities with wards, seven are nonpartisan, and eighteen are mayor only or mayor and finance director with no CAO. Although there is little difference in partisanship between governments in group 4 with good solvency and slack and the twenty-six governments with poor solvency and slack, the former tend to have a more corporate structure according to qualitative evidence. However, three of the governments in group 4 are not corporate, and several of the nonoutlying governments were corporate, which indicate that governance structure is not a necessary condition for good financial condition. In this case, home rule gives governments with high revenue burden relative to spending effort an important advantage in maintaining financial condition.

What do governments in the four groups in table 7.10 tell us about municipal government financial condition overall? First, corporate governance structures, low political conflict, conservative fiscal decisions (low capital and debt), low vulnerability to the 2001 recession, but adequate funding of services (high revenue burden) seem to encourage good financial condition in governments with low fiscal capacity. Second, governments with high fiscal capacity but low solvency and slack tend to be more political than corporate, or have strong political features that encourage officials to follow high-powered incentives and use political heuristics to resolve financial problems rather than follow low-powered incentives and use corporate heuristics. Many of these governments also are more vulnerable to recessionary effects and other fiscal threats due to their dependence on sales taxes. Third, governments that are spending more than they are financing and have low solvency and slack also tend to depend on sales taxes for most of their revenue, and they rely more on political solutions to financial problems than corporate solutions. However, political conflict seems to be more prevalent in these governments and therefore a greater factor in their financial problems. By comparison, governments that have difficulty meeting and financing spending needs but are able to maintain high budgetary solvency tend to be more corporate and have less reliance on sales taxes.

More generally, the findings seem to be that, in the extreme, a corporate institutional structure with low-powered incentives and professional solutions to financial problems helps governments maintain better financial condition. Being less vulnerable to fiscal threats associated with declines in sales taxes is also critical here, but it is important to keep in mind that there are many municipal governments that depend highly on sales taxes and are in very good financial condition. Likewise, there may be some governments that are clearly on the corporate end of the institutional continuum, yet have bad financial condition. The next section assesses how solutions to financial problems and financial condition vary among similar governments with different governing structures to better investigate the impact of governance on fiscal policy, practice, and financial condition.

Does Governance Structure Matter?

Table 7.11 shows seven of the ten control groups from appendix 7 and summarizes findings about the effects of governance, including conflict, and fiscal administrative capacity on financial condition in each group presented. Financial decision structure is the primary governance or administrative capacity feature examined here, and the table shows how it varies for each municipal group. Notice that primary groups A, I, and J and secondary groups 5 and 11 from appendix 7 are excluded from this table. All of these groups except A are wealthier and larger than the other groups, and all of

TABLE 7.11 Summary of Findings about Financial Condition and Fiscal Governance

Main Description	Group[a]	Secondary Description	FDS Category (No. of governments)[b]	Summary
(B) White-collar, wealthy, various growth	3	Very small and small commercial	1(4), 2(4), 3(4), 5(1)	Form of government and governance matters to practice and outcome, but it is moderated by pressure from the public and elected officials to alter fiscal practices in particular ways. However, all have the capacity to easily recover from their fiscal problems, especially those that are home rule.
	4	Small and medium, residential	1(5), 2(2), 3(10), 4(1), 5(3)	Form of government and governance has little direct impact on fiscal outcomes, but fiscal expertise may provide an advantage in certain situations, especially growth. These governments are less vulnerable to economic events, but also have the capacity to easily recover from fiscal stress.
(C) Small, blue-collar, low or no growth	6	Some commerce or industry, no growth, poor, inner ring	3(3), 4(2), 5(7)	Corruption and political governance features do not always lead to a poor financial condition, and governments with administrators and more corporate features do not always have good financial condition. However, fiscal expertise and control appear to be an important factor in improving or maintaining financial condition and fiscal practices in governments that are not insolvent.
		Industry, no growth, poor	1(1), 2(1), 3(1), 4(1), 5(4)	Corporate governments with a more professional form encourage economic development and higher capital investment, which is funded through debt and higher revenue burden. These governments also have higher government budgetary balance, but they may rely on their enterprise funds to subsidize these financial demands. This mixed picture of financial condition may demonstrate the trade-offs that such governments are forced to make to maintain capital investment and their long-term fiscal position.
	7	More commercial, higher wealth, low growth	3(3), 5(3)	Similar to subgroup 6 form of government appears to have little effect on finances or handling of growth, but some municipalities with high political conflict, as reported in the news, are worse off financially. The strong political features of these governments may counteract the effects of form of government and make it difficult to assess the broader features of governance structure on financial condition.
	8	Residential, poor, low growth	3(5), 5(5)	The evidence suggests that corporate governance with administrators helps to improve fiscal position across the indicators, but it is neither a necessary nor sufficient

(D) Moderate size and wealth, blue–white collar mix, low growth	9	Residential	1(4), 2(1), 3(3), 4(1)	condition. In addition, the lack of consistency in form of government over time makes it difficult to assess its impact. Fiscal direction and control is important to these governments' fiscal position, but turnover in professional staff, political conflict, and many political governance features make it difficult to maintain corporate fiscal practices or to encourage broad-based, proactive, and investment-oriented financial choices at a policy level.
	10	Commercial and industrial	1(1), 2(3), 3(3), 4(1), 5(3)	There seems to be very little relationship between form of government and fiscal position in these governments, but they have many strong political governance features, which may limit the implementation of corporate fiscal practices over a sustained period of time.
	12	Blue–collar, low wealth, residential; Blue–collar, low wealth, commercial	1(2), 2(2), 3(4), 4(2), 5(4)	These municipalities demonstrate that fiscal expertise and administrative guidance in the area of planning and managing growth, and corporate governance, can be very effective in helping governments that are experiencing high growth to improve their financial condition. However, these features may not be necessary in the earlier stages of growth. It is also apparent that negotiating the fiscal and service demands of growth and planning for a sound fiscal position in the future is the primary challenge facing these governments and that the switch to more corporate governance can be difficult for the current political system.
(E) Small, low–moderate wealth, high growth	13	White-collar, residential, lower wealth (no sales); White-collar, residential, higher wealth (high income); White–blue mix, higher wealth (high sales)	1(1), 2(4), 3(9), 4(1), 5(4)	There is no clear indication that fiscal decision structure has an effect on short-term fiscal condition of municipalities in subgroup 13, although interviews and news reports in this subgroup indicate that a CAO and finance director help to change fiscal practices and policies to focus more on long-term fiscal condition. However, political conflict, turnover among professional staff, and the circuitous route these municipalities take in becoming more corporate obscure the effects of form of government and corporate governance on financial condition in this group. High growth often forces municipalities to make unpleasant political trade-offs between improving or maintaining fiscal solvency (attracting commerce and raising taxes and fees to support growth) and the demands of residents (less commerce, traffic, and lower taxes and fees), which leads to political conflict that make it difficult to work with developers efficiently and pursue consistent goals, which in turn leads to lawsuits. Growth increases water, sewer, and drainage demands exponentially, which, if poorly funded and planned, can lead to significant water, sewer, and drainage problems and additional lawsuits.

TABLE 7.11 Summary of Findings about Financial Condition and Fiscal Governance

Main Description	Group[a]	Secondary Description	FDS Category (No. of governments)[b]	Summary
(F) Mod.–large size, mod. Income, blue–white collar mix, high growth	14	Lower wealth (residential)	1(3), 2(6), 3(1), 5(1)	This group demonstrates how bad fiscal practices, turnover in staff, political conflict, political governance, and lack of fiscal planning for growth may worsen a government's financial condition. However, the increasing revenues from growth allows some municipalities to remain relatively well off by comparison to others, at least in the short run. The primary challenges governments face here are making growth pay for itself, establishing the correct fiscal structure to do this, planning for the end of growth, and diversifying revenue structure to reduce pressure on property taxes. With the exception of one municipality, all those in the top half of the fiscal position indicators have very active economic development programs and units according to websites and news reports. The three lowest municipalities are less active in economic development. Fiscal data also show that finance directors are associated with more debt, higher capital spending, and better enterprise funds, which probably leads to their higher revenue burdens. Interviews and news reports demonstrate that administrators, and especially finance directors, encourage revenue increases to accommodate growth and prepare for their fiscal future. In contrast, mayoral and less corporate forms of governance are more wedded to no-debt policies and limiting capital spending. Political forms of government also borrow more from enterprises to run governmental operations.
	15	Higher wealth (sales)	1(2), 2(5), 3(3)	

			FDS[b]	
(G) Mod.–large size, industrial, blue collar, no growth	17	Moderate size, low wealth	1(3), 3(1), 4(3), 5(6)	Governments with mayors or finance directors only and significant political features are in the worst position, and those with administrators, finance directors, and more corporate features have better fiscal practices and better financial condition. However, the strong political features of the latter muddle the connection between form of government and fiscal outcome. The interviews clearly indicate how fiscal practices can change in governments that have adopted strong fiscal direction and are trying to become more corporate, but their political features prevent full implementation or reverse the implementation of recommended fiscal practices. Municipalities with political governance features seem to value responsiveness to constituents over efficiency, and define accountability in terms of political control. Interviews and news reports also indicate that the relatively good financial position of some of these municipalities may be due to very conservative fiscal policies (low debt, capital spending from reserves only, and low tax/low revenue burden), a stable government, and cooperation among elected officials.
	18	Large, low wealth	1(1), 4(5), 5(4)	
	19	Large, moderate wealth	1(4), 2(1), 3(1), 4(3), 5(1)	
(H) Mod.–very large size, poor, blue-collar, no growth	20	Mostly residential, moderate size	1(2), 3(1), 5(3)	Many of the stories and experiences of these municipalities as related by the interviews and news reports are the same as those of group G, but there is less evidence that municipalities with fewer political features or more corporate forms are better off financially.
	21	Mostly residential, large	1(3), 2(2), 5(1)	Form of government seems to have little direct effect on financial condition, possibly due to political and financial instability in these governments and the strong influence of political governance features.
	22	Mostly industrial or commercial, very large	1(2), 2(1), 4(2), 5(1)	

[a]See appendix 5.

[b]Financial decision structure (FDS); 1 = manager and finance director; 2 = administrator and finance director; 3 = administrator or manager only; 4 = finance director only; 5 = mayor only.

the groups except A had both a CAO and a finance director, which makes it impossible to assess the effects of FDS in these groups. By comparison, all governments in group A are too small to have either an administrator, manager, or finance director.

The financial condition indicators examined for governments within each group in table 7.11 are the same as those examined in the prior section. All available qualitative data were assessed for governments in each group using coded statements in the interviews and news reports. Narratives were written for each type of government in each group incorporating information from the financial indicators and qualitative data. Table 7.11 summarizes these narratives, showing conclusions about the effects of institutional features of governance and other factors on the financial condition of governments in each primary group.

The thirty-four municipalities in group B (white-collar and wealthy) are divided into those with high levels of commerce versus those that are more residential. Among the commercial municipalities, the government with a mayor only is clearly in the worst fiscal position, and the municipalities that are the best off have finance directors. Most of the residential municipalities have few service responsibilities (no water, sewer, fire, library, or park services because they are in special districts), and they are highly dependent upon property taxes.

Two significant patterns emerge from the financial condition indicators, interviews, and news articles concerning the link between fiscal governance, financial practice, and financial outcome in the commercial subgroup of group B. One is the tension between political demands and sound fiscal practice, even in more corporate types of government. Election and political issues in at least four of these governments revolved around fiscal practices, such as not using debt to finance capital infrastructure, dramatically lowering the fund balance, increasing reliance on sales taxes to maintain low or no property taxes, and maintaining artificially low water rates. One of the interviewees talked at length about the board micromanaging the financial staff but had little to say about overall fiscal policy. He also talked about having to work to "bring new boards along" to understand the government's fiscal affairs and not "suspend the laws of economics."

The second pattern, which has been noted before, is that governments that are highly dependent on sales taxes are vulnerable to economic declines, which impact their budgetary and service-level solvency. The fiscal stress experienced by four of the corporate governments in this group of thirteen (subgroup 3) that were relatively dependent on sales taxes due to the 2002–3 recession engendered significant political turmoil, turnover in elected and appointed officials, and a worse fiscal position. However, all of these municipalities have the capacity to easily recover from their fiscal problems, especially those that are home rule. The lesson here is that form of government and governance structure matter to practice and outcome, but their effects are moderated by pressure from the public and elected officials that alters fiscal practices and policies in particular ways.

In contrast, the residential communities in subgroup 4 display no such clear pattern of effect, although some events suggest that fiscal expertise may provide advantages in certain situations. Many of these municipalities, especially those with low growth and stable fiscal resources, face few fiscal problems that require high levels of fiscal expertise or control. Fiscal practices are often informal and not performed according to professional standards. Auditors and board members with expertise in particular areas also may provide enough fiscal guidance in some cases, and some are small enough that they require no full-time administrator. However, some face significant fiscal threats, especially regarding development, where fiscal expertise seems to matter.

The thirty-six municipalities in group C in table 7.11 are divided into four groups, one of which is not very homogenous. The first subgroup of twelve municipalities includes some of the poorest municipal governments in the region, all have very high revenue burden, and two might be classified as generally insolvent. Three of the four interviews of governments in this group indicate the extent to which change to a more corporate form of government has little effect on budgetary and service-level solvency, and the difficulties of improving short-term solvency under conditions of very poor long-term solvency. Four of the seven mayor-only municipalities in this group experienced corruption, fraud, or stealing by a government official during the period of study, which corresponded to news reports of problems of transparency and lack of internal controls in these governments. News reports also indicate that these four governments have many other characteristics that make them political rather than corporate.

Two of the twelve governments in subgroup 6 have relatively good budgetary and service-level solvency by comparison to the others, and interviews with officials in these governments show they are attempting to move their governments toward better fiscal practices. However, several others with a more corporate structure do not have good financial condition. Thus, the conclusion here is that corruption and political governance features do not always lead to a poor financial condition, and governments with administrators and more corporate features do not always have good financial condition. However, fiscal expertise and control appear to be an important factor in improving fiscal practices in all governments and maintaining financial condition in governments that are not at the lowest levels of long-term solvency.

All eight governments in the second group of subgroup 6 are home rule. Governments with finance directors have higher governmental budgetary slack, but those with mayors only clearly have better enterprise budgetary slack. Municipalities with a mayor only have lower debt and lower revenue burden but also less capital investment. The government that is clearly the worst off financially in this group has a finance director only, there are new reports documenting the misuse and inappropriate use of funds in the government, and it had no website in 2003 or 2010. The two other governments with evidence of corruption do not have poor financial condition relative to the others, and the three governments with many corporate features are not necessarily better off.

In conclusion, it seems that corporate governments in this industrial subgroup tend to pursue economic development more and have higher capital investment than political governments, which is funded through debt and higher revenue burden. Corporate governments also have higher government budgetary slack, but they may be relying on their enterprise funds to subsidize these financial demands. This mixed picture of financial condition in corporate governments in this group seems to demonstrate the trade-offs such governments are forced to make to maintain capital investment and long-term fiscal position.

Unfortunately, none of the municipalities in subgroup 7 of group C were interviewed, and they are not very homogenous so it is difficult to separate out the effects of governance from other factors. Also the strong political features of all governments in subgroup 7 confound and may counteract the effects of fiscal decision structure, which make it difficult to assess the broader features of governance structure on financial condition.

The last subgroup in group C with ten municipalities (subgroup 8) demonstrates that fiscal decision structure is not constant and that the evolution toward a more corporate structure is not smooth, which makes it difficult to determine the effects of this factor on financial condition. Some municipalities in this subgroup did not replace their administrators when they left voluntarily or involuntarily after the election of a new mayor or board. In this case, the CAO duties may be assumed by a police chief, fire chief, or finance director for an extended period of time. In one government, the mayor became full time when he retired from his "real" job to avoid hiring an administrator. The municipal attorney also shares significant administrative responsibilities with the administrator in another government, and with the mayor in a third government. This practice of sharing executive and administrative duties in multiple departments coupled with inconsistency in fiscal decision structure seems to be driven by the need for trust in chief administrators and fiscal expediency.

Group D has twenty municipalities divided into a residential subgroup in which the governments are all non–home rule and a commercial subgroup. The interviews and news reports on the residential governments demonstrate the extent to which political governance and political conflict can affect fiscal practices and outcomes. The three governments with administrators only are ranked at the bottom of the others on fiscal condition, and the interview with one was very useful for revealing the dynamics of trying to change fiscal policy and practice from political to corporate in a government with many political features. High professional staff turnover is seen in two other governments in this subgroup, but it does not appear to guarantee a poor fiscal position because one is relatively well-off. Overall, one can conclude that fiscal control and planning is important to governments in subgroup 9 for maintaining budgetary and service-level solvency. However, turnover in professional staff, political conflict, and a political perspective on fiscal governance make it more difficult to maintain good solvency and discourage broad-based, proactive, and investment-oriented financial choices at a policy level.

All eleven municipal governments in subgroup 10 of group D have many political governance features. These suburbs are older, inner ring, and commercial or industrial and are very active politically. One government is a commission form, three are cities, and five more have had the same mayor for twenty or more years. In addition, many of the administrators or managers are political rather than merit appointees. However, the worst government has a mayor only and, as related in the press, numerous deficiencies in its fiscal practices, including relying on long-term auditors for fiscal advice (and to determine their fiscal position) and misappropriations of pension funds. Another government in poor financial condition in this group also has a mayor only, but a third mayor-only government is relatively well-off.

The two municipalities interviewed in subgroup 10 both had professional administrators and finance directors, some corporate features, but not very good budgetary solvency. Both interviewees discussed the difficulties of promoting recommended fiscal practices in their government, including strategic and capital planning, raising fees and charges to cover costs, outsourcing, and reducing dependence on sales taxes. The municipality with the best fiscal position in this subgroup is a true council-manager form of government, but political controversy between the mayor and council over firing and hiring of the village manager and finance director is very apparent. The other municipalities that are well-off have no finance director but have significant fiscal guidance from knowledgeable elected officials. Based on all the evidence for subgroup 10, a corporate fiscal decision structure does not ensure good financial condition because the strong political governance features in many appear to limit implementation of recommended fiscal practices over a sustained period of time.

All municipal governments in group E in table 7.11 have experienced high growth from 1990 to 2000 and or from 2000 to 2005. Their experiences were assessed previously using a somewhat different set of criteria in chapter 5 and so will not be reviewed here in great detail. In total, the municipal governments in subgroup 12 demonstrate that fiscal expertise, corporate approaches to planning and managing growth, and corporate governance can be very effective in helping those that are experiencing high growth to maintain and improve financial condition, but it may not be as necessary in the early stages of growth. It is also apparent that negotiating the fiscal and service demands of growth and planning for good financial condition in the future is the primary challenge these governments face and that the switch from political to more corporate governance can be difficult. In contrast, there is no clear indication that fiscal decision structure has an effect on the short-term solvency of municipalities in subgroup 13, although interviews and news reports on governments in this subgroup indicate that a CAO and a finance director help to change fiscal practices and policies to focus more on financial condition in the future. Data on governments in this subgroup also demonstrate the strain that growth places on these municipalities and the extent to which governments in group E struggle to become more corporate.

High growth often forces municipalities in group E to make unpleasant political trade-offs between improving or maintaining fiscal solvency (attracting commerce and raising taxes and fees to support growth) and the demands of residents (less commerce, traffic, and lower taxes and fees), which leads to political conflict that makes it difficult to work with developers efficiently and pursue consistent goals. These problems, in turn, can lead to lawsuits and mismanaged or uncontrolled development. Growth increases water, sewer, and drainage demands exponentially, which, if poorly funded and planned, can lead to significant water, sewer, and drainage problems and more lawsuits in the future.

Group F has 21 municipalities divided into two subgroups, and almost all have aggregate fiscal indicators that are above the median for the region. In other words, they all have reasonably good budgetary and short-term solvency. Municipalities in both subgroups had experienced high growth prior to 2003 but are now close to being built-out and nearing the end of their growth period. Thus these municipalities represent the future state for municipalities in group E and demonstrate the trend toward growing municipalities eventually hiring an administrator or manager and finance director. The majority of municipalities in this group have persons in both positions, one government has a mayor only, and the other four have an administrator only. Thus there is some basis for determining the effects of financial decision structure on financial condition in this group.

The mayor-only municipality, which was interviewed and is in the worst fiscal shape among the residential subgroup, provides an interesting contrast to others in group F. It is the only municipality with no significant economic development program. In fact, it had no website during the time period examined. The mayor of this town had been in office thirty years until he lost to a candidate that was promoting the need for economic development. The interview indicated that the mayor relied on auditors for financial advice, and the government instituted few recommended fiscal practices. In fact, the police chief answered many of the financial questions in the interview.

Group F also provides an opportunity to examine the effects of political conflict on financial practices and condition independent of financial decision structure. In this case, significant political conflict in one government led to its having seven different finance directors and ten different village managers between 1999 and 2005. The government's finances were also in disarray, and it did not have a clean audit for several years during this time period. News reports also indicate that political factors are driving fiscal practices regarding their fund balance, interfund transfers, water rates, capital maintenance, internal controls, and insurance costs.

Based on the evidence here, group F demonstrates how bad fiscal practices, turnover in staff, political conflict, political governance, and lack of fiscal planning for growth may threaten even a wealthy government's financial condition. However, the increasing revenues from growth allow some municipalities with these conditions to remain relatively well-off, at least in the short run. The primary challenges governments face here are making growth pay for itself, establishing the correct fiscal structure to do this, strategically positioning the organization to transition to a new fiscal structure when growth ends, and diversifying revenue structure to reduce pressure on property taxes. The three municipalities with the lowest financial condition also have less active economic development programs.

Most of the thirty-three municipalities in Group G have aggregate fiscal indicators that are worse than the median for the region. The smaller governments tend to have mayors only and the larger governments have administrators or managers and finance directors. Many of the governments demonstrate how political governance features counteract corporate forms of governance and attempts to implement recommended fiscal practices. These municipalities also demonstrate the struggle between corporate and political governance that exists in many circumstances.

For instance, the mayor and board in one council-manager government that was interviewed in subgroup 17 continued to function as a mayor-council form with respect to the staff and departmental operations. The council-manager form was established by voters in response to past corruption by elected officials, but that did not deter elected officials from promoting ballot measures to return to a mayoral form, which had been defeated previously. Not surprisingly, turnover of administrative staff is high, and both the manager and finance director changed jobs shortly after the interview. The interview with the finance director, which was a relatively new position, indicated the wide range of financial management practices she was trying to change and the fiscal problems that resulted from past practices. As reported on previously, Maywood is another municipality in group G (subgroup 18) with a similar story of elected officials in a council-manager government trying to operate as if it were a mayor-council form, cycling through numerous managers and finance directors and having unsound fiscal practices and policies that professionals were trying to change.

Two other municipalities in subgroup 17 demonstrate the link between type of governance, financial practices, and fiscal condition based on interviews that document the experiences of new finance directors in governments that were mayor-only several years prior to the interview. Although these municipalities have very low revenue wealth, improvements can be seen in the short-term fiscal indicators over time in both cases. Both interviews documented the fiscal practices that existed prior to and after the finance director was hired, and most reforms instituted by these individuals focused on improving internal and fiscal controls.

Unfortunately, the other municipalities in group G demonstrate a mixture of corporate and political features, fiscal practices, and levels of financial condition that are hard to untangle. The strong political features of many governments with a CAO and finance director muddle the connection between fiscal decision structure and financial condition. Although the interviews clearly indicate how fiscal practices and heuristics can change in governments that are trying to become more corporate, their political features often prevent full implementation or reverse the implementation of corporate approaches. Generally speaking, however, governments in group G that have mayors or finance directors only and significant political governance features are the worst off, and those with administrators, finance directors, and more corporate features have better fiscal practices and better financial condition. However, the relatively good financial condition of some of the more political municipal governments may be due to their conservative fiscal policies (low debt, capital spending from reserves only, and low tax/low revenue burden), stable government, and cooperation among elected officials as revealed in the qualitative and quantitative data. Thus, good financial condition can be achieved in other ways than the advancement of corporate fiscal practices and policies.

As with group G, the governments in group H in table 7.11 have significant political features that conflict with the corporate tendencies of professional managers, administrators, and finance directors. Although many of the stories and experiences of these municipalities, as related by the interviews and news reports, are the same as those of group G, there is less consistent evidence that municipalities with fewer political features or more corporate forms are better off financially.

For instance, the municipality in group H that is in the worst financial position consistently during the time period examined has a manager and a finance director, but the mayor (who has been in office for many years) is attempting to change his position to full time to increase political control. In contrast, three of the mayor-only governments in this group, one of which was interviewed, have relatively good financial condition. They are very stable governments, good cooperation seems to exist between the mayor and board or elected treasurer, and they have very conservative fiscal policies that include no debt and low capital spending.

In contrast, two other municipal governments in group H with a manager or administrator and finance director are in relatively good shape, although they have significant political features. One of these governments presents another example of a mayor and board trying to manipulate the managerial form to increase political control, in this case by making the manager position part time and appointing the police chief, a political supporter, to both positions. The administrator in the other municipality in this comparison is a political appointee and is known for Chicago-style politics. The interview with the finance director (their first one) revealed that she uncovered long-term corruption by the public works director. Although she has been in the position for ten years, she stated that maintaining internal and fiscal controls was her biggest battle.

All the governments in subgroup 22 have very political governance systems but a mixture of different levels of financial condition. Three have corruption problems that relate to fiscal controls (e.g., abuse of open purchase orders, illegal spending, stealing funds, ghost payrolling). The board in another municipality, which has a manager and a finance director, fired the entire economic development department contrary to the wishes of the mayor. Overall, fiscal decision structure of governments in this subgroup seem to have little direct effect on their financial condition, possibly due to the strong influence of political governance features on fiscal practices and policies.

When outcomes and conditions in all groups in table 7.11 are considered, the major finding is that having a CAO and a finance director is not a necessary or sufficient condition for good short-term financial condition (budgetary and service-level solvency) in all instances, but professional and qualified administrators, managers, and finance directors do influence financial practices in ways that increase the likelihood of improving and maintaining financial condition. It is apparent that finance directors provide a level of fiscal expertise and control that is helpful in many situations, and administrators and managers are critical for managing the threats and opportunities of population growth and development. The analysis also demonstrates the extent to which political governance features, high-powered incentives, political conflict, and turnover in government officials (elected or appointed) threaten financial condition and confound the effects of fiscal decision structure on fiscal practices and financial condition. Thus, a corporate decision structure does not always produce sound fiscal practices and good financial condition, and political governance features do not necessarily produce poor fiscal condition even though fiscal practices may be unsound. While these findings are not very satisfying, they demonstrate the complexity of municipal government financial condition and the contingent nature of the key factors identified here.

Conclusion

This chapter identifies some of the strategies that Chicago municipal governments use to maintain or improve financial condition in the long run and solve long-term financial problems. It also examines the effects of key factors from the model in figure 4.1 on financial condition, paying particular attention to the effects of governance structure and fiscal administrative capacity. Chapter 6 focuses on the tools these governments use to manage fiscal stress and munificence and finds that they have an order of operations or choice of tools that fits their political environment and fiscal structure. Chapter 7 focuses on documenting the fiscal policies and practice tools that they use to manage financial condition for the long haul and offers some explanations of the tools chosen and the tools' effects.

Two of the most important tools identified in this chapter for maintaining and improving financial condition, which are related, are capital investment and its method of finance. The analyses show that use of these tools varies significantly across municipal governments in the Chicago region. In this case, the level of capital investment by governments is a function primarily of fiscal capacity, including intergovernmental revenue, size of government, fiscal stress, and fiscal decision structure to a lesser extent. Capital spending is funded primary through debt or existing revenues and surplus funds. Use of debt is determined by specific features of fiscal capacity (sales receipts, grants, and home rule), size of government, population growth, miles of roads, and fiscal decision structure.

All other things being equal, governments with both a CAO and a finance director invest more in capital infrastructure and are much more likely to use debt and dedicated revenues to finance capital spending than governments that are administered by a mayor according to the regression analyses. These findings and the qualitative evidence suggest that more corporate and professionally administered governments place greater emphasis on maintaining and improving capital infrastructure to maintain and improve financial condition and are less likely to view debt as undesirable. In the context of financial problem solving, these results also suggest that governments with a CAO and finance director may have different assessments of the risks of underfunding capital infrastructure for maintaining financial condition and using debt to finance these investments. By comparison, governments that are administered by mayors only may see debt and high capital spending as politically risky, which would be of less concern to professional administrators. Consistent with this outcome, governments that are administered by mayors only spend less and collect less revenue, relatively speaking, than governments with both a CAO and a finance director.

Economic development is another very important financial tool for improving and maintaining financial condition, which was discussed at length in the interviews and the news reports. Both data sources were coded for different subjects related to economic development and population growth, and these tools were documented in chapter 3 primarily in the context of high growth and development. As described there, sales tax–generating enterprises are highly valued by municipal governments in the region because they generate sales taxes that diversify revenue structure and reduce dependence on property taxes. Voters' dislike of the property tax provides much incentive for governments to increase their reliance on sales taxes, which make them more vulnerable to recessions and increases competition between them for commercial businesses. All of this affects a wide range of fiscal policies that these governments pursue to maintain or improve financial condition, including capital investment and methods of financing these investments.

A comprehensive discussion of economic development policies to maintain or improve financial condition is beyond the scope of this book, but it is clear from the analyses here that competition in economic development and competition to maintain low taxes and charges should be incorporated directly into explanations of the fiscal policies implemented by municipal government (Hendrick, Wu, and Jacob 2007; Wu and Hendrick 2007). In fact, the extent to which competition was a factor in decisions about taxation, charges, fees, and even spending was very apparent from both the interviews and news reports. This trend clearly cannot be discounted in explanations of the fiscal policies of suburban municipal governments in this region. One important question in this case, which cannot be answered here, is the extent to which the regional and state governing environment in Illinois facilitates these outcomes more than in other regions or states.

It is clear from both the qualitative and quantitative analysis that sales receipts and home rule, which are important components of fiscal capacity, greatly affect decisions about revenue and operational and capital spending by municipal governments in the Chicago region. More important, these effects are not linear or straightforward. Home rule governments clearly take advantage of their status to raise sales tax rates, reduce reliance on property taxes, and increase GO debt. Reliance on sales taxes seems to improve financial condition overall and in specific areas such as capital investment, even during recessions, unless the government does not adequately balance slack with sales tax risks. But fiscal capacity is the most important factor in financial condition overall, and in particular areas such as capital investment and budgetary solvency.

With respect to the financial management tools these governments use to maintain financial condition, one would expect them to be more directly linked to internal governance structure than other types of fiscal tools. Unfortunately, this link cannot be established as systematically or as definitively as other relationships, as the interviews were not comprehensive with respect to financial management practices. The exception here was for budgeting as this subject was covered in all interviews. In addition, reports and interviews from nine governments that underwent or were undergoing changes from political to corporate forms were very useful in indentifying common trends. Concerning the budgeting process and documents, political governments and small governments were more likely to operate without a meaningful budget. These governments also were less likely to use planning, analysis, monitoring, and other characteristics associated with professional standards and rational heuristics and were more likely to use heuristics associated with boundedly rational problem solving.

Two other noteworthy findings about budgeting were reported here. First, governments in constant fiscal crisis and without tools for managing fiscal stress cannot engage in meaningful planning or budgeting. Their budgeting process is similar to what was described by a study of budgeting in poor countries in the early 1970s (Caiden and Wildavsky 1974). Second, governments' budgeting processes become more top-down during times of fiscal stress. That is, government budgeting is less driven by the wish lists of departments and more driven by the wishes of the CAO or CEO in response to threats of changes in financial condition.

Two other areas of financial management practice seemed particularly important to the nine governments mentioned previously. First, change agents and new finance directors focused on moving the locus of control of operations and fiscal transactions in the government from the political and personal realm to the corporate and administrative realm. Second, they focused on trying to clarify their government's fiscal structure and financial position. Along with planning and preparedness, financial professionals in these positions worked to determine the size and content of the fiscal toolbox and institute practices to better ensure that the tools chosen were implemented as planned and intended.

With respect to the effects of governing structure, political conflict, and administrative capacity (professional heuristics) on municipal financial condition and practices, the evidence is fairly clear that hiring knowledgeable and professional chief administration and financial officers and adopting corporate approaches to governance will, over time, improve financial management and lead to implementation of more professional practices. However, elected officials have significant authority over many fiscal policies and often establish policies that are not financially sound or consistent with professional standards. In addition, some political policies may improve some areas of financial condition. The finding that some political governments operate very conservatively with respect to capital spending and debt is a good example of political policies that help governments to maintain low revenue burden even when fiscal capacity is low. Conversely, overt political conflict, which often reflects a clash between political and corporate approaches to governance, is found to be a significant threat to financial condition due to turnover of policymakers and chief administrators and the inconsistency this produces in financial policies and overtime practices.

Notes

1. The following statutes explain these bonds in more detail: 65 ILCS 5/8-7-1 through 65 ILCS 5/8-7-7.
2. GFOA also recommends that this level of fund balance be maintained at higher levels in governments in which major revenue sources are volatile or unpredictable, those with significant exposure to higher outlays (e.g., disasters or immediate capital needs), or those with deficits in other funds.
3. Another explanation is that many unexpected threats or costs (outlay exposure) are the same irrespective of size of government (e.g., lawsuit), so smaller governments must keep a higher proportion of funds in their reserves than do larger governments.
4. By comparison, 60 percent of the municipalities had no bond ratings through Standard and Poor's in 2009, but 65 percent of them had bond ratings through either Moody's or Standard and Poor's in 2009.
5. GO, alternate revenue, and revenue bonds. At the time of these analyses, data were not available after 2005.
6. www.standardandpoors.com/products-services/RatingsDirect-Global-Credit-Portal/en/us (accessed December 2009).
7. Many governments seemed particularly sensitive and knowledgeable about capital deficiencies during the interviews, possibly due to the implementation of GASB 34 during that time. This standard required governments, many of which had not done this in the past, to inventory and assess their physical assets.
8. Due to PTELL restrictions, once non–home rule governments pay off GO debt they lose the portion of the property tax levy devoted to that debt unless they go to referendum. Thus some municipalities continuously issue GO debt, whether they need it or not, to maintain GO debt payments on their property tax levy.
9. Data on revenue dedicated to capital spending are available only for 2001 to 2005, so results for this equation reflect a somewhat different time period.
10. Total budget might have been a better measure of government size, but this variable is endogenous in most equations.
11. Percent of population voting for Bush vote in 2004 and percent of population with at least some college education were also tested in the model as crude indicators of service and revenue preferences of the voting population but were significant only in the own-source revenue and operational spending equations. Thus they are excluded here.

12. Robust standard errors present valid estimates of the standard errors in the presence of heteroskedasticity (White 1980). Also tests of serial correlation in the pooled data were estimated and found to be insignificant for all equations (Wooldridge 2002, 176–77).

13. The values of β and the betas are calculated using variables that are standardized on different scales. Because both the independent (X) and dependent variables (Y) are logged, β is interpreted as the percent change in Y for a 1 percent change in X. Betas show those effects in standard deviation units, which take into account the different variances of X and Y. Betas are considered more comparable in this case for continuous Xs, but the values of β for binary Xs are more meaningful.

14. Interestingly, the β for reliance on sales taxes (percent sales tax of own-source revenue) when substituted for revenue diversification in the budgetary solvency model is statistically insignificant, as it is for the same model when fund balance is used as a dependent variable in place of budgetary solvency. Thus governments that rely more on sales taxes are not really maintaining higher surpluses, contrary to expectations.

15. www.gfoa.org/index.php?option=com_content&task=view&id=118&Itemid=130.

16. The mayor, who was interviewed, was a high-level executive of a large bank in Chicago that had local governments as customers.

17. One part-time finance director who used to audit many local governments in the region expressed discomfort with this practice and so discontinued auditing to focus only on financial consulting.

18. It seemed especially tempting for long-term mayors in smaller governments to want to have complete discretion over financial practices at the managerial level. The expressed sentiment was that the mayor's time in office had provided him with enough experience and information to know what the financial problems are and how to handle them.

19. One interviewee's prophecy that he would be fired by his board for his initiatives came true six months after the interview. Another interviewee in a different city had also been the finance director in a municipality where she had functioned as a change agent. She talked off the record but at length about her experience there and the disappointment of dealing with the political environment in trying to change governing at the management level.

20. Many of these governments carried commercial catastrophic insurance for health and liability.

Chapter 8

Municipal Fiscal Health
Practice, Governance, and Policies

The introduction identifies the following four broad questions about fiscal stress and financial condition in Chicago suburban municipal governments: (1) What are the sources of fiscal threats and opportunities in these governments? (2) What tools (policies and practices) do they use to manage fiscal stress and maintain financial condition? (3) What effect do contextual factors such as fiscal capacity and governance have on the tools available to them and the tools they use to manage fiscal threats and opportunities and maintain financial condition? (4) What effect do particular tools have on their ability to manage fiscal threats and opportunities and maintain financial condition?

Chapter 2 lays out the conceptual framework for measuring fiscal stress and financial condition. Chapters 3 and 4 provide complementary theoretical frameworks for explaining officials' choice of tools, focusing on their problem-solving approaches (chapter 3) and governments' immediate political, fiscal, and organizational environments (chapter 4). Chapter 4 also examines macrolevel fiscal rules and governing structures that also affect the contents of the suburban governments' fiscal toolboxes and choice of tools by suburban governments. All four questions are investigated using extensive qualitative and quantitative data analyses in chapters 5, 6, and 7 based on the frameworks presented in chapters 2, 3, and 4. Chapters 5 focuses on answering question 1, and chapters 6 and 7 address different aspects of questions 2 and 3. Question 4 is the primary subject of chapter 7 and possibly the most difficult one to answer.

Keeping in mind that this investigation applies to municipal governments in the Chicago metropolitan region, what do we know about the effect of particular tools and events on financial condition? We know from the qualitative and quantitative evidence from chapters 6 and 7 that fiscal health and solvency depend primarily on the fiscal tools available to government and that the most effective tools for managing fiscal stress and maintaining financial condition depend on government fiscal capacity (revenue wealth, spending needs, and home rule). We also know from chapter 5 that the effects of fiscal threats and opportunities on financial condition can be permanent, temporary, and enhanced by government fiscal structure. Recessions that reduce sales tax revenues, for instance, are often temporary but have a greater effect on the financial condition of governments that rely heavily on such revenue, and these effects can become permanent if major commercial enterprises close during the recessionary period. As both threat and opportunity, population growth and development were found to have profound effects on these governments' financial condition, fiscal structure, and internal governing institutions.

Chapter 7 also demonstrates that government fiscal health depends to some extent on how governments manage these threats and opportunities and whether they can adapt their fiscal structure to changes in the fiscal environment. In other words, financial condition depends, in part, on the appropriateness of fiscal policies and practices to the existing fiscal environment and whether government fiscal policies and practices can restore, maintain, or improve the balance between their fiscal structure and environment. Unless the government has much revenue capacity and few fiscal threats, choice of appropriate fiscal policies often depends on the outcome of the battle between political pressures to increase spending and reduce taxes.

As demonstrated in chapter 6, the incentive structure in many governments, which is exacerbated by yardstick competition, favors a reduction in revenue burden but increases in service effort, which is not possible in perpetuity. Other governments are not shy about increasing revenue burden and decreasing service effort to manage fiscal stress, which are more sound fiscal tools during recessionary periods. However, revenue burden may be increased too much or in inefficient ways, such as when governments implement multiple new charges and fees that yield little revenue relative to their costs. Service effort also can be decreased too much, such as when governments do not maintain critical infrastructure in time to prevent more costly fixes in the future in the quest to have the lowest property taxes and charges in the region.

More generally, the analyses in the book show that fiscal health depends on the following: (1) government fiscal capacity (e.g., ability to increase sales taxes and the level of revenues this will generate); (2) the fiscal threats and opportunities governments face (e.g., a recession that lowers sales tax revenue); and (3) whether they choose sound financial tools (e.g., lowering capital spending) that balance their fiscal structure (e.g., level of investment in capital infrastructure) with their fiscal environment (age and condition of infrastructure). In this case, the effects of governing structure and administrative capacity are particularly important to the choice of sound financial tools. Political and corporate governments establish different incentives for financial policies (high-powered versus low-powered incentives), and they foster a different set of financial practices and strategies that are tied to the heuristics of professionalism in the case of corporate governments and politics in the case of political governments. Thus, what fiscal tools are considered to be sound by different governments vary by type of governance structure. For instance, governments with a political structure appear to spend either much more or much less than governments with a corporate structure, and political governments prefer less debt overall than corporate governments.

Moving forward, what are the most important or interesting observations and findings of this study? First is the extent to which generating sales taxes drives financial policies, financial condition, and financial structure of municipal governments in the Chicago region. Property taxes are politically unpopular, so elected officials chase sales-tax-generating business to provide higher levels of services to their constituents that are paid for in part by persons outside the jurisdiction, which lowers the tax burden on property owners in the jurisdiction. This strategy pays off if the government protects itself adequately from the risk of recessionary declines in sales receipts and other fiscal threats associated with commercial and enterprise failure. However, the Great Recession may show the limits and downside of this strategy as many governments that rely heavily on such taxes appear to have reached the bottom of their fiscal toolboxes, especially those that are not home rule. Although raising property taxes is the last resort for most governments, it is important to remember that this tool is available to home rule governments and is an important safety valve in helping these governments maintain financial condition as demonstrated by the Village of Schaumburg, which instituted its first property tax in its history in December 2009.

A second important finding is that governments have first, second, third, and last resorts for managing fiscal stress and that the order of operations is similar to what was observed thirty years ago (Levine 1978). Governments start with the easiest and least disruptive tools for adapting to fiscal threats and then move toward harder and more disruptive options as the threat increases or continues or if they have used up tools at a higher level. More specifically, there is a hierarchical preference in the order of tools to employ in managing fiscal threats that varies by governing structure, heuristics, and political values. The order is fairly consistent for most governments unless the dimensions of the toolbox change (e.g., government becomes home rule or begins high growth) or the political and governing environment changes. What is more likely to change is how far governments have to go in their order of fiscal tools before the threat is alleviated. The Great Recession may require many governments in the region to go further than they have gone before, which could dramatically change the fiscal structure of many.

A third important finding is the tremendously different financial experiences of governments in different stages of growth. Governments in different stages of growth have different financial problems and different streams of revenues and spending. Thus the tools available for maintaining and improving financial condition will vary for governments according to their stage of growth, as will the likelihood of success of different financial policies and practices in each stage. This research posited four stages of growth for metropolitan regions: growth initiation, rapid growth, built-out, and redevelopment. One might also distinguish rural municipalities that have no growth, which are most likely to exist outside of metropolitan regions, from governments in one of these four categories, as rural municipal governments are likely to have a different set of financial experiences than urban governments (Weber, Hendrick, and Thompson 2008). These categories of growth experience should be recognized in future financial research on suburbs and explored in more depth. However, there is also evidence that these phases may not be as prevalent or widespread in the future, as development has slowed greatly in the region, and there is an expectation among many that this change may be permanent.

A fourth important finding is the extent to which overt competition for sales tax enterprises, especially in growing communities, and less overt forms of competition drive many financial policies and strategies in Chicago municipal governments. Chapter 5 documented the extent to which these governments compete for businesses that produce sales tax revenues, especially the "dancing" stores and automobile dealerships, as one interviewee noted. The interviews in 2003 and the news reports for that period also document extensive use of tax incentives (tax payments) and other measures such as tax incremental finance districts to attract strong sales tax generators to their jurisdictions to prevent becoming the "donut hole" of commercial development once the municipality is built-out. Less obvious forms of competition among municipalities to attract businesses, residents, and even the rights to provide water and sewer to unincorporated areas also were noted.

However, the most surprising manifestation of competition was the extent to which these governments compared themselves to each other in news reports and interviews. These comparisons were primarily on the revenue side, but also every other area of fiscal policy and practice. These practices, which are evidence of *yardstick competition* (Kenyon 1997), are exhibited by the phrases "our tax rates and fees are very competitive compared to surrounding communities" or "we have the lowest taxes and fees in the county." In total, these sentiments were expressed by twenty-five different municipalities in the news report and twenty-eight governments in the interviews. In yardstick competition, governments compare their own revenue rates to other governments' and then use the information to adjust their own rates.

Yardstick comparisons also were observed in many other areas regarding spending and financial management practices. Governments often rely on surveys from their COGs and their own efforts to see what comparable communities are doing to obtain ideas about new revenue sources or ways of trimming costs, but also to make sure that what they are doing is consistent with similar governments. This is a form of benchmarking, especially for services levels, debt, and spending, but not necessarily to improve performance. Governments want to know that they are not too different from their neighbors or whether their policies and practices are contrary to the norm.

As discussed in chapter 4, such competition should lead to lower revenue rates throughout the region and may even create pressure to lower charges to the point where public goods and services are being underprovided or underfunded (Rork 2003). These dysfunctional effects on water and sewer charges were apparent from the qualitative data. Chapter 6 describes a trend in some governments of not raising water and sewer rates enough to cover costs, especially the maintenance of infrastructure, which can lead to lawsuits from individuals or other governments to improve infrastructure and dramatic increases in rates to meet these obligations. It is apparent from quotes from the news reports and interviews that water and sewer are treated competitively, although they are structured as enterprises. Yet, water and sewer services also have significant public health and safety implications. As was demonstrated in the suburb of Crestwood, yardstick competition to lower charges for such goods can have disastrous results.

In June 2009 the Illinois EPA found that Crestwood had knowingly supplemented up to 20 percent of their water supply with highly toxic drinking water from a contaminated well for more than twenty years. The state attorney general filed a lawsuit against the village at that time that outlined a systematic cover-up of their use of the tainted water. The prior mayor of Crestwood and the certified water operator had signed official reports telling residents and state regulators that Crestwood relied exclusively on Lake Michigan.[1] But records show they kept using the polluted well. As reported by the *Chicago Tribune,* these policies helped the village save money, as the mayor boasted that he ran Crestwood like a business, and the village "attracted national recognition for pinching pennies, rebating property taxes and maintaining the lowest water rates in Cook County" (Hawthorne 2009). In this case, using the contaminated well enabled officials to cut back on their purchases of lake water and freed them from expensive testing of the well, which seriously undermined the health and safety of the residents.[2]

Monitoring Financial Condition and Identifying At-Risk Governments

Although observations about the effects of governance, fiscal capacity, and other factors (e.g., dependence on sales taxes) on municipal government financial condition may be interesting, why should people other than scholars and local practitioners care about such matters? Why should we care about the effects of the fiscal toolbox, governance, and administrative capacity on how or whether these governments manage fiscal stress and maintain financial condition? In an area the size of the Chicago metropolitan region, each suburban municipality is such a small portion of the total population and economic base. Do we care if some of them do not provide adequate health and safety services to citizens and visitors because they do not have the fiscal capacity to do so, or because they have managed their finances badly and sometimes illegally for a long time? Do we care that some local governments in metropolitan regions are incapable of adapting to their fiscal environment, and do we care more generally whether municipal suburban government finances are managed well and with probity? Assuming that we do care, should state government have the authority to intervene in the financial policies and practices of local governments, especially if voters approve of officials' decisions and the officials who made them?

Our answers to these questions depend, in part, on how many suburbs throughout metropolitan regions are in this position, how many people are affected, the extent to which the financial problems of these governments have regional impact, and our feelings about what is equitable and right. Investigation of answers to the last two questions is beyond the scope of this book. Answers to the first two questions require that we have a means of assessing the number of municipal governments that either cannot provide basic services or are at risk of not being able to provide basic services. Such governments do not have the tools to adapt to their fiscal environment in a manner that allows them to adequately meet their service obligations.

The analyses presented here have demonstrated that external fiscal capacity is the most important factor to the overall fiscal health of municipal governments, followed by service-level solvency and budgetary solvency. Thus, this factor should be examined first to determine the most important tools in an arsenal. The problem is that measuring fiscal capacity for municipal governments in different states, and even within the same state, is not always straightforward, as what determines these features varies tremendously by state and other factors such as home rule status. In this case, the measures of fiscal capacity developed for municipal governments in the Chicago region would not apply to municipal governments in other states that can levy an income tax or cannot levy a sales tax. But these measures could be adapted to municipal governments in other states or even other types of local governments using the basic principles presented here.

Ranking municipal governments in the Chicago metropolitan region according to the primary measure of external fiscal capacity developed here—the ratio of revenue wealth to spending needs in 2000—governments that are lowest on this scale (low wealth and high spending needs) can be examined further on other dimensions of financial condition to assess their adaptability and risk of becoming insolvent. For instance, governments in the lowest quintile of this indicator include the four very large satellite cities, which are somewhat unique compared to other governments in the region, and two governments that have exceedingly high levels of commercial and industrial activity (McCook and Rosemont), which distorts this ratio. Ten other governments in this quintile are rural, very small (populations below or near one thousand), and have very high population growth.

Close examination of other factors besides external fiscal capacity on this ranking show numerous outlying governments that do not have poor financial condition. Eliminating these outliers leaves thirty-nine governments that were probably facing significant fiscal problems in the early 2000s. Examining other financial condition indicators of service-level and budgetary solvency from appendix 1 (2000 to 2005) for these thirty-nine governments reveal twenty-five governments that were likely in danger of becoming fiscally insolvent. Eight of these governments were especially at risk due to some combination of the following: high debt, high revenue burden, low spending effort, low change or declines in revenue base, and populations less than ten thousand.[3]

Half of the eight governments have home rule, which is an important advantage in managing fiscal stress, as claimed by the interviewees from two of them. However, the extremely low revenue wealth and solvency of one of these governments likely counteracts its home rule status, which makes it impossible for this government to ever adapt financially. The other interviewed government is wealthier by comparison, but the interview demonstrates how precarious their financial condition is and the struggle to get control over the government's financial affairs through new policies and practices.

Of the larger governments in this group of twenty-five with low wealth-to-need ratios, low budgetary solvency, and low governmental budgetary balance, there are eight that have very high revenue burden. Their larger size may give them greater flexibility to manage fiscal threats and opportunities than smaller at-risk governments, and their home rule status certainly increases their fiscal capacity. But the financial conditions of these eight were very precarious in the early 2000s, and some may not be providing adequate core services according to the spending effort index.[4]

It is interesting that, according to news reports and interviews, all of these eight larger governments except Park Forest have institutional governing structures that are primarily political, although several others have important corporate elements. Moreover, government officials in all eight except Park Forest were reported to have been investigated or indicted for illegal activities and/or had significant problems with fiscal improprieties sometime between the mid-1990s and the middle of the first decade of the 2000s. As noted in chapter 5, the financial condition of two of these governments had improved during the period of study as documented in the data in conjunction with changes in fiscal practices noted in the interviews.

Adding the populations of these sixteen fiscally precarious governments reveals that more than 250,000 residents in the Chicago metropolitan region were likely living in municipalities where the governments were not providing adequate services or were facing insurmountable challenges in maintaining financial condition. The Chicago metropolitan region had a population of about 7.4 million in 2000 in six counties, which means that about 3.4 percent of the population in the region were being affected in this manner. Although the financial condition of several governments identified here may not have been as precarious as suggested according to the interviews in 2003, the poor long-term solvency of all and the unsound fiscal policies and practices in many will make adapting to the financial environment very difficult for many of them. It is also the case that many governments in this position have no choice but to engage in unsound policies and practices because their fiscal capacity and structure offer no other options in the toolbox.

Unfortunately, assessing the financial condition and at-risk status of municipal or other local governments in the region centrally and on a regular basis is not easy using the methods and indicators used here. As argued in chapter 2, local financial condition is complex, with many dimensions and components that do not fit together in a linear or straightforward manner. Moreover, high or low levels of financial indicators in one situation may not be meaningful in others, and different dimensions of financial condition may be more important than others to overall fiscal health. Thus assessing financial condition comprehensively may not be reduced to a simple formula that can be applied in a straightforward manner in all situations.

The Illinois Office of the Comptroller (IOC) and Department of Revenue already collect much of the data that could be used to assess the financial condition of Illinois local governments (not school districts) in the state, but developing a system as comprehensive as what is presented here would be very costly. The IOC produces a fiscal responsibility report card on local governments, but the report presents aggregate financial conditions of different types of local government, not the financial condition of individual governments.[5] However, the IOC does make data on all local governments in Illinois available to the public, which is very important for local government transparency and to groups and individuals who have the desire and capacity to investigate the financial affairs of their own local government or other local governments.[6]

The Illinois State Board of Education (IBHE) developed a school district financial profile index based on the five different financial indicators shown below, some of which are similar to those used in this book:

▼ Fund balance-to-revenue ratio
▼ Expenditure-to-revenue ratio
▼ Days of cash on hand
▼ Percent of short-term borrowing ability remaining
▼ Percent of long-term debt margin remaining

Each component is categorized in an ordinal manner to reflect different fundamental levels of risk, and components are weighted before they are summed to produce a total profile score. This method recognizes the nonlinear and complex nature of financial condition in school districts, but it focuses on aspects of financial condition that are very short term. It overlooks the external fiscal capacity of school districts, which is generally acknowledged to be the most critical financial problem faced by many school districts in the state. By the time school districts reach the highest risk category of financial watch or even the next highest category of financial early warning on the IBHE index, it may be too late or difficult to turn their financial condition around, especially if they have very low external fiscal capacity. In this case, the IBHE should consider the external fiscal capacity of school districts more directly in their index.

An important question at this juncture is which municipal governments are likely to face the highest level of fiscal stress as a result of the Great Recession? As with measuring fiscal capacity, what constitutes a fiscal threat and opportunity also varies tremendously across states and sometimes local governments in the same state. An obvious answer to this question for municipal governments in the Chicago metropolitan area is that local governments that depend highly on sales tax revenue, especially from dealerships, will be hit the hardest. Second, governments that depend highly on sales taxes and have little budgetary solvency or slack to absorb the loss of this major revenue source will have the most difficulty managing the threat of declining sales receipts. In addition, governments in this position that do not have home rule and/or have high revenue burden (e.g., at their maximum rates for all utility taxes) will have an even harder time managing this recession because they have fewer replacements for sales tax revenue in their toolboxes.

Municipal governments that were experiencing very high levels of population growth prior to the recession and then saw an abrupt halt to residential and commercial development also are likely to have very high levels of fiscal stress. One of the executive directors of the COGs interviewed in 2009 talked about a member municipality that had recently built infrastructure that it had financed with bonds to accommodate a development with 1,500 new homes and commercial properties. Only 150 homes had been built, and completion of the project in the near future seemed unlikely. This municipal government now has the obligation to repay this debt, and the expected revenue stream of fees from development (e.g., impact fees, tap-on fees, and building inspection fees) will not occur and must be replaced with other revenue sources. Given that municipalities that faced such threats from the Great Recession are likely to be non–home rule, their ability to manage these threats will be limited and their financial condition may become very precarious in the future.

Solutions and Examinations for the Future

As noted in the 2009 interviews, collaboration and other forms of collective action between governments and between governments and nonprofit organizations are being investigated and promoted in the Chicago metropolitan region (Metropolitan Mayors Caucus 2009) as a tool for dealing with the fiscal threat of the Great Recession. It is also being advocated nationwide (Parr, Riehm, and McFarland 2006; Eichenthal 2010; Muro and Rahman 2010; Boris and Steuerle 2006) as a means of increasing the efficiency of providing local services. But as discussed in chapter 4, the Chicago metropolitan region is structurally fragmented and fiscally dispersed, state-local relations are decentralized, and its population is highly sorted. Although structural fragmentation may increase the opportunity for collective action, it also promotes competition. In conjunction, these features may suppress collective action among municipal governments in the region and produce only the easiest forms of collaboration such as informal cooperation, regional councils, and bilateral interlocal service contracts (Feiock 2009; Basalo 2003; Hendrick and Jimenez 2010).

The summary of conditions that promote or hinder cooperation presented in Hendrick and Jimenez (2010) indicate that more difficult forms of collaboration, especially for core services, may be too costly to implement in this region. Population sorting and other structural features create very divergent interests among local governments and unique organizational structures that increase transaction costs and reduce the benefits of collaboration. However, according to the interviews with the executive directors of the area COGs, the depth and severity of the Great Recession may have altered the payoffs of collaboration such that the benefits now outweigh the costs. Thus the Chicago region might indeed begin to see the voluntary consolidation of local governments and more multilateral arrangements for the delivery of core services in the near future, especially if civic organizations and state government can facilitate such actions. The regional COGS are in a good position to act as leaders and champions and help reduce transaction and other costs of collaboration. State government also might create incentives for collaboration among local governments in service delivery and cost sharing by utilizing criteria that promote collaboration and regional solutions in awarding grants (Lindstrom 1997).

Another important question is whether the Great Recession will permanently alter the financial condition of municipal governments in the region and their fiscal policies, practices, and structure. Answers to this question are elusive at this point as many local and state governments are still being affected by the recession, and it is unclear what factors may change permanently as a result of it. For instance, several interviewees in 2009 expressed the sentiment that the frenetic pace of development observed in many municipalities in the Chicago region from 1990 to 2000 would not resume. If this happens, this source of threats and opportunities could be minimized permanently for municipal governments in the outer areas of the region where such development was occurring. Furthermore, this could reduce competition for commercial and residential development throughout the region. In addition, governments in the region may now adapt better to growth and development, as their environments will change more slowly.

It is apparent that many municipal governments in the United States will not be affected as dramatically by the Great Recession as Chicago governments that rely highly on sales taxes or growth revenue. Because the state of Illinois, unlike most other states, allows their municipal governments to levy a sales tax, many Chicago municipalities have a unique financial structure compared to other suburban governments in the United States. More important, Illinois distributes state sales tax to municipal governments based on point of sale, which intensifies the competition among them to attract commercial enterprises. In this case, Chicago municipal governments face somewhat unique fiscal threats compared to municipal governments elsewhere in large part because of their access to more recession-prone revenue sources and because competitive pressures associated with these revenues are high. As noted previously, sales taxes are exportable to nonresidents, which makes them very attractive to governments that are under pressure to increase spending and keep revenue burden on property owners low, but such revenue is risky.

Does this mean that local governments should be prevented from relying on risky revenue and exporting their revenue burden to others? No, because the evidence presented here shows that a diversified revenue structure improves many components of financial condition for municipal governments in the Chicago region. However, it does mean that greater consideration should be given to the dysfunctional effects of the incentives created by sales tax on the revenue fiscal capacity, fiscal policies, and financial structure of municipal governments in Illinois. This is especially true for municipal governments in the Chicago metropolitan region where fragmentation, competition, and variation in fiscal capacity seem to be quite high.

In effect, distributing state sales taxes to municipal governments based on point of sale enhances competition among these governments and promotes higher levels of disparity in fiscal capacity overall. In addition, allowing only home rule governments the freedom to levy a sales tax at will gives them an unfair advantage in reaping the rewards from this competition. Thus state institutional rules may enhance or even promote inequality in local fiscal capacity and have other harmful effects. For instance, competition among local governments for sales tax generators can promote sprawl that is detrimental to the region as a whole (Rusk 1995).

The point, however, is not to deny municipal governments methods of diversifying their revenue, but there may be ways of giving them access to sales tax revenue that even out the competitive playing field and do not make competition for sales tax revenue so intense. Such solutions may involve some level of sharing of sales tax revenues among municipalities and other local governments or incorporating need into the formula for distributing sales tax revenues to municipalities and other local governments.

Similarly, the distribution of state income tax to local governments based only on population proportions rewards municipal governments for increasing population within their boundaries and increases the revenue distributed to these governments at a time when most do not need it. The analyses presented here show that the rates of increase in most types of revenue to municipal governments are higher in growing municipalities, and such governments tend to be more fiscally healthy. In this case, the State of Illinois might consider distributing shared income tax to local governments based, in part, on need rather than population alone. These considerations are now incorporated into how state-shared revenue in Illinois is distributed to school districts, and there are other states that take need into consideration when distributing revenue to their local governments. But Illinois is not recognized as a state that equalizes funding for primary and secondary education (Kenyon 2007; Gardener et al. 2002), and its political climate is not likely to favor redistributing state income and sales tax to other local governments using a need-based formula (Gove and Nowlan 1996).

Ultimately, municipal government officials have a great level of responsibility to ensure that their governments are well-managed financially and make sound financial decisions that do not worsen financial condition or place their governments at high risk of being severely affected by fiscal threats. Dependence on sales taxes and intergovernmental revenue and dealing with population growth and development are particularly challenging for municipal governments when managing fiscal threats and maintaining financial condition, and so is capital investment. Financial decisions about capital investments also are linked to decisions about how to finance these investments, which often are concomitant with population growth and development, pursuit of sales tax generators, and increasing reliance on sales taxes. The analyses presented here show that many of the policy choices governments make in these areas vary systematically by governing structure. Fiscal practices that support these decisions and their implementation, such as budgeting and capital planning, also vary by governing structure with corporate governments that follow professional standards more than political governments.

Irrespective of their governing approach, many municipal and other local governments undoubtedly pushed spending obligations for capital infrastructure, debt, and pensions off into the future and used other unsound solutions to manage the effects of the Great Recession. But what can municipal governments do to increase the likelihood they will be well managed financially and have good financial condition in the long run? Unless governments are very small or have very low fiscal capacity, all other things being equal, most governments can improve financial management practice and raise the soundness of fiscal policies by progressing toward a more corporate approach to financial problem solving. One way of accomplishing this if the government is small is to contract out for managerial and fiscal expertise, as was observed in several cases, to bring experience and knowledge of professional standards (heuristics) to the financial decisions and operations of government.

Larger municipal governments are more likely to have financial and managerial professionals involved in governance, yet struggle with financial condition, although they have reasonably good fiscal capacity. The analyses presented here have suggested several reasons why this might occur. First, governments may underestimate the risks associated with fiscal threats such as recessions, the closing of a major property tax-payer, lawsuits related to development and other matters, and underinvestment in capital infrastructure. Because they underestimate these risks, governments may not compensate by giving themselves enough slack, insurance, or tools in their fiscal toolbox to maintain financial condition to deal with serious threats if they become reality.

Second, governments of all sizes experience dysfunctional conflicts, and discontinuity of fiscal practices and strategies for maintaining financial condition. Although change is sometimes good, much qualitative evidence was presented here that shows how political conflict leads to high turnover of elected and appointed officials, which leads to chaotic fiscal policies and operations that undermine the government's ability to maintain financial condition and follow through with plans for managing growth. In this case, the policy of changing village managers and administrators every time a new mayor or board is elected can be very destabilizing to the fiscal and administrative operations of government in a way that weakens the government's capacity to maintain or improve financial condition. Elected officials should strive to minimize conflict and promote continuity of sound policies and practices and also realize that the policy of political appointments, which promotes replacement of top administrators with the election of a new mayor or board, contributes to these problems. In this case, voters are not just observers in this process and can help in this regard by electing qualified individuals and advocating a council-manager form or the hiring of a professional administrator, where this is appropriate. Voters also should demand that their governments have transparency and pass a meaningful budget and not just an appropriations ordinance.

The depth of the Great Recession, its potential effects on property taxes, and the expectation that the economy may not rebound to the same levels as in prior recessions may be unique. It may also mean that financial condition in many municipal governments may never be as good as prior to the recession and may always be more precarious. These changes, in conjunction with the knowledge that more than a few municipal governments in the Chicago metropolitan region may be insolvent and do not provide adequate core services, suggests that state government should be paying closer attention to the financial health of its municipal governments. Illinois state government should also consider whether the enforcement of both local government fiscal assistance laws—one for home rule and one for non–home rule governments—should be by invitation alone. As demonstrated by the case of East St. Louis, there are conditions under which the state should intervene unilaterally in the fiscal affairs of a local government. However, with the financial condition of Illinois state government at great peril currently, the likelihood of it taking on additional responsibilities in this area is very low. Moreover, the decentralized nature of state-local relations in Illinois and the state's hands–off approach to local governance will be difficult to overcome to implement this kind of change.

Finally, this last section has said little about where the future study of local government financial condition should be headed in general, or in the Chicago region in particular. This study has demonstrated the importance and role of governance and administrative capacity to financial policies and fiscal practices, but its findings do not offer much understanding of the process of how different governing structures and administrative capacities change financial problem solving. In fact, this study does not really separate the effects of governance from administrative capacity on financial policies and practices. These tasks could be accomplished with case studies that examine events and changes in governments over time, and with more precise measurement and observation of these two features.

This study has shown what types of governments might yield productive insights from case study analysis and further exploration of the differences between governance and administrative capacity. Specifically, municipal governments with growing populations and increasing development could be examined and contrasted with government in municipalities that have stable populations and little development. Also the governmental groups in appendix 7 could provide a framework for identifying cases for further analysis and exploration, and governments that experience change in governing structure and administration provide a natural experimental design that is very useful for this purpose. However, the challenge will be to find governments in which these features are stable for a long enough period of time for impacts to occur and be observed.

Undoubtedly, there will be much research in the near future on the effects of the Great Recession on local governments in the United States. In this case, continued observation and study of municipalities in this region will be very useful given the record laid down here. Specifically, it will be interesting to observe how governments with high growth and development prior to the recession coped with a halt to these activities, how far municipalities that are highly dependent on sales taxes fall as a result of the recession, the extent to which municipal government and services contract overall, and whether collaborative arrangements or even consolidation of governments becomes more the norm than the exception in this region. Some have predicted that a permanent reduction in growth and development in the outer areas of metropolitan regions brought about by the recession will reduce sprawl and other negative spillovers from these events. Others have argued that local governments around the United States will be experiencing a new normal in their fiscal environment, which could dramatically change their fiscal structure, fiscal toolboxes, and the ways they manage fiscal stress and maintain financial condition. Only time will tell if these predictions come true.

Notes

1. Chester Stranczek was mayor from 1969 to 2007, when his son was elected mayor.

2. Investigations and lawsuits in this case are still continuing, and the exact motivation for the actions of Crestwood has not been established. The village is now facing significant fiscal threat from the costs of fighting these lawsuits.

3. The eight governments are Burnham, Dixmoor, East Hazel Crest, Ford Heights, Phoenix, Stone Park, Robbins, and Willow Springs.

4. The following municipal governments are in this group: Bellwood, Berwyn, Chicago Heights, Dolton, Harvey, Maywood, North Chicago, and Park Forest. Others that could be placed in this group are Markham, Riverdale, Sauk Village, and Schiller Park.

5. www.ioc.state.il.us/Office/LocalGovtDev/index.cfm?DisplayPage=51.

6. The website of the local government division of the IOC has a great deal of useful information on all local governments in Illinois, including financial data from the annual financial reports and statutes.

Appendix 1: Operationalization of Financial Condition Measures and All Other Variables

Most financial variables, with the exception of those indicated below, are calculated as three-year moving averages for the years encompassing 1998–2006. Variables in the year 2000, for instance, are calculated as the average of years 1999 to 2001. Rate and percent changes in financial variables use three-year averaged amounts for year t and year t − 1. Unless indicated otherwise, all financial variables represent totals for all governmental operating funds: general, special revenue, debt, and expendable trust (capital funds are excluded except where indicated). Governmental operating funds do not include enterprise funds. Capital funds are for all purposes (governmental and enterprise). EAV is corrected for the underassessment of residential and commercial properties in Cook County in order to calculate variables that show the percentage of EAV, such as percent residential EAV. The source for most financial data is the Illinois Office of the Comptroller (IOC) www.ioc.state.il.us/index.cfm/departments/local-government-division/download-center/financial-databases/. Other financial data were obtained from the Illinois Department of Revenue (IDOR) over many years. Most socioeconomic and demographic data are downloaded from the US Bureau of the Census for 1990 and 2000. Population figures for 1998–2000 are extrapolated from census figures for 1990 and 2000. Population estimates from the census are used for 2001 to 2006. As indicated below, many per capita measures are weighted by multiplying them by percent residential EAV to correct for the distortion of per capita measures in nonresidential municipalities. Items that are enumerated by ▼ were considered but not used here. The following municipalities are not included in the analysis because they were incorporated after 2000 or because much of the jurisdiction is in a county outside of the six-county region: Big Rock, Bull Valley, Coal City, Diamond, Greenwood, Homer Glen, Minooka, and Trout Valley.

IGR: state and federal grants and shared revenue

TOSR (total own-source revenue) = property tax + sales tax + other tax + nontax

(I) Long-Term Solvency

(1) Revenue wealth: capacity to generate own-source revenues from available revenue bases. EAV (property tax) and sales receipts (sales tax) are the primary revenue bases. Personal income is a revenue base for many other revenues. Access to these revenue bases varies greatly depending on home rule status of the municipality. The indicators below are used separately to examine trends in fiscal stress and as independent variables in regression analyses. The variables are also combined into an index that represents overall revenue wealth for 2000. The indices are constructed as the sum of Z scores (or percent of the median) weighted by standardized regression slopes. The regression coefficients were obtained from a regression analysis with TOSR per capita (★% residential EAV) as the dependent variable, the three component indicators (A–C) below as independent variables, and run separately for home rule and non–home rule governments.

(A) Per capita personal income: 1999, US Census

(B) Sales receipts per capita (weighted): [sales receipts/population] × [residential EAV/total EAV]

(C) Equalized assessed value per square mile: EAV/square miles

Index for home rule municipalities: $.441zA + .314zB + .047zC, R^2 = .38$

Index for non–home rule municipalities: $.417zA + .507zB + .144zC, R^2 = .61$

(2) Spending needs: service pressure due to responsibilities and need. Costs of providing services, such as labor and supplies, are assumed to be equal for municipalities in the Chicago region (macrolevel effects). Spending demands are considered to be a function of tastes rather than needs and so are not included here. The indicators below are used separately as independent variables in regression analyses, and they are combined into an index that represents overall spending needs for 2000. The indices are constructed as the sum of Z scores (or percent of the median) weighted by standardized regression slopes. The regression coefficients were obtained from a regression analysis using weighted operational expenditures per capita (*% residential EAV) as the dependent variable, the seven indicators (E–K) below as independent variables, and controlling for per capita personal income (as a measure of demand for services).

(E) Crime per 1,000 population (weighted): violent crime (State of Illinois Crime Report, 1998–2006) [number serious crimes/population] ★ [residential EAV/total EAV]. These values are estimated for twenty-five municipalities for which no crime statistics are reported using expected values calculated from regression analyses of governments with reported crime figures.

(F) Median age housing: 2000, US Census; reversed for index by subtracting the value from 2000.

(G) Miles of roads for square mile: roads that the municipality is responsible for (IL Dept. of Transportation, 1997–2006)/square miles.

(H) Population density: [population/square miles]; logged and reversed for index by subtracting it from 10.

(I) Fire district: whether municipality is in a fire district; 1 = yes, 0 = no (2003).

(J) Park district: whether municipality is in a park district; 1 = yes, 0 = no (2003).

(K) Library district: whether municipality is in a library district; 1 = yes, 0 = no (2003).

Index: $126zE + .160zF + .133zG + .333zH + .155I + .065J + .085K, R^2 = .62$

(3) Balance of revenue wealth and spending needs: ratio of revenue wealth to spending needs, 2000.

(4) GO debt, total bonds, and total debt per capita (weighted): debt/population ★ % residential EAV.

Change in Long-Term Solvency Conditions

(5) Change in revenue sources: 2000 to 2005. The indices are constructed as the sum of Z scores (or % of the median) weighted by standardized regression slopes. The regression coefficients were obtained from a regression analysis using ratio change in total revenue as the dependent variable, the three variables below (L–N) as independent variables, and run separately for home rule and non–home rule governments.

(L) Ratio change sales receipts (weighted by dependence on sales taxes): (sales receipts$_t$/sales receipts$_{t-1}$) ★ % sales tax of total revenue.

(M) Ratio change EAV (weighted by dependence on property taxes): (EAV$_t$/EAV$_{t-1}$) ★ % property tax of total revenue.

(N) Ratio change IGR (weighted by dependence on IGR): (IGR$_t$/IGR$_{t-1}$) ★ % IGR of total revenue</LL.

Index for home rule municipalities: $.273zL + .487zM + .331zN$, $R^2 = .25$

Index for non–home rule municipalities: $.064zL + .027zM + .461zN$, $R^2 = .24$

    (6) Ratio change in population: $\text{Population}_t / \text{population}_{t-1}$

(II) Service-Level Solvency

Overall

    (7) Revenue burden: (2000), TOSR per capita (weighted)/revenue wealth.

    (8) Spending effort: (2000), operational spending (noncapital) per capita (weighted)/ spending needs.

    (9) Own-source revenue per capita (weighted): [TOSR/population] ★ [residential EAV/ total EAV].

    (10) Operational spending per capita (weighted): [total spending, no capital/population] ★ [residential EAV/total EAV].

Specific Revenues

    (11) Other own-source revenues per capita (weighted): [other own-source revenue/population] ★ [residential EAV/total EAV].

    (12) Sales tax effort: sales taxes/sales receipts.

    (13) Property tax rate for regular funds: sum of all component regular fund rates as reported by IDOR.

    (14) Nongrant, state-shared revenue per capita (weighted): [(income tax + motor fuel tax)/population] ★ [residential EAV/total EAV].

    (15) Federal and state grants per capita (weighted): [(federal IGR + state IGR that is not shared)/population] ★ [residential EAV/total EAV].

Capital Investment: For All Purposes, Governmental and Enterprise Funds Combined

    (16) Percent capital spending: capital spending/(operational + capital spending).

    (17) Capital spending per capita (weighted): [capital spending/ population] ★ [residential EAV/total EAV].

    (18) Own-source capital revenue per capita (weighted): [own-source capital revenue/ population] ★ [residential EAV/total EAV].

Revenue Slack (Fungibility)

▼ Percent enterprise of own-source revenues
▼ Enterprise charges coverage

Spending Slack (Fixity)

▼ Percent debt service spending
▼ Percent spending for personnel

Revenue Risk

(19) Revenue diversification: based on the Hirschman-Herfindahl index: $[1 - ([\text{property tax}/\text{TOSR}]^2 + [\text{sales tax}/\text{TOSR}]^2 + [\text{other tax}/\text{TOSR}]^2 + [\text{nontax}/\text{TOSR}]^2)]/.75$.
(20) Dependence on IGR: IGR/total revenue.
(21) Dependence on sales taxes: sales taxes/TOSR.
(22) Dependence on other own-source revenue—non-tax revenue, other taxes, property tax: own-source revenue/TOSR.

Change in Service-level Solvency

(23) Ratio change own-source revenue: own-source revenue$_t$/own source revenue$_{t-1}$.
(24) Ratio change operational spending and capital spending: spending$_t$/spending$_{t-1}$.
(25) Ratio change in property tax levy and property tax levy per capita: tax levy$_t$/tax levy$_{t-1}$.
(26) Ratio change IGR: IGR$_t$/IGR$_{t-1}$.

(III) Budgetary Solvency

(27) Budgetary solvency: (fund balance + total revenue)/operational spending.
(28) Percent fund balance: reserved and unreserved fund balance (governmental funds) as percent of operational spending.
(29) Percent deficit or surplus: excess or deficiency of revenues over spending (governmental funds) before transfers, as percent of total operational spending.

▼ Percent income or loss: excess or deficiency of revenues over expenses (enterprise funds) before transfers, as percent of total expenses.

(30) Governmental budgetary slack: (fund balance − deficit or surplus)/total operational expenditures; fund balance with deficit added or surplus removed to account for planned deficits or surpluses.

▼ Enterprise budgetary slack: net assets minus income or loss (neg.) as percent of total operational expense; fund balance with loss added or income removed (planned loss or income).

Change in Budgetary Solvency

(31) Ratio change budgetary solvency: budgetary solvency$_t$/budgetary solvency$_{t-1}$.

Variables Used in Calculation of Indices and in Analyses

(32) Square miles: 1990 and 2000 (US Census); 2005 (Chicago Metropolitan Agency for Planning).
(33) Home rule: 1998 and 2006 (Illinois Municipal League); 2007 (Illinois Secretary of State). Both sources list the date that home rule referendums passed and whether home rule was obtained due to population reaching 25,000. If the latter occurred, the date of municipality becoming home rule was determined from municipal website or news sources.
(34) Percent residential EAV: residential EAV/total EAV (IDOR).

Other Variables Used in Analyses of Chicago Municipalities

Percent of Resident Population with Managerial or Professional Occupations: US Census, 2000

Cook County: This county is exceptional among the other six metropolitan counties due to unique property assessment formulas and other factors.

Miles from central city.

Date of incorporation: Illinois Secretary of State.

Percent vote for Bush, 2004: county clerk elections results (canvas reports) available from county clerk websites.

Size of government: total spending for governmental and enterprise funds (no capital).

Financial decision structure (FDS), 2003 and 2009: measures governing structure and administrative capacity that affects financial decision making and financial decisions (1) manager and finance director; (2) administrator and finance director; (3) administrator or manager, no finance director; (4) finance director, no manager or administrator; and (5) no finance director, manager, or finance director (determined from websites, news reports, or phone calls to municipalities).

Elected treasurer: (1) yes; (0) no (determined from municipal code, website, or phone calls to municipalities).

Partisan elections: (1) nonpartisan elections; (2) partisan elections but all candidates run as independents in consolidated elections in 2003, 2005, and 2007; (3) partisan elections (county clerk elections results or canvas reports available from websites).

City or village: (1) city (board elected by ward or district);(0) village (board elected at large).

Structure of government: (1) village, council-manager form; (2) village, council-mayor form; (3) city or commission, council-manager form; (4) city or commission, council-weak mayor form; (5) city or commission, council-strong mayor form (determined from municipal code, website, or phone calls to municipalities).

Moody's Bond Rating, 2003 and 2009.

Standard and Poor's Bond Rating, 2003 and 2009.

GFOA Budget Award, 2003: www.gfoa.org/index.php?option=com_content&task=view&id=1401&Itemid=1.

GFOA CAFR Award, 2002: http://www.gfoa.org/index.php?option=com_content&task=view&id=35&Itemid=58.

Appendix 2: Sampling Methodology for Interviews of Municipal Governments, 2003

Given the difficulties of interviewing a large number of municipalities and the numerous conditions likely to affect financial practices, policies, and condition, a purposive sampling protocol was developed based on information from prior studies of suburbs in the region (Hendrick 2002, 2003). These studies suggested factors that should be used to stratify the population for sampling to ensure the broadest range of conditions in the observations, and which ones should be oversampled to target critical relationships. It was also important to have enough cases in each stratum and the entire sample to hold key variables constant for qualitative analysis.[1]

Some of the variables chosen for stratification are a function of the high degree of fragmentation and specialization of suburban municipalities relative to rural municipalities and central cities (Rusk 1995). As explained elsewhere (Hendrick 2011), individual suburban jurisdictions tend to be homogenous socioeconomically and demographically within their boundaries, but heterogeneous by comparison to one another. In addition, their economic role within the region can be very specialized. For instance, some suburbs may be residential, bedroom-type communities, while others that are mostly industrial or commercial provide jobs and services to the rest of the region. As a result, suburbs' features can vary tremendously, and this must be accounted for in choosing municipalities in which to interview government officials.

Governments were sampled for the interviews by dividing all 264 municipalities into mutually exclusive categories based on the stratification variables of population size (A), revenue wealth/spending needs (B), and population growth (C), and then choosing suburbs based on the distribution of the other stratification variables within these categories. (See the following tables.) These three base variables were expected to be the most critical in affecting financial decisions and condition. As expected, some categories have few cases and others have many cases. For instance, municipalities that are low wealth and high need tend to have little growth and be smaller. High-wealth and high-need governments tend to have lower growth, and municipalities with high levels of professional and managerial residents (white collar) tend not to be low residential. Conversely, municipalities with high levels of nonprofessional residents (blue collar) can be high residential or low residential (often industrial). Although categories with few cases were targeted less for sampling, the large number of factors and categories with many cases required a relatively large sample size by comparison to most studies that employ interview and case study methodologies.

Some categories were also oversampled to observe relationships important to this study or undersampled because of the lack of variance in their fiscal affairs. For instance, very small municipalities were undersampled because not much happens financially in these governments. However, small governments with home rule were oversampled to ensure an adequate comparison with non–home rule governments to determine whether having home rule really makes a difference in the financial decisions and condition of smaller governments. Municipalities in the outer ring of the region that were not growing, which tend to be small, were undersampled and replaced with similar governments nearer to the city of Chicago (and less distance to travel to the interview). Most important, governments that were low wealth and high need were oversampled to be able to observe all the variety in their operations and problems. The use of the targeted sampling here resulted in oversampling of governments that grew more than 14 percent and undersampling of governments with population decline or less than 5 percent growth.

Fifty-three municipalities were chosen initially for the study, and interviews were begun in early 2003 with, as requested, the "person most knowledgeable or responsible for financial management and implementing fiscal policies" in the government. However, it quickly became apparent that professionally managed governments had very different fiscal practices than governments without a professional CFO or CEO. Nine suburbs were then added to the original sample to better capture the variation in this condition. Given the high number of governments interviewed and the fact that many only have one person responsible for implementing fiscal policies in the government, a decision was made to interview only one person per suburb and supplement information about the suburb with news reports and secondary documents.[2] If a suburb declined to be interviewed, a similar one was chosen from the same group. However, municipal governments with no CEO or CFO had the highest rate of decline that resulted in an undersampling of these suburbs.

The following tables present the seven variables on which the stratification was based and show how suburbs are distributed on each variable for the population (N = 264), the full sample (N = 62), and governments that were not interviewed. See appendix 1 for definitions of the variables in the following tables. Table A2.8 shows the title of the person interviewed and table A2.9 shows the list of municipalities where an interview occurred. Regulation and approval of the interviews by the Institutional Review Board at the University of Illinois at Chicago prevents identifying specific municipalities in analyses in the book that could reveal the identity of the person interviewed.

TABLE A2.1 Size: Population, 2000

	Interview	Not Interview	Population
<9,000	17/27%★	103/51%	120/46%
9,000–25,000	32/52%	55/27%	87/33%
>25,000	13/21%	44/22%	57/22%
Total	62	202	264

Note: ★Undersampled.

TABLE A2.2 Revenue Wealth/Spending Needs

	Interview	Not Interview	Population
Low wealth/low need	15/24%	49/25%	64/25%
Low wealth/high need	19/31%★	47/24%	66/25%
High wealth/low need	14/23%	53/27%	67/26%
High wealth/high need	14/23%	49/25%	63/24%
Total	62	198	260

Note: ★Oversampled; division of high and low based on medians.

TABLE A2.3 Growth: Percent Change Population, 1990–2000

	Interview	Not Interview	Population
<5%	26/42%	50/25%	76/29%
5–13.9%	19/30%	56/28%	75/29%
14–39.9%	7/11%	46/23%	53/21%
≥40%	10/16%	45/23%	55/21%
Median	7	12	10
Mean	22	34	31

TABLE A2.4 Home Rule Status, 2003

	Interview	Not Interview	Population
Not home rule	34/55%	126/62%	160/60%
Home rule	28/45%	76/38%	104/39%
Home rule, <25,000	16/26%★	33/16%	49/19%

Note: ★Oversampled.

TABLE A2.5 Location

	Interview	Not Interview	Population
Inner ring	27/44%	62/31%	89/34%
Middle ring	24/39%	60/30%	84/32%
Outer ring	11/16%★	80/40%	91/34%

Note: ★Undersampled.

TABLE A2.6 Occupation of Population/% Residential EAV

	Interview	Not Interview	Population
Low professional and manager/ low residential	22/36%	64/32%	86/33%
Low professional and manager/ high residential	10/16%	52/26%	62/23%
High professional and manager/ low residential	11/18%	24/12%	35/13%
High professional and manager/ high residential	19/31%	62/31%	81/31%

Note: Division of high and low based on means.

TABLE A2.7 Financial Decision Structure

	Interview	Not Interview	Population
Manager and finance director	21/34%	54/27%	75/28%
Administrator and finance director	13/21%	27/13%	40/15%
Administrator or manager, no finance director	12/19%	44/22%	56/21%
No administrator or manager, finance director	5/8%	13/6%	18/7%
No administrator or finance director	11/18%★	64/32%	75/28%

Note: ★Many governments that were chosen initially declined to be interviewed.

TABLE A2.8 Title of Person Interviewed

Mayor	10/16%
Administrator/manager (AM)	12/19%
Finance director (FD)	33/53%
Treasurer (T)	6/10%
Other (O)	1/3%

TABLE A2.9 List of Municipalities Interviewed, 2003

Alsip	Forest Park	Morton Grove	Sauk Village
Arlington Heights	Frankfort	North Riverside	Schaumburg
Barrington Hills	Golf	Northlake	Schiller Park
Bellwood	Harvey	Oak Brook	Skokie
Berkeley	Hazel Crest	Oak Forest	South Barrington
Brookfield	Indian Head Park	Oak Park	South Elgin
Burr Ridge	Justice	Orland Park	Steger
Calumet City	La Grange Park	Palos Heights	Sugar Grove
Channahon	Lake Forest	Palos Hills	Summit
Chicago Heights	Lake in the Hills	Park Forest	Thornton
Crest Hill	Lincolnshire	Plainfield	Vernon Hills
Deerfield	Lindenhurst	Riverdale	West Chicago
Deer Park	Lombard	River Forest	Wilmette
Downers Grove	Lynwood	Robbins	Zion
East Hazel Crest	Lyons	Roselle	
Elk Grove Village	Montgomery	Round Lake Park	

Notes

1. This method of sampling ensures that the unit homogeneity or constant effects assumption for determining causal effects is met (King, Keohane, and Verba 1994).
2. Some interviews were attended by two people from the same suburb.

Appendix 3: Interview Questions, 2003

Following is a summary of the questions asked and topics covered in the interviews. The interviews were open-ended and structured. Most lasted about $1^{1}/_{2}$ hours and were conducted at the municipal offices, which provided an opportunity to tour the suburb and note the condition of its infrastructure and type of properties in the community. The interviews were taped and transcribed, and notes were written within one day of the interview to record impressions about the government and observations about the interview that were not recorded. Most of the governments also provided a copy of their budget (or appropriations ordinance) and annual financial report. Financial and demographic data and news reports about the government and municipality were reviewed prior to conducting the interview.

▼ Roles and responsibilities of primary actors in determining fiscal practices and policies: mayor, board, treasurer, finance director, manager/administrator, comptroller
▼ Philosophy toward service provision and revenues on a continuum: (1) underspend services and infrastructure to keep taxes and fees low, (2) service provision at whatever cost (e.g., plow sidewalks, vacation watch, garbage can retrieval)
▼ Factors affecting current fiscal health: revenues (e.g., cuts from state, sales, assessment appeals, commercial and industrial closings), spending (e.g., lawsuits, workers' comp claims, underfunded pensions, insurance)
▼ Fiscal strategies/practices to cope
   1. At budget time: spending (e.g., cut or slow capital, attrition or layoffs, other discretionary), revenues (e.g., taxes, fees, grants), fund surpluses
   2. During the fiscal year: for example, short-term borrowing, fund subsidy or sharing
   3. Future: improve revenues (e.g., economic development), reduce costs (e.g., shared services, risk and purchasing pools, cost analyses), alter constraints (e.g., home rule)
▼ Financial management practices: focus on budget process, but interviews covered many other areas of financial management, including financial control problems and solutions, fund balance uses, capital financing policies, role of auditors, and assessment of financial factors (e.g., how they determined taxes, charges, performance, spending).
▼ Miscellaneous
   1. Impact and fiscal practices during the good times of the late 1990s
   2. Fiscal impacts and interactions between municipality and wide host of special districts (e.g., school, park, library, fire)
   3. Competition with neighbors and others in region (e.g., tax abatements, comparables)
   4. Interaction with subregional council of governments and professional organizations (e.g., IML, IGFOA, mayors caucuses, municipal conferences)
   5. GASB 34 and TIFs
   6. Economic development: role, financing, impact, policies

Appendix 4: Interview Codes, 2003

Coding of Themes

Fiscal Stress
  Assessment of
  Causes
  How manage

Practices and Policies
  Planning and budgeting
  Accountability
  Monitor and assess
  Financial stability and
  health (overall)
  Economic development
  (future)

Governance
  Authority and
  responsibility
  Expertise and membership
  Conflict and turnover
  Structure

Coding of Content

Budgeting
  Advanced methods
  Bottom-up process
  Top-down process
  Follow budget act
  Follow appropriate
  ordinance
  CIP
  Financial planning
  Strategic planning
  Comprehensive and
  prioritized
  Minimal process and
  document
Fiscal Stress
  Yes
  No
  Affect
    Cash flow
    Deficit
  Sources
    Growth
    Income tax down
    Increasing costs
    Insurance up
    Low spending
    flexibility
  Mandates

P-tax appeal board
Pension funding
Revenues down
Sales tax down
State or county actions
Tax caps
Tax delinquents
ST strategies
  Charge backs
  Cuts
  Delay hiring
  Defer capital and
  maintenance
  Fund balance
  Increase or add revenue
  Reduce taxes, charges,
  or fees
  Short-term borrow or
  subsidize
Interaction with Neighbors
  Cooperative agreements
  Compare to others
  Competition
  Disputes with others
  Fire district
  Park district
  School district

Capital Finance and
Spending
  Capital investing
  Capital needs
  Debt
  Fund balance
  Grants
  Property tax
  Other taxes
  Pay as you go
  Abate property tax debt
Financial Practices
  Advanced practices
  Assess costs
  Billing
  Cash
  Deposit
  Earmarking
  Forecasting
  Fund balance level
  GASB 34
  Internal controls
  Liability insurance
  Payroll
  Purchasing
  Reporting
  Risk management
  Self-insured

Revenues
  Property tax
  Sales tax
  Utility tax
  Other tax
  Fees and charges
  Vehicle sticker
  Revenue diversify
Miscellaneous
  Auditors
  Conflict
  Dealerships
  Educate and options to
  board
  Flooding & drainage
  Home rule
  Illegal activities
  Lawsuit
  Referendum
  Role of staff and elected
  officials
  Turnover of staff and
  elected
  Unions

Development and Growth
  Aggressive ED
  ED not important
  Annexation
  Building and impact fees
  Developer contributions
  Incentives
  Risky venture
  Downtown
  TIF
  Residential
  Commercial
  Manage growth
  Built out
  Image
Information and Reporting
  Deficiencies with
  Difficulty with
  Goals and objectives
  Monitoring
  Outcomes and outputs
  Policies about practices
LT Fiscal Strategies
  Balance services and
  revenues

Casino
Diversify revenue
Export taxes
Fiscal conservative
Pursue grants
Low or no property tax
Low or no other tax
Maximize property tax
One-time revenue
Privatize or contract out
Raise taxes or charges
Rely on sales tax
Save during good times
Spend during good times
Spending priorities
Special census
Special assessment district
Value businesses
Value high service levels
Enterprises
  Water and sewer
  Housing
  Parking
  Other

Appendix 5: News Article Codes, 2001–6

Capital Infrastructure
  Building and impact fees
  Capital investing
  Capital needs
  CIP
  Debt
  High spending on capital
  Fund with savings
  Fund with taxes
Fiscal Problems
  Elastic revenue
  Flooding and drainage
  Growth
  Late state payments
  Lawsuit
  Mandates
  Pension
  Property tax appeals
  Reduced building fees
  Sewer and wastewater
  Tax caps
  Unions
  Water provision
  Workers' comp
Financial Manage. Problems
  Illegal activities
  Miscellaneous problems
Financial Manage. Strategies
  Fiscal analysis
  Planning
  Miscellaneous strategy
Special Districts
  Fire
  Library
  Parks
  Schools
  Other

Miscellaneous
  Higher authority
  Hire CAO?
  Hire other professional?
  Home rule
  Insurance
  Referendum
Collaboration
  Chamber of commerce
  Dispute with others
  Formal
  Informal
Development and Growth
  Annexation
  Balance commercial and
  residential
  Built out
  Casino
  Commercial
  Residential
  Dealerships
  Developers pay own
  way
  Development strategy
  Downtown
  Goals dispute
  Obligation dispute
  Growth control
  Image
  Incentives and rebates
  Risky venture
  Pursue growth and
  develop
  Too much growth
  Strict zoning
  TIF
  Vacant commercial

Revenues
  Diversified
  Charges and fees, other
  Water fees
  Gasoline
  Income tax
  Other tax
  Property tax
  Sales tax
  Utility tax
  Vehicle sticker
Enterprises
  Water and sewer
  Golf
  Parking
  Other
Fiscal Strategies
  Compare to others
  Conservative spending
  Conservative taxes
  and fees
  Court businesses
  Create or dissolve sp.
  district
  Export taxes
  High service levels
  Obtain grants
  Privatize and contract
  out
  Rely on risky revenue
  Special census
  Special service area
Politics and Governance
  Board cooperate
  Conflict
  Election challenge—

Election challenge—low
Corporate/administrative
Political governance
Long-term CAO
Long-term mayor
Strategies
Turnover in
administration
Turnover in elected

Role of official
  Attorney
  Board
  CAO
  Finance officer
  Mayor
  Chief—fire or police
Fiscal Stress
  Add taxes and fees

Make cuts
Use fund balance
Short-term fixes
Reduce taxes and fees
Taxes too high
Priorities for handling
Fiscal stress—yes
Fiscal stress—no

Appendix 6: Interviewed Agencies, 2009–10

DuPage Mayors and Managers Conference

Lake County Municipal League

McHenry County Council of Governments

Metropolitan Mayors Caucus

Metro West Council of Governments

Northwest Municipal Conference

South Suburban Mayors and Managers Association

Southwest Conference of Mayors

West Central Municipal Conference

Not Interviewed

Barrington Area Council of Governments

Will County Government League

Appendix 7: Grouping of Municipalities and Their Features

Description: Primary Group		Description	Number of Municipalities	Number of Interviews
(A) Very small, residential, rural, various growth	1	White-collar, mod. wealth	8	0
	2	Blue-collar, poor	13	0
(B) White-collar, wealthy, various growth	3	Very small and small commercial	13	2
	4	Small and medium, residential	21	5
	5	Mod. to large size; residential	6	2
(C) Small, blue-collar, low or no growth	6	Industrial, some commercial, no growth, poor, inner ring	12	4
			8	1
	7	More commercial, higher wealth, low growth	6	0
	8	Residential, poor, low growth	10	3
(D) Moderate size and wealth, blue-white collar mix, low growth	9	Residential	9	3
	10	Commercial and industrial	11	2
	11	Larger, high industry and/or commercial	7	3
(E) Small, low-moderate wealth, high growth	12	Blue-collar, low wealth, residential	9	2
		Blue-collar, low wealth, commercial	5	1
	13	White-collar, residential, lower wealth (no sales)	5	1
		White-collar, residential, higher wealth (high income)	5	1
		White-blue collar mix, higher wealth (high sales)	9	0
(F) Mod.–large size, mod. income, blue-white collar mix, high growth	14	Lower wealth (residential)	11	5
	15	Higher wealth (sales)	10	1
	16	Highest wealth, white-collar	6	3
(G) Mod.–large size, industrial, blue-collar, no growth	17	Moderate size, low wealth	13	5
	18	Large, low wealth	10	7
	19	Large, moderate wealth	10	0

Description: Primary Group		Description	Number of Municipalities	Number of Interviews
(H) Mod.–very large size, poor, blue-collar, no growth	20	Mostly residential, moderate size	6	4
	21	Mostly residential, large	6	2
	22	Mostly industrial or commercial, very large	6	1
(I) High growth, balanced residential sales, wealthy	23	Medium and large size	8	1
(J) Built-out, balanced residential sales, mod.–large, wealthy	24	Moderate size, high sales	7	1
	25	Large, high sales	11	5
	26	Large, lower sales	5	1

Note: Some groups are not mutually exclusive, as some municipalities are assigned to more than one group.

Population Categories, 2000

Very small = population less than 1,500 (10th percentile)

Small = population 1,500 to 7,000 (10th–35th percentiles)

Moderate = population 7,000 to 20,000 (35th–65th percentiles)

Large = population 20,000 to 40,000 (65th–90th percentiles)

Very large = population greater than 40,000 (90th percentile)

Glossary

Actual revenues: The amount of revenues (taxes, charges, fees, etc.) government collects via chosen tax rates, fee rates, and charges. See *revenue capacity* and *revenue base.*

Administrative capacity: Characteristics of government personnel and processes that increase performance and success (service effectiveness and improved financial condition) through attention to the development of strategies and competencies to solve problems, maximize opportunities, and minimize threats.

Agent: The party hired by the principal to fulfill a contact. In the local government setting, elected officials are agents and voters are principals, or departmental heads are agents and elected officials are principals.

Alternate revenue debt: Local government debt in Illinois that is guaranteed by taxes other than property tax. It is different from revenue debt that is guaranteed by changes for services or other revenues generated by the services.

Asset: Anything that is owned by the government that can produce an economic benefit. Any form of wealth including external resources that the government has access to or that gives it the capacity to meet obligations and improve financial condition.

Budgetary solvency: The ability to balance the budget or generate enough resources to cover expenditures in the current fiscal year.

Cash solvency: The ability to generate enough cash over thirty or sixty days to pay bills during that time period.

Economic base: The set of economic resources from which government draws own-source revenue.

Equalized assessed property value: The assessed value of a property after the county equalization factor has been applied to bring the value up to 33.3 percent of market value (in Illinois).

Ex ante controls: Mechanisms used by the principal to control the agent's discretionary and opportunistic behavior before it occurs. For instance, the authorization of purchases over a certain amount of money by the municipal board is an ex ante control.

Ex post controls: Mechanisms used by the principal to control the agent's discretionary and opportunistic behavior by judging the behavior after it occurs. For instance, the principal reviewing an in-depth report of the purchases made by the department at the end of the fiscal year is an ex post control.

Financial condition: Generally, it is a government's ability to meet current and future obligations as assessed at a particular period of time. Specifically, it is the state of equilibrium or balance that exists between different dimensions or components of government's financial sphere of spending pressures and obligations, external fiscal resources, revenues and internal resources, and actual spending (see figure 2.1).

Financial decisions: Financial policies and practices that are conceptualized as solutions to financial problems.

Financial decision structure: See Other Variables Used in Analyses of Chicago Municipalities in appendix 1.

Financial health: A general term that refers to a government's financial condition (static) and fiscal stress/munificence (dynamic).

Fiscal capacity: External—revenue wealth relative to spending needs; internal—internal resources relative to short-term spending flexibility.

Fiscal governance: Structure, process, and institutions that affect financial decisions. (See *governance.*)

Fiscal munificence: An improvement in financial condition brought about by positive changes in the fiscal environment and related opportunities. It is the opposite of *fiscal stress.*

Fiscal opportunities: External chances to improve the financial condition of government.

Fiscal policy space: The set of available options and choices officials can make about government fiscal structure for the purpose of solving financial problems. It is also called the *fiscal toolbox.*

Fiscal stress: A worsening of financial condition brought about by negative changes in the fiscal environment and related threats. It is the opposite of *fiscal munificence.*

Fiscal structure: Financial policies and choices about government characteristics within the primary areas of the financial policy space (see figure 2.2). Combined outcome of financial policies and choices about the primary areas of the financial policy space (see figure 2.2). It has many features that are usually represented in relative terms, such as fund balance relative to total spending and property tax as a percentage of total revenue.

Fiscal threats: External factors in the environment that could make financial condition worse for the government.

Fiscal toolbox: The options available to governments to respond to fiscal threats and opportunities. The set of all financial policies and practices governments could adopt at a point in time to solve financial problems. The policy space in figure 2.2 that also can be conceptualized according the components of the fiscal equation in figure 4.1.

Fund balance: The unencumbered cash remaining in a fund at the end of a fiscal year. According to the accounting framework, it is measured as total assets minus total liabilities in a fund.

Governance: "The traditions, institutions, and processes that determine how power is exercised, how citizens are given a voice, and how decisions are made on issues of public concern," as defined by the Institute of Governance (http://iog.ca/about-us/governance/governance-definition).

Heuristic: "Any principle or device that contributes to the reduction in the average search for solutions" (Simon, Newell, and Shaw 1962, 152). Techniques and cognitive shortcuts government officials use to simplify problem solving.

High-powered incentives: As structured by the institutional environment, benefits from transactions flow directly to the parties in the transaction, such as in an election where candidates trade decisions for votes and electoral resources from supporters.

Institutions: Formal and informal constraints, rules, and expectations about behavior and decisions that structure interaction among government officials and their relationship to citizens and other stakeholders.

Intergovernmental revenue: Funds received from the state or federal governments for specific functions (grants) or for general financial assistance (aid).

Liability: Anything that is owed by the government to another party. The sacrifice of current or future economic benefits to satisfy current and past obligations.

Long-run solvency: The long-term balance between government revenues and spending; emphasizes the ability of government to meet future obligations and handle unknown fiscal challenges for an extended period.

Low-powered incentives: As structured by the institutional environment, where the benefits of transactions do not flow directly to the parties in the transaction, such as on the administrative end of the governing continuum in table 4.2 where appointed officials gain benefit through raises, promotions, and professional reputation and satisfaction.

Own-source revenue: Generated from resources within the local government's jurisdiction, although they can be collected by other governments and distributed to the owner government at regular intervals.

Principal: The party that hires an agent to fulfill a contract. In the local government setting, voters are principals and elected officials are agents, or elected officials can be principals and departmental heads are agents.

Revenue base: The portion of the economic base government has access to through specific revenue-raising mechanisms as established by state statute and other legal and institutional constraints.

Revenue burden: The ratio of actual revenues to revenue base or revenue capacity. Reflects how much of its revenue capacity a government is using, or how much burden the government is placing on the revenue capacity. Also called revenue effort.

Revenue capacity: The portion of the revenue base government can actually tax; also established in most cases by state statute. The maximum level of revenue it could raise from all sources.

Revenue elasticity: The responsiveness of a particular revenue base or revenue source to changes in the national economy, personal income, tax rates, or other economic quantity.

Revenue fungibility: The extent to which revenues from one source can be substituted for revenues from another source.

Revenue reserves: Excess or slack revenue capacity that the government has access to, but has not used or tapped into. Revenue reserves = revenue capacity − actual revenues.

Revenue wealth: The capacity of a government to generate revenue from available sources. Governments with high revenue wealth have the capacity to generate high levels of revenue at a low rate of taxation and charge (low revenue burden).

Risk: The government's exposure or vulnerability to detrimental fiscal shocks and changes in the environment (fiscal stress).

Satellite city: A city located within or near a large metropolitan area that is somewhat independent of the region and central city economically. It often has its own suburbs.

Service-level solvency: The ability to provide adequate services to meet the health, safety, and welfare needs of its citizens given its revenue resources.

Shared revenue: Revenue drawn from one source, such as income tax, that one government shares with other governments using a formula such as proportion of population or level of need. State-shared revenue with municipalities in Illinois includes income tax, motor fuel tax, and grants.

Slack: Pool of resources in excess of the minimum necessary to produce a given level of output. Resources can be internal, such as a fund balance or excess employees, or external in the form of excess revenue capacity (wealth).

Spending demands: Spending priorities of residents, clients, and other stakeholders who influence government through the political process.

Spending effort: The extent to which its service obligations are being met. Actual spending relative to spending needs.

Spending fixity: The degree to which spending for particular obligations and liabilities is fixed and inflexible.

Spending needs: Spending responsibilities and obligations. Governments have an obligation to adequately provide certain services. Municipal governments' primary responsibilities are the health and safety of the population they serve. They also have obligations to creditors.

Spillover effects: Positive or negative side effects of activity or processes in one entity upon another entity that is not involved directly. Also called externalities.

Transaction costs: Any cost that is incurred in an economic exchange or contractual relationship. Both the principal and agent incur costs in establishing and enforcing the contract, but principals incur higher costs of controlling the agent. Mechanisms used by principals to control agents have been classified as ex post and ex ante.

Yardstick competition: A form of competition between governments that is generated when voters and taxpayers compare the goods and services of different governments and, based on these benchmarks, pressure their own government to improve its performance. The yardstick competition observed here is focused primarily on taxes, fees, and charges rather than goods and services and is expressed by elected officials.

References

Abney, Glenn, and Thomas P. Lauth. 1986. *The Politics of State and Local Administration.* Albany, NY: SUNY Press.

Advisory Commission on Intergovernmental Relations (ACIR). 1962. *Measures of State and Local Fiscal Capacity and Effort,* M-16. Washington, DC: ACIR.

———. 1971. *Measuring the Fiscal Capacity and Effort of State and Local Areas,* M-58. Washington, DC: ACIR.

———. 1979. *Measuring the Fiscal Blood Pressure of the States: 1964–1975,* M-111. Washington, DC: ACIR.

———. 1988. *State Fiscal Capacity and Effort,* M165. Washington, DC: ACIR.

———. 1990. *Mandates: Cases in State-Local Relations,* M173. Washington, DC: ACIR.

———. 1993. *State Law Foundations of Local Self Government: Constitutional, Statutory, and Judicial Issues.*

Agranoff, Robert, and Michael McGuire. 2003. *Collaborative Public Management: New Strategies for Local Governments.* Washington, DC: Georgetown University Press.

Alabama Policy Institute. 2008. *Jefferson County on Verge of Making Bankruptcy History.* Birmingham: Alabama Policy Institute, March 14. www.alabamapolicy.org/gary_blog/article.php?id _art=290.

Altshuler, Alan, William Morril, Harold Wolman, and Faith Mitchell. 1999. *Governance and Opportunity in Metropolitan America.* Washington, DC: National Academy Press.

Ammons, David N. 2008. "City Manager and City Administrator Role Similarities and Difference." *American Review of Public Administration* 38 (1): 24–40.

Andrews, Rhys, George A. Boyne, Jennifer Law, and Richard M. Walker. 2009. "Centralization, Organizational Strategy, and Public Service Performance." *Journal of Public Administration Research and Theory* 19 (January): 57–80.

Anthony, LaRita, Jonathan Becks, Jeanne Chi, and Jessica Mitton. 2009. *The Village of Riverside Budget, 2009.* Report completed for Budgeting for Public Management, spring 2009, Public Administration, UIC.

Appleton, Lynn M., and Bruce A. Williams. 1986. "Community and Collective Goods: How Sunbelt Cities Respond to Austerity." In *Fiscal Austerity and Urban Management, Research in Urban Policy,* vol. 2, pt. A, edited by T. Clark, 3–23. Greenwich, CT: JAI Press.

Aronson, J. Richard. 1984. "Municipal Fiscal Indicators." In *Crisis and Constraint in Municipal Finance: Local Fiscal Prospects in a Period of Uncertainty,* edited by J. Carr, 3–53. New Brunswick, NJ: Center for Urban Policy Research.

Badu, Yaw A., and Sheng Y. Li. 1994. "Fiscal Stress in Local Government: A Case Study of the Tri-Cities in the Commonwealth of Virginia." *Review of Black Political Economy* 22 (Winter): 5–17.

Bahl, Roy W. 1984. *Financing State and Local Government in the 1980's.* New York: Oxford University Press.

Baldassare, Mark. 1998. *When Government Fails: The Orange County Bankruptcy.* Berkeley, CA: University of California Press.

Banovetz, James M. 2002. "Illinois Home Rule: A Case Study in Fiscal Responsibility." *Journal of Regional Analysis and Policy* 32 (1): 79–98.

Barrett, Katherine, and Richard Greene. 2000. "The Government Performance Project: Grading the Cities; A Management Report Card." *Governing Magazine* 13 (February): 22.

Bartle, John R., and Ronnie LaCourse Korosec. 1996. "Are City Managers Greedy Bureaucrats?" *Public Administration Quarterly* 20 (Spring): 89–102.

Basalo, Victoria. 2003. "US Regionalism and Rationality." *Urban Studies* 40 (March): 447–62.

Berman, David R. 2003. *Local Government and the States: Autonomy, Politics, and Policy.* Armonk, NY: M. E. Sharpe.

Berne, Robert, and Richard Schramm. 1986. *The Financial Analysis of Governments.* Englewood Cliffs, NJ: Prentice Hall.

Berry, Christopher. 2007. "Piling On: Multilevel Government and the Fiscal Common-Pool." *American Journal of Political Science* 52 (October): 802–20.

Bluedorn, Allen C., Richard A. Johnson, Debra K. Cartwright, and Bruce R. Barringer. 1994. "The Interface and Convergence of the Strategic Management and Organizational Environment Domains." *Journal of Management* 20 (Summer): 201–62.

Bollen, Kenneth A., Barbara Entwisle, and Arthur S. Alderson. 1993. "Macrocomparative Research Methods." *Annual Review of Sociology* 19: 321–51.

Boris, C. Elizabeth T., and Eugene Steuerle. 2006. *Nonprofits and Government: Collaboration and Conflict.* 2nd ed. Washington, DC: Urban Institute Press.

Bowman, Woods, Roland Calia, and Judd Metzgar. 1999. *Evaluating Local Government Financial Health: Financial Indicators for Major Municipalities in Northeastern Illinois.* Chicago: Civic Federation.

Boyne, George A. 1992. "Is There a Relationship between Fragmentation and Local Government Cost?" *Urban Affairs Quarterly* 28 (December): 317–22.

———. 1996. *Constraints, Choice, and Public Policies* Greenwich, CT: JAI Press,

Boyne, George A., and Richard M. Walker. 2004. "Strategy Content and Public Service Organizations." *Journal of Public Administration Research and Theory* 14 (April): 231–52.

Braun, Martin Z. 2003. "N.Y. State Comptroller Pushes Financial Oversight for Buffalo." *Bond Buyer* 344(31645). May 29.

Brecher, Charles, and Raymond D. Horton. 1985. "Retrenchment and Recovery: American Cities and the New York Experience." *Public Administration Review* 45 (March–April): 267–74.

Brennan, Geoffrey, and Richard E. Wagner. 1977. *Democracy in Deficit: The Political Legacy of Lord Keynes.* New York: Academic Press.

Brown, Ken W. 1993. "The 10-Point Test of Financial Condition: Toward an Easy-to-Use Assessment Tool for Smaller Governments." *Government Finance Review* 9 (February): 21–25.

Bruton, Garry D., and W. Bartley Hildreth. 1993. "Strategic Public Planning: External Orientations and Strategic Planning Team Members." *American Review of Public Administration* 23 (December): 308–9.

Buffalo News. 2001. "A New Fiscal Reality," September 25.

Bunch, Beverly S. and Robert R. Ducker. 2003. "Implications of Using Enterprise Funds to Account for Public Works Services." *Public Works Management and Policy* 7 (January): 216–225.

Burchell, Robert W., David Listokin, George Sternlieb, James W. Hughs, and Stephen C. Casey. 1981. "Measuring Urban Distress: A Summary of the Major Urban Hardship Indices and Resource Allocation Systems." In *Cities under Stress,* edited by R. Burchell and D. Listokin, 159–229. Piscataway, NJ: Center for Urban Policy Research.

Busenitz, Lowell W. 1999. "Entrepreneurial Risk and Strategic Decision Making." *Journal of Applied Behavioral Science* 35 (September): 325–40.

Busenitz, Lowell W., and Jay B. Barney. 1997. "Differences between Entrepreneurs and Managers in Large Organizations: Biases and Heuristics in Strategic Decision-Making." *Journal of Business Venturing* 12 (January): 9–30.

Caiden, Naomi, and Aaron Wildavsky. 1974. *Planning and Budgeting in Poor Countries.* New York: John Wiley & Sons.

Carr, Gloria 2003. "'Extreme Failure' in C'ville's Finances: 'Extraordinarily Serious' Issues; Village's New Finance Director Outlines Problems in Report." *Courier News* (Elgin, IL), September 27.

———. 2005. "Faces Change in East Dundee." *Courier News* (Elgin, IL), April 30.

Chapman, Jeffrey. 1999. *Local Government, Fiscal Autonomy, and Fiscal Stress: The Case of California.* Cambridge, MA: Lincoln Institute of Land Policy, WP99JC1.

Chattopadhyay, Prithviraj, William H. Glick, and George P. Huber. 2001. "Organizational Actions in Response to Threats and Opportunities." *Academy of Management Journal* 44 (October): 937–55.

Child, John. S. 1972. "Organizational Structure, Environment, and Performance." *Sociology* 6, (January): 1–22.

———. 1997. "Strategic Choice in the Analysis of Action, Structure, Organizations and Environment: Retrospect and Prospect." *Organization Studies* 18 (1): 43–76.

Chow, Gregory C. 1960. "Tests of Equality between Sets of Coefficients in Two Linear Equations." *Econometrica* 28 (July): 591–605.

Civic Federation. 2008. *Effective Property Tax Rates, 1999–2006: Selected Municipalities in Northeastern IL.* Chicago: Civic Federation, September 17.

———. 2009. *Status of Local Pension Funding Fiscal Year 2007: An Evaluation of Ten Local Government Employee Pensions Funds in Cook County.* Chicago: Civic Federation.

Clark, Cal, and Liver B. Walter. 1991. "Urban Political Cultures, Financial Stress, and City Fiscal Austerity Strategies." *Western Political Quarterly* 44 (September): 676–97.

Clark, Terry Nichols. 2000. "Old and New Paradigms for Urban Research: Globalization and the Fiscal Austerity Urban Innovation Project." *Urban Affairs Review* 36 (September): 3–45.

Clark, Terry N., and Lorna C. Ferguson. 1983. *City Money: Political Processes, Fiscal Strain and Retrenchment.* New York: Columbia University Press.

Clingermayer, James C., and Richard C. Feiock. 2001. *Institutional Constraints and Policy Choice: An Exploration of Local Governance.* Albany, NY: SUNY Press.

Conte, Andrew. 2001. "Debts Refinanced to Balance Budget." *Pittsburgh Tribune-Review,* November 14.

Cooper, Steven D. 1996. "Local Government Budgeting Responses to Fiscal Pressures." *Public Administration Quarterly* 20 (Fall): 305–19.

Cyert, Richard M., and James G. March. 1963. *A Behavioral Theory of the Firm.* Englewood Cliffs, NJ: Prentice Hall.

Daily Herald (Arlington Heights, IL). 2005. "Bensenville Candidates Focus on O'Hare, Business Growth." March 7.

———. 2010a. "Welcome to 2010: Northwest Suburban Mayors Take a Look Forward." January 1.

———. 2010b. "Your Town's Toughest Challenge Northwest Suburban Mayors Say as One: Money, Money, Money." January 4.

Day, David V., and Robert G. Lord. 1992. "Expertise and Problem Categorization: The Role of Expert Processing in Organizational Sense-Making." *Journal of Management Studies* 29 (March): 35–47.

Deephouse, David L., and Robert M. Wiseman. 2000. "Comparing Alternative Explanations for Accounting Risk-Return Relations." *Journal of Economic Behavior & Organization* 42 (August): 463–82.

DeHoog, Ruth Hoogland, and Gordon P. Whitaker. 1990. "Political Conflict or Professional Advancement: Alternative Explanations of City Manager Turnover." *Journal of Urban Affairs* 12 (4): 367–77.

Deno, Kevin T., and Stephen L. Mehay. 1987. "Municipal Management Structure and Fiscal Performance: Do City Managers Make a Difference?" *Southern Economics Journal* 53:627–42.

DeSantis, Victor S., and Tari Renner. 2002. "City Government Structures: An Attempt at Clarification." In *The Future of Local Government Administration: The Hansell Symposium,* edited by H. G. Frederickson and J. Nalbandian, 71–80. Washington, DC: ICMA.

DeSarbo, Wayne S., C. Anthony Di Benedetto, Michael Song, and Indrajit Sinha. 2005. "Revisiting the Miles and Snow Strategic Framework: Uncovering Interrelationships between Strategic Types, Capabilities, Environmental Uncertainty, and Firm Performance." *Strategic Management Journal* 26 (1): 47–74.

Dewan, Shaila. 2009. "Alabama Reeling in Face of Fiscal Crisis." *New York Times,* July 31.

Dluhy, Milan J., and Howard A. Frank. 2002. *The Miami Fiscal Crisis: Can a Poor City Regain Prosperity?* Westport, CT: Praeger.

Dowding, Keith, Peter John, and Stephen Biggs. 1994. "Tiebout: A Survey of the Empirical Literature." *Urban Studies* 31 (May): 767–97.

Dowding, Keith, and Thanos Mergoupis. 2003. "Fragmentation, Fiscal Mobility, and Efficiency." *Journal of Politics* 65 (2003): 1190–1207.

Downing, Rondal G. 1991. "Urban County Fiscal Stress: A Survey of Public Officials' Perceptions and Government Experiences." *Urban Affairs Quarterly* 27 (2): 314–25.

Downs, Anthony. 1994. *New Vision for Metropolitan America.* Washington, DC: Brookings Institution.

Dubrow, David L. 2009. *The Treatment of Municipal Debt under Chapter 9 of the Bankruptcy Code.* Washington, DC: Arent Fox. www.arentfox.com/email/dubrow/Chapter%209%20Article.pdf.

Dunn, Delmer D., and Jerome S. Legge Jr. 2002. "Politics and Administration in U.S. Local Governments." *Journal of Public Administration Research & Theory* 12 (July): 401–22.

Dye, Richard F., and Therese J. McGuire. 1997. "The Effect of Property Tax Limitation Measures on Local Government Fiscal Behavior." *Journal of Public Economics* 66 (3): 469–87.

Ebdon, Carol, and Peter F. Brucato. 2000. "Government Structure in Large US Cities: Are Forms Converging?" *International Journal of Public Administration* 23 no. 12, 2209–35.

Eichenthal, David. 2010. "Is There a Case for Consolidation or Collaboration? The Ochs Center for Metropolitan Studies." 211/311. An ICMA white paper, June. http://icma.org/en/icma/knowledge_network/documents/kn/Document/301482/211311_Is_There_a_Case_for_Consolidation_or_Collaboration.

Elejalde-Ruiz, Alexia. 2005a. "E. Dundee Subdivision Scrapped after Three Years of Planning, Cambridge Homes Calls Off Development Project." *Daily Herald* (Arlington Heights, IL), April 12.

———. 2005b. "Village Loath to Raise Water, Sewer Rates: Study Says Hike Needed to Balance Expenses." *Daily Herald* (Arlington Heights, IL), September 18.

Esser, Jeffrey L. 1997. "A New Standard of Excellence in Budgeting: National Advisory Council on State and Local Budgeting New Budget Practices." *Government Finance Review* 13 (5): 5.

Farnham, Paul G. 1987. "Form of Government and the Median Voter." *Social Science Quarterly* 68 (September): 569–82.

Feiock, Richard C. 2009. "Metropolitan Governance and Institutional Collective Action." *Urban Affairs Review* 44 (January): 356–77.

Feiock, Richard C., Moon-GI Jeong, and Jaehoon Kim. 2003. "Credible Commitment and Council-Manager Government: Implications for Policy Instrument Choices." *Public Administration Review* 63 (September): 616–25.

Feiock, Richard C., and Jae-Hoon Kim. 2001. "Form of Government, Administrative Organization, and Local Economic Development Policy." *Journal of Public Administration Research and Theory* 11 (January): 29–49.

Feiock, Richard, and Christopher Stream. 2002. "Local Government Structure, Council Change, and City Manager Turnover." In *The Future of Local Government Administration: The Hansell Symposium,* edited by H. G. Frederickson and J. Nalbandian, 118–23. Washington, DC: International City/County Managers Association.

Feldman, Martha S., and Anne M. Khademian. 2002. "To Manage Is to Govern." *Public Administration Review* 62 (September–October): 541–54 .

Fields, Greg. 1996. "Ripples of Scandal Can Rock Economy, but City Hall Crisis Survivable Analysts Say." *Miami Herald,* September 29.

Flickinger, Ted, and Peter M. Murphy. 1990. "Special Districts." In *Illinois Local Government: A Handbook,* edited by J. Keane and G. Koch, 151–201. Carbondale, IL: Southern Illinois University Press.

Flynn, Courtney. 2005. "North Chicago in for a Fight: 3 Mayoral Challengers Heat Up Race for the Incumbent." *Chicago Tribune,* February 4.

Folz, David H., and P. Edward French. 2005. *Managing America's Small Communities: People, Politics, and Performance.* New York: Rowman & Littlefield.

Forrester, John P., and Charles J. Spindler. 1990. "Managing Municipal Services in an Era of Declining Federal Assistance." *Policy Studies Review* 10 (Fall): 63–84.

Foster, Kathryn. 1997. *The Political Economy of Special Purpose Governments.* Washington, DC: Georgetown University Press.

Frant, Howard. 1996. "High-Powered and Low-Powered Incentives in the Public Sector." *Journal of Public Administration Research and Theory* 6 (July): 365–81.

Frederickson, H. George, Gary A. Johnson, and Curtis H. Wood. 2004. *The Adapted City: Institutional Dynamics and Structural Change.* Armonk, NY: M. E. Sharpe.

Frederickson, H. George, and John Nalbandian, eds. 2002. *The Future of Local Government Administration.* Washington, DC: International City/County Managers Association.

Fuchs, Ester R. 1992. *Mayors and Money: Fiscal Policy in New York and Chicago.* Chicago: University of Chicago Press.

Gainsborough, Juliet F. 2001. *Fenced Off: The Suburbanization of American Politics.* Washington, DC: Georgetown University Press.

Gardener, Mathew, Robert G. Lynch, Richard Sims, Ben Schweigert, and Amy Meek. 2002. *Balancing Act: Tax Reform Options for Illinois.* Washington, DC: Institute on Taxation and Economic Policy. www.ctj.org/itep/ilfinal.pdf.

Gigerenzer, Gerd. 2004. "Fast and Frugal Heuristics: The Tools of Bounded Rationality." In *Blackwell Handbook of Judgment and Decision Making,* edited by D. Koehler and N. Harvey, 62–88. Oxford, UK: Blackwell.

Gove, Samuel K., and James D. Nowlan. 1996. *Illinois Politics and Government: The Expanding Metropolitan Frontier.* Lincoln: University of Nebraska.

Government Finance Officers Association. 2001. *Recommended Practices for State and Local Government.* Chicago: GFOA.

Gramlich, Edward M. 1976. "The New York City Fiscal Crisis: What Happened and What Is to Be Done?" *American Economic Review* 66 (2): 415–29.

Graydon Megan. 2009. "Property-Tax Plan Draws Fire: Schaumburg Receives Earful over Proposal to Begin Assessments." *Chicago Tribune,* December 18.

Groark, Virginia. 2002. "Oak Brook Mayor Will Not Seek Re-Election: Trustee Also Says He Will Not Run." *Chicago Tribune,* October 30.

Groves, Sanford M., and Maureen Godsey Valente. 2003. *Evaluating Financial Condition: A Handbook for Local Government.* 4th ed. Revised by Karl Nollenberger Washington, DC: International City/County Managers Association.

Groves, Sanford M. W., Maureen Godsey, and Martha Shulman. 1981. "Financial Indicators for Government." *Public Budgeting and Finance* 1 (June): 5–19.

Hansell, William H. 2002. "Professionalism in Local Government Administration." In *The Future of Local Government Administration: The Hansell Symposium,* edited by H. G. Frederickson and J. Nalbandian, 181–95. Washington, DC: International City/County Managers Association.

Hawkins, Brett W. 1989. "A Comparison of Local and External Influences on City Strategies for Coping with Fiscal Stress." In *Decisions on Urban Dollars, Research in Urban Policy,* vol. 3, edited by T. Clark and R. Fitzgerald, 73–90. Greenwich, CT: JAI Press.

Hawkins, Brett W., Keith J. Ward, and Mary P. Becker. 1991. "Government Consolidation as a Strategy for Metropolitan Development." *Public Administration Quarterly* 15 (Summer): 253–67.

Hawthorne, Michael. 2009. "Madigan: Crestwood Lied about Tainted Well: State Alleges in Lawsuit That Officials Misled EPA, Residents about Source of Water." *Chicago Tribune,* June 10.

Hayes, Kathy, and Semoon Chang. 1990. "The Relative Efficiency of City Manager and Mayor-Council Forms of Government." *Southern Economic Journal* 57 (July): 167–77.

Heinrich, Carolyn J., and Laurence E. Lynn Jr., eds. 2000. *Governance and Performance: New Perspectives.* Washington, DC: Georgetown University Press.

Hendrick, Rebecca. 2002. "Revenue Diversification: Fiscal Illusion of Flexible Financial Management." *Public Budgeting and Finance* 22 (Winter): 52–72.

———. 2003. "Professional Management and Variations in Fiscal Practices among Fiscally Threatened Suburban Municipalities." Paper presented at the annual conference of the Association of Budgeting and Financial Management, Washington, DC, September 18–20, and at the National Public Management Research Conference, Washington, DC, October 9–11.

———. 2004. "Assessing and Measuring the Fiscal Health of Local Governments: Focus on Chicago Suburban Municipalities." *Urban Affairs Review* 40 (September): 78–114.

———. 2006. "Role of Slack in Managing Local Government Fiscal Conditions." *Public Budgeting and Finance* 26 (Spring): 14–46.

———. 2011. "Reinvention of Local Governance in the US Through Collective Action." http://tigger.uic.edu/cuppa/pa/faculty/vitae_pdf/Reinvention%20of%20Local%20 Governance%20in%20the%20US%20Through%20Collective%20Action.pdf

Hendrick, Rebecca, Michael DeLorenzo, Meg Haller, Laura Husarek, Benoy Jacob, Kseniya Khovanova, and Gena Miller. 2006. "Assessing the Financial Condition of Local Governments: What Is Financial Condition and How Is It Measured?" Working paper produced from graduate class PA 554: Advanced Seminar in Financial Management, Fall 2006.

Hendrick, Rebecca, and Benedict Jimenez. 2010. "Are All Interlocal Government Agreements (ILGAs) Created Equal?" Paper presented at annual conference of the Association of Budgeting and Financial Management, Omaha, NE, October 7–9.

Hendrick, Rebecca, Benedict Jimenez, and Kamna Lal. 2011. "Does Local Government Fragmentation Increase Local Spending?" *Urban Affairs Review* 47 (4): 467–510. Available at http://uar.sagepub.com/content/early/recent.

Hendrick, Rebecca, and Bonnie Lindstrom. 2002. "Stress, Structure, and Strategy: Fiscal Management in Chicago Suburbs." Paper delivered at the annual conference of the American Society of Public Administration, Phoenix, AZ, March 23–26.

Hendrick, Rebecca, Yonghong Wu, and Benoy Jacob. 2007. "Tax Competition among Municipal Governments: Exit vs. Voice." *Urban Affairs Review* 43 (November): 221–55.

Hickson, David J., D. C. Wilson, D. Cray, G. R. Mallory, and R. J. Butler. 1986. *Top Decisions: Strategic Decision Making in Organizations.* San Francisco: Jossey-Bass.

Hildreth, W. Bartley. 1997. "Financial Management: The Centrality of the Fiscal in Local Government and Politics." In *Handbook of Local Government Administration,* edited by J. Gargan, 159–90. New York: Marcel Dekker.

Hill, Carolyn J., and Laurence E. Lynn Jr. 2004. "Governance and Public Management: An Introduction." *Journal of Public Administration Research and Theory* 23 (January): 3–11.

Hill, Melvin 1978. *State Laws Governing Local Government Structure and Administration,* M-186. Washington, DC: Advisory Commission on Intergovernmental Relations.

Hirschman, Albert O. 1970. *Exit, Voice, Loyalty: Responses to Declines in Firms, Organizations, and States.* Cambridge, MA: Harvard University Press.

Hirth, Diane. 1996. "Financial Watchdog Will Help Out Miami." *Orlando Sentinel,* December 4.

Hobbs, Frank, and Nicole Stoops. 2002. "Demographic Trends in the 20th Century." *Census 2000 Special Reports,* Series CENSR-4. Washington, DC: US Government Printing Office.

Hoene, Christopher, and Michael A. Pagano. 2010. *City Fiscal Conditions in 2010.* Washington, DC: National League of Cities.

Holcombe, Randall G., and Russell S. Sobel. 1997. *Growth and Variability in State Tax Revenue: An Anatomy of State Fiscal Crises.* Westport, CT: Greenwood Press.

Honadle, Beth Walter. 2003. "The States' Role in US Local Government Fiscal Crises: A Theoretical Model and Results of a National Survey." *International Journal of Public Administration* 26 (13): 1431–72.

Hou, Yilin. 2003. "What Stabilizes State General Fund Expenditures in Downturn Years: Budget Stabilization Fund or General Fund Unreserved Undesignated Balance?" *Public Budgeting and Finance* 23 (Summer): 64–85.

Howell-Moroney, Michael. 2008. "The Tiebout Hypothesis 50 Years Later: Lessons and Lingering Challenges for Metropolitan Governance in the 21st Century." *Public Administration Review* 68 (January–February): 97–109.

Huber, George P., C. Chet Miller, and William H. Glick. 1990. "Developing More Encompassing Theories about Organizations: The Centralization/Effectiveness Relationship." *Organization Science* 1 (February): 11–40.

Illinois Municipal League. 2007. *Fiscal Analysis of the Downstate Police, Fire, and IMRF Pension System.* Springfield, IL: IML.

Illinois Office of the Comptroller. 2010. *The Illinois State Comptroller Quarterly,* October, no. 37.

Ingraham, Patricia W., and Laurence E. Lynn. 2004. *The Art of Governance: Analyzing Management and Administration.* Washington, DC: Georgetown University Press.

Inman, Robert P. 1995. "How to Have a Fiscal Crisis: Lessons from Philadelphia." *American Economic Review* 85 (May): 378–83.

Jones, Bryan D. 2001. *Politics and the Architecture of Choice: Bounded Rationality and Governance.* Chicago: University of Chicago Press.

Jones, Sandra M. 2009. "Shopping Takes Sharp Downturn: Holiday Season Looks Bleak after Record Decline in Sales." *Chicago Tribune,* September 18.

———. 2010. "Area Retail Recovering Slowly: 2010 Has Seen Rebound, But Still Below '08 Level." *Chicago Tribune,* September 21.

Kahneman, Daniel, Paul Slovic, and Amos Tversky, eds. 1982. *Judgement under Uncertainty: Heuristics and Biases.* Cambridge: Cambridge University Press.

Kahneman, Daniel, and Amos Tversky. 1979. "Prospect Theory: An Analysis of Decision under Risk." *Econometrica* 47 (2): 263–91.

Keane, James F., and Gary Koch 1990. *Illinois Local Government: A Handbook.* Carbondale: Southern Illinois University Press.

Kee, James Edwin. 2004. "Fiscal Decentralization Theory as Reform." In *Financial Management Theory in the Public Sector,* edited by A. Khan and W. B. Hildreth, 165–85. Westport, CT: Praeger Press.

Kelly, Janet. 1994. "Mandate Reimbursement Measures in the States." *American Review of Public Administration* 24 (December): 351–73.

Kenyon, Daphne. 1997. "Theories of Interjurisdictional Competition." *New England Economic Review* 97 (2): 13–28.

———. 2007. *The Property Tax: School Funding Dilemma.* Cambridge, MA: Lincoln Institute of Land Policy. Policy Focus Report, PF015. www.lincolninst.edu/pubs/PubDetail.aspx?pubid=1308.

Keren, Gideon, and Karl H. Teigen. 2004. "Yet Another Look at the Heuristics and Biases Approach." In *Blackwell Handbook of Judgment and Decision Making,* edited by D. Koehler and N. Harvey, 89–109. Oxford, UK: Blackwell.

King, Gary, Robert O. Keohane, and Sidney Verba. 1994. *Designing Social Inquiry: Scientific Inference in Qualitative Research.* Princeton, NJ: Princeton University Press.

Kloha, Philip, Carol S. Weissert, and Robert Kleine. 2005. "Developing and Testing a Composite Model to Predict Local Fiscal Distress." *Public Administration Review* 65 (May–June): 313–23

Krane, Dale, Platon N. Rigos, Melvin B. Hill Jr., eds. 2001. *Home Rule in America: A Fifty-State Handbook.* Washington, DC: CQ Press.

Krause, George A. 2003. "Coping with Uncertainty: Analyzing Risk Propensities of SEC Budgetary Decisions, 1949–97." *American Political Science Review* 97 (February): 171–88.

Kreiser, Patrick M., Louis D. Marino, and K. Mark Weaver. 2002. "Reassessing the Environmen-EO Link: The Impact of Environmental Hostility on the Dimensions of Entrepreneurial Orientation." *Academy of Management Proceedings:* G1–G6.

Kuczka, Susan. 2005. "Island Lake Is a Sea of Unrest: Village Government Seeks Calm after Rift." *Chicago Tribune,* November 18.

Ladd, Helen F., and J. Milton Yinger. 1989. *America's Ailing Cities: Fiscal Health and the Design of Urban Policy.* Baltimore, MD: John Hopkins University Press.

Lawrence, Peter R., and J. W. Lorsch. 1967. *Organization and Environment.* Homewood, IL: Irwin.

Lenhoff, Pat. 2001. "The Short Version of Vernon Hills Budget Surplus." *Naperville Sun* (IL), March 1.

Levin, Martin A., and Mary Bryna Sanger. 1994. *Making Government Work: How Entrepreneurial Executives Turn Bright Ideas into Real Results.* San Francisco: Jossey-Bass.

Levine, Charles H. 1978. "A Symposium: Organizational Decline and Cutback Management." *Public Administration Review* 38 (July–August): entire issue.

———, ed. 1980. *Managing Fiscal Stress.* New York: Chatham House.

Levine, Charles H., Irene S. Rubin, and George Wolohojian. 1981. *The Politics of Retrenchment: How Local Governments Manage Fiscal Stress.* Beverly Hills, CA: Sage Publications.

———. 1982. "Managing Organizational Retrenchment." *Administration and Society* 14 (May): 101–36.

Lewis, Paul G. 1996. *Shaping Suburbia: How Political Institutions Organize Urban Development.* Pittsburgh, PA: University of Pittsburgh.

Lindstrom, Bonnie. 1997. "Regional Cooperation and Sustainable Growth: A Study of Nine Council of Governments in the Northeastern Illinois Region." *Journal of Urban Affairs* 20 no. 3, 327–42.

Logan, John R., and Mark Schneider. 1981. "The Stratification of Metropolitan Suburbs." *American Sociological Review* 46 (April): 175–86.

Lowery, David. 2000. "A Transactions Costs Model of Metropolitan Governance: Allocation versus Redistribution in Urban America." *Journal of Public Administration Research and Theory* 10 (January): 49–78.

Lubell, Mark, Richard Feiock, and Edgar Ramirez. 2005. "Political Institutions and Conservation by Local Governments." *Urban Affairs Review* 40 (July): 706–29.

Luce, R. Duncan, and Howard Raiffa. 1957. *Games and Decisions.* New York: John Wiley and Sons.

Lynn, Laurence E., Jr., Carolyn J. Heinrich, and Carolyn J. Hill. 2001. *Improving Governance: A New Logic for Empirical Research.* Washington, DC: Georgetown University Press.

Lynn, Laurence E., and Patricia Ingraham. 2004. "Governance and Public Management: A Symposium." *Journal of Policy Analysis and Management* 23 (Winter): entire issue.

Macmanus, Susan A. 2004. "'Bricks and Mortar' Politics: How Infrastructure Decisions Defeat Incumbents." *Public Budgeting & Finance* 24 (Spring): 96–112.

MacManus, Susan A., and William J. Pammer Jr. 1990. "Cutbacks in the Country: Retrenchment in Rural Villages, Townships, and Counties." *Public Administration Quarterly* 14 (Fall): 302–23.

Maher, Craig S., and Steven C. Deller. 2007. "Municipal Responses to Fiscal Stress." *International Journal of Public Administration* 30 (12–14): 1549–72.

Malone, Mark. 2005. "Crest Hill Candidates Speak Out: Election Forum." *Herald News* (Joliet, IL), March 14.

March, James G., and Herbert A. Simon. 1958. *Organizations.* New York: John Wiley & Sons.

March, James G., and Zur Shapira. 1987. "Managerial Perspectives on Risk and Risk Taking." *Management Science* 33 (November): 1404–18.

Marlowe, Justin. 2005. "Fiscal Slack and Counter-Cyclical Expenditure Stabilization: A First Look at the Local Level." *Public Budgeting and Finance* 25 (Fall): 48–72.

Mattson, Gary A. 1994. "Retrenchment and Fiscal Policy Planning: The Political Culture of Small Southern Towns." *Public Productivity and Management Review* 17 (Spring): 265–79.

McCabe, Barbara, and Richard C. Feiock. 2005. "Nested Levels of Institutions: State Rules and City Property Taxes." *Urban Affairs Review* 40 (May): 634–54.

McCabe, Barbara Coyle, Richard C. Feiock, James C. Clingermayer, and Christopher Stream. 2008. "Turnover among City Managers: The Role of Political and Economic Change." *Public Administration Review* 69 (March): 380–86.

McCue, Clifford P. 2000. "The Risk-Return Paradox in Local Government Investing." *Public Budgeting and Finance* 20 (Fall): 80–101.

McEvily, Bill, Vincenzo Perrone, and Akbar Zaheer. 2003. "Trust as an Organizing Principle." *Organization Science* 14 (January–February): 91–103.

McGuire, Therese. 1991. "Federal Aid to States and Localities and the Appropriate Competitive Framework." In *Competition among States and Local Governments: Efficiency and Equity in American Federalism,* edited by D. Kenyon and J. Kincaid, 153–66. Washington, DC: Urban Institute Press.

Meier, Kenneth J., Laurence J. O'Toole, George A. Boyne, and Richard M. Walker. 2007. "Strategic Management and the Performance of Public Organizations: Testing Venerable Ideas against Recent Theories." *Journal of Public Administration Research and Theory* 17 (April): 357–77.

Metropolitan Mayors Caucus. 2009. Service Delivery Task Force First Report to the Full Caucus. Chicago, IL, December 14.

Meyers, Dan. 1990. "The Banks May Call the Shots in Bailout." *Philadelphia Inquirer,* December 23.

Miles, Mathew B., and A. Michael Huberman. 1994. *Qualitative Data Analysis: An Expanded Sourcebook.* 2nd ed. Thousand Oaks, CA: Sage Publications.

Miles, Raymond E., and Charles C. Snow. 1978. *Organizational Strategy, Structure and Process.* New York: McGraw-Hill.

Mintzberg, Henry. 1979. *The Structuring of Organizations.* Englewood Cliffs, NJ: Prentice Hall.

———. 1990. "The Design School: Reconsidering the Basic Premises of Strategic Management." *Strategic Management Journal* 11 (March–April): 171–95.

Mintzberg, Henry, and Joseph Lampel. 1999. "Reflecting on the Strategy Process." *Sloan Management Review* 40 (Spring): 21–30.

Mintzberg, Henry, Duru Raisinghani, and Andre Theroet. 1976. "The Structure of Unstructured Decision Processes." *Administrative Science Quarterly* 21 (June): 246–75.

Moe, Terry 1997. "The Positive Theory of Public Bureaucracy." In *Perspectives in Public Choice,* edited by D. Mueller, 455–80. Cambridge: Cambridge University Press.

Molotch, Harvey. 1976. "The City as a Growth Machine." *American Journal of Sociology* 82 (September): 309–32.

Moody's Investor Services. 2000. *Moody's Rating Methodology Handbook.* New York: Moody's Investor Services.

Morgan, David R., and Kenneth Kickham. 1999. "Changing the Form of County Government: Effects on Revenue and Expenditure Policy." *Public Administration Review* 59 (July–August): 315–24.

Morgan, David R., and William J. Pammer Jr. 1988. "Coping with Fiscal Stress: Predicting the Use of Financial Management Practices among US Cities." *Urban Affairs Quarterly* 24 (September): 69–86.

Morgan, David R., and John P. Pelissero. 1980. "Urban Policy: Does Political Structure Matter?" *American Political Science Review* 74 (December): 999–1006.

Municipal Finance Officers Association in conjunction with Peat, Marwick, Mitchell & Co. 1978. *Is Your City Heading for Financial Difficulty? A Guidebook for Small Cities and Other Governmental Units.* Athens: Institute of Government, University of Georgia.

Muro, Mark, and Sarah Rahman. 2010. "Encouraging Innovation through Creative Governance Cities, Growth through Innovation, Metropolitan Recovery and Spending Priorities, Regions and States." Brookings Institution, May 5, Up Front Blog. www.brookings.edu/opinions/2010/0505_innovation_muro_rahman.aspx.

Musso, Juliet Ann. 1998. "Fiscal Federalism as a Framework for Governance." In *Handbook of Public Finance,* edited by F. Thompson and M. Green, 347–96. New York: Marcel Dekker.

Nalbandian, John. 1992. *Professionalism in Local Government: Roles, Responsibilities, and Values of City Managers.* San Francisco: Jossey-Bass.

Nelson, Kimberly L., and James H. Svara. 2010. "Adaptation of Models versus Variations in Form: Classifying Structures of City Government." *Urban Affairs Review* 45 (March): 544–62.

Newell, Allen, and Herbert A. Simon. 1972. *Human Problem Solving.* Englewood Cliffs, NJ: Prentice Hall.

News Sun (Waukegan, IL). 2001. "Lawsuit Could Be Costly: Antioch-Neumann Development; Officials Say Assessments May Be Needed for Legal Fees." June 30.

Niskanen, William A. 1975. "Bureaucrats and Politicians." *Journal of Law and Economics* 18 (December): 617–59.

Nohria, Nitin, and Ranjay Gulati. 1996. "Is Slack Good or Bad for Innovation?" *Academy of Management Journal* 39 (October): 1245–64.

Nooteboom, Bart. 1996. "Trust, Opportunism and Governance: A Process and Control Model." *Organization Studies* 17 (6): 986–1010.

North, Douglass C. 1991. "Institutions." *Journal of Economic Perspectives* 5 (Winter): 97–112.

Nutt, Paul C., and Robert W. Backoff. 1987. "A Strategic Management Process for Public Sector and Third-Sector Organizations." *American Planning Association Journal* 53 (Winter): 44–57.

———. 1992. *Strategic Management of Public and Third Sector Organizations.* San Francisco: Jossey-Bass.

Oakerson, Ronald J. 1999. *Governing Local Public Economies: Creating the Civic Metropolis.* Oakland, CA: ICS Press.

Oakerson, Ronald J., and Roger B. Parks. 1989. "Local Government Constitutions: A Different View of Metropolitan Government." *American Review of Public Administration* 19 (December): 279–94.

Oates, Wallace. 1972. *Fiscal Federalism.* New York: Harcourt Brace Jovanovich.

———. 1977. *The Political Economy of Fiscal Federalism.* Lexington, MA: Lexington Books.

————. 2006. "On the Theory and Practice of Fiscal Decentralization." Institute for Federalism and Intergovernmental Relations Working Paper Series, no. 2006-05. www.ifigr.org/publication/ifir_working_papers/IFIR-WP-2006-05.pdf.

Oates, Wallace, and Robert M. Schwab. 1991. "The Allocative and Distributive Implications of Local Fiscal Competition." In *Competition among States and Local Governments: Efficiency and Equity in American Federalism,* edited by D. Kenyon and J. Kincaid, 127–45. Washington, DC. Urban Institute Press.

Oliver, Eric J. 2001. *Democracy in Suburbia.* Princeton, NJ: Princeton University Press.

Orfield, Myron. 2002. *American Metropolitics: The New Suburban Reality.* Washington, DC: Brookings Institution.

Ostrom, Elinor. 1990. *Governing the Commons: The Evolution of Institutions for Collective Action.* Cambridge: Cambridge University Press.

Pagano, Michael A., and Christopher Hoene. 2010. "States and the Fiscal Policy Space of Cities." In *The Property Tax and Local Autonom,* edited by M. Bell, D. Brunori, and J. Youngman, 243–84. Cambridge, MA: Lincoln Institute of Land Policy.

Pammer, William J. 1990. *Managing Fiscal Strain in Major American Cities: Understanding Retrenchment in the Public Sector.* New York: Greenwood Press.

Parr, John, Joan Riehm, and Christiana McFarland. 2006. "Guide to Successful Local Government Collaboration in America's Regions." National League of Cities, CityFutures Program.

Perry, Tony. 2006. "San Diego Officials Indicted for Fraud: 5 OKd Risky Plan That Drained Pension Fund." *Chicago Tribune,* January 8.

Peterson, Paul. 1981. *City Limits.* Chicago: University of Chicago Press.

Pfeffer, Jeffrey, and Gerald Salancik. 1978. *The External Control of Organizations.* New York: Harper & Row.

Pindyck, Robert S., and Daniel L. Rubinfeld. 1990. *Econometric Models and Economic Forecasts.* 3rd ed. New York: McGraw-Hill.

Pinfield, Lawrence T. 1986. "A Field Evaluation of Perspectives on Organizational Decision Making." *Administrative Science Quarterly* 31 (September): 365–88.

Pittsburgh Post-Gazette. 2002. "Fiscal Friction: Council Must Be Part of the City's Solution," August 14.

Poister, Theodore H., and Gregory Streib. 1989. "Management Tools in Municipal Government: Trends over the Past Decade." *Public Administration Review* 49 (May–June): 240–48.

————. 2005. "Elements of Strategic Planning and Management in Municipal Government: Status after Two Decades." *Public Administration Review* 65 (January): 45–56.

Pollard, David. 2005. "Quitting Time: Finance Chief Leaves Over Trustee 'Interference.'" *Maywood Herald* (IL), August 24.

Post, Stephanie S. 2004. "Metropolitan Area Governance and Institutional Collective Action." In *Metropolitan Governance: Conflict, Competition, and Cooperation,* edited by R. Feiock, 67–91. Washington, DC: Georgetown University Press.

Poterba, James M. 1994. "State Responses to Fiscal Crises: The Effects of Budgetary Institutions and Politics." *Journal of Political Economy* 102 (August): 799–821.

Rachlinski, Jeffrey J. 2004. "Heuristics, Biases, and Governance." In *Blackwell Handbook of Judgment and Decision Making,* edited by D. Koehler and N. Harvey, 567–84. Oxford, UK: Blackwell.

Rafuse, Robert W., Jr., and Laurence R. Marks. 1991. *A Comparative Analysis of Fiscal Capacity, Tax Effort, and Public Spending among Localities in the Chicago Metropolitan Region.* Washington, DC: US Advisory Commission on Intergovernmental Relations.

Rajagopalan, Nandini., Abdul M. A. Rasheed, and Deepak K. Datta. 1993. "Strategic Decision Processes: Critical Review and Future Directions." *Journal of Management* 19 (June): 349–84.

Reardon, Kenneth M. 1997. "State and Local Revitalization Efforts in East St. Louis Illinois." *Annals of the American Academy of Political and Social Science* 551: 235–47

Ring, Peter Smith, and Andrew H. Van De Ven. 1992. "Structuring Cooperative Relationships between Organizations." *Management Journal* 13 (October): 483–98.

Ritholtz, Barry. 2009. "Bear Market Comparisons, 1929–2009." *Big Picture,* February 29. www.ritholtz.com/blog/2009/02/bear-market-comparisons-1929-2009/.

Robinson, Karen. 2003. "Fiscal Struggle Likely to Worsen as Crisis Engulfs City, Experts Say." *Buffalo News,* November 16.

Rork, Jonathan C. 2003. "Coveting Thy Neighbors' Taxation." *National Tax Journal* (December): 775–87.

Ross, John P., and James Greenfield. 1980. "Measuring the Health of Cities." In *Fiscal Stress and Public Policy,* edited by C. Levine and I. Rubin, 89–110. Beverly Hills, CA: Sage Publications.

Routliffe, Kathy. 2006. "Rules for Finance, Investment Finally on Village Books." *Lincolnwood Review* (IL), February 2.

Rubin, Irene. 1992. "Budget Reform and Political Reform: Conclusions from Six Cities." *Public Administration Review* 52 (September–October): 454–66.ß

Ruffatto, Natalie. 2003. "Common Sense: Crest Hill Can Be a Better Place to Live." *Herald News* (Joliet, IL), February 27.

Rusk, David. 1995. *Cities without Suburbs.* Washington, DC: Woodrow Wilson Center Press.

Ryan, Joseph. 2005. "Bitter Feelings over S. Barrington Land Drive Campaigns." *Daily Herald* (Arlington Heights, IL), March 31.

San Diego Union-Tribune. 2006. "Questions Linger on Pension Autonomy: Lack of Independence from City Blamed for Problems," February 6.

Schick, Allen. 1980. "Budgetary Adaptations to Resource Scarcity." In *Fiscal Stress and Public Policy,* edited by Charles Levine and Irene S. Rubin, 113–34. Beverly Hills: Sage Publications.

Schilling, Edward G. 1995. "The Values of City Management." In *Ideal & Practice in Council-Manager Government,* 2nd ed., edited by H. G. Frederickson, 108–19. Washington, DC: International City/County Managers Association.

Schmidlkofer, C. M. 2005. "More Cash May Flow: Village Board May OK Significant Increase in Water, Sewer Rates." *Wauconda Courier* (IL), May 19.

Schneider, Mark. 1989. *The Competitive City: The Political Economy of Suburbia.* Pittsburgh, PA: University of Pittsburgh Press.

———. 1992. "Undermining the Growth Machine: The Missing Link between Local Economic Development and Fiscal Payoffs." *Journal of Politics* 54 (1): 214–30.

Schneider, Mark, and Paul Teske. 1992. "Toward a Theory of the Political Entrepreneur: Evidence from Local Government." *American Political Science Review* 86 (September): 737–47.

Schneider, Mark, Paul Teske, and Michael Mintrom. 1995. *Public Entrepreneurs: Agents for Change in American Government.* Princeton, NJ: Princeton University Press.

Schwenk, Charles R. 1984. "Cognitive Simplification Processes in Strategic Decision-Making." *Strategic Management Journal* 5 (April–June): 111–28.

———. 1988. *The Essence of Strategic Decision Making.* Lexington, MA: Lexington Books.

Scott, W. Richard 1998. *Organizations: Rational, Natural, and Open Systems.* 4th ed. Englewood Cliffs, NJ: Prentice Hall.

Sharfman, Mark P., Gerrit Wold, Richard B. Chase, and David A. Tansik. 1988. "Antecedents of Organizational Slack." *Academy of Management Review* 13 (October): 601–14.

Sharp, Elaine B., and David Elkins. 1987. "The Impact of Fiscal Limitations: A Tale of Seven Cities." *Public Administration Review* 47 (September–October): 385–92.

Shefter, Martin. 1992. *Political Crisis/Fiscal Crisis: The Collapse and Revival of New York City.* New York: Columbia University Press.

Simon, Herbert A. 1962. "The Architecture of Complexity." *American Philosophical Society Proceedings* 106 (December): 467–82.

———. 1991. "Bounded Rationality and Organizational Learning." *Organization Science* 2 (1): 125–34.

Simon, Herbert A., and Associates. 1986. "Decision Making and Problem Solving," *Research Briefings 1986: Report of the Research Briefing Panel on Decision Making and Problem Solving.* Washington, DC: National Academy Press.

Simon, Herbert A., Allen Newell, and J. C. Shaw. 1962. "The Process of Creative Thinking." In *Models of Thought,* H. Simon, 144–74. New Haven, CT: Yale University Press.

Singh, Jitendra. 1986. "Performance, Slack, Risk Taking in Organizational Decision Making." *Academy of Management Journal* 29 (September): 562–85.

Smith, Gerald. 1988. "Towards a Heuristic Theory of Problem Structuring." *Management Science* 34 (December): 1489–1506.

Standard and Poor's. 2002. *Public Finance.* New York: McGraw-Hill.

Star (Chicago Heights, IL). 2005. "Editorials: Endorsements: Molski Favored in Flossmoor." March 27.

Stein, Robert M. 1987. "Tiebout's Sorting Hypothesis." *Urban Affairs Quarterly* 23 (September): 140–60.

Stephens, G. Ross. 1974. "State Centralization and the Erosion of Local Autonomy." *Journal of Politics* 36 (February): 44–76.

Stephens, G. Ross, and Nelson Wikstrom. 2000. *Metropolitan Government and Governance: Theoretical Perspectives, Empirical Analysis, and the Future.* New York: Oxford University Press.

Stonecash, Jeffrey, and Patrick McAfee. 1981. "Ambiguities and Limits of Fiscal Strain Indicators." *Policy Studies Journal* 10 (December): 379–95.

Stumm, Theodore J., and Matthew T. Corrigan. 1998. "City Managers: Do They Promote Fiscal Efficiency?" *Journal of Urban Affairs* 20 (Fall): 343–51.

Suyderhoud, Jack P. 1994. "State-Local Revenue Diversification, Balance, and Fiscal Performance." *Public Finance Quarterly* 22 (2): 168–94.

Svara, James H. 1990. *Official Leadership in the City: Patterns of Conflict and Cooperation.* Oxford: Oxford University Press.

———. 1999. "The Shifting Boundary between Elected Officials and City Managers in Large Cities." *Public Administration Review* 59 (January–February): 44–53.

———. 2001. "The Myth of the Dichotomy: Complementarity of Politics and Administration in the Past and Future of Public Administration." *Public Administration Review* 16 (March–April): 176–83

Tabb, William K. 1982. *The Long Default: New York City and the Urban Fiscal Crisis.* New York: Monthly Review Press.

Tan, Justin, and William M. Peng. 2003. "Organizational Slack and Firm Performance during Economic Transitions: Two Studies from an Emerging Economy." *Strategic Management Journal* 24 (December): 1249–64.

Tannenwald, Robert, and Jonathan Cowan. 1997. "Fiscal Capacity, Fiscal Need, and Fiscal Comfort among U.S. States: New Evidence." *Publius* 27 (3): 113–25.

Theising, Andrew J. 2003. *Made in USA: East St. Louis, the Rise and Fall of an Industrial River Town.* St. Louis, MO: Virginia.

Thompson, James. 1967. *Organizations in Action.* New York: McGraw-Hill.

Thurmaier, Kurt, and Curtis Wood. 2002. "Interlocal Agreements as Overlapping Social Networks: Picket-Fence Regionalism in Metropolitan Kansas City." *Public Administration Review* 62 (September–October): 585–98.

Tiebout, Charles M. 1956. "A Pure Theory of Local Expenditure." *Journal of Political Economy* 64: 416–24.

Tsetsekos, George P. 1995. "The Cost and Value of Slack." In *Advances in Financial Planning and Forecasting,* vol. 6, edited by C. Lee, 135–51. Greenwich, CT: JAI Press.

Tversky, Amos, and Daniel Kahneman. 1974. "Judgment under Uncertainty: Heuristics and Biases." *Science* 185 (September 27): 1124–31.

———. 1981. "The Framing of Decisions and the Psychology of Choice." *Science* 211 (January 30): 453–58.

———. 1991. "Loss Aversion in Riskless Choice: A Reference Dependence Model." *Quarterly Journal of Economics* 107 (November): 1039–61.

Walsh, James P. 1995. "Managerial and Organizational Cognition: Notes from a Trip Down Memory Lane." *Organization Science* 6 (May–June): 280–321.

Wandling, Richard. 2001. "Illinois." In *Home Rule in America: A Fifty-State Handbook,* edited by D. Krane, P. Rigos, and M. Hill Jr., 128–38. Washington, DC: CQ Press.

Weber, Rachel, Rebecca Hendrick, and Jeremy Thompson. 2008. "The Effect of Tax Incremental Financing on School District Revenues." *State and Local Government Review* 40 (1): 27–41.

Weiher, Gregory R. 1991. *The Fractured Metropolis: Political Fragmentation and Metropolitan Segregation.* Albany, NY: SUNY Press.

Weitzel, William, and Ellen Jonsson. 1989. "Decline in Organizations: A Literature Integration and Extension." *Administrative Science Quarterly* 34 (March): 91–109.

Westchester Herald (IL). 2005. Editorial, August 24.

Wheeland, Craig M. 2000. "City Management in the 1990s: Responsibilities, Roles, and Practices." *Administration and Society* 32 (July): 255–81.

Whetten, David A. 1987. "Organizational Growth and Decline Processes." *Annual Review of Sociology,* 13:335–58.

Whitaker, Gordon P., and Ruth Hoogland DeHoog. 1991. "City Managers under Fire: How Conflict Leads to Turnover." *Public Administration Review* 51 (March–April): 156–65.

White, Halbert. 1980. "A Heteroscedasticity-Consistent Covariance Matrix Estimator and a Direct Test for Heteroscedasticity." *Econometrica* 48 (May): 817–38.

Whitmire, Kyle, and Mary Williams Walsh. 2008. "High Finances Backfires on Alabama County." *New York Times,* March 12.

Wildavsky, Aaron. 1984. *The Politics of the Budgetary Process.* 4th ed. Boston: Little Brown.

Williams, Vanessa. 1991. "Bad Politics Caused City Crisis, Hafer Says." *Philadelphia Inquirer,* March 28.

Williamson, Oliver E. 1985. *The Economic Institutions of Capitalism.* New York: Free Press.

———. 1996. *The Mechanisms of Governance.* New York: Oxford University Press.

Wilson, John Douglas. 1999. "Theories of Tax Competition." *National Tax Journal* 52 (June): 269–304.

Wiseman, Robert M., and Philip Bromiley. 1996. "Toward a Model of Risk in Declining Organizations: An Empirical Examination of Risk, Performance and Decline." *Organization Science* 7 (September–October): 524–43.

Wiseman, Robert M., and Luis R. Gomez-Mejia. 1998. "A Behavioral Agency Model of Managerial Risk Taking." *Academy of Management Review* 23 (January): 133–53.

Wooldridge, Jeffrey M. 2002. *Econometric Analysis of Cross Section and Panel Data.* Cambridge, MA: MIT Press.

Wu, Yonghong, and Rebecca Hendrick. 2009. "Vertical and Horizontal Tax Competition among Florida Local Governments." *Public Finance Review* 37 (May): 289–311.

Index

Page numbers in italics refer to tables and graphs.